Symbolizing and Communicating in Mathematics Classrooms

Perspectives on Discourse, Tools, and Instructional Design

Symbolizing and Communicating in Mathematics Classrooms

Perspectives on Discourse, Tools, and Instructional Design

Edited by

Paul Cobb
Vanderbilt University

Erna Yackel
Purdue University–Calumet

Kay McClain
Vanderbilt University

LAWRENCE ERLBAUM ASSOCIATES, PUBLISHERS
2000   Mahwah, New Jersey   London

#40543245

Lawrence Erlbaum Associates, Inc., Publishers
10 Industrial Avenue
Mahwah, NJ 07430

Cover design by Kathryn Houghtaling Lacey

Library of Congress Cataloging-in-Publication Data

Symbolizing and communication in mathematics classrooms :
perspectives on discourse, tools, and instructional design /
edited by Paul Cobb, Erna Yackel, and Kay McClain.

p. cm.

Includes bibliographical references and index.
ISBN 0-8058-2975-X (hb : alk. paper) —
ISBN 0-8058-2976-8 (pb : alk. paper)
1. Mathematics—Study and teaching. 2. Mathematical notation.
I. Cobb, Paul. II. Yackel, Erna. III. McClain, Kay.
QA11.S873 1999
510'.71—dc21   99-52381
                                                   CIP

Books published by Lawrence Erlbaum Associates are printed on
acid-free paper, and their bindings are chosen for strength and
durability.

Printed in the United States of America
10 9 8 7 6 5 4 3 2 1

*We dedicate this book to Jenny Cobb
with thanks for the numerous and varied
ways in which she has supported our work
over the years.*

Contents

Preface

In 1993, we, in collaboration with Koeno Gravemeijer of the Fruedenthal Institute, Utrecht, The Netherlands, began working on a National Science Foundation-funded project titled "Mathematizing, Modeling, and Communicating in Reform Classrooms." A major purpose of the project was to investigate the role of models and symbols in mathematical learning, thereby addressing a previously underdeveloped area of learning theory. Our intention was to build on and extend previous research by coordinating a cognitive analysis of the role of modeling in mathematical development with an analysis of the fundamentally social nature of model and symbol use in innovative classrooms. To that end, we conducted a series of classroom teaching experiments in first-, second-, and third-grade mathematics classes where mathematics instruction followed an inquiry tradition. These teaching experiments differed significantly from those that we had conducted in our previous work in that, in these, we were guided not only by our understanding of individual students' mathematical conceptual development, but also by the instructional design theory of Realistic Mathematics Education (RME). Of particular importance in each case was developing one or more realistic (in the sense of RME) scenarios that could serve as starting points for students' initial informal activity and that had the potential to facilitate students' development of more formal mathematical reasoning. In the process we were able to investigate the role that student-generated models can play in supporting their transition from informal, situated problem solving to more formal yet personally-meaningful mathematical activity.

As the project progressed it became apparent to us that it would be helpful to engage in in-depth discussions with others who were also grappling with issues of communicating, symbolizing, modeling, and mathematizing, particularly as these issues relate to learning in the classroom. It was for this purpose that we assembled a small international group at Vanderbilt University in the fall of 1995 for a symposium on symbolizing, communicating, and mathematizing. This volume is a result of that symposium.

This book is intended for those who are seeking to expand their understanding of the complexity of learning as we are, so that we can enhance the learning experiences students have in schools.

ACKNOWLEDGMENTS

We wish to acknowledge the assistance of a number of people who contributed significantly to the successful production of this book. We are grateful to the National Science Foundation, and especially to our program officers, Richard Lesh and Barbara Lovitts, for supporting the symposium which led to preparation of the book itself. We also thank the Office of Educational Research and Improvement and especially Thomas Romberg, Director of the National Research and Development Center on Achievement in School Mathematics and Science, for supporting the development of the book. We are grateful to Andy Anderson, for providing a detailed review that contributed significantly to the improvement of this volume, and to Naomi Silverman of Lawrence Erlbaum Associates for her assistance with the preparation and publication of this book. We are also indebted to Cheryl Burkey for formatting the manuscript, and Pamela Hunter, for her invaluable assistance with the editing process. Finally, we thank members of our families for their support throughout this entire project.

—Paul Cobb
—Erna Yackel
—Kay McClain

1

Introduction: Perspectives on Semiotics and Instructional Design

Erna Yackel
Purdue University–Calumet, Hammond, Indiana

> *Mathematical work is work with ideas. Symbols are used as aids to thinking just as musical scores are used as aids to music. The music comes first, the score comes later.*
>
> (Hersh, 1986, pp. 18–19)

This book grew out of a symposium on discourse, tools, and instructional design held at Vanderbilt University in the fall of 1995. The symposium brought together a small international group of mathematics educators whose work and interests relate to the symposium theme. In organizing the conference, we purposefully included researchers who represent a wide range of theoretical perspectives including constructivism, cognitive science, sociocultural theory, and discourse theory. Symposium participants discussed papers that were prepared and read in advance of the conference, shared videotape analyses of classroom episodes and interviews, and wrestled with the complexities of theoretical considerations and pragmatic implications of the conference theme. The discussions were permeated by questions such as: How do symbols acquire meaning? How is meaning achieved? What do we mean by "meaning"? What role do symbols play in the (mathematician's) development of mathematical concepts? What role do symbols play in students' mathematical learning? The chapters in this book are tangible products of our deliberations. They span the range of theoretical perspectives represented at the symposium. Each paper was extensively revised in light of the discussions and with an eye toward developing a coherent volume that would invite the broader community into the deliberations by setting out the various perspectives and insights of the symposium participants.

Symbolizing and communicating are not new areas of investigation. There is a long history of study in both semiotics and communication, much of which is reviewed in chapters in this book (Sfard, chap. 3, this volume). Yet the role of semiotic mediation has been an underdeveloped theme within mathematics education and, at a broader level, within several of the theoretical perspectives that form the basis for much of the current work in mathematics education. In addition, the relationship between symbolizing as a central aspect of the evolution of classroom mathematical practices and the mathematics learning of individual children as they participate in and contribute to the development of those practices is an important issue that relates specifically to instructional design (cf. Gravemeijer, Cobb, Bowers, & Whitenack, chap. 7, this volume, for a detailed discussion of this issue). This book represents an important step forward in responding to the need to develop semiotic theories for mathematics, as expressed by Dörfler (chap. 4, this volume), and the need to develop approaches to instructional design informed by those theories, as expressed by Gravemeijer et al. (chap. 7, this volume).

This volume might be viewed as a successor to the book *Problems of Representation in the Learning and Teaching of Mathematics*, edited by C. Janvier (1987), which resulted from a conference held at the University of Québec in 1984. The purpose of the Québec conference was to bring together what was considered at that time to be state-of-the-art work on representation in mathematics. Several of the chapters in the Janvier book were devoted to the attempt to develop an adequate theory of representation. The authors of those chapters addressed issues relating to translations among representations, the role of symbols in representation, and the relationship of external and internal representations. Other contributors challenged the notion of representation, because it can be interpreted in conveyor and container metaphors of communication, and instead argued that the focus should be on the process of symbolizing. In the decade since the Janvier book was published, static views of representation have given way to more dynamic, action-oriented views (Kaput, 1994). It is for this reason that the title of this volume emphasizes the processes of *communicating* and *symbolizing*. Further, the dichotomy between internal and external representations has been displaced by nondualist views. In addition, knowing and doing mathematics is now seen as socially and culturally situated activity (Bauersfeld, Krummheuer, & Voigt, 1988; Schoenfeld, 1987; van Oers, 1996). This volume reflects these developments and extends the focus from that of merely analyzing students' mathematical activity to that of proactively supporting their mathematical learning.

TWO CONTRASTING APPROACHES
TO SYMBOLIZING AND COMMUNICATING

Before presenting an overview of the book, we invite the readers to consider two contrasting approaches to the analysis of symbolizing and communicating by presenting an example from outside of mathematics. These two general approaches are sometimes called the objectivist approach and the interpretivist approach. To emphasize the distinction between these two contrasting approaches and to highlight the complexity of the issues involved, we consider the case of music and the musical score. In a poignant essay entitled "Score: Imagination and Reality," noted French conductor and educator Pierre Boulez (1995) described the difference as follows: "There are generally two approaches for composers and performers—the first is that everything is within the notes, and of course, the opposite is that everything is behind or *beyond* the notes" (p. 19). Boulez went on to elaborate that those who take the first approach see the score as an object with precise data, including pitches, rhythm, dynamics, and tempos. In this approach the individual (musician) is seen as a transmitter. The musicians' task is to reproduce mechanically what they see and nothing more. Those who take this position think that they are "being faithful to the score" (p. 20). Composers such as Stravinsky and Ravel, who have taken this position, have been highly critical of what they referred to as the freedom of the performer. Stravinsky went so far as to compose a piece for a mechanical piano.

The other point of view is that the score is simply a convenient and accepted method of notating that which cannot possibly be easily or fully notated. The composers who take this point of view are aware from the very beginning that they cannot put into written or notational form all of the information they want to give the performer.[1] Many aspects go beyond notation. According to this view, "All notations—as precise as they can be, are just indications—the beginning of a process which leads to a higher level of understanding" (p. 20). Boulez referred to this attitude as interpretivist. In this view the performing musician must develop a personal understanding of the score. Otherwise, the musician just plays notes.

As the essay continues, Boulez makes it clear that he takes the interpretivist position. He argues that even though the language of signs in music is relatively simple to learn, performing goes beyond "reading" the signs and symbols. When performing, a musician must combine the

---

[1]This same idea was expressed by G. Spencer Brown (1969) (as quoted by John Richards, 1991, in a chapter on mathematical discussions) when he said, "Music is a similar art form, the composer does not even attempt to describe the set of sounds he has in mind, much less the set of feelings occasioned through them" (p. 77).

numerical proportions of rhythm and the pitch of the notes specified in the score with tempo, phrasing, articulation, and dynamics. Thus, musicians bring to the performance their own understanding of the music. Boulez's own attempts to take the objective approach, including incorporating a mechanical piano into a concert performance, convinced him that such an approach is not viable.

The distinction made by Boulez is similar to one that Richards (1991) made between derivation and proof in mathematics. In the same way as a musical score functions to guide a musician as he or she reproduces a melody, a mathematical derivation functions as a logical reconstruction intended to make a proof objective and repeatable. However, as Richards noted, "A derivation entices, or leads us into seeing a proof. It does not tell us (communicate directly) the proof" (p. 23). In this sense, proof, like music, involves an act of interpretation.

In the quotation that begins this chapter, Hersh also draws an analogy between mathematics and music. Like Boulez, Hersh takes an interpretivist approach to symbolizing. All of the contributing authors to this book take this approach as well. However, not all would agree with Hersh's clear distinction about precedence, that "The music comes first, the score comes later." In fact, a number of contributors to this book take up the challenge of explicating the dynamic interplay between mathematical thinking and symbolizing. For example, Sfard argues that there is an inherent problem of circularity in a discourse, such as mathematics, that creates its own objects. After presenting examples from the history of mathematics in which symbols were introduced before there were well-defined concepts that they signified, she suggests that rather than ask which comes first, symbols or concepts, we should investigate the dynamic interplay between symbolizing and meaning making.

OVERVIEW OF THE BOOK

The goal of this book is to present a variety of views and perspectives on symbolizing and communicating that derive from emerging theoretical perspectives in mathematics education as well as from field-based research. In the process we advance our understanding of classroom discourse and tool use as they relate to mathematical learning. Each of the chapters presents a theoretical or empirical analysis of some aspect of symbolizing and communicating within mathematics education.

The book is organized into two sections. The chapters in the first section focus on theoretical issues and theory development, and those in the second section are devoted to symbolizing and communicating as they relate to instructional design. The theoretical section begins with an introductory chapter by Paul Cobb that serves as an advance organizer for the four chapters that follow. In this chapter, Cobb highlights commonalities and differences in the theoretical perspectives taken by the authors and raises issues that emerge as important themes. Each of the chapters in the second section of the book is based on specific examples taken from research in classrooms or from instructional development projects. Finally, the book ends with an integrative summary by Bowers in which she delineates themes that cut across both sections of the book and uses those themes as the basis for drawing implications for the future.

Part I: Theoretical Considerations

The four main chapters in the first section of the two-part book focus on the role of discourse and semiotic processes in mathematics learning. The authors of these chapters capitalize on recent developments in semiotics and communication theory to advance new and challenging viewpoints that are informed by a deep understanding of both mathematics and classrooms. To aid communication with the reader, the authors all ground their theoretical discussions in a number of specific examples and cases. Although they each take distinct positions, the authors all broadly define symbolizing to include reasoning with physical materials, pictures, diagrams, computer graphics, and verbal expressions, as well as with conventional and nonstandard written symbols. In addition, they all focus on discourse and tool use as it occurs in the social context of the classroom. They all also challenge the traditional dichotomy between external mathematical representations or symbols and internal, mental processes. Indeed, the authors take the view that tools and symbols are integral to mathematical reasoning and that reasoning is not located entirely in the head. In this regard, their work shares a number of assumptions in common with distributed theories of intelligence (Pea, 1993). A theme shared by all of the authors is that symbols do not stand for something in and of themselves. Thus, the focus is not on symbols and their meaning, but on the activity of symbolizing and meaning making.

In her chapter, Sfard elaborates a theory of symbol use and symbolizing and thus extends the notion of reification that she introduced and developed in her earlier work. Previously, Sfard (1991) used the term *reification* to describe the process by which individuals come to take mathematical actions and processes as mathematical objects. The notion of reification is a psychological notion in that it refers to an individual's cognitive activity. In this chapter, Sfard extends the discussion to include the place of symbol use and symbolizing, not only in the individual's development of mathematical concepts, but also in the historical development of these concepts. In doing so, Sfard addresses the question of circularity, that is, which comes first, the meaning or the symbol. This question is also taken up, in one way or another, by Dörfler, van Oers, and Nemirovsky and Monk. As Sfard puts it, we cannot avoid the problem of circularity because it is "inherent in discourse that creates its own objects" (p. 92). She proposes that rather than ask which comes first, "we [should] rather give thought to the question of how to orchestrate and facilitate the back-and-forth movement between symbols and meanings" (p. 92). She uses examples from the historical development of mathematical concepts, such as function and complex number, to argue that symbols do not always develop as a means of recording already-defined notions and concepts. Instead, as in the case of the examples cited, symbols may be introduced and used initially for ill-defined notions, the meanings of which evolve over time, partly due to the symbols used. Likewise, in the case of students' learning of mathematical concepts, Sfard argues that students may initially use symbols effectively and communicate with others with little difficulty even before they conceive of the signifier as standing for something else. Sfard refers to such usage as *templates-driven*. According to Sfard, in a second phase the use becomes semantically mediated. Thus, in promoting the thesis that introducing a new symbol is a decisive step in the creation of a new concept, Sfard is making a strong claim. The claim, as suggested by the title of her chapter, "Symbolizing Mathematical Reality Into Being," is that (well-developed) meaning does not necessarily precede the use of a symbol. Instead, the relationship is reflexive. Symbols and meaning are mutually constitutive.

Dörfler's chapter, more than any other in the book, will appeal to mathematicians and mathematics educators who are interested in the development of meaning for more advanced mathematical concepts. Unlike Sfard, Dörfler does not discuss the historical development of such meaning. His discussion of the "means for meaning" centers on how individuals develop meaning for concepts that are already part of conventional mathematical knowledge. He uses concepts such as vector space and the identity element to illustrate and elaborate his theoretical position. Dörfler argues convincingly that concepts such as these do not (cannot) gain meaning (for individuals) simply through precise (mathematical) definition. Rather, meaning develops as individuals participate in discursive activity. For Dörfler, a main goal of cognitive learning is the ability to participate in a discourse according to its implicit and explicit rules, norms, and conventions. In his chapter, Dörfler discusses types of experiences that have potential for introducing a learner into mathematical discourse, that is, for developing meaning for mathematical terms. Finally, he argues that any discourse presupposes implicit assumptions and beliefs. In particular, for mathematics this necessitates accepting what he calls an "as-if attitude" (e.g., we speak "as if" all of the natural numbers were given with well-determined properties). In doing so, Dörfler, like Sfard, posits a dynamic interplay between discursive activity and mathematical meaning.

van Oers' chapter brings a Vygotskian perspective to the discussion of symbolizing, communication, and mathematizing. From this point of view, mathematizing is seen as a culturally developing activity that can be appropriated by assisted participation and constructive imitation on the part of the learner. For van Oers, symbolizing is the heart of mathematizing. It is an activity of forming and using symbols, including constructing both the sign and the meaning of the symbol. In his chapter, van Oers attempts to deepen the psychological analysis of the symbolizing process by explicating the process of appropriation. A central tenet of his position is that symbolizing entails tagging a situation in some way to characterize it and make it distinct from others. van Oers calls this aspect of symbolizing *predication* and argues that the appropriation of symbols consists of acquiring insight into and proficiency in the predication process. His position is that this acquisition is based on semiotic activity, that is, reflection on the reflexive relationship between sign and meaning, as well as on the development of this interrelationship. van Oers argues that one complicating factor in this process of symbol use and construction is the immediacy of this symbol-based predication. He explains that this immediacy is a result of abbreviating the actions that constitute the predication process and claims that the improvement of the predication activity related with symbols should begin with the explicit execution or construction of this predicative act.

For van Oers, the implications for instruction of his position are that a developmental approach is required for promoting the improvement of symbolizing and mathematizing at school. That is, there must be serious attention to explicit, socially distributed semiotic activity and predication from an early age. To clarify and explicate his theoretical claims and to illustrate the developmental approach that he advocates, van Oers uses the example of a group of young children attempting to devise a means for organizing boxes of shoes of various types (and sizes). With the assistance of the teacher, the children first develop the need for some means of symbolizing the type of shoe in a box and then develop symbols that they find useful. In the process, the semiotic actions are made explicit. According to the perspective that van Oers takes, the teacher is viewed as a semiotically more capable individual who promotes semiotic actions when the latter are relevant and who evokes communicative and reflective actions that result in the pupils making public symbols. Thus, the teacher plays a critical role in the predicating activity of the children.

The final chapter in the first part of the book is, in a sense, a bridge between the theoretical chapters and those that focus on instructional design. Unlike in the chapters by Sfard, Dörfler, and van Oers, where each author develops a theoretical position and illustrates it with examples from his or her empirical work, the theoretical position that Nemirovsky and Monk advance in their chapter developed out of their analysis of classroom and interview data. They explore the nature of symbolizing by focusing on two notions: fusion and trail-making. In their chapter, Nemirovsky and Monk use examples of children's make-believe play to illustrate and clarify these notions. For example, fusion is illustrated by children's acting, talking, and gesturing, without distinguishing between a symbol and what it represents (e.g., treating a stick as if it were a horse), and the notion of trail-making is illustrated by how the play is enacted by the child(ren) without following a script. Here, the make-believe play is an ongoing creation in which actions and words emerge from the activity itself in open-ended ways and not from a planned sequence. Nemirovsky and Monk use an interview conversation between Lin, a 10-year-old girl, and a researcher as the basis for developing and explicating their theoretical position. They propose that fusion and trail-making are central qualities in the use of mathematical symbols, using a trace of Lin's changing interpretations of motion graphs to elucidate their position. They then explain how their theoretical notions can be used as the foundation for instructional design. For them, the core task of design is the creation of environments for a future that cannot be fully anticipated. Nemirovsky and Monk see symbols and symbolizing as playing a role in the creation of such environments without imposing meaning (i.e., the lived-in space where symbolizing takes place is not predetermined). Symbols and symbolizing activity can be constraining and, at the same time, can be instrumental in bringing unintended aspects of the situation to the forefront. Thus, the position these authors take is consistent with that of the others in this volume, all of whom highlight the dynamic interplay between symbols and symbolizing activity and meaning making.

As a whole, the chapters in this section present distinct but complementary views of the process of symbolizing and the development of meaning. The challenge for mathematics educators is to incorporate these theoretical perspectives into an understanding of the teaching and learning process and to use them to advance students' mathematical learning. The chapters in the second section of the book take up this challenge.

Part II: Instructional Design Issues Related to Symbolizing, Communicating, and Mathematizing

The authors of the four chapters in the second section of the book directly address issues of instructional design. In doing so, they discuss how semiotic processes can be exploited to proactively support students' development of the types of mathematical reasoning advocated in current reform documents. The authors all draw on their extensive firsthand experience of working in classrooms to give detailed analyses of students' mathematical learning in instructional situations. Common themes include taking students' authentic experience as the starting point for the learning process and describing how students might eventually come to reason powerfully with conventional mathematical symbols. Differences between the authors' positions concern the types of tools and symbols that students use and the extent to which these tools and symbols emerge from students' activity. In one approach, students are encouraged to develop their own increasingly sophisticated symbols and notations with only an occasional nudge from the teacher. In a contrasting approach, conventional ways of symbolizing are introduced from the outset but are related to students' authentic activities via computer linkages. Collectively, the four chapters on instructional design illustrate a variety of ways in which the vision of reformers can be realized in mathematics classrooms.

In their chapter, Gravemeijer, Cobb, Bowers, and Whitenack describe an approach to instructional design that involves coordinating three aspects of learning: psychological issues that focus on conceptual development, social issues that involve the interactive constitution of collective ways of knowing, and design issues that focus on developing hypothetical learning trajectories (Simon, 1995) that direct the development of instructional sequences. They begin by expanding Doerr's (1995) distinction between expressive and exploratory computer models. Their goal is to distinguish the underlying assumptions between the expressive and exploratory approaches by describing the ways in which each approach addresses the tension between capitalizing on students' own self-developed models and introducing the more culturally accepted ways of notating. The authors describe the expressive approach as one that, in general, supports students' efforts to invent ways of symbolizing, with occasional assistance from the teacher, and the exploratory approach as one that supports students' efforts to discover the culturally approved meaning of conventional ways of symbolizing that are introduced ready-made by the designer or teacher.

Gravemeijer et al. then outline an alternative approach to instructional design grounded in the tradition of the Dutch Realistic Mathematics Education (RME) instructional theory. In doing so, they address the tension between the expressive and the exploratory approaches by describing their work in one first-grade classroom teaching experiment. In this experiment, they attempted to create a proposed learning trajectory that begins with the students' own models, but also forecasts a vision of how the teacher and students might collectively progress, through a series of social negotiations, toward the more conventionally accepted ways of notating. For Gravemeijer et al., instructional design is inextricably linked with a vision of the classroom as a social setting. For them, the design process cannot be executed as a straightforward application of theory. Instead, it has to take the form of transformational or developmental research that considers the social aspects of the classroom microculture.

Bransford, Zech, Schwartz, Barron, Vye, and the Cognition and Technology Group at Vanderbilt discuss a set of theoretical principles that guide their attempts to design environments that invite and sustain mathematical thinking. They first discuss several analyses of meaning, understanding, and social environments that provide the foundation for their thinking about instruction. They then illustrate how different sets of principles can be combined to create different kinds of learning environments. After outlining environments that incorporate only a few of the principles, they describe environments that incorporate all of them. In this way, they demonstrate the changes in thinking that they have made as they attempt to synthesize insights from what they describe as the "regular" cognitive literature and the "situative" cognitive literature. Thus, these authors give us a window into the evolution of their own work in instructional design as their perspective on meaning has evolved from that of helping students understand the meaning or significance of new information to that of facilitating students' development of meaning in terms of relationships between and among things, events, or situations. In doing so, the authors take the position that the meaningfulness of something is determined by its place in a system of relationships. Finally, Bransford et al. give a detailed description of an instructional environment that embodies their most recent thinking about design—the use of "Smart Tools"—and they discuss some of their initial findings from classroom experiences with this environment.

Lehrer, Schauble, Carpenter, and Penner focus on the importance of inscription and symbolizing for teaching and learning mathematics and science. By contrasting two different cases in which children's learning in the classroom was organized around design activity, they underscore the importance of a shared history of inscription, as well as the necessity to align forms of inscription with classroom learning and design goals. The first case they discuss involves a situation in which second graders designed and then constructed "race cars" to roll down an inclined plane at different speeds. The second case involves third graders designing experiments that explored factors affecting the growth rate of Wisconsin "Fast Plants." In both cases, Lehrer et al. track the evolution and interdependence of students' forms of inscription and their conceptual understanding. For example, initially students used various means of recording data, solely for the purpose of keeping a record. However, these records then became means for the students' developing understanding of patterns of growth or of change and for communicating about the situations, such as the steepness of the ramps for the cars or the variability in the growth of the plants. Using Latour's (1990) notion of "cascades of inscriptions" as a framework, the analysis by Lehrer et al. shows that the students understood the natural world through a progression of increasingly powerful inscriptions. That is, as children's inscriptions evolved, so did their understanding of the world. In both examples discussed by these authors, attention to the potential of various means of symbolizing for contributing to students' meaning making was an integral aspect of the instructional design from the outset.

In contrast, Lesh and Doerr use the language of models and modeling, which is well established in both mathematics and mathematics education literature, as a basis for discussing issues of instructional design that relate to symbolizing, communicating, and mathematizing. Their intention in doing so is to link their discussion to existing notions and to explicate in which ways their current thinking differs from or extends those notions. After elaborating what they mean by *models* and *a modeling approach* and discussing their view of how models and representations are related, they address the relationship between a models and modeling perspective and cognitive constructivism, social constructivism, and mathematizing. Finally, they illustrate a models and modeling approach to instructional design by presenting an example from the classroom. In the example, seventh-grade students worked on a "Summer Jobs" investigation in which they used employee data from a previous year to make decisions about which individuals to hire again for the next summer. Lesh and Doerr focus their discussion on the modeling activity of the students and on the series of models students developed as they progressed through the problem. In the same way that Lehrer et al. focused on the increasing sophistication in the inscriptions that students developed and on the way in which these inscriptions contributed to students' understanding, Lesh and Doerr are interested in the increasing sophistication in the models that students develop as they work through a complex investigation and in the implications for students' mathematical development. For example, Lesh and Doerr have found that an important characteristic of model development is that students' later models are characterized by greater stability than their earlier models. Also, like Lehrer et al., Lesh and Doerr note that the means of symbolizing that students use (Lesh and Doerr use the term *representations* whereas Lehrer et al. use the term *inscriptions*) organizes the situation so that other information might be noticed, thus making it possible, for example, to direct attention towards underlying patterns and regularities. In this way, the symbolizing activity and the resulting symbols have the potential to lead to further conceptual development. Lesh and Doerr thus argue that a perspective to instructional design that emphasizes models and modeling integrates issues related to symbolizing, communicating and mathematizing.

As a whole, the chapters of this section serve the important function of explicating the complexities that arise when taking symbolizing and communicating into account in instructional design. Further, these chapters provide the reader with concrete examples of instructional situations in which explicit attention to symbolizing, communicating, and mathematizing has been a part of the instructional design, and they give evidence of how such explicit attention plays out in the realization of the instructional design in the (classroom) learning situation.

CONCLUDING REMARKS

The contributions to this book indicate the diversity of views on symbolizing and communicating that exist within mathematics education both at the theoretical level and within instructional design. The chapters illustrate the complexities of the issues involved and demonstrate how perspectives within the field of mathematics education have evolved over the past few years. Together, the primary chapters and the commentary chapters are intended to provide an emerging framework for considering how symbolizing and communicating contribute to the advancement of mathematical concepts, both individually and collectively. In this sense, the ideas presented in this volume are not limited to theory development but also have important implications for designing instructional activities and strategies. In particular, all of the contributors to this book take the position that it is the activity of symbolizing, not the symbols themselves, that should be the central focus of attention. Thus, rather than focusing on how individuals interpret symbols and use them to represent and convey meaning, the focus is on means for developing meaning and for recording and communicating that meaning. The implication of this focus for instructional design is seen in the chapters in the second section of the book. There, the authors draw attention not only to the activity of the cognizing individual as a participant in a community, but also to the collective activity of the community (see especially, Gravemeijer et al., chap. 7, this volume). These activities are seen as mutually constitutive. Thus, both psychological and sociological means are used in developing explanations and theories that account for the role of symbolizing and communicating in mathematical conceptual development and used in designing instruction that gives explicit attention to the role of symbolizing, communicating, and mathematizing as key aspects of the learning process.

ACKNOWLEDGMENTS

The preparation of this chapter was supported by the National Science Foundation under grants DMS-9057141 and RED-9353587 and by the Office of Educational Research and Improvement under grant R305A60007. The opinions expressed are solely those of the author.

REFERENCES

Bauersfeld, H., Krummheuer, G., & Voigt, J. (1988). Interactional theory of learning and teaching mathematics and related microethnographical studies. In H.-G. Steiner & A. Vermandel (Eds.), *Foundations and methodology of the discipline of mathematics education* (pp. 174–188). Antwerp, Belgium: Proceedings of the TME Conference.

Boulez, P. (1995, December 14, 15, 16). Score: Imagination and reality. *Chicago Symphony Orchestra Program Notes*, pp. 19–28.

Doerr, H. (1995, April). *An integrated approach to mathematical modeling: A classroom study.* Paper presented at the annual meeting of the American Educational Research Association, San Francisco.

Hersh, R. (1986). Some proposals for reviving the philosophy of mathematics. In T. Tymoczko (Ed.), *New directions in the philosophy of mathematics* (pp. 9–28). Boston: Birkhäuser.

Janvier, C. (1987). *Problems of representation in the teaching and learning of mathematics.* Hillsdale, NJ: Lawrence Erlbaum Associates.

Kaput, J. J. (1994). The representational roles of technology in connecting mathematics with authentic experience. In R. Biehler, R. W. Scholz, R. Strässer, & B.Winkelmann (Eds.), *Didactics of mathematics as a scientific discipline* (pp. 379–397). Dordrecht, The Netherlands: Kluwer Academic Press.

Latour, B. (1990). Drawing things together. In M. Lynch & S. Woolgar (Eds.), *Representation in scientific practice* (pp. 19–68). Cambridge, MA: MIT Press.

Pea, R. D. (1993). Practices of distributed intelligence and designs for education. In G. Solomon (Ed.), *Distributed cognition* (pp. 47–87). New York: Cambridge University Press.

Richards, J. (1991). Mathematical discussions. In E. von Glasersfeld (Ed.), *Constructivism in mathematics education* (pp. 13–52). Dordrecht, The Netherlands: Kluwer Academic Press.

Schoenfeld, A. H. (1987). What's all the fuss about metacognition? In A. H. Schoenfeld (Ed.), *Cognitive science and mathematics education* (pp. 189–216). Hillsdale, NJ: Lawrence Erlbaum Associates.

Sfard, A. (1991). On the dual nature of mathematical conceptions: Reflections on processes and objects as different sides of the same coin. *Educational Studies in Mathematics, 22,* 1–36.

Simon, M. A. (1995). Reconstructing mathematics pedagogy from a constructivist perspective. *Journal for Research in Mathematics Education, 26,* 114–145.

van Oers, B. (1996). Learning mathematics as meaningful activity. In L. P. Steffe, P. Nesher, P. Cobb, G. A. Goldin, & B. Greer (Eds.), *Theories of mathematical learning* (pp. 91–113). Mahwah, NJ: Lawrence Erlbaum Associates.

I

THEORETICAL CONSIDERATIONS

2

From Representations to Symbolizing: Introductory Comments on Semiotics and Mathematical Learning

Paul Cobb
Vanderbilt University

The four chapters in this section of the book all focus on semiotics as it relates to mathematical learning. The authors are therefore concerned with symbols and their role in mathematical communication. Each chapter offers a perspective on the subtle interplay between the modification and use of symbols on the one hand and the development of mathematical meaning on the other. In this introduction, I first consider common assumptions that cut across all four chapters and then compare and contrast the specific perspectives developed in each chapter. My purpose in doing so is to orient the reader to the general theoretical commitments made by the various authors. As Dörfler observes in his chapter (chap. 4), these differing theoretical conceptions of meaning constrain the research questions addressed and thus what is describable and observable. Dörfler goes on to note that theoretical commitments of this type have pedagogical impact in that teachers' preconceptions of mathematical understanding and of the meaning of the subject matter strongly influence the judgments they make about students' mathematical activity (cf. Thompson, 1992).

CROSS-CUTTING THEMES

It is important to note at the outset that the authors use the term *symbol* broadly to denote any situation in which a concrete entity such as a mark on paper, an icon on a computer screen, or an arrangement of physical materials is interpreted as standing for or signifying something else. Thus, to cite a well-known example discussed by Vygotsky, a knot in the corner of a handkerchief serves a symbolic function when we tie it to remind ourselves to run an errand. Similarly, a first grader who uses blocks to solve an arithmetical word problem is using the blocks symbolically in that they signify numerical quantities. As these two examples illustrate, symbols for the authors are not restricted to conventional mathematical signs but can include physical materials as well as charts, tables, graphs, and nonstandard notations.

A second point common to the four chapters concerns the authors' focus on the activity of symbolizing. This can be contrasted with an alternative approach in which the properties of symbols are analyzed independently of their use. Nemirovsky (1994) highlighted this difference by distinguishing between *symbol systems* and *symbol use*:

> With "symbol system" I refer to the analysis of mathematical representations in terms of rules. For example, Cartesian graphs can be considered as a symbol system; that is, a rule-governed set of elements, such as points being determined by coordinate values in specific ways or scales demarking units regularly. On the other hand, with "symbol use" I refer to the actual concrete use of mathematical symbols by someone, for a purpose, and as part of a chain of meaningful events. (p. 390)

This focus on symbol use emphasizes that the same concrete entity can serve different symbolizing functions and might, in fact, be used nonsymbolically. For example, the child who used the blocks while solving the word problem might subsequently stack them while building. In the latter case, the blocks do not necessarily symbolize anything beyond themselves. An important consequence of this focus on the activity of symbolizing is that it challenges the notion that symbols can serve as unambiguous carriers of meaning in the classroom. Instead, the authors emphasize that students' use of an entity as a symbol to communicate their reasoning involves a process of negotiation.

In drawing on contemporary semiotics to develop their viewpoints, the authors question several assumptions about meaning that are commonly made by mathematics educators. For example, they all reject the view that the process of constructing meaning for symbols involves associating them with separate, self-contained referents. Instead, they all argue that the ways that symbols are used and the meanings they come to have are mutually constitutive and emerge together. It is important to caution against translating this general theoretical commitment into an instructional prescription that bears directly on the issue of whether instruction should focus first on meaning or on symbols. Rather, this theoretical commitment provides a general orientation for both teaching and instructional design by emphasizing that symbolizing is integral to mathematical activity. The assumed reflexive relationship between symbol use and mathematical meaning implies that a student's use of symbols involves some type of meaning, and that the development of meaning involves modifications in ways of symbolizing. Viewed in these terms, teaching and instructional design both involve attempts to support the development of students' ways of symbolizing as part of the process of supporting the development of mathematical meaning (cf. Kaput, 1994). The chapters in the second section of this book, which focus on instructional design, illustrate several approaches in which designers consciously exploit semiotic processes to promote mathematical learning.

In addition to challenging the traditional relationship between symbol and referent, the authors of all four chapters also question a distinction central to mainstream psychology, that between external representations or symbols on the one hand and internal representations or concepts on the other (cf. Lesh & Doerr, chap. 10, this volume). The dissolution of this mainstream distinction is in fact a direct consequence of the focus on symbol use and symbolizing rather than on the properties of symbols per se. In particular, analyses that focus on people's activity with symbols treat them as an integral aspect of their mathematical reasoning rather than as external aids to it. For example, the reasoning of a mathematician working alone would not, from this point of view, be located in his or her head. Instead, the mathematician's reasoning would be located in the person's activity and would therefore encompass that person's use of symbols (cf. Hutchins, 1995).

A final cross-cutting theme concerns the significance that all the authors attribute to discourse. As becomes apparent, they develop a range of perspectives on discourse. Despite these differences, the authors all take social exchanges with others as constituting a primary occasion in which students modify their ways of symbolizing and thus their mathematical meanings. In addition, the authors all highlight the communicative function of symbols, thereby emphasizing that symbolizing is integral to collective as well as individual activity. Cast in this way, the process of learning to use symbols in general, and conventional mathematical symbols in particular, is seen to have a participatory aspect. Symbol use is then seen not so much as something to be mastered, but as a constituent part of mathematical activity in which students come to participate. In bringing the discursive aspect of symbolizing to the fore, the authors draw together the three overarching themes addressed in this book—those of symbolizing, communicating, and mathematizing.

It might appear from this initial overview that the authors' positions are relatively similar. There are, however, significant differences in both the theoretical perspectives they develop and the specific questions they address. Taken together, the chapters offer a multifaceted view of semiotics as it relates to mathematics education. In contrast to the quest for a single, overarching theory, this plurality of approaches offers greater flexibility when developing instructional designs and analyzing mathematical activity in classrooms. My focus in the remainder of this chapter is on the relationships and contrasts between the chapters. To this end, I first consider the contributions of Nemirovsky and Monk and of van Oers, and then those of Sfard and Dörfler.

MATHEMATICAL EXPERIENCE
AND CULTURAL ACTIVITIES

In both the chapters by Nemirovsky and Monk and by van Oers, the authors analyze the face-to-face negotiation of mathematical meanings and of ways of symbolizing. However, they do so from sharply differing perspectives. Nemirovsky and Monk's orientation is phenomenological and focuses on the nature of individual students' mathematical experience as they negotiate meanings with others. The issue they address is that of developing ways to describe the experience of engaging in mathematical activity, and it is to this end that they propose two theoretical constructs, *fusion* and *trail-making*. They illustrate the relevance of these constructs by analyzing several short episodes involving a 10-year-old student, Lin, and an interviewer, Tracy. In the course of the analysis, they take what might be called the actor's viewpoint (MacKay, 1969) as they strive to describe the quality of Lin's experience as she modified her ways of symbolizing while interacting with Tracy.

van Oers, for his part, presents a sociocultural approach in which human activity is treated primarily as a cultural phenomenon. From this perspective, mathematics is viewed as a cultural activity that involves inventing, using, and improving symbols. The issue that van Oers addresses is that of students' appropriation of ways of symbolizing as a central aspect of their enculturation into established mathematical practices. In approaching this issue, he emphasizes the adult's role in proactively supporting students' learning within the zone of proximal development. However, in doing so, he questions individualistic characterizations of this zone that stress the difference between what a student can do unaided and with the assistance of more knowledgeable others. He argues that Vygotsky instead viewed the zone of proximal development as a dynamic context that emerges in interaction between students and adults and that involves the joint reenactment of preexisting cultural activities. In this theoretical scheme, students are seen to appropriate mathematical ways of symbolizing as they move from peripheral to more substantial participation in the meaningful reenactment of established mathematical practices. A key theoretical construct that van Oers proposes, that of *predication*, serves to clarify this process of appropriation as it occurs during students' participation in culturally organized activities.

In contrast to Nemirovsky and Monk, who take the actor's viewpoint and focus on the experience of the symbolizer, van Oers takes the observer's viewpoint and focuses on the students' actions with symbols as they relate to established mathematical practices. Despite this sharp contrast in their overall viewpoints, their positions are not necessarily oppositional. For example, van Oers follows Vygotsky in stressing that culturally established meanings cannot be transmitted ready made. Instead, the students have to figure out with others' help the generally accepted meaning of conventional ways of using mathematical symbols, thereby making their own meaning. In other words, students actively construct meaning as they participate in increasingly substantial ways in the reenactments of established mathematical practices. This acknowledgment of students' meaning-making activity would seem to leave room for phenomenological analyses of the type developed by Nemirovsky and Monk. Significantly, the sample transcripts presented in each of the two chapters lend themselves to interpretations developed in terms of the theoretical constructs proposed in the other chapter. van Oers, for example, might argue that the exchanges between Lin and Tracy presented by Nemirovsky and Monk involve the meaningful reenactment of the culturally established mathematical practice of graphing. Similarly, Nemirovsky and Monk would have little difficulty in using their key constructs to develop conjectures about the mathematical experiences of the children in some of the episodes presented by van Oers. This juxtaposition of interpretations developed from the actor's and the observer's viewpoints is intriguing for those of us who are willing to admit a multiplicity of perspectives. The two interpretations can in fact be seen to complement each other if one accepts that, although phenomenological and constructivist analyses do not go far enough in locating students' activity in social and cultural context, sociocultural analyses do not go far enough in delineating students' socially and culturally situated mathematical experience.

A further point of contact between the two chapters emerges when we focus specifically on symbolizing in that Nemirovsky and Monk and van Oers both develop their positions by drawing analogies with play. Nemirovsky and Monk argue that symbolizing is typically experienced by the symbolizer as "making the absent present." They take care to distinguish this characterization from one in which the meaning of a symbol is said to emerge as it is associated with another entity that serves as its referent. To clarify the distinction between this associationist characterization of meaning and their own position, Nemirovsky and Monk introduce the example of two girls who are playing with stuffed animals by pretending that they are pets looking for food. The authors argue that the girls do not merely associate terms such as *cat* and *bear* with the toys. Instead, the girls act, talk, and gesture as though the stuffed animals really are pets looking for food, while remaining aware that the stuffed animals are not real pets. Nemirovsky and Monk note that in symbolic play of this type, the signifiers (the stuffed animals) and the signifieds (the pets) are fused in children's experience. Their fundamental contention is that the *fusion* of symbol and meaning is characteristic of symbol use in mathematics as well as in children's play. Thus, they argue that the distance–time graphs that Lin and Tracy created were fused in their experience with what they signified (the speeds of toy bears). In making these claims about the quality of the symbolizer's experience, Nemirovsky and Monk question the more common metaphor of transparency wherein symbols are described as being meaningful when they become invisible and the symbolizer sees through them to what is signified. For Nemirovsky and Monk, in contrast, the visual attributes of symbols remain in the foreground and can be distinguished from the signifieds with which they are fused.

Nemirovsky and Monk discuss children's play in order to clarify the experience of reasoning with mathematical symbols, whereas van Oers views children's participation in culturally determined play activities as a developmental source of mathematical symbolizing. He argues that mathematical activity is a special form of semiotic activity and that it first emerges from early symbolic play activities. In developing his position, van Oers clarifies that semiotic activity is concerned with symbol–meaning relationships and involves both the construction of meaning and the constructive improvement of symbols (cf. Lehrer, Schauble, Carpenter, & Penner, chap. 9, this volume). He stresses that this concurrent process of making meaning and making symbols involves reflecting on the consequences of modifying a symbol for the corresponding meaning, and vice versa. To illustrate this process, van Oers describes an instructional situation in which small groups of children were first encouraged to draw a diagram of a railway track that they had built. The teacher then supported their reflection on the relationship between their diagrams and the railway track by asking them what specific parts of their drawings signified and then encouraging them to verify whether there was, say, a bridge at a particular location on the track. In participating in this reenactment of the cultural activity of making diagrams, the children reflected on the adequacy of symbols with respect to what they signified and adjusted them accordingly.

In addition to investigating whether young children can reflect on symbol–meaning relations, van Oers also explores opportunities for teaching by focusing on the "mathematics-like actions" that occur in semiotic play activities. The theoretical construct that he introduces when analyzing teacher–child interactions in play situations is that of *predication*. He argues that in describing a situation of joint interest symbolically, the teacher and children predicate the situation by attributing additional features or qualities to the situation, thereby distinguishing it from other situations. As an example, van Oers discusses a standard textbook task in which seven birds are shown sitting on a roof, two more are shown coming to join them, and students are asked to find out how many birds will eventually be on the roof. In van Oers' terms, a student who writes a number sentence such as $7 + 2 =$ predicates the situation by attributing an additional feature to it (i.e., it is an adding situation) that serves to distinguish it from other situations in which one might subtract, multiply, or whatever. In more familiar terms, this act of predication is an act of mathematization that involves interpreting the situation in terms of relations between quantities. For van Oers, predication does not first involve developing a mathematical interpretation and then expressing the interpretation symbolically. Instead, symbolizing is integral to the act of mathematizing a situation. His notion of predication encompasses both the use of symbols and the development of the corresponding mathematical interpretation. van Oers goes on to characterize negotiation in these terms by describing it as the process of offering and testing predicates in order to develop a topic of joint attention. As van Oers makes clear, this process of coming to agree upon predicates involves both cooperatively figuring out what can be said and struggling for taken-as-shared meaning. Given this interdependence of meaning and symbols, whether written or spoken, the sequence of predicates offered during negotiation simultaneously traces the evolution of interpretations and of symbolizations.

A comparison of Nemirovsky and Monk's and van Oers' treatments of symbol use in mathematics indicates a potential conflict. Nemirovsky and Monk emphasize the experienced fusion of signifier and signified, whereas van Oers stresses the importance of reflecting on the relation between symbol and meaning. Nemirovsky and Monk might argue that van Oers' approach is associationist in that it implies a correspondence between symbols and meanings that are treated as separate entities. Conversely, van Oers might counter that Nemirovsky and Monk fail to acknowledge the importance of reflecting on relations between symbols and meaning. The difference in their positions plays out in their contrasting assessments of Werner and Kaplan's (1963) theory of the development of semiotic activity. van Oers cites Werner and Kaplan's work approvingly, whereas Nemirovsky and Monk criticize a key aspect of the theory. Werner and Kaplan speak of the fusion and unity of meaning and symbolic form but also use fusion to describe the child's inability to differentiate between symbol and meaning. Thus, Werner and Kaplan view fusion as an indicator of a relatively primitive level of development, whereas Nemirovsky and Monk contend that fusion is a pervasive quality of the symbol use of mathematicians as well as of young children.

In clarifying this conflict, it is important to note that in the episodes presented by Nemirovsky and Monk, Lin and Tracy did occasionally speak as associationists. This occurred when they became consciously aware that they did not understand each other's interpretation of a graph. Nemirovsky and Monk take this as evidence that Lin and Tracy could both step back and explicitly distinguish between symbol and the signified situation when the need arose to do so. However, one can also conjecture that this capability to step back when conversational breakdowns occur is a developmental achievement. In other words, one can agree with Nemirovsky and Monk that fusion typifies the symbol use of both expert mathematicians and young children while accepting that young children might not initially be able to step back and reflect on relations between signifiers and signifieds either when breakdowns in communication occur or when explicitly encouraged to do so by an adult.

Nemirovsky and Monk supplement their discussion of fusion by proposing a second construct, *trail-making*. They contrast this with path-following as a way of solving problems. As path-following involves executing a sequence of directions, the solver's attention tends to focus on cues as to the next step to be taken in order to complete a solution. In contrast, trail-making is a more creative activity in which the solver continually assesses how to deal with immediate circumstances in order to move closer to the final goal. Trail-making, therefore, involves an openness to what might happen next, and is characterized by an awareness of the broader situation that is not restricted to scanning for specific cues. Following Suchman (1987), Nemirovsky and Monk go on to stress that although trail-making does not involve following a well-defined plan, it should not be equated with merely reacting to each local situation in an ad hoc manner. Instead, a vision of the final goal and a general sense of how to achieve it serve to orient local judgments, which can in turn lead to unanticipated modifications in both the envisioned goal and the means of achieving it.

Nemirovsky and Monk's discussion of trail-making is intriguing given its compatibility with aspects of Lave's (1988) analysis of the problem-solving activity of "just plain folks" in such settings as shopping for groceries in a supermarket. For example, Lave argued that the shoppers' activity of solving price-comparison problems involved closing the gap between the anticipated resolution and immediate circumstances by repeatedly modifying both. Further, Lave demonstrated that the shoppers often capitalized opportunistically on aspects of the immediate situation such as the availability of priced packages of different amounts of the same product. Similarly, Nemirovsky and Monk demonstrate that Lin, the student, capitalized opportunistically on the grid that happened to be marked on the only paper that was readily available during one of her exchanges with Tracy. More generally, Nemirovsky and Monk echo Lave's remarks about the emerging significance of aspects of the local situation when they argue that, in trail-making, initially unintended background details often move into the foreground and become integral to the problem-solving process.

This relationship between Nemirovsky and Monk's analysis and Lave's work might seem surprising, given that Lave emphasizes the socially and culturally situated nature of activity. Her overall theoretical position is in fact closer to van Oers' perspective than to Nemirovsky and Monk's focus on individual experience. Lave has, for example, been outspoken in criticizing the individualistic emphasis of mainstream cognitive psychology. The key in resolving this apparent anomaly is to tease out the assumptions that underlie Nemirovsky and Monk's characterization of the individual. In their portrayal, Lin and Tracy are not the putative creatures of mainstream psychology who create internal representations and perform cognitive skills. Instead, Lin's and Tracy's intelligence is seen to be embodied, or to be located, in their activity. Further, rather than representing a world, they are characterized as enacting a taken-as-shared world of signification (cf. Varela, Thompson, & Rosch, 1991). The unit of analysis for Nemirovsky and Monk is therefore the person acting in the lived-in world rather than cognitive processes located in the head that intervene between perceptual input and observed output responses. In this regard, their approach is consistent with that of Lave (1988), who discussed the need "to incorporate the active character of experience into the unit of analysis" (p. 180). She also observed that "the choice of the experienced, lived-in world as one element in the dialectical constitution of the sociocultural order places emphasis on the notion that persons are directly engaged with the world" (p. 180). It is this common focus on the self as embodied and located in the world that accounts for areas of compatibility between Lave's and Nemirovsky and Monk's work. This again indicates that a focus on individual experience need not conflict with sociocultural approaches. In fact, one of the contributions of Nemirovsky and Monk's chapter is to demonstrate that mathematically significant activity such as that engaged in by Lin and Tracy is amenable to analysis in terms of acting in a lived-in world. This goes some way toward clarifying that Lave's treatment of problem solving is not restricted to such situations as shopping for groceries in which the mathematical significance of the reasoning involved has been open to debate.

The final issue I consider concerns the relevance of Nemirovsky and Monk's and van Oers' analyses to instructional design. Nemirovsky and Monk view design as the creation of artifacts such as instructional activities and software environments that open up domains of contact between teachers, students, and historically developed mathematical practices. However, they argue that these artifacts do not, by themselves, determine what they are going to mean for students, but instead make possible a variety of trajectories that can be realized by trail-making. In addition, the authors caution that we can never totally anticipate how students will deal with a problem when symbols are used in a trail-making fashion. Given this lack of determinism, Nemirovsky and Monk's notions of fusion and trail-making can best be viewed as conceptual resources that can be used when engaging in the process of design. In particular, these theoretical constructs offer a way of interpreting students' mathematical activity in classrooms. They therefore serve to inform pedagogical judgments that are made when experimenting in classrooms and thus influence the modifications that are made to initial designs. In my judgment, Nemirovsky and Monk's adoption of the actor's viewpoint is appropriate to this purpose, given that such experimenting involves coparticipating in learning–teaching activities with teachers and their students. To coparticipate is to engage in communicative interactions that involve a reciprocity of perspectives characteristic of the actor's perspective (cf. Rommetveit, 1992; Schutz, 1962).

In contrast to Nemirovsky and Monk's nondeterminist position, van Oers argues that mathematical constructions are produced by the practices and sociocultural activities in which students are involved. Thus, although students make their own meanings, they do so as they participate in preexisting cultural practices that generate the qualities of their thinking (van Oers, 1996). This contention has direct instructional consequences in that it implies that the structure of the reasoning that students are to develop should be present in the interactions between the teacher and students as a precondition for its development. More generally, the relatively direct relation that van Oers posits between the structure of the practices in which students participate and the forms of reasoning they develop enables him to outline a theory of mathematics education. He describes this theory as a developmental pedagogy for the appropriation of mathematizing. Such a theory would specify an evolving sequence of practices that are to be created discursively in the classroom. van Oers contributes to the realization of a theory of this type when he suggests that mathematics, viewed as a developing form of semiosis, is rooted in culturally organized semiotic play activities. Thus, where Nemirovsky and Monk offer designers a conceptual resource that is useful at the micro-level of classroom experimentation, van Oers offers a sketch of broad phases in a developmental pedagogy. Nemirovsky and Monk's notion of trail-making is helpful in clarifying this distinction given its emphasis on the interplay of long-term plans and local judgments. In these terms, van Oers' work serves to inform the development of long-term design plans that orient local judgments, whereas Nemirovsky and Monk's work informs local design judgments that can lead to a revision of these plans.

DISCOURSE AND MATHEMATICAL LEARNING

I have noted several significant differences in the theoretical perspectives developed by Nemirovsky and Monk and by van Oers. In contrast, the chapters by Sfard and Dörfler are in many ways complementary. Both authors view mathematics as discourse and argue that mathematical learning involves appropriating the use of conventional mathematical terms and symbols. In taking this approach, they are both careful not to reduce discourse to language use. Instead, discourse for them encompasses perceiving and doing as well as speaking and writing. Both therefore appear to follow Bruner (1986) in emphasizing the constitutiveness of language wherein what is spoken and the world spoken about are seen to be mutually constitutive. On the one hand, the world comes into being through discourse, and on the other hand, the world thus constituted constrains what can be said about and done in it. In defining mathematical discourse in this relatively broad manner, Sfard and Dörfler are both concerned with the development of mathematical meaning—with what teachers and students are speaking about as well as how they speak.

Further commonalities become apparent when we consider Sfard's and Dörfler's treatments of mathematical meaning. In taking a discourse perspective, they both reject the view that the meaning of symbols, words, and sentences can be isolated and described in the same way that one would describe the properties of physical objects. They instead both draw on Wittgenstein's claim that the meaning of a term is synonymous with how it is used. For example, Dörfler argues that, in practice, we infer that a student has grasped the meaning of a mathematical term only when the student has a thorough command of its social use (i.e., when the student consistently uses the term in socially accepted ways). It is, however, important to note that a strict adherence to Wittgenstein's view that meaning can be reduced to social use leads to an epistemological behaviorist position in which understanding involves nothing more than acting in accordance with the established norms or conventions of a discourse (cf. Rorty, 1979). As Sfard and Dörfler both observe, exclusive focus on social usage ignores the experiential aspect of meaning that includes imagery and emotions. Thus, although they define mathematical learning as enculturation into mathematical discourse, they also acknowledge the importance of focusing on the nature of individual students' experience as they actively participate in their mathematical enculturation. Thus, like van Oers, both appear to leave room for an analysis of the type conducted by Nemirovsky and Monk.

The degree to which Sfard and Dörfler analyze this experiential aspect serves to differentiate their contributions. Sfard focuses to a greater extent on how students use mathematical terms and in doing so distinguishes between what she calls *templates-driven* and *object-mediated* usage. To be sure, this distinction in symbol use implies a corresponding distinction in the quality of students' mathematical experience. However, Sfard's primary concern in her chapter is to account for mathematical development in terms of changes in the ways that students are observed to use symbols. In taking this approach, she is careful to clarify that her focus on social use does not translate into a philosophical claim about the essence of mathematical meaning. Instead, based on the assumption that meaning has much to do with linguistic use, her purpose is to illustrate how the development of mathematical meaning might actually be investigated. The motivation for her focus on symbol use is therefore primarily methodological.

In concert with Sfard, Dörfler contends that a theory of students' development of mathematical meaning should explain how they come to participate successfully in mathematical discourse. However, rather than focusing on students' observable use of symbols, Dörfler is concerned with the evolving nature of their mathematical experience as they learn to participate successfully in mathematical discourse. He clarifies that his purpose in introducing two theoretical notions, *prototypes* and *protocols*, is to delineate an experiential basis with concrete and perceivable entities (including symbols) that mathematical discourse can be viewed as being about. Thus, Sfard repeatedly points to the experiential aspect of meaning while focusing primarily on symbol use, whereas Dörfler attempts to describe the experience of the symbolizer, frequently by reflecting on his own activity as a practicing mathematician. It is in this respect that their contributions can be viewed as complementary. There is therefore a parallel with the first two chapters discussed in that Sfard, like van Oers, adopts the observer's viewpoint, whereas Dörfler, like Nemirovsky and Monk, develops his theoretical approach from the actor's perspective.

An issue addressed by both Sfard and Dörfler is that of how students come to have the experience of talking about and acting on mathematical objects when they participate in mathematical discourse. Sfard approaches this issue by analyzing the metaphorical relations between everyday discourse about physical objects and the mathematical discourse about experienced mathematical objects. Her analysis can therefore be interpreted as an elaboration of Bloor's (1976) observation that physical reality constitutes the ultimate metaphor with which we think. In her view, the process by which mathematical reality is constructed in the image of physical reality involves a metaphorical projection in which the virtual reality discourse of mathematics is built in the image of actual reality discourse. In developing her position, Sfard uses a rigorous criterion for the meaningfulness of mathematical terms, namely, that the terms are experienced as signifying mathematical objects. It is with reference to this criterion that she argues that "in the beginning was the word," before terms are experienced as signifying mathematical objects and thus before fully developed meanings have been established. A central question for her is therefore that of explaining the process by which experientially real mathematical objects retroactively come into being for students as a consequence of their use of symbols that are said to represent them. The distinction that she makes between the templates-driven and object-mediated use of symbols bears directly on this question.

Sfard argues that students' use of a mathematical term necessarily involves an initial templates-driven phase in which the term is not experienced as signifying a mathematical object and is therefore relatively empty of meaning. In this phase, students can only use the term in already-familiar phrases or linguistic templates. She contrasts this with the subsequent object-mediated phase in which the more flexible and creative use of the term is mediated by the mathematical object it is experienced as signifying. For Sfard, it is students' attempts to participate in discourse in which mathematical terms are used as though they signify independently existing mathematical entities that account for the terms eventually becoming fully meaningful. The strong discourse perspective that Sfard develops in her chapter therefore challenges more traditional psychological approaches that treat changes in how students speak as expressions of internal conceptual developments.

Dörfler follows Sfard in arguing that experienced mathematical objects come into being exclusively within a discourse that attributes to them both an existence and properties of an objective character. He therefore concurs with Sfard's claim that it is not until students attempt to speak as if such objects exist that they can become experientially real for the students. One of the important contributions that Dörfler makes in his chapter is to describe an experiential basis that might make it possible for students to eventually use mathematical terms in an object-mediated way. It is to this end that he introduces the theoretical notions of protocols and prototypes, both of which can serve as a means of supporting students' induction into mathematical discourse.

Dörfler describes a protocol as a cognitive process in which one reconstructs the stages, phases, and results of a prior activity when interpreting a symbolic record of that activity. It is important to note that in giving this definition, Dörfler emphasizes the students' interpretative activity.

The protocol is not the symbolic record per se but is instead a particular way of interpreting the record. The subtlety of this distinction between the symbolic record as the carrier of the protocol and the interpretation of that record as the protocol serves to illustrate Nemirovsky and Monk's observation that the signifier (the record) and signified (the phases of prior activity) are frequently fused in the experience of the symbolizer. We can also note that, in van Oers' terms, the protocol serves to predicate the prior activity by attributing to it stages and phases that serve to differentiate it from other activities.

The significance that Dörfler attributes to protocols as a means of supporting the development of mathematical meaning stems from his view that certain specific actions and their results constitute the developmental origins of many mathematical concepts and symbolizations. Thus, for Dörfler, mathematical development is a process of reorganizing activity rather than of abstracting structures from specific situations in the world. In this regard, he rejects what Dewey called the spectator view of knowledge and instead treats knowing as activity in which one engages. It is also important to note that Dörfler uses the term *action* broadly to encompass conceptual actions as well as physical actions. For example, a symbolic record of a permutation serves as a protocol if it is interpreted as signifying phases in the process of arranging the relevant elements. Based on this view of the origin of mathematical concepts, Dörfler proposes that students' induction into mathematical discourse should involve first carrying out the relevant actions and then reflecting on the actions and their results. In this approach, protocols function as a means of reflecting on just those aspects of the actions that constitute what Dörfler calls the *germ* of the intended mathematical concepts. Throughout the discussion, Dörfler stresses that it is the student who constructs the protocol as a cognitive tool by coming to interpret the symbolic record in a particular way. He also clarifies that this requires appropriate social guidance. Given the significance that he attributes to discourse, one can infer that the construction of protocols involves coming to speak about symbolic records in a way that makes reference only to schematized and general aspects of the actions that they signify.

In introducing the related construct of prototype, Dörfler differentiates it from Rosch's (1981) analysis of meaning in which the notion of prototype also features prominently. For Rosch, a prototype is a central, paradigmatic case in a category of referents associated with a particular term. In contrast, the important aspect of a prototype for Dörfler is that it serves to guide mathematical activity such as calculating, proving, and arguing. As an initial example, Dörfler notes that the number line can serve as a prototype for Z, the integers, in that one can use it to think about integers and their relations. As he did in the case of protocols, Dörfler stresses students' interpretive activity by observing that students must develop a specific way of viewing the number line in order for it to serve this function. He illustrates this point by noting that the number line can also serve as a prototype for Q, the rationals, provided that it is viewed as a continuous line composed of points rather than as a line broken into segments of equal length.

Dörfler argues that prototypes should not be viewed as representations of abstract mathematical concepts such as Z and Q. Instead, when students use the number line to support their thinking, it serves to regulate mathematical activity that is viewed as meaningful by others. In other words, although the students speak about integers, they are actually thinking about the number line. Cast in this way, a prototype is a means of relying on experiences with specific objects and activities in order to use linguistic terms in a socially accepted manner. It would therefore seem that a student's initial use of mathematical terms based on a prototype is consistent with Sfard's discussion of templates-driven use in which new terms are utilized only in already familiar phrases. In the case of the integers, for example, the new terms might first be employed in phrases previously used to talk about the number line. The two analyses therefore complement each other in that Dörfler clarifies the source and nature of meaning in Sfard's templates-driven phase whereas Sfard delineates observable features of students' use of symbols. The compatibility of the analyses becomes even more apparent when we note that both Sfard and Dörfler highlight the role of metaphors in the development of mathematical meaning. Sfard, for example, argues that certain metaphors came into play and specific expectations are established as to the nature of the signified when a new term is used for the first time. Dörfler's example of the number line illustrates this phenomenon in that the number line becomes a metaphor that makes it possible to use integer terminology in a socially accepted manner.

In discussing students' subsequent mathematical development, Dörfler suggests that once students have acquired, say, "integer theory" discourse, they can reason independently of the prototype. By this point, the students' use of mathematical terms has taken on a life of its own in that it no longer requires the guidance that the imagery of specific objects and activities such as the number line provide. This type of symbol use appears to correspond to Sfard's object-mediated phase in which mathematical terms are experienced as signifying mathematical objects. In discussing these experienced abstract entities, Dörfler notes that the discourse proceeds as though the signifieds of mathematical terms are unique entities that determine what is to count as a representation of them (e.g., the number line counts as a representation of the integers because it captures important properties and relations of the integers). However, both his and Sfard's contention that mathematical objects come into existence exclusively within discourse calls this apparently self-evident intuition into question. In Dörfler's view, it is the so-called representations, and the relationships between them, that determine the discourse about abstract objects, rather than the other way around. He argues, for example, that a prototype such as the number line suggests properties and operations that are formulated in discourse as properties and operations of the integers. In this view, abstractness is a quality of mathematical discourse. A symbol such as "–5" does not refer to an entity that exists independently of the discourse. Instead, it is used to express experiences with various prototypical objects in a general manner. As a consequence of this way of speaking, "–5" is experienced as signifying an entity with numerous properties that are, for Dörfler, suggested by prototypes such as the number line. The implication of this view is that induction into mathematical discourse requires a willingness on the part of students to speak as if there are independently existing mathematical entities as a precondition for such entities becoming experientially real. In this regard, Dörfler concurs with Sfard that students' attempts to use mathematical terms necessarily precede the full development of meaning. This general point of agreement has far-reaching pedagogical implications.

In discussing pedagogical issues, Sfard argues that it is impossible to prepare what she calls an easy, meaningful landing for students by first supporting their development of mature mathematical meanings that the new terms are then introduced to baptize. In addition, she critiques instructional approaches in which everyday discourse about physical reality is viewed as the only possible source of mathematical meaning. She contends that although the roots of all language games go back to everyday discourse, the sequence of links between this discourse and the discourse of mathematics might be too extensive to reconstruct during 10 or 12 years of schooling. This leads her to consider what she calls intradiscursive sources of meaning—sources that originate within mathematical discourse and that do not reach beyond it to everyday discourse. Dörfler's example of the number line as a prototype for the integers illustrates this notion in that discourse about the number line is of a mathematical rather than everyday nature. Sfard supports her position by observing that mathematical ideas that are firmly situated in a mathematical context can be as meaningful and relevant as those from everyday-life situations. Her point in making this argument appears to be that, although the instructional starting points might involve mathematical rather than everyday discourse, they should nonetheless be experientially real for students. In this regard, it is worth recalling that, strictly speaking, the number line itself is not a prototype for the integers. Instead, the prototype is a particular way of interpreting and talking about the number line. This indicates that the number line cannot serve as an intradiscursive source of meaning for the integers until students have developed these ways of interpreting it. Sfard subsequently elaborates her view of intradiscursive sources of mathematical meaning by suggesting that in time it might eventually be possible to return to everyday discourse that would then be endowed with new mathematical significance. She argues that, in such an approach, the physical world would seem to students more orderly than before in that real-world structures do not come into existence by themselves, but instead have to be symbolized into being. One can imagine an illustration of this approach in which students who have been successfully inducted into discourse about the integers subsequently mathematize everyday situations in these terms. In such a case, the process of mathematizing would symbolize into being relationships between quantities in the everyday situations.

We have already noted that Dörfler's analysis complements Sfard's focus on symbol use by describing the experiential basis for induction into mathematical discourse. For example, he clarifies that protocols can serve as an important means of supporting students' reflection on and restructuring of prior activity. In addition, he discusses the value of offering students appropriate carriers of prototypes and of negotiating ways of interpreting and talking about them so that students might construct viable prototypes. Thus, Sfard's theoretical analysis gives rise to general reflections that alert us to potential pitfalls in several currently popular approaches to instructional design, whereas Dörfler outlines a particular approach to design in which symbolizing serves as a means of supporting students' induction into mathematical discourse.

SUMMARY

Two broad ways of contrasting the four contributions in part one of this book become apparent when we review the authors' theoretical stances. The first concerns the distinction between the actor's and the observer's viewpoints. Nemirovsky and Monk and Dörfler both focus on the quality of students' experience as the latter engage in mathematical activity. In contrast, van Oers and Sfard both adopt the observer's viewpoint and focus on students' observed activity. However, both also seem to leave open the possibility of conducting analyses from the actor's perspective. Sfard, for example, repeatedly points to the experiential aspects of mathematical meaning. Similarly, there is nothing in van Oers' theoretical approach that appears to delegitimatize an experiential analysis of students' participation in culturally organized activities.

The second contrast concerns the way in which the authors characterize mathematical learning. Sfard and Dörfler both characterize it as a process of induction into mathematical discourse. For his part, van Oers treats mathematical learning as a process of coming to participate in preexisting, historically developed mathematical activities. In all three cases, learning is viewed as a process of enculturation, and individual students' mathematical activity is framed as an act of participating in communal practices. This contrasts with Nemirovsky and Monk's contribution in that they treat mathematical learning primarily as a process of construction and locate students' activity within ongoing communicative interactions rather than within broader communal practices. The distinction can be clarified by comparing Nemirovsky and Monk's contribution with Dörfler's in that both adopt the actor's perspective and focus on students' mathematical experience. In their discussion of the sample episodes involving Lin and Tracy, Nemirovsky and Monk analyze Lin's mathematical experience as she interacts with Tracy in the immediate here and now. Dörfler, however, is concerned with students' mathematical experience at a broader macro-level as it relates to their induction into mathematical discourse. Thus, in contrast to Nemirovsky and Monk, he might describe Lin's experience while graphing in terms of her development of a prototype that might subsequently support her induction into discourse about functions. Described in this way, the contrasting characterizations of learning lead to differences both in the detail with which the experiential aspect of symbol use is analyzed and in the overall scope of the analysis.

A final issue concerns the relationship between Sfard's and Dörfler's interests in discourse on the one hand, and van Oers' focus on historically developed mathematical practices on the other. It is worth reemphasizing that neither Sfard nor Dörfler equates discourse solely with language use. Instead, discourse for both encompasses perceiving and doing as well as speaking and writing. This broad definition might in fact be acceptable to van Oers as a general characterization of a communal mathematical activity. Despite this broad area of compatibility, it does seem possible to differentiate between the three contributions in terms of the extent to which they focus on symbolizing per se or on symbolizing-in-interaction.

Sfard and Dörfler both focus on students' induction into mathematical discourse. To this end, they explain how students are able to participate in this discourse in a peripheral manner before they have developed the full, mature meanings for mathematical terms, and how they are eventually able to participate in the discourse in a more substantial fashion. Although Sfard and Dörfler repeatedly indicate that this process involves interactions with more competent symbolizers, the detailed analysis of such interactions is not part of their agenda. In contrast, van Oers brings to the fore the process of negotiating mathematical interpretations and ways of symbolizing when he develops his notion of predication. In doing so, he focuses on the cultural activity that the teacher and students reenact in the course of their interactions rather than on students' symbolizing in relation to the developmental endpoint—mathematical discourse. Thus, for example, he describes the students' symbolizing as they and the teacher participate in culturally organized play activity and discusses how, with the teacher's guidance, it might become a mathematics-producing activity. In taking this approach, van Oers characterizes students' mathematical enculturation in terms of their participation in a sequence of cultural activities with the support of more competent others (cf. the Gravemeijer et al. discussion of the proactive role of the teacher, chap 7, this volume). Sfard and Dörfler follow an alternative approach and view students as participating in mathematical discourse when they use mathematical terms. The issue for them is how students' ways of participating in this cultural activity evolve.

At the beginning of this chapter, I suggested that the authors together offer us a multifaceted view of semiotics as it relates to mathematics education. The distinctions I have drawn when summarizing their contributions indicate that they do not fall into neat, oppositional camps. Instead, we have a network of commonalities and contrasts. This might be disturbing to those who revel in "paradigm wars" and who continue to argue that their own favored position constitutes an overarching viewpoint that gets things right independently of history, situation, and purpose. In my view, essentialist arguments of this type indicate a striking lack of self-awareness that contributes to the relative immaturity of mathematics education as a field of inquiry. Rather than playing the contributions off each other, I have instead drawn contrasts in order to tease out some of the interests, concerns, suppositions, and assumptions that underlie the various theoretical perspectives. In addition, I have discussed the potential relevance of each perspective to instructional design. My intent in doing so is to demonstrate that the authors collectively offer us a range of theoretical constructs and approaches that allows considerable flexibility when we frame issues that emerge while developing specific instructional designs and while analyzing mathematical activity in classrooms. To be sure, we might well view one theoretical perspective as more appropriate than another for a particular purpose. However, in taking this pragmatic stance toward theorizing, we give up the quest for a God's-eye point of view once and for all.

ACKNOWLEDGMENTS

The analysis reported in this chapter was supported by the National Science Foundation under grant RED-9353587 and by the Office of Educational

Research and Improvement under grant R305A60007. The opinions expressed do not necessarily reflect the views of either the NSF or OERI.

REFERENCES

Bloor, D. (1976). *Knowledge and social imagery*. London: Routledge and Kegan Paul.

Bruner, J. (1986). *Actual minds, possible worlds*. Cambridge, MA: Harvard University Press.

Hutchins, E. (1995). *Cognition in the wild*. Cambridge, MA: MIT Press.

Kaput, J. J. (1994). The representational roles of technology in connecting mathematics with authentic experience. In R. Biehler, R. W. Scholz, R. Strasser, & B. Winkelmann (Eds.), *Didactics of mathematics as a scientific discipline* (pp. 379–397). Dordrecht, The Netherlands: Kluwer Academic Press.

Lave, J. (1988). *Cognition in practice: Mind, mathematics, and culture in everyday life*. New York: Cambridge University Press.

MacKay, D. M. (1969). *Information, mechanism, and meaning*. Cambridge, MA: MIT Press.

Nemirovsky, R. (1994). On ways of symbolizing: The case of Laura and the velocity sign. *Journal of Mathematical Behavior, 13*, 389–422.

Rommetveit, R. (1992). Outlines of a dialogically based social-cognitive approach to human cognition and communication. In A. Heen Wold (Ed.), *The dialogical alternative towards a theory of language and mind* (pp. 19–44). Oslo, Norway: Scandinavian University Press.

Rorty, R. (1979). *Philosophy and the mirror of nature*. Princeton, NJ: Princeton University Press.

Rosch, E. (1981). Prototype classification and logical classification: The two systems. In E. Scholnick (Ed.), *New trends in cognitive representation: Challenges to Piaget's theory* (pp. 73–86). Hillsdale, NJ: Lawrence Erlbaum Associates.

Schutz, A. (1962). *The problem of social reality*. The Hague, The Netherlands: Martinus Nijhoff.

Suchman, L. A. (1987). *Plans and situated actions: The problem of human–machine communication*. New York: Cambridge University Press.

Thompson, A. (1992). Teachers' beliefs and conceptions: A synthesis of the research. In D. A. Grouws (Ed.), *Handbook of research on mathematics teaching and learning* (pp. 127–146). New York: Macmillan.

van Oers, B. (1996). Learning mathematics as meaningful activity. In P. Nesher, L. Steffe, P. Cobb, G. Goldin, & B. Greer (Eds.), *Theories of mathematical learning* (pp. 91–114). Mahwah, NJ: Lawrence Erlbaum Associates.

Varela, F. J., Thompson, E., & Rosch, E. (1991). *The embodied mind: Cognitive science and human experience*. Cambridge, MA: MIT Press.

Werner, H., & Kaplan, B. (1963). *Symbol formation: An organismic developmental approach to language and the expression of thought*. New York: Wiley.

3

Symbolizing Mathematical Reality Into Being—Or How Mathematical Discourse and Mathematical Objects Create Each Other

Anna Sfard
The University of Haifa, Haifa, Israel

THE QUESTION OF MEANING IN VIRTUAL REALITY DISCOURSE

According to Bertrand Russell (1904), "Mathematics may be defined as a subject in which we never know what we are talking about, nor whether what we are saying is true" (p. 84). Thus, for Russell, "not knowing what we are talking about" is the unique characteristic of mathematics, something that sets mathematical discourse apart from other discursive formations. To have a better grasp of what Russell might have had in mind, let us compare the following two utterances:

1. The expressions "the founder of psychoanalysis" and "Sigmund Freud" mean the same because they refer to the same person.
2. The symbols "$\frac{2}{3}$" and "$\frac{12}{18}$" mean the same because they refer to the same number.

The two sentences are similar in many ways. Both speak about something being signified by something else. Both lead the attention of the reader from one kind of thing to another: from objects that refer to something (the name *Sigmund Freud*, the symbol $\frac{2}{3}$) to those that are referred to (the person, the number). Thus, on the face of it, the way to understand a sentence and to decide about its truth value should be basically the same in the two cases. Summoning one's knowledge of the history of modern psychological thought or of mathematics, one has to verify that in each of the sentences the two referring objects (e.g., *Sigmund Freud* and *the founder of psychoanalysis*) have the same object as their referent.

Those, however, who take the verifying business seriously will soon discover a subtle difference between the two instances. In the first, all one has to do to convince an interlocutor of the equivalence of the two expressions is to point out the person who is supposed to be their common referent. This straightforward method would not work for the second. Unlike the Austrian psychiatrist, rational numbers are not palpable objects that can be seen, heard, and touched. Thus, the only way to prove the equivalence of the symbols ⅔ and ¹²⁄₁₈ is to use an indirect procedure, such as the one that shows how the fraction ⅔ may be obtained from ¹²⁄₁₈ by dividing the numerator and denominator by the same number. This method is neither immediate nor does it display the object whose existence is presupposed by the sentence. Throughout the whole procedure, the implied entity remains behind the scene and its existence can only be inferred from the processes performed on its "representations."

To put it more succinctly, whereas the referent of "Sigmund Freud" and of "The founder of psychoanalysis" may be identified "ostensively"[1] (e.g., by showing Freud's portrait), the object allegedly referred to by the symbols ⅔ and ¹²⁄₁₈ can at best be imagined. Unlike the former, the latter cannot be communicated to others just by pointing to something. In this case, a straightforward appeal to one's senses would be useless.[2] The common referent of the symbols ⅔ and ¹²⁄₁₈ is an elusive entity, the ontological status of which has been puzzling philosophers for ages.

One may highlight the difference between utterances 1 and 2 metaphorically, by saying that the two sentences belong to fundamentally different types of discourse: The first comes from actual reality (AR) discourse whereas the second belongs to virtual reality (VR) discourse.

[1]As argued by Wittgenstein (1953), the apparent straightforwardness of ostensive definitions is misleading and, in fact, it is impossible to determine the meaning of words by simply pointing to their referents. Please note, however, the difference between the present use of the term *ostensive* and the use made by Wittgenstein in *Philosophical Investigations* (Wittgenstein, 1953). Although Wittgenstein is concerned with the logical soundness of the idea of "ostensive definition" (which he rightly views as problematic), I am dealing with an entirely different and more practical issue of the means that keeps a discourse in focus and which makes the different utterances meaningful to the discourse participants.

[2]At this point, one may object by saying that the equivalence of the symbols ⅔ and ¹²⁄₁₈ can be demonstrated by pointing to two pieces of a whole (of a pie, say), one of them being composed of two-thirds of the whole and the other of 12 eighteenth parts, and by showing that these two pieces are equal. However, none of the particular pieces of a particular whole may be regarded as a proper referent of the symbols, because in this case, the referent is conceived of as a universal entity.

This figurative description underlines the basic disparity in the ways the meaning of the two types of sentences is constructed and communicated. To put it in a somewhat simplistic way, actual reality communication may be perceptually mediated by the objects that are being discussed, whereas in the virtual reality discourse perceptual mediation is scarce and is only possible with the help of what is understood as symbolic substitutes of objects under consideration. This description should not be read as a statement on an ontological status of the "realms" underlying the discourses. In introducing the metaphor of the two realities, I was psychologically, rather than philosophically, minded. That is, the distinction was drawn with an eye to the differing actions and experiences of the participants of the discourses rather than to ontological questions.

When seen in this light, the virtual reality metaphor not only gives an idea about the rather unique mode of communication characteristic to mathematics, but also conveys a message as to the particular rights and obligations the mathematical discourse confers upon the participants. The demands seem more obvious than the rights. Those who really wish to communicate, not being able to rely on their senses, have to use all their mental faculties in an attempt to reconstruct for themselves the realm within which the moves of their interlocutors make sense. On the other hand, VR discourse frees its participants from responsibilities typical of the AR discourse. The latter kind of discourse mediates concrete human actions and, as such, may have a tangible influence on people's physical condition and on their environment. Think, for example, about possible effects of a medical prescription on a patient or about the influence of an architectural plan of a house on the lives of its inhabitants (cf. Nemirovsky & Monk, chap. 6, this volume). The VR discourse, in contrast, being much less likely to have an immediate impact on the actual reality, creates an atmosphere of freedom that for some students is a source of enjoyment whereas for some others seems rather disturbing. For learners of the latter type, lack of real-life responsibility and constraints may mean lack of importance, and thus lack of interest.

To sum up, the mathematical discourse was presented here as a VR discourse, which can be defined in opposition to the AR discourse. The distinction, drawn along the experiential axis, proved quite fundamental. In light of this, the question may rightly be asked why the AR discourse was juxtaposed to mathematical discourse in the first place. Indeed, why AR discourse and not, say, scientific or literary discourse?

AR discourse may not be the only one against which the particularities of mathematical discourse would stand in full relief, but for my present purpose it is certainly the most appropriate. First and foremost, in the fervor of pinpointing differences, we should not overlook striking similarities. One example substantiating this claim has already been given in the form of sentences 1 and 2. Clearly, the two are almost identical structurally. They both speak about two objects being, in fact, the same entity. This surface similarity is so great that we had to make a certain effort to notice and understand the way in which they differ. An additional glimpse at mathematical textbooks or classroom exchanges should be enough to convince ourselves that the similarity is quite general and that mathematical discourse, in almost all its manifestations, is structurally very close to AR discourse. Indeed, in descriptions of mathematical processes and objects, the same linguistic forms are used as in AR narrative, even though the AR narrative is concerned with physical procedures performed on concrete material objects.

Another way to characterize the similarity between AR and VR discourses is to say that, in both, *the use of symbols is often mediated by objects*. Within our present discussion, in which a psychological perspective has been adopted, object mediation means a certain distinctive way of manipulating symbols, of solving problems and of communicating—a mode that reminds us of what can be observed when people talk about physical objects, whether actually present or only recalled. The claim that a discourse is object mediated signifies that in their attempt to communicate, interlocutors can help themselves with a reference to entities conceived as external to, and independent of, the discourse itself (this is what people do, e.g., when discussing the appropriateness of a given kind of fabric for a certain type of garment, or when they judge the applicability of a given function as a model for a certain biological phenomenon). My use of the phrase "*conceived as* external" rather than "which *are* external" with regard to the mediating entities (objects) comes to emphasize that in the present discussion, the question of the "real" ontological status of these entities is of no relevance, if not entirely out of place. It is very important to understand that in our context, the word *objects* does not stand alone and does not signal an existence of special entities which regulate the discourse. In phrases such as "the discourse is object mediated," "the student has constructed a mathematical object," or "a new object emerged (in discourse)," its use is essentially metaphorical. The term *object mediation* refers, metaphorically, to a certain set of discursive competencies and underlying psychological processes, and should by no means be read as a statement on the nature or the extradiscursive existence (or nonexistence) of the mediating entities.

A detailed description of this mode of symbol use and discursive competencies is given later. Here, I restrict myself to illustrating the idea with the example presented in Fig. 3.1. A 12-year-old boy named George, who has learned about linear functions but has never before tackled a linear equation, is given a problem that he is only able to solve thanks to his ability to "see" more than algebraic expressions themselves. He

This example comes from a study recently completed by Carolyn Kieran and me in Montreal. In our experiment, twelve-year-olds took their first steps in algebra. Our approach was functional, and the learning was massively supported with computer graphics. In the final interview, a boy named George was asked to solve the equation

$$7x + 4 = 5x + 8.$$

Here is our exchange with George:

G: Well, you could see, it would be like, . . . Start at 4 and 8, this one would go up 7, hold on, 8 and 7, hold on . . . no, 4 and 7; 4 and 7 is 11. . . . they will be equal at 2 or 3 or something like that.
I: How are you getting that 2 or 3?
G: I am just graphing in my head.

FIG. 3.1. Object-mediated mathematical discourse—a sample.

speaks and acts as if the symbols were mere representations of some invisible objects. He clearly refers to a structure that cannot be seen on the paper. What is remarkable about George's behavior is that he is able to manipulate this structure "in his head" exactly as he does in the case of concrete objects. His actions may be compared, for example, to those of a person who speaks about moving furniture in a room and tries to figure out the final outcome. As can be learned from mathematicians' testimonies (Sfard, 1994a), what George is able to attain by "drawing in his head" is often achieved by expert practitioners by imagining objects that cannot be actually drawn on paper or even on a computer screen.

As can be seen from this example and from those that follow, object-mediated use of mathematical symbols is the use that gives the VR discourse the leading characteristics of AR discourse: Object-mediated mathematical discourse is conducted as if "with an eye to" a certain entity that keeps this discourse *in focus* and *integrated* (cf. Dörfler, chap. 4, this volume). The expression *in focus* refers to a discourse in which the participant has a clear sense of knowing what his or her utterances are all about. A discourse is *integrated* if there is a general agreement between interlocutors about the focus of the conversation. In AR discourse, thanks to object mediation, that is, to the perceptual accessibility of concrete objects to which participants refer, both of these features are attained without particular difficulty. Indeed, when the discourse is about "a table," there is little danger that the interlocutors would have doubts about the focus of the conversation (and this is true even if the table in question cannot be seen at the moment). Focus and integration are much more difficult to attain in mathematical discourse, in which object names and symbols bring almost no perceptual hints as to the relevant aspects of the situation—those aspects that should be attended to in the conversation. Thus, for example, young students asked to formulate a question for which the answer could be ⅔ would often reply with something like the following: "The cake was divided into nine equal parts; children ate seven of them. How many parts were left?"[3] This is a classical example of an out-of-focus response, which shows that "two ninths" does not yet refer to a well-defined mathematical object for the students; rather, it signifies a certain type of situation.

Let me add that the decision to contrast mathematics with AR discourse has also to do with a possible developmental connection between the two. Because of the already mentioned similarities in structure and in use on the one hand, and in light of the primary, basic character of AR discourse on the other hand, one has good reason to hypothesize that AR discourse may be the earliest link in the long developmental chain from which mathematical discourse eventually emerges. The hypothesis of a developmental connection between AR and VR discourses is examined in the reminder of this chapter with particular attention to mathematical symbols and to the role they play in the construction of mathematical meaning.

WHAT IS IN THE SYMBOL AND HOW DOES IT GET THERE?

The Problem

When stating that in mathematics we do not know what we are talking about, Russell certainly did not intend to say that mathematical symbols have no meaning or that mathematicians talk about nothing. Indeed, it seems that his only claim was that, unlike in AR discourse, the participants of the mathematical discourse have no direct access to this special "something" which is supposed to be signified by mathematical expressions. Using the traditional language of theories of meaning, one may say that the question Russell was posing was that of the *referent*: Mathematical symbols refer to something—but to what?

Let me put the problem in clearer terms. Traditionally, symbol has been understood to be an entity that points to another entity (the referent). Encouraged by Eco (1976), one of the central figures in today's semiotics, we may say that symbol "is a lie" because *it stands for something else*. This classical dichotomy imposes a series of questions about the nature of the entities to which mathematical symbols are supposed to refer. What is

---

[3]The example is taken from my experiments with students of different ages. The experiment has shown that this kind of utterance is very frequent, and not only among young children.

the ontological status of these entities? Where do they come from? How can one get hold of them (or construct them)? These are the most prominent of the issues to be dealt with.

In the preceding section, I argued that the words *mathematical object* are only meaningful in certain phrases and have, at best, some metaphorical meaning. As a consequence, I objected to ontological questions such as those asked earlier. This objection, far from being immediately obvious, is nevertheless an inevitable conclusion from centuries-long debates on the nature of the relation between symbol and its referent. Before we continue our deliberations on the object mediation in mathematical discourse, it would be useful to have a quick look at the way this debate evolved.

Parting From the Referent: A Brief History

What follows is a story of the gradual shift from the objectivist symbol/referent dichotomy to the relativist theories of signification based on penetrating insights into sociocultural mechanisms of meaning production. Three basic positions on the nature of meaning have been proposed over the centuries. First, there is the classical *realist/objectivist* viewpoint, according to which the referents of mathematical symbols have a real existence of a kind, whereas seeking the objective truth about these abstract entities is the mission of the mathematician. For the followers of Plato and Descartes it was, therefore, only natural to view meaning as independent of, and primary to, symbols that, consequently, were regarded as mere vehicles for forwarding an external semantic "load" from one person to another (cf. Reddy, 1979). Taking the realist position as a point of departure, it was only natural to ask what should come first in the process of learning: the knowledge of mathematical objects, or the use of the symbols representing these objects. Should the student "have the idea" of, say, negative numbers, before the student can actually talk about them or symbolize them? The problem is a theoretical one, but with a potential for crucially important pedagogical implications. Many would say that, even if not absolutely necessary, this previous knowledge of the object denoted by the new symbol would be as helpful to learners of mathematics as having an experience of a physical object is useful to a child who learns the word signifying this object. The belief that, indeed, the knowledge of the world is helpful in the acquisition of language has been aptly expressed in Bruner's *Alerting Hypothesis*: "It is immeasurably valuable, in learning a code, to know already what the code stands for" (Bruner, 1983, p. 29). It is only natural that this maxim would be extended by realistically minded educators to the learning of mathematics.

The realist/objectivist position has been questioned first by the founders of the *constructivist* movement, who denied the possibility of a God's-eye view and transmitted the power of creation from God and nature to the individual human mind; and then by the *interactionists*, who claimed that "the meaning . . . is derived from, or arises out of, the social interaction that one has with one's fellows" (Blumer, 1969, p. 2). Both these changes of view were concurrent with a shift of general attention from ontological questions to the mechanisms underlying human experience. The old conceptions of symbolic content as an externally determined "cargo" carried by the signifier gave way to the vision of meaning as lying "in the eyes of the beholder" or in an interpersonal sphere. From now on, one of the focal issues will be the question of to what degree the experience (the knowledge) of a mathematical object depends on symbolic representation of this object.

Be the constructivist and the interactionist paradigms as far removed from the objectivist framework as they might, they still have proven to be compatible, at least initially, with Platonism and with theories of meaning that have sustained a clear-cut distinction between symbols and meaning.[4] These theories have tended to admit that meaning, whether received or constructed, is quite independent of symbols and may, in principle, develop prior to the introduction of any kind of notation. This applies, of course, to mathematical objects—this principal manifestation of mathematical meaning. There is therefore no reason why the maxim of "objects before symbols" should not find its advocates also among constructivists and interactionists. Indeed, many would agree with Thompson's advice that, as teachers, we should better "focus on having students use signs and symbols only when they (students) have something to say through them (symbols)" (Thompson & Sfard, 1994, p. 8).

Further revision of the objectivist doctrine and the advent of semiotics put a question mark on the clear-cut distinction between the symbol and its referent and eventually led to a reconceptualization of the issue of the construction of meaning in general, and of mathematical objects in particular. The conception of a sign and its meaning as independent entities was replaced with the claim of an indissoluble unity of the two. This was the message brought almost simultaneously, although quite independently and in different ways, by the founders of semiotics, Saussure (1916/1986) and Peirce (1931–1935).[5] It was also promoted by the Russian school of thought that originated in the work of Vygotsky (1962, 1987).

---

[4]Radical constructivists, who take a clear antiobjectivist position on epistemological issues, are likely to say that ontological questions are of no relevance to their project. Most of them would simply refuse to make any ontological commitments (cf. von Glasersfeld, 1991, 1995; see also Cobb, 1994, 1995; Cobb, Jaworski, & Presmeg, 1996), which means that they would not describe themselves as either realists or nonrealists. It also implies, however, that if a constructivist wishes to take an ontological position, realism is a viable option.

[5]French linguist Saussure lived from 1857 to 1913, and the American philosopher Peirce was born in 1839 and died in 1914.

The rejection of the classical dualist view expressed itself, above all, in the Saussurian change of terminology. Defining the notion of sign as denoting an indissoluble union of signified and signifier, Saussure exorcised the idea of symbol as an empty container and of an independent referent that fills it with meaning. The emphasis here is at the untenability of the traditional dichotomy of sign and meaning. A similar idea is conveyed by Vygotsky through the metaphor of decomposing water into its components: Just like there is no possibility to learn about properties of water by simply studying properties of oxygen and hydrogen, there is no way to understand human conceptual thinking by severing signifieds from signifiers and by their separate investigations (Vygotsky, 1987, p. 45).

This reconceptualization of the relation between semiotic form and content made it necessary to revise common conceptions about mechanisms underlying production of meaning. The claim that one cannot consider signifieds independently of signifiers implies untenability of the belief in "meaning before symbols." It is only natural that Vygotsky (1962) thought of language, and symbols at large, as having a constitutive, rather than only a representational, role. He claimed: "Thought is not merely translated in words; it comes into existence through them" (p. 125).[6] Approximately at the same time, Peirce began to pursue the idea of meaning as originating in the intricate interplay of signifiers. The American semiotician viewed the signification and construction of meaning as an ongoing process in which an *interpretant* of one sign becomes a *representamen* of another. (The *interpretant* and *representamen* are Peirce's terms for two of his three components of sign; the last element in the triple is *object*; see Peirce, 1955.) Thus, for example, in response to the symbol (representamen) x^2, one may draw a parabola. The parabola would be an interpretant of the sign. When seeing the graph, another person may say, "This function has no negative values." This utterance is an interpretant of the parabola, which, in the context of the new sign (the utterance), functions as a representamen.[7] The motif of such "cyclic," hierarchic signification recurs in works of the French semiotician and psychoanalyst Lacan (1977), who may be viewed as both a successor and a reformer of Saussure. In Lacan's writings, one finds the idea of a sign turning into a signified of another sign. Thus, for instance, in the preceding example,

---

[6]In Vygotsky (1987), this sentence appears in a different translation: "Thought is not expressed but completed in the word" (p. 250). The message about the priority of word with respect to meaning becomes slightly weakened. Without consulting the Russian original, I would opt for the earlier translation because it seems to me more in tune with the rest of Vygotsky's writings.

[7]Please note that in semiotics every linguistic expression, as well as every action, thought, or feeling, counts as a sign. Thus, an utterance "This function has no negative values" can be treated as a sign, or as representamen.

the symbol x^2, in itself a signifier (of the basic quadratic function), may be viewed as a signified of parabola. In turn, the parabola may become a signified of the expression "the basic quadratic curve." Excellent illustrations of such "chains of signification" were given by Walkerdine (1988) and by Cobb, Gravemeijer, Yackel, McClain, and Whitenack (1997) (see also Gravemeijer, Cobb, Bowers, & Whitenack, chap. 7, this volume).

The notion of meaning as emerging from an interplay of signs was a significant step toward freeing the theory of meaning from the need to consider externally given, preexisting referents. The antireferent position has been explicitly declared in this way or another by almost all contemporary semioticians (cf. Gottdiener, 1995). For example, French thinker Michael Foucault (1972, 1973) objected to "treating discourses as groups of signs (signifying elements referring to contents or representations)" and preferred to treat them "as practices that systematically form the objects of which they speak" (p. 49). Referring specifically to the theme of madness, he explained that its "object" (mental illness), like all the other objects around which discourses are built,

> was constituted by all that was said in all the statements that named it, divided it up, described it, explained it, traced its developments, indicated its various correlations, judged it, and possibly gave it speech by articulating, in its name, discourses that were to be taken as its own. (Foucault, 1972, p. 47)

For Foucault the conclusion is obvious: "There can be no question of interpreting discourse with a view to writing a history of the referent" (Foucault, 1972, p. 47).

Dreyfus and Rabinow (1982) translated this position into "practical" advice by stating that "The tendency to think of language in terms both of referents, and of words pointing to objects, must be resisted" (p. 62). If not referents, however, then what? How can one investigate the issue of meaning when, on the one hand, the idea of a referent as a meaning-rendering device has been given up and, on the other hand, the conception of meaning as beginning and ending in the free play of signifiers (as Derrida, 1967/1976, and other deconstructivists would have it) does not seem to tell all of the story? One viable alternative to both of these positions may be found in Wittgenstein's famous statement, "The meaning of a word is its *use* in the language" (1953, Remark 43, p. 20). The use, in turn, is not unrestricted and arbitrary. It has a well-defined, although infinitely complex, set of rules, which, by determining discursive forms, also determines their meaning.

The assumption that meaning has much to do with linguistic use is central to this chapter. It is also important to stress, however, that the position adopted along these pages is much less formal and less restrictive than implied by the equation of "meaning = use in language." Although there is full agreement as to the utmost importance of linguistic use, there is also a conviction that from a psychological point of view, the issue of meaning cannot be captured through linguistic analysis alone. In such an analysis, the gestalt effect, which seems to be the gist of the *experience of meaningfulness* (and of "having a mathematical object"), is inevitably lost. The experiential facet of meaning includes imagery and emotions, among others. As Lotman observed while referring to the exclusive use of linguistic analysis, "If we put together lots of veal cutlets, we do not obtain a calf. But if we cut up a calf, we obtain lots of veal cutlets" (quoted in Eco, 1990). To say it differently (and in a less "bloody" way!), understanding the parts of a whole, which is the kind of understanding we gain while analyzing use, does not translate automatically into an understanding of the whole. The collection of pieces is not enough to reconstruct the "living creature," this unique experience of "seeing" a meaning of a symbol.

In the Beginning Was the Word: The Role of Signifier

In the rest of this chapter, I grapple with the question of what it means to participate in a discourse on mathematical objects and how this participation is made possible by an appropriate use of mathematical symbols. The central thesis that is expounded and examined among these pages is that mathematical discourse and its objects are *mutually constitutive*: It is the discursive activity, including its continuous production of symbols, that creates the need for mathematical objects; and these are mathematical objects (or rather the object-mediated use of symbols) that, in turn, influence the discourse and push it into new directions.

Before I start explaining this thesis and examining its implications, I must make some lexical preparations. The vocabulary that we all use to speak about issues of meaning still brings to mind the old symbol/referent dichotomy and is, therefore, somehow incompatible with the general spirit of the present dispute. The objectivist approach, which rendered the referent a separate existence and primacy over the symbol, is immortalized in the notions that are still in use. Whether we talk about symbols, signs, or representations, we always imply the existence of another entity for which the entity at hand (a mark on paper, a word) is intended to be a discursive replacement. Indeed, each one of these terms invites the follow-up phrase "of something" (see Lesh and Doerr's use of *model* and *representation*, chap. 10, this volume). For instance, a symbol is always a symbol *of something*, as are sign and representation. Thus, if there is room for the word *representation* in the present framework, it is under the condition that we interpret it in a novel way, tacitly agreeing that representations are not necessarily born as such, and more often than not earn their "representational" status only much later, if at all.[8]

To be able to tackle the process through which the objects "represented" by the symbols come retroactively into being, I need a vocabulary that can be trusted to minimize the impact of the objectivist metaphors for meaning. Not having much choice, I decided to use the words sign, signifier, and signified in the sense similar to those of Saussure and Lacan. The word *sign* should be understood as anything experienced as meaningful, whether it is a spoken word, a written symbol, or any other artifact used for communication. The words *signifier* and *signified* refer to two inseparable aspects of human relation to signs: The former implies that a sign must have a perceptually accessible form, and the latter makes it clear that from the user's point of view there is more to the sign than what meets the eye (or ear). In this chapter I refer mainly to three types of mathematical signifiers: names (words), algebraic symbols, and graphs.

Having made these lexical clarifications, we are now in a position to delve into a more detailed analysis of the role of signifiers in the development of discourses on numbers, on functions, and on sets. Within our present framework, naming and symbolizing can no longer be considered "baptizing an object" (Wittgenstein, 1953, p. 38), a mere introduction of linguistic pointers to already existing entities. Rather, they must be viewed as crucial components of acts of creation. Although generally true, nowhere is this claim more prominent than in VR discourse. Unlike in AR discourse, in which the way toward a new concept (object) may sometimes begin not with the help of symbolic tools but with a visually accessible physical object, in VR discourse name and symbol are the only public means for focusing attention—indeed, for creating the discourse that, in its turn, creates the object that we speak about. Thus, we can metaphorically say that in the process of learning mathematics, the role of discourse

---

[8]While I was embarking on the present project, these limitations of the existing terminology gave me quite a headache. I put much effort into an attempt to find a word that would denote a written or spoken sign without the connotation of something standing for something else; but in vain. None of the candidates—be it representation, symbol, sign, ideogram, or mark—proved free of the unwanted semantic load. One word that looked more promising than the others, from this point of view, was the term *inscription* (see Lehrer, Schauble, Carpenter, & Penner, chap. 9, this volume). I rejected this possibility because of the restriction to the written signs that it clearly imposes. It may well be that my problem was aggravated by the limitation of my English. I invite the readers to think about better alternatives. In the meantime, I have to settle on the generally accepted terminology, hoping that I will manage to convey some innovative messages in spite of the unwanted connotations it brings. Incidentally, this little story may serve as a case study for those interested in the dynamics of discourse evolution. It brings into full relief the phenomenon of language constraints influencing conceptual change.

in creating the virtual reality of mathematics is no less significant than the role of this reality in creating the discourse.

As may be learned from the history of mathematics, the introduction of new mathematical signifiers is rarely preceded by formal definitions. Moreover, when a new symbol is introduced, the mathematicians may be unable to give any description at all of the "object represented by" this symbol. Contrary to what seems to be a quite common conviction, mathematical names and symbols may become a regular part of mathematical discourse at the stage when mathematicians have only a very faint notion of their signifieds.

In this chapter, I am trying to promote the idea that the introduction of a new structural signifier, and thus the creation of a new discursive focus, can be seen as an act of conception of a new mathematical object. The words *structural signifier* refer to those mathematical symbols that appear in propositions dealing with objects—as opposed to propositions that focus on, say, operations. Thus, for example, while $+$, $-$, $*$, $\sqrt{}$ and $\frac{d}{dx}$ play the role of operational signifiers in most of their appearances (such as in "In order to find the area of a rectangle, you have to perform the multiplication: *width* $*$ *length*"), the symbols -3 and $f(x)$ would more often than not be used as structural (such as in "$-3 < 0$" or in "Multiply $f(x)$ by 7"). The distinction, therefore, is made with regard to the linguistic uses of the symbols. This means that the suggested categorization of symbols is not absolute: The distinction between structural and operational signifiers is relative to the discursive context in which they are employed, and the same symbol may sometimes be used as operational, and sometimes as structural. As argued elsewhere (e.g., Sfard, 1991; Sfard & Linchevski, 1994), most of the known mathematical symbols display such structural/operational dualism (this dualism has been epitomized in the notion of "procept" introduced by Gray and Tall, 1994). It should be understood, therefore, that while using the adjectives *structural* and *operational* with reference to symbols, I am hinting at the way they are used in the discourse under consideration.

It can be shown that many important historical developments in mathematics occurred due to ontological turns that followed an introduction of structural symbols into a discourse that until now focused on operations. This is certainly what happened when such symbols as -3 and i were proposed. But the lives of negative and complex numbers began even earlier than that. These two types of numbers emerged from symbolic operations such as those that can be presented by the expressions $5 - 8$ or $\sqrt{-1}$. These operations led to talking about objects that did not seem to exist; they enabled discursive activities where the interlocutors seemed to be manipulating these nonexistent entities. Surprisingly, the discursive manipulations over the "empty symbols" occasionally produced perfectly legitimate objects. (This is what happens when, for example, Cardan's algorithms are applied to such an equation as $x^3 = 15x + 4$, producing $\sqrt{-121}$ as an intermediate result and $x = 4$ as a final solution.) Sometimes, the structural upheaval in discourse would be an almost inevitable result of the inner dynamics of the existing symbolic system. Talk about negative numbers could begin by admitting into mathematics nonstandard combinations of existing symbols (e.g., 5 − 8), which owed their existence to the fact that the rules of operating over the known symbols could be usefully extended. As is customary in mathematics, the expression "5 − 8" itself could be used both operationally, as denoting an operation, and structurally, as signifying an object (the result of an operation). The fact, however, that the same signifier had to be employed in two seemingly incompatible roles, operational and structural, certainly aggravated the difficulty of *reification* (transition to the structural mode). Indeed, process/object duality defies our perceptually conceived intuitions. In the perceptual reality, processes and objects are two different things. The questions, "But what is [the result of] $\sqrt{-2}$?" or "How much is $\sqrt{-2}$?," which we can often hear from students, show that the learners of mathematics may experience exactly this kind of difficulty. No wonder, then, that special symbols were evidently necessary to play the role of objects, as opposed to symbols that signified the operations. The structural turn in discourse was completed and the new types of numbers were generally accepted only after the numerals preceded by minus were introduced to denote "the result" of some subtractions and the letter i was proposed by Euler to stand for "the result" of square root extraction from −1.

The history of negative and complex numbers shows how a symbolically induced ontological change in mathematical discourse may bring about the emergence of new mathematical objects. As another example, let me take the concept of function. The biography of this notion has been analyzed many times in many different ways. Here, it is dealt with from a semiotic point of view.[9] Looking at the earliest events in the history of function through the lens of the theories of meaning summarized earlier, one immediately notices that this central mathematical concept, like many others, began its life as a symbol, and as quite an empty symbol at that. ("Empty" does not imply "meaningless"; it only says that those who agreed to use the symbol and knew how to do so were, nevertheless, puzzled about the nature of its signified; the signified was supposed to be an object, but they could not figure out the nature of this object.) Let us examine, for example, the first two definitions of function that are known in the history of mathematics, presented in Fig. 3.2.

---

[9]The analysis presented here should not be regarded as an alternative to these earlier analyses, but rather as a complement to them.

Jean Bernoulli, 1718:
One calls here Function of a variable a quantity composed in any manner whatever of this variable and of constants.

Leonard Euler, 1748:
A function of a variable quantity is an analytical expression composed in any manner from that variable quantity and numbers or constant quantities.

(after Kleiner, 1989)

FIG. 3.2. Early definitions of function.

In order to understand the point I wish to make here, one has to look *at* the language used in the two definitions rather than *through* this language. This change from looking-through to looking-at may be metaphorically compared to the shift of focus that occurs when one switches from looking through a window to looking at the window (cf. Lave & Wenger, 1991, on the use of tools; see also Nemirovsky & Monk, chap. 6, this volume). The surface features of the phrases used by both Bernoulli and Euler are what indicate the ontological status of function. Both of these phrases contain the same message: they point to certain symbolic expressions as *genus proximum* of function. To put it in a simpler language, function is identified with a certain type of algebraic symbol and not with anything that might be represented by this symbol. This is obviously true for Euler's definition, which explicitly equates function with an analytical expression. Some of the readers may remain unconvinced about the accuracy of this statement with regard to Bernoulli's definition because of the use it makes of the term *quantity*. (Ontologically speaking, quantity is not a symbol.) These readers are advised to consider the fact that this quantity is said to be composed of variables and constants. Because the distinction between *variable* and *constant* can only have sense with respect to algebraic symbols, one has good reasons to conclude that, indeed, Bernoulli's definition is similar in its implicated ontology to that of Euler, even though its message is conveyed in a less direct way.

The emergence of the notion of function has, therefore, much to do with the advent of algebraic symbolism. By the end of the 16th century, and due mainly to the work of Vieta and Descartes, "analytical expressions" involving letters, numerals, and operators began deluging mathematical texts in spite of widespread doubts about their exact meaning and about the validity of their use (see, e.g., Kline, 1980). The doubts, it seems, stemmed precisely from the fact that the introduction of the symbolism preceded a good idea of what the symbols stand for, and about the exact nature of the rules of their use. As a result, the newborn algebra was treated with caution. Newton, who used it quite extensively, described it as the "analysis of bunglers."

Let me dwell a little longer on the nature of these historical doubts. On the face of it, there is no reason why the symbols themselves could not serve as objects called *functions*. This is, evidently, what Euler believed possible when he conferred the title of function on the multifarious algebraic expressions that, in the late 16th century, grew out of the mathematical discourse as if by themselves. If his definition were accepted, the transformation of the discourse from purely operational to structural would be accomplished in no time. After all, anything one wants to know about mathematical objects—their properties and the ways in which they can be manipulated—could be easily derived from the former "language games." Indeed, the rules of use imposed themselves on the users. Why is it, therefore, that mathematicians could not, in fact, relax and acknowledge these new symbols as being the thing itself, not standing for anything else? Why couldn't they do what Hilbert and other formalists tried to do over 200 years later? What were they looking for when complaining that they were compelled to deal with "empty" symbols?

It is interesting to note that it was Euler himself who questioned his definition of 1748. Seven years after he equated function with *analytic expression*, he announced that one is dealing with function whenever "some quantities depend on others in such a way that if the latter are changed that former undergo changes themselves." He went on to formulate a new definition: "If . . . x denotes a variable quantity then all the quantities which depend on x in any manner whatever, or are determined by it, are called its functions" (Ruthing, 1984, pp. 72–73). The ontology of this new description is dramatically different from that of the old one. This time, there is no mention of symbols. Rather than being a mark on paper, function presents itself now as a disembodied abstract entity, existing independently of its perceptually accessible "avatars." It is enlightening to look at the events that brought about this conceptual turn. They reveal the reason why mathematicians cannot accept the idea that symbols, as such, are the objects they are talking about.

It was his famous dispute with d'Alembert on the possible solutions of the problem of a vibrating string (see, e.g., Kleiner, 1989) that eventually forced Euler to reconsider his idea of function. While analyzing the possible solutions to the problem, Euler faced a dilemma. There were two basic assumptions that appeared to contradict each other. On the one hand, each state of the vibrating string, and thus every continuous line in a plane, was supposed to correspond to a function; on the other hand, there were shapes that could not be described by any (single) "analytical expression." There were only two ways out of this quandary: Either some states of the string were not functional, or the definition of function as an analytic expression had to be changed. Euler chose the latter solution and decided that, in order to broaden his conception of function, he must make it independent of any kind of symbolism. (As an aside, let me note that d'Alembert went the other way; that is, he decided to adhere to the idea of function as an expression.) It was, therefore, the attempt to bridge the two different kinds of symbolism—algebraic and graphical—that brought about a conclusion that one needs a symbol-independent entity if one wants to account for the complex relationships between the symbols themselves.

Once again, we are witnessing here the effects of metaphorical projection from AR discourse to VR discourse. In order to account for the isomorphism between symbolic systems, one brings into play a mathematical object that unifies the respective symbols the way that Sigmund Freud, the person, unifies the pictures presented in Fig. 3.3b. It is for a similar reason that teachers and textbook authors feel compelled to talk to children about function when they try to account for symbolic equivalencies, such as $2 + x + 3x = 2 + 4x$ or $3(x + 2) = 3x + 6$. They need these intangible objects in order to answer the question, "What is it that remains the same when the symbols themselves change?" The question, in fact, could be reformulated: "What is it that makes two symbolic expressions such as $3(x + 2)$ and $3x + 6$ fully interchangeable in mathematical discourse?" It is this discursive interchangeability, therefore, that makes the introduction of mathematical objects indispensable.[10]

Let me finish with a general remark on possible reasons for the introduction of structural symbolism. Whether we are talking about numbers or functions, these symbols played a crucial role in turning the discourse onto itself and making its former practices an object of reflection. In all the cases discussed here, the new signifiers did fulfill the mission for which they were meant: They helped to thematize the former discursive processes and turn them into the focus of the mathematical conversation. In this way, they catalyzed a new discursive formation and raised the discourse to a metalevel where mathematical processes previously merely executed became a reified object of study. At this higher level, the process could be reflected on and combined into ever more complex units. Because the discourse itself was new, however, the signifieds of the new signifiers were yet to be built. The process of construction would often lead into directions unforeseen by those who introduced the signifier in the first place. It is in this sense, therefore, that the phrase *signifier before signified*

---

[10]Another possible way to define the equivalence is to specify the operations that transform formulae into equivalent ones. If this approach is to work, the rules of transformations must be introduced axiomatically. Thus, rather than trying to explain the roots of the observed linguistic equivalence, the axiomatic treatment carries the message of the arbitrariness of the rules of algebra.

1.

x	y
−1	1
0	0
1	1
2	4
3	9
4	16

2. $y = x^2$

3. read(x);
    x: = x*x;
    write('$f(x) =$', x);

4.

a. VR discourse: All the above symbols are representations of the same function: *the basic quadratic function.*

b. AR discourse: All the above pictures are representations of the same person: *Sigmund Freud.*

FIG. 3.3. Symbols as *representations* in VR discourse and in AR discourse.

is being used in this chapter. Although meaning construction is an ongoing process with no beginning and no end, there are, nevertheless, certain events that influence the course of further development in a crucial way and may, therefore, count as beginnings of a "new chapter." These are events that redirect the discourse and bring a new discursive focus. Introduction of a new signifier is one of these events. In the long run, it is bound to bring about the development of a new signified. The exact course of this development, especially as it takes place in the process of learning mathematics, is the topic of the next section.

Pump Mechanism: How Signified
Is Built out of Signifier

Notwithstanding the generally accepted view of learning as construction, there is a substantial difference between historical and individual symbolizing. Whereas mathematicians were the first inventors of mathematical symbols and the pioneer builders of the structural discourse, today's student is usually thrown straight into a predetermined mathematical conversation, governed by a set of ready-made rules (cf. Freudenthal's notion of anti-didactical inversion as discussed by Gravemeijer et al., chap. 7, this volume). In this discourse, many symbols are readily available and their use is structural from the moment of their introduction. In other words, the structural interpretation of symbols is imposed by the way in which the symbols are used—the ontological assumptions are implicit in the expert-participants' language. In most cases, the act of introduction is performed by a teacher. No special effort has to be made by the latter in order to evoke the metaphor of, say, –3 as an object. This metaphor is inherent in the language the teacher uses. The way in which –3 is incorporated into mathematical discourse puts it naturally into one category with the numbers the student already has used before. The realization of this fact may well be the beginning of the dialectic process of object construction that is going to be carried out from now on. This process will be fueled and shaped by social interactions all along the way. Aside, perhaps, from the extremely rare cases of exceptional creativity (and the radical interactionists are likely to argue against the very possibility of this exception), eventual transition to object-mediated use of symbols is only made possible by students' ongoing exchange with others. The "others" may be teachers, peers, parents, or the authors of the texts the student is reading.

Introduction of negative numbers, as it is usually done in schools, is a good illustration. When the negative numbers are first mentioned in the process of teaching, they are usually defined by a reference to some symbols. Figure 3.4 presents a sample of an introduction to signed numbers, taken from a Hebrew textbook. If the look-at-the-language approach is assumed, one immediately realizes that negative numbers are presented here as new symbols. Indeed, they are introduced as names for points on an extended number line (the points themselves are not the numbers!). In view of the previous claims on the use of symbolism and object mediation, this approach, even if seemingly undesirable, could not, in fact, be easily modified.

> Let's choose a point on a straight line and name it "zero." Let's choose a segment and call it "the unit of length." Let's place the unit head-to-tail repeatedly on the line to the right of the point "zero." The points made this way will be denoted by 1, 2, 3 and so on (or +1, +2, +3, . . .). To the left of the point "zero," we put the unit segment head-to-tail again and denote the points obtained in this way with *numbers* –1, –2, –3, . . . The set of *numbers* created in this way is called the set of negative numbers.

FIG. 3.4. Introduction of negative numbers in a Hebrew textbook. From Mashler (1976). Translation and emphasis added.

As strange as it may seem, this state of affairs is not but one possibility out of many. In view of the basic assumptions about meaning adopted in this study, at certain levels of VR discourse this order of things—signifiers before signified—is the only possibility. If we agree with Wittgenstein and Foucault that discourse creates its own objects and that discursive relations and uses of symbols are perhaps most crucial components of what we previously called the signified, then there are no mathematical objects without designated signifiers; or, to put it differently, before a symbol enters the language and becomes a full-fledged element of the discourse, there is simply no object to talk about.

All of this means that any discourse, and mathematical discourse in particular, suffers from an inherent circularity. Signifieds can only be built through discursive use of the signifiers, but at the same time the existence of these signifieds is a prerequisite for the meaningful use of the signifiers. This circularity, seemingly a serious trap for the prospective participants of the discourse, is in fact the driving force behind its incessant growth. This is what fuels the process of coemergence in which the new discursive practices and the new signified spur each other's development. In this process, the discursive forms and the meaning, as practiced and experienced by interlocutors, are like two legs that make moving forward possible due to the fact that they are never in exactly the same place, and at any given time one of them is ahead of the other.

In this section I take a closer look at this intricate, somehow circular, process of object construction that follows introduction of a new structural signifier. This process consists, basically, of two stages. These stages differ from each other by the type of use that is made of the symbol under consideration. The first hint of the distinction I have in mind may be found in the study carried out early in this century by two psychologists, Woodrow and Lowell (1916), and repeated later with similar results by many others (Brown & Berko, 1960; Ervin, 1961; Palermo, 1963; Palermo & Jenkins, 1963). The researchers tested the free associations arising in children and adults in reaction to simple everyday words. They found an interesting age-related difference: The children tended to make associations with words that would usually follow the stimulus word in a sentence; in contrast, the majority of adults thought of words with a related or opposite meaning. Thus, for example, the young subjects would follow *table* with *eat*, and *deep* with *hole*, whereas adults associated *table* with *chair*, and *deep* with *shallow*. One may say that the words presented to the children activated in them ready-made linguistic templates in which the stimulus word and the response word represented different parts of speech and together formed a meaningful phrase. Adults, on the other hand, associated words belonging to the same semantic categories, words that fit the same "slots" within propositional structures. To put it differently, the children's associations brought syntactic complements of the stimulus words, whereas grown-ups' associations led to syntactic equivalents. Using Sausserian language, one may say that the children associated *syntagmatically*, whereas the adults associated *paradigmatically*.[11]

This interesting result indicates a substantial difference between the way children and adults control the use of words in language. Children's use of words may be termed *templates-driven*, whereas that of the adults is mediated by their former knowledge and by their ability to classify words into semantic categories. This difference is the basis for my characterization of the two stages of meaning production in general, and of the development of object-mediated use in particular.[12]

In this chapter, the focus is on structural signs. According to what has been said before, an act of introducing a new structural name or a new symbol cannot be viewed as a "finishing touch" in the creation of a new mathematical object. On the contrary, this operation is often a beginning rather than an end of the process. As mentioned before, when the symbol of the fraction, say ⅞, is presented to children for the first time, one can hardly expect the young students to have the underlying abstract object,

---

[11]Syntagmatic relationship is the relationship that occurs between words that can be combined together to create a sentence. Thus, the words *she*, *is*, and *hungry* are syntagmatically related. The relationship is paradigmatic if, from a grammatical point of view, the words may replace each other in a sentence. Thus, *he* and *she*, or *hungry* and *heavy* are paradigmatically related.

[12]All this brings to mind Vygotsky's (1978) claim that, *"For the young child, to think means to recall; but for the adolescent, to recall means to think"* (p. 51; italics in the original). What Vygotsky seems to be saying is that children's thinking is grounded in collections of concrete instances, whereas adolescents and adults have recourse to abstraction, which effectively mediates the use (and recall) of concrete instances. Thus, thinking-by-recall means, among others, solving problems with the help of concrete recipes fitting these particular problems. Recalling-by-thinking refers to summoning general algorithms and heuristics to tackle the concrete cases at hand. In this chapter, this difference is not considered to be solely age related. On the contrary, it is expected to be found repeatedly in the processes of symbolization, whether the person who symbolizes is a child or an adult.

that is, to view the symbol as but an "avatar" of another, intangible, entity. In spite of this, the students do not remain idle until the new mathematical object is fully formed. They do use the new signifier even though they may still only be able to see the symbol and not what should be seen *through* the symbol. However, the way they use the symbol at this early stage is quite different from the way they will do so later, when the symbol develops in their minds as a fully fledged, signifier–signified couple. It is the central thesis of this chapter that *when structural symbols (symbols that refer to objects) are introduced for the first time, their use is mainly templates driven, and it is only some time later that it becomes object mediated.* Moreover, I claim that this order of things, far from being undesirable, is inherent in the logic of the process of symbolization. If this sounds somehow too strong, let me add that in certain cases the period of templates-driven use may be so brief that it goes virtually unnoticed.[13] In some other instances object mediation would be very slow to develop, and in most extreme cases it would remain out of reach forever.

Of particular interest to us in the present discussion is the phase in which the discursive practices outgrow the meaning, which takes place during the period immediately following the introduction of a new signifier. This act of introduction creates a "semantic space" yet to be filled with meaning. The signifier enters the language game before the rules of this game have been sufficiently specified and before the signifier has acquired the power of evoking a familiar experiential resonance (cf. Dörfler's notion of protocols, chap. 4, this volume). "Filling in" the semantic space occurs in a gradual manner. At the first stage, the symbol starts establishing its place within the discourse in the only way possible—by following in the footsteps of some other, already well-established, element of this discourse. If sneaking into old discursive "slots" is an opening move, slipping out of these slots, due to some basic misfit, marks the beginning of a new stage—a stage at which new discursive forms are generated. These new forms are what eventually defines the symbol's unique use and, thus, its particular meaning. The meaning of mathematical symbols may come from within the mathematical discourse itself—from gradual realization of its relations with other mathematical signs. Such an intradiscursive creation of meaning is known only too well to today's mathematicians. However, the meaning of a symbol may often

---

[13]Moreover, one cannot exclude the possibility of some *experience of mathematical objects* prior to the introduction of any symbolism. According to mathematicians' testimonies (Hadamard, 1949; Sfard, 1994a), a sensation of mathematical objects would sometimes appear without any symbolical support, simply as a result of a long period of particularly intensive thinking. It is evident, however, that even among mathematicians this is a rather rare event and, in any case, one that, in the absence of symbolism, cannot be adequately communicated and studied.

originate in the interdiscursive space, in the process of carrying a symbol over from one discourse to another. In the latter case, the links with the AR discourse are the most significant. Endogenous mathematical signification—creation of new signifieds that occur exclusively within the closed system of mathematical discourse—may be a common practice since the advent of the formalist movement, but for many centuries the links between the AR and VR discourses were a central source of mathematical meaning. They may still be indispensable in today's mathematics classroom. As shown in the next sections, the mechanisms of reification (Sfard, 1991, 1992) and of metaphorical projection (Johnson, 1987; Lakoff, 1987; Sfard, 1997) underlie the creation of mathematical chains of signification, both those internal to mathematical discourse and those that link the latter to AR discourse.

This whole process, drawn here in very rough strokes, brings to mind the mechanism of a pump. Introduction of a symbol is like lifting the piston in that it creates a new semantic space. The gradual emergence of object mediation is analogous to the procedure of filling in the space thus created. Based on this metaphor, I talk about the process of symbolization as governed by the pump mechanism. It is through an intermittent creation of a space "hungry" for new objects and through its subsequent replenishment with new discursive forms and relations that the participants of mathematical discourse steadily expand its limits.

In the next section I focus on the phase of "lifting the piston"—the phase of creating semantic space by the introduction of new structural signifiers. This is the stage in which the use of a new symbol is governed by old rules. The subsequent stage, in which the new sign gets life of its own and becomes an integrated signifier–signified unit, is presented in the section that follows. Theoretical reflections on both of these phases are illustrated, among others, with vignettes taken from my recent studies.

MEANING FROM SYMBOLS, ACT ONE: CREATING OBJECT SPACE

Templates-Driven Use

Summing up what has been said up to this point, the VR discourse of mathematics may be viewed as an autopoietic system, which is continually self-producing.[14] The discursive practices and mathematical objects have been presented as being mutually constitutive and as being in a constant dialectic process of coemergence. As is always the case with

---

[14]For discussion of autopoietic systems, see Maturana and Varela (1987).

autopoietic systems, by adopting this model we doom ourselves to the dilemma: How does the ongoing process of coemergence begin? According to what has been said, structural symbols cannot become fully meaningful before they are used; however, how can one use a symbol before it becomes meaningful?[15] On the face of it, reducing meaning to use, as Wittgenstein suggested, may help us out of the entanglement. In the reductionist case, in which there is no longer any use–meaning dichotomy, the question of "What comes first?" seems to lose its grounds. However, the problem still exists except that this time it is translated into the question of "How does old use produce new use?"

There can be no question that new uses originate in old uses. To illustrate this claim, let us help ourselves with a thought experiment.

Thought Experiment. You have never heard the word *krasnal* before, but you have just read the sentence: *A krasnal woke up and got up from his bed.* Does the sentence tell you what krasnal means? Certainly not. However, the fact that you do not know the meaning of the word does not leave you unable to make certain uses of this word. Indeed, after hearing only one accidental sentence about krasnals, you are certainly able to take some steps toward incorporating it into a discourse. Even though no one told you what krasnals are, you may be expected to be able to distinguish between meaningful and absurd sentences about krasnals, and even say a few things about krasnals that you believe must be true. Did you shrug at my use of *what* rather than *who* in this last sentence? Well, this is the first evidence of your having recourse to certain well-established propositional templates. You expect *krasnal* to point to a person rather than to a thing; thus, for you the use of the word *krasnal* along with the word *what* is incorrect. Let us test it further.

Which of the following propositions seem to you to be correct and meaningful sentences about krasnals, and which of them do not?

Yesterday, a krasnal went to a supermarket.

A krasnal was divided by three and then squared.

Some of the krasnals were cheerful, some of them sang.

This krasnal is raised by public subscription.

A krasnal begins at 5:30 p.m.

This krasnal is younger than this one.

---

[15]We seem doomed to entanglement in vicious circles. The present quandary immediately brings to mind the other circles known from literature: the hermeneutic circle (see e.g., Bauman, 1978), the learning paradox (see e.g., Bereiter, 1985). The present dilemma is, in fact, equivalent to the circle of reification, as presented in Sfard (1991).

All these expressions are syntactically correct propositions, but only some of them seem meaningful (possibly true). Now, can you complete the following sentence in a meaningful way?

Krasnal A is wise, whereas krasnal B is . . .

Finally, try to construct a possibly meaningful sentence about krasnals yourself. Build one you believe cannot be meaningful.

The example we have just seen shows that the way out of the autopoietic circle leads through old habits—through language games that are already well known and deeply rooted. Indeed, it is only natural that in order to circumvent the dilemma of having to use new words before we are aware of their unique uses, we resort to uses with which we are already familiar. We do it by putting the new words and symbols into slots of well-known, remembered-by-heart, propositional templates (e.g., "____ is younger than ____", "____ is cheerful") into which they seem to fit. (It is interesting to explore the sources of our intimations about this linguistic fit. This is done a little later.) This is why I called this early kind of use *templates-driven*.[16]

Let me immediately follow this decision about terminology with the following disclaimer: *Templates-driven* does not mean meaningless. Rather, we are talking here about a certain special, even if not most effective, type of meaning. (Indeed, because, for pragmatic purposes, meaning can be equated to use, and because we are talking here about a kind of reasonable use, it clearly follows that we are also talking about a kind of meaning.) As was shown in the thought experiment earlier, this is the kind of meaning that we may acquire through an exposure to just one sentence containing the new name. It expresses itself in our ability to make some limited linguistic use of the new signifier. This use is characterized by rigidity. The new signifier does not have existence of its own and it can only appear within certain ready-made phrases. Often, we use and complete such phrases mechanically, just as we complete a familiar melodic piece after hearing its first notes. There are no general rules for the use, only a number of concrete cases. Thus, at this point the signifier certainly does not have a well-developed signified. I am tempted to paraphrase Derrida's famous maxim and say that at the stage of templates-driven use, the signifier is the thing itself.[17]

---

[16]As was remarked by a reader of the early draft of this chapter, the templates-driven use may be mediated by imagery—by sometimes quite vivid mental images evoked by the first utterance. As reported by this reader, the sentence *A krasnal woke up and got up from his bed* brought to mind a cartoon-like vision of a little creature getting up from a bed.

[17]Derrida (1967/1976) declared that in spite of our need of an "absolute object" that would safely put an end to the free play of signifiers, we have no choice but to admit that there is "nothing but the text" and that "the thing itself is the sign" (pp. 48–49).

The ability to make use of symbols that were never seen before was observed many times by my colleagues and me in studies with children who were not yet acquainted with algebra but, nevertheless, displayed a certain intuitive understanding of algebraic symbolism (see, e.g., Sfard & Linchevski, 1994). When faced for the first time with an expression $2x + 3x =$ _____, many students would spontaneously complete it to the proposition $2x + 3x = 5x$. As reported by Demby (1994), students usually explain their decision by saying, "Two apples and three apples make five apples." Clearly, the new symbol, x, was substituted here instead of "apples" and thus x took the role of a label rather than of a number. This tendency to view algebraic variables as fitting label slots in nonmathematical discourse may account for a frequently observed error of completing such expressions as $2x + 3$ to $2x + 3 = 5x$. This error was observed many times in the study Carolyn Kieran and I carried out in Montreal. We conjectured that the mistaken completion may have been due to the underlying reliance on the template of "Two _____ and three more make five _____" (e.g., Two apples and three more make five apples). The plausibility of this explanation was then reinforced by the fact that, when the multiplication sign was explicitly written in the expression ($2 \cdot x + 3$), the error usually disappeared. Indeed, the multiplication sign redirects the student to a different discourse and associates the expression with a cluster of mathematical, rather than everyday, templates. In the arithmetical templates, a slot on either side of an operator can only be filled with a number. Thus, once the multiplication sign appeared, it became clear that the x is a replacement for a number and that $2x + 3$ should be used according to rules differing from those that had been initially assumed.

Interestingly, at a later stage in the study, our 12-year-old Montreal students who were just introduced to algebra provided an explicit confirmation of this interpretation in a classroom discussion that developed around the expression "$15000 - 300w$." This expression was constructed by the children and was supposed to present one person's dwindling savings as a function of time measured in weeks (thus the letter w). A difference of opinions developed when one of the students requested inclusion of $300w$ in brackets, hinting that otherwise, in the absence of the multiplication sign, the w might be interpreted as "weeks" rather than as "number of weeks." The excerpt in Fig. 3.5 speaks for itself and requires no comment. I added italics in order to stress those students' utterances that were most revealing.

Later in our course, we saw how the letter-as-a-label use hindered the understanding of the rule $2x + 3x = 5x$ as a special case of distributive law application. Obviously, one does not "take a common divisor out of brackets" when adding apples! Even the teacher seemed startled when we first mentioned the connection between the formula and the rule.

[95]	Teacher:	Would anyone do anything differently? Martha?
[96]	Martha:	I'd do 15 thousand minus brackets 300 and number of weeks.
. . .		
[100]	Teacher:	. . . All right. Do we need brackets around this?
[101]	A student:	No.
[102]	Teacher:	Why not?
. . .		
[104]	Simon:	Yes, you do, *because you have to know that there's an operation. A person, now, he'll probably think 300 weeks, not 300 times weeks.*
[105]	Teacher:	OK, anyone who now knows algebra will know there is an operation.
. . .		
[110]	Simon:	Well, how do you know . . .
[111]	Martha (?):	So, do you need the brackets or not?
[112]	Simon:	Maybe he is trying to say 300 weeks.
[113]	Stephanie:	Yes . . .

FIG. 3.5. A classroom discussion on the need of brackets in the expression "15000 − 300*w*."

The fact that the introduction of a multiplication sign brought about such a radical change in the further use of the formula brings into full relief another important feature of the templates-driven use. *Templates come in clusters.* As we saw in the thought experiment, certain uses of words go along with some other uses, yet clearly disagree with still others. This phenomenon underlies our ability to judge meaningfulness of the propositions about krasnals. We could see how the very first use of a word directed us to a particular kind of discourse—to a cluster of templates that seemed to come together with the one underlying the original proposition. To put it more simply, the very first use already *framed* the discourse and greatly delineated the set of possible linguistic applications.

Co-occurrence of templates is a matter of former experience and habit. The bond between the co-occurring templates is not necessarily that of logical dependence. The templates in a given cluster have been brought together in former uses, where their slots were filled with well-established signs. (It seems that certain prototypical uses are particularly forceful in this respect. In the case of discourse about numbers, all types of meaningful propositions about, say, a prototypical number 5 will tend to cluster together also when the signifier "5" is replaced with a new symbol.) Templates cumulated around each sign, and as time went by the clusters thus formed acquired a cohesion that still keeps them together when a new signifier is substituted for the old. This helps to account for the fact that mathematicians knew how to manipulate such symbols as −3 or $\sqrt{-1}$ even before the negative and complex numbers entered their discourse as fully fledged mathematical objects.

To give yet another example, let me recount a very restricted informal experiment that I recently carried out among my colleagues. I approached them with the following sentence:

a and b are pexons and $a + b = c$.

Pexon is a word I invented myself so, naturally, none of my respondents could know any more about it than was available through this one sentence. Nevertheless, when asked to decide among other propositions containing the word *pexon*, which could, under certain circumstances, be true or which could only be meaningless, they had their answers and none of them claimed that the task was impossible. First and foremost, nobody seemed to doubt the fact that pexons belong to a mathematical discourse and that they signify an object (rather than, say, an operation or a relation). Moreover, it was evident that most respondents associated it with algebraic or maybe even with arithmetic templates. Pexons were expected to appear within propositions that contain operations of all kinds, even operations that were not explicitly mentioned in the original sentence ("John often makes mistakes when multiplying pexons"). Similarly, it did not seem impossible that pexons might be combined with the inequality symbol ("$a > b$"). On the other hand, and in contrast to krasnals, pexons appeared unlikely to go along with adjectives such as *wise* or *cheerful* or with verbs such as *sing* or *type*. Notably, all the respondents univocally claimed that the proposition, "If a and b are pexons then $a + b$ is a pexon," is meaningful, and probably true. A similar conviction may well be the source of the idea of negative number. If the first two slots in a template of the form "_____ − _____ = _____" are filled with numbers, then the sign in the last slot must also be a number. When negative numbers are introduced as mere symbols (historically, as signifiers that replace expressions such as $5 - 8$; in today's classroom as "names of points" on the number line), it is their placement within arithmetic templates that frames them as numbers (conceived as abstract objects).

As can be seen from the examples already given, the old templates for new uses may come from many different kinds of discourse. Thus, for example, the word "function" appeared initially in the context of computational processes on the one hand (as we have seen, Bernoulli and Euler associated it with variable quantities), and in relation to geometric shapes on the other hand (Leibnitz applied it in the context of curves in the plane; compare Kleiner, 1989; Sfard, 1991). This multiplicity of discursive sources will play a key role at the later stage. As a result of a crossbreeding between discourses, a new, unique kind of discourse will eventually emerge. It will include language games that only the new signifiers can play. Sometimes, the discursive crossbreeding will be a relatively straightforward cumulative process, with an immediate acceptance of the new transplant and no adverse side effects. At other times, when there is a clash between the uses within different discourses (as happened many times in the history of function, before the geometric and the algebraic discourses agreed to combine), it will require a total restructuring of all the discourses involved.

Another important aspect to stress is that the new uses may be endogenous—coming from purely mathematical templates (e.g., the uses of a variable originating in arithmetic discourse), and they may be exogenous—formed by habits acquired outside mathematical discourse (e.g., templates within which a letter is a label). Clearly, wherever new uses have their roots, the mechanism at work is that of a metaphorical projection (Johnson, 1987; Lakoff & Johnson, 1980; Sfard, 1994a, 1997). The family resemblance between AR and VR discourses is the recurring theme in this chapter. The virtual reality of mathematics that emerges from VR discourse is made in the image of actual reality. In light of the preceding discussion, the reason for this seems to be clear. AR discourse, due to the fact that it certainly was here before all other kinds of discourse, seems to be the primary source of all the templates we use and of all our linguistic habits, and therefore may be regarded as a great-grandmother of all the other discourses.

Let me now make a summarizing comment. Throughout this section, I have been describing and analyzing processes that take place following the introduction of a new mathematical signifier. I tried to make my point with a fairly artificial example—that of the word *krasnal*, the meaning of which has been significantly framed by a single sentence. In this final remark, I wish to stress the fact that the artificiality of the example only fortifies its message. Unlike in a real learning situation, the sentence about *krasnal* came as if out of nowhere, completely detached from the ongoing discourse, and thus almost entirely context free. Even so, it managed to evoke responses that show that already in this very limited and uninformative appearance it did not remain devoid of any meaning. Let us now consider the fact that real learning is never a matter of one isolated sentence, and whatever new symbols we encounter usually appear within the context of some ongoing discourse. In this situation, the mechanism that proved quite effective in the least favorable circumstances may be expected to become truly powerful. After all, this is the mechanism that underlies children's learning of their mother tongue. Let me also stress that, when I am talking about context, I mean more than purely linguistic elements of the discourse. The general circumstances in which the new signifier appears may play a crucial role in the process of meaning construction. Thus, for example, when the term *color* is encountered within the context of a physics lesson, it is understood differently than when it is introduced in, say, an art lesson. Except for the dramatic difference in the immediate treatment of the concept, these two situations provide noncomparable sets of expectations as to the possible uses of the notion. Moreover, the word *color* itself when introduced as a scientific concept (in the sense of Vygotsky) is already laden with meaning constructed through its use in everyday discourse. When it comes to construction of a new meaning within a new discursive context, this former meaning is both a prop and a hurdle. The same mechanism through which contexts shape new meaning helps overcome polysemy, which is so ubiquitous in mathematics.[18] To sum up, if a single sentence proves so powerful as a "meaning activator," the effectiveness of a rich, thoughtfully engineered discursive context can hardly be overestimated.

Before closing this section, let me raise again the issue of the social nature of the processes that have been presented. The mechanism of templates-driven meaning construction is only effective because it is accompanied by an ongoing discursive interaction. It is through this interaction that public signifiers are turned into private signs. Conversational feedback plays a central role in preparing discursive and experiential background for the introduction of the sign. It is essential in the act of bringing the signifier to the learner, and it remains crucially important during the subsequent meaning-building. In particular, the templates-driven use becomes increasingly successful due to its being regulated by discursive negotiations.

Expectations and Verifications

One consequence of the things said in the last section is that the very first use of a new signifier frames the discourse, that is, has the power of directing us toward certain uses rather than toward other uses. Together with old templates come old uses, old meanings. The new and the old are now linked together for better and for worse (cf. Nemirovsky & Monk's discussion of *fusion* and *confusion*, chap. 6, this volume). The effects of the permanent link between the old and the new will be scrutinized in this section.

We may say that we are dealing here with the issue of *expectations* and *verifications*. With the first appearance of a new signifier, certain metaphors come into play and some expectations as to the nature of its signified are conceived. From then on, we are testing the expectations, sometimes finding that they were justified and at other times proving that they were

---

[18]The word *polysemy* refers to the phenomenon of the same signifier having a number of different meanings (signifieds). Mathematics, which has been described by Poincaré (1929) as "the science that calls different things the same names," seems to be afflicted by the phenomenon of polysemy in a particularly acute way.

untenable. As shown in this section, the expectations may come from the very first use of the new signifier, or they may arise from associations evoked by the signifier itself. In any case, the mechanism of metaphorical projection from familiar to unknown is at work.

In her recent book devoted to framing in discourse, Tannen (1993) emphasized the centrality of expectations in shaping both our perception and our abstract thinking. As she explained, talk about expectations deals, in fact, with the well-known truth that old knowledge shapes new knowledge.

> I have been struck lately by the recurrence of a single theme in a wide variety of contexts: the power of expectation. . . . The emphasis on expectation seems to corroborate a nearly self-evident truth: in order to function in the world, people cannot treat each new person, object, or event as unique and separate. The only way we can make sense of the world is to see the connections between things, and between present things and things we have experienced before or heard about. These vital connections are learned as we grow up and live in a given culture. As soon as we measure a new perception against what we know of the world from prior experience, we are dealing with expectations. (pp. 14–15)

Expectations are known also as *prejudgements, prejudices, intimations,* or *intuitions.* The motif of meaning constructed through the to-and-fro movement between what we expect and what we find goes back to Heidegger and Gadamer, on the one hand, and to Bartlett, Piaget, and Vygotsky on the other hand. In the immediate context of mathematics, it became known as an issue of conjecturing versus proving/refuting (Lakatos, 1976; Lampert, 1990). In the present chapter the focus is on linguistically induced expectations.[19]

Ontological Framing and Reification.   If I do not wish to end up writing a book, I should refrain from discussing the possible types of expectations and framing. Indeed, if framing (or expecting) is understood to be directing toward particular discursive formations and hinting at the statements that may be made about the signifier, then the issue is much too rich and complex to be treated in passing. Different discourses overlap and interact with each other in such intricate ways that any attempt to isolate and categorize them is doomed to failure. (Compare Wittgenstein's reflections on language games.) Moreover, any sign belongs simultaneously to many different discourses, and these discourses, in turn, may be

---

[19]Those who identify meaning with linguistic use would say that there can be almost no other source for our expectations. I use this opportunity again to warn against such reductionism.

classified and stratified according to such diverse criteria as theme, level (e.g., one may distinguish between object level and metalevel), ontological status of the focal notions, and so forth. Let me only tackle this last type of framing, because it is of particular importance for the present discussion. In the following paragraph, I elaborate on the theme that has earlier been dealt with only in passing—that of the "ontological upheaval" caused by an appearance of a new structural signifier.

It has already been said that when it comes to mathematical objects, introduction of a new name should be viewed as an act of conception rather than of baptism. Indeed, naming plays a most crucial role in the process of reification. Introduction of nouns into those places in which, until now, people had only been talking about processes (e.g., counting or subtracting 8 from 5) refocuses the discourse. If there was nothing but a certain process up to this point, now the attention may split between the process and its hitherto nonexistent product (a natural number, a negative number). This ontological shift from an operational to a structural focus is well felt, for example, in the transition from the expression *These things cost five dollars* to the expression *The cost of these things is five dollars.* It is echoed in the more abstract example—the transition from *The class numbers twenty students* to *The number of students in the class is twenty.* Because nouns fit those template slots that are reserved for objects (as opposed to verbs or adjectives that refer speakers and listeners to different ontological categories), it is expected that the new signified will have the properties of an object: existence, permanence, manipulability. The anticipation of these features is reinforced repeatedly by the way in which the new name is used within language. The templates activated by nouns are direct descendants of templates coming from AR discourse, in which, more often than not, nouns are names of perceptually accessible material objects. As mentioned before, the effect of transferring templates from discourse to discourse is known as metaphor. We may say, therefore, that what we call *mathematical objects* are metaphors resulting from certain linguistic transplants. As may have been already learned from our discussion about function, introduction of a new mathematical symbol is often enough to spur an ontological shift in the discourse—and to bring about reification. In the case of function, focusing the discourse on "analytical expression" was a decisive step in reification of computational processes which had been in use for many centuries. Introduction of the name *function* gave a further push in the direction of the structural approach.

To summarize, templates we use bring with them ontological messages. If we write a new name or a new symbol in the slot reserved for objects, the new signifier will eventually spur an emergence of a new mathematical object. The history of negative and complex numbers, of functions, and of groups may certainly be read this way.

Expectations That Work—Building New Uses for a New Signifier. Let me now turn to an example that will show the dialectic process of expecting and verifying in an action. The episode is taken from my recent study in which a mathematically precocious 14-year-old student—let us call him Dan—learned a number of new mathematical notions.

The aim of the experiment was to try to understand more clearly the discursive construction of mathematical objects and, more specifically, to expose the linguistic elements of this mechanism. I wanted to see the "wheels of the symbolism" turning on their own. To put it differently, I strove to see how much could be attained by a formal introduction of symbols, unsupported by a meaningful context. This is why I created a learning situation that, by constructivist standards (in fact, any standards), must appear extremely "unfriendly." I created teaching material in which new symbols were introduced within a sterile context of formal manipulations. Examples of operations that could be performed on these symbols were the only available source of their meaning. In this experiment, therefore, the new concept was presented to the student as purely artificial in the Vygotskian sense, that is, as one that grows neither from a network of already-constructed concepts nor from its earlier "spontaneous" version.[20] Thus, while solving the problems that were presented to him after a brief exposure to the examples, Dan could only rely on deductive reasoning and on his linguistic associations. In this clinically sterile setting, I had hoped to be able to find out how much could be achieved through "symbol games" alone, unsupported by links to previous knowledge or by relation to a student's needs. It was Dan's job to build these links for himself, and it was my job as a researcher to watch the processes through which these links were constructed—if they were constructed at all.[21]

The first of a series of new mathematical notions to which Dan was exposed in the course of the experiment is presented in Fig. 3.6. Because

---

[20]Although I prefer, as probably most of the readers do, to see this "clinical" situation as purely theoretical and far removed from the reality of today's classrooms, the sad truth is that many would recognize it as only too familiar. Even if it becomes more and more rare in schools, it is still quite frequent in colleges and at universities. I am also sure that the conversation between Dan and me, which resulted from my experimental script, is likely to be considered by some people as a classical mathematical discourse—the kind of discourse that is generated by those who transmit mathematics to others by lecturing or through professional mathematical texts.

[21]It is important to remark that Dan made truly impressive progress in this extremely "unfriendly" situation. Not every student could be expected to reach the point he did. It seems that Dan was exceptionally motivated. His outstanding ability to cope with mathematical problems was evidently a very important element of his self-image, and this made him a willing participant in the kind of discourse we led. Dan seemed to recognize the situation as normal, and he complied with the rules of the symbolic game, never questioning them or wondering about them.

During the present meeting we will define addition and multiplication between *pairs of whole numbers*. Here are a few examples:

a. (2,3)·(5,4) = (10, 12)   b. (11,2)·(5,6) = (55, 12)
c. (3,4)+(2,5) = (23, 20)   d. (5,2)+(1,7) = (37, 14)

1. Complete:
    (a,b)·(c,d) =
    (a,b)+(c,d) =

2. Compute:
a. (1,3)·(2,5)   b. (5,1)+(2,3)   c. (3,5)+(7,5)
d. (2,15)·(10,3)   e. (8,3)+(0,5)   f. (7,8)+(3,12)
g. (5,4) : (1,2)   h. (8,15) : (2,3)   i. (11,9)–(5,3)

3. Complete:
    (a,b):(c,d) =
    (a,b)–(c,d) =

FIG. 3.6.   Introducing calculus of whole-number pairs.

the intention of the study was to observe an intramathematical production of meaning, the whole process began with a formal introduction of a new signifier. In the experiment, I acted both as an instructor and a researcher. During ten 1-hr-long meetings, I observed Dan closely while he worked his way toward meaning.

The new signifiers introduced during the first meeting were pairs of whole numbers that could be multiplied and added in certain well-defined ways.[22] A careful reader will immediately recognize the pairs as another "representation" of rational numbers. For Dan, however, the isomorphism with rational numbers remained unnoticed until the third meeting. Therefore, for more than 2 hr he acted as a *tabula rasa* as far as the new signifiers were concerned. It is important to stress that during the first two meetings I refrained from referring to the pairs as "numbers," lest this particular name frame the discourse in ways that might distort the processes I wished to observe. I wanted Dan to arrive at certain conclusions totally on his own and not just because some particular kinds of behavior could be expected from objects called numbers. The dialogue between Dan and me was in Hebrew.

After Dan discovered the general formulas for addition and multiplication (problem 1 in Fig. 3.6) and applied them to a number of concrete cases (items *a–f* in problem 2), he unexpectedly encountered the operation

_____

[22]In full accordance with the theory of chains of signification, the new signifier made a reference to previously-established signs.

> [1] D: . . . I have a problem here.
> [2] A: ?
> [3] D: Am I supposed to try now?
> [4] A: Do what you can. Write this down [points to item 2*g*], read it.
> [5] D: OK, five comma two divided by . . . I think I will do the same [as in the case of multiplication], only I will change to division instead of multiplication, 'cause the symbol of operation here . . .
> [6] A: What do you mean? What are you going to do?
> [7] D: Five divided by one, comma, four divided by two, equals five comma two [writes: $(5,4):(1,2) = (\frac{5}{1}, \frac{4}{2}) = (5, 2)$].
> [8] A: OK, now I would like you to explain why you did what you did.
> [9] D: My reason . . . In principle, I wouldn't . . . It is only because you gave me these operations . . . In fact, I wanted to remark already in the beginning that you shouldn't have used the symbols of addition and multiplication 'cause it is confusing . . . 'cause here [points to the inside of brackets] we use multiplication as one operation, and here in the equality [points to the multiplication sign appearing outside the brackets, between two pairs] we used it for a different operation. But since you gave me this in that form, I tried to solve it according to what I know . . . that division is an inverse of multiplication. So I just did reverse operations . . .

FIG. 3.7. Dan defines division between whole-number pairs.

of division (*g*), which had not been introduced to him thus far. The conversation that followed is presented in Fig. 3.7.

As can be seen, Dan did not have much difficulty deciding how division should be performed. Moreover, he was also very eloquent about the reasons for his decisions. In [9], after criticizing the teacher (me) for using the familiar multiplication sign to denote a nonstandard kind of operation (between pairs), he stated that this was that very sign that had made him act the way he did. ("Since you gave me this in that form [with multiplication sign], I tried to solve it according to what I know . . . that division is an inverse of multiplication.") In an exchange that took place a few minutes later, after Dan had successfully verified his result by multiplying (1,2) and (5, 2), he explicitly confirmed the role of signifier-induced expectations (Fig. 3.8, utterances [25] and [27]–[29]).

It is noteworthy that Dan's decision was grounded exclusively in linguistically evoked expectations. The appearance of signs with some previous meaning was the only reason for the way in which he chose to broaden the use of the new signifiers. Rather than stick to deduction (which, in this case, would leave him empty-handed because of the insufficiency of the information at hand), he decided to rely on intuition and analogy.

What Dan created constituted a consistent whole. It was now up to me as a teacher to confirm his interpretation or try to change it. The role

[24] A: Listen, I defined the addition and the multiplication as I wanted. I had my reasons to do it the way I did, but I will keep them to myself for now. The question is . . . could you do the same when defining the division? Were you free to define it as you wanted?

[25] D: No, I was restricted by my associations.

[26] A: What do you mean? What kind of associations?

[27] D: That this sign is a multiplication . . .

[28] A: And this one is division? . . .

[29] D: Yes, and for all I know, they are related.

FIG. 3.8. Dan explains why he defined division the way he did.

of the social aspect in the process of sign-building stands in full relief again. My instructional interaction with Dan was an interplay between Dan's individual constructions and my regulatory interventions.

Expectations That Do Not Work. After demonstrating the strength of linguistically driven expectations, let me turn to the obvious pitfalls of projecting the old to the new. First, by activating old uses, the new signifiers may lead to beliefs that obstruct creation of new meaning, and create interdiscursive contradictions. Second, the expectations may be superficial and fuzzy, so that their implications are difficult to implement or test.

The overprojection of old uses results in the phenomena known as misconceptions. This may be best illustrated by the example of the notion of infinity. One may envision the following scenario. A person first becomes familiar with utterances of the form, "Function f grows infinitely." This may well be the phrase through which "infinity" makes its first appearance. At this point the new signifier has no existence of its own. The basic meaningful units are the expressions "function f" and "grows infinitely." Then, borrowing the template "Function f grows/tends to _____" from the discourse on functions and numbers ("Function f grows/tends to a number y_0 (when x tends to x_0)."), the learner would say, "Function f grows/tends to infinity" or even in the symbolic form, "Function f grows/tends to ∞." Once inserted into a slot originally meant for numbers, the word *infinity* and the symbol ∞ have a tendency to sneak into any place destined for numbers. Thus, because the phrase "Function f tends to a number y_0" may be translated into "The limit of function f equals y_0," it seems only natural to say, "The limit of function f equals ∞." Here, because of a clear ontological shift (from operational *grows infinitely* to the structural *equals (is) infinity*), the name *infinity* and the symbol ∞ acquire a life of their own and start acting in language as signifiers of an independently existing object. This is a perfect example of hypostasis—bringing a new mathematical object into existence just by a change in the rules of the language game. To this point, everything seems fine. However, if not restricted, the expectation that ∞ should fit any slot meant for numbers would soon produce statements creating intradiscursive anomalies and contradictions. The common error $\infty/\infty = 1$ is a good example.

The fact that using an old template is a "package deal" finds its other expression in the common expectation that whatever appears within expressions with arithmetic operators must also be applicable in utterances about quantities and magnitudes. Thus, the fact that complex numbers are not ordered appears counterintuitive.

The other weakness of expectations—the one resulting from their blurred inexact nature—may be illustrated with yet another episode taken from the study with Dan. I have just shown how the appearance of known signs (operators · and :) enabled Dan to act in a meaningful way in an unknown situation (division of pairs of whole numbers). Dan's expectation that division should be "an inverse of multiplication" proved sufficient as a basis for constructing a working definition of this new operation. As may be seen from the excerpt in Fig. 3.9, this was not the case with the operation of subtraction. The mention of subtraction (the appearance of the sign –) invoked the phrase "Subtraction is the inverse of addition" but did not give precise directives about the way the term *inverse* should be applied. Thus, Dan's first impulse was to reverse anything that could be reversed—all the operations on numbers that appeared in the formula for addition of the pairs. After all, reversing the component operations did work in the case of division. The only difficulty in the present case was that there seemed to be more possibilities for combining different reversals.

By testing the suggested formula in a concrete case, Dan soon realized that reversing all the operations did not work—it did not result in a pair of whole numbers that when added to the subtrahend would produce the minuend. Thus, he ventured a new conjecture, as presented in Fig. 3.10.

---

[1] A: Good . . . now, would you, please, do [problem 2] i [(11,9)–(5,3)=]?

[2] D: OK, This is already more complicated. Would you mind if I made side notes?

[3] A: On the contrary, suit yourself.

[4] D: (a,d) minus (c,d) equals . . . This is a problem . . . a problem . . . there are . . . there are many more possibilities for the inverse operation and I have to check them.

[5] A: Fine. Let's see. Continue.

[6] D: I will try to do [it]. Suppose, *a* equals . . . equals *a* divided by *d* minus *b* divided by *c*, comma, *b* divided by *d* [writes ($a/d - b/c, b/d$)], and I reverse all the operations that are here.

FIG. 3.9. Dan looks for a definition of subtraction—first trial.

---

[56] A: Yes, good. It seems that the conjecture did not prove itself, did it? What next? Where were we?

[57] D: I have to derive the operation of subtraction.

. . .

[66] D: Now, I have an idea.

[67] A: A brilliant idea, of course . . .

[68] D: No, I am not sure. Now, when I have seen . . . When I tried to perform this operation here, I reversed all the signs and the right-hand side answer was correct, the answer that did not require reversal of the operation of addition. So perhaps I only have to reverse the multiplication sign in order to get . . .

[69] A: Namely? . . .

[70] D: Namely, that I will do (a, b) minus (c, d) equals a divided by d plus b divided by c comma b divided by d. [writes $(a/d + b/c, b/d)$]

[71] A: So the difference between this and what we had before is that we now have plus instead of minus?

[72] D: Yes.

FIG. 3.10. Dan looks for a definition of subtraction—second trial.

More often than not, the certain difficulty stemming from an inexact nature of expectations is not an insurmountable obstacle. Substantial progress may be made either in a gradual way, by a succession of trials and errors, or in one big step—by translating the anticipation into an algorithm for finding a working definition. The latter is how Dan eventually overcame the present difficulty. He translated the claim about the relation between addition and subtraction into a symbolic statement:

$$(a, b) - (c, d) = (x, y) \qquad \text{iff} \qquad (x, y) + (c, d) = (a, b)$$

and then, after applying the formula for addition, solved the resulting equations for x and y.

Can Definitions Help?

The limitations of reasoning based on analogy are obvious. It is an ambition of mathematicians to ground the mathematical discourse in more reliable principles. Indeed, mathematical discourse may be the only one that aspires to derive decisions about co-occurrence of different templates (and utterances) from purely deductive considerations. Here, an introduction of a new signifier is usually accompanied (or at least, according to the rules of the mathematical discourse, should be accompanied) by a *definition*. Like any other utterance, a definition is a statement that has the power of activating clusters of other of utterances. The way it operates, however, is intended to be quite special. Definition is an utterance that formally minded mathematicians would like to regard as the sole generator of the entire discourse involving the signifier that it defines. Mathematicians recognize as legitimate only those utterances that may be presented as a result of formal deductive derivation from definitions, or at least that may be shown to be consistent with these definitions.[23]

Thus, those who reduce meaning to linguistic use would claim that definitions fully determine the meaning of signifiers. As teachers and researchers, we know only too well that, in practice, this is hardly the case. Definitions certainly help in establishing meaning of signifiers, but they do not tell the whole story. It is a well-known fact that people often hold to certain beliefs about scientific and mathematical signs in spite of the dictum of definitions. On the face of it, it may seem truly surprising that people may have robust preconceptions about a signifier they have never seen before. The following example shows, however, that even in the case of mathematical inventions, the mechanism of expectations is not only possible, but may even play a very central role. In fact, the power of framing and analogy may be greater than that of deductive reasoning (cf. Dörfler's notions of prototypes and protocols, chap. 4, this volume).

In a new mathematics text for schools that I was recently asked to review, I found a curious redundancy. Aiming at the concept of derivative, the authors first introduced the concept of the slope of a graph at a point (presented as the slope of the tangent to the graph at that point). Then, in the very next sentence, they defined a derivative at a point as the slope of the graph of the function at this point. At the meeting with the project team, I pointed out the double naming (slope, derivative) of exactly the same thing and asked the authors for the reason underlying their decision to pass through slope on their way toward derivative.

This question incited a fierce discussion. Quite clearly, all the participants felt intuitively that, in spite of the mathematical equivalence of *slope* and *derivative*, these two do not bring the same message. One of the speakers, G., put it this way:

> No, they are not the same . . . 'cause slope is the basic notion and derivative exists only as a function [rather than in its local sense of "derivative in a point"]. *Slope tells them* [the students] *something. . . .* They know this is a number from the beginning. *You tell them "slope" and they see something—an angle.* "Derivative" does not tell them anything. It's a function dependent on [another] function. Yeah, everything must start with the slope. [With slope] the kids understand something. *They have something in their head.* [Translation from Hebrew and emphasis mine]

---

[23]To put it in a slightly weaker form, a definition of a signifier S regulates the entire discourse about S by being a touchstone against which the admissibility of another statement about S is tested.

What G. was clearly trying to say is that the different names have a different framing power. They evoke different expectations and connect the new notion to different discursive formations and different template clusters. With the term *slope*, one is directed toward the geometric context within which the new notion comes complete with connections to other related notions and with well-developed mental images. In the case of derivative, all these helpful links and pictures are initially absent. The difference may be as great as expressing itself in the possibility that within one frame the notion will be semantically mediated while in the other its use will continue to be templates-driven.

This example brings quite a number of noteworthy messages. First, it shows in a persuasive way that definitions are not the only source of signifieds. Definitions as such introduce new signs in a skeletonized form, with almost no links to previous discourses. Indeed, cutting such links seems to be the very essence of formalization and abstraction. Using an expression Bruner (1987) applied in a different context, we may say that formal mathematical definitions are "all reference and no sense" (p. 119).[24] These definitions, therefore, may be very well suited as tools for testing hypotheses and expectations, but they are not equally effective as generators of the expectations themselves. Thus, contrary to what some people may believe, definitions cannot be regarded as always effective short-cuts to meaning.[25]

More often than not, the signifiers themselves become more or less powerful meaning activators, with their signifying strength depending on their history. Thus, the name *slope* obviously brings a much richer semantic heritage than the word *derivative*.[26] The same distinctions can often be made when it comes to mathematical symbols. For example, the symbol a/b for a rational number is certainly a more powerful meaning generator than the symbol (a,b). The former brings an immediate association with division, thus connecting rational numbers to the computational processes that constitute their operational source.

---

[24]The terms *sense* and *reference* are to be understood, after Frege, as referring to "relation to other things and other concepts" and to "extension of the concept to the world of instances," respectively (Frege's original German terms, often used by those who quote him, are *Bedeutung* for reference and *Sinn* for sense).

[25]Bakhtin spoke to this effect when he contrasted "contextual meaning" with definitions that only "contain potential meaning" (Bakhtin, 1986, p. 145).

[26]In our work as researchers, the awareness of a potential impact of names and symbols makes us very careful in choosing terminology for new theoretical frameworks. It has already been observed that researchers are analogical reasoners who, in creating new theories, avail themselves of metaphors (Knorr, 1980). The decisions about names and symbols may have far-reaching consequences. A felicitous choice, through a chain of associations with previous meanings, will bring important new insights; an unlucky choice will result in a cluster of counterproductive connotations.

The final implication regards the nature of the meaning. An important moral of the story of slope and derivative is that there is much more to meaning than logically regulated use. The example casts doubt on the reductionist position that tries to do without reference to anything but forms of use. Except for saying that different names activate different discourses, G. was stressing that they evoke different experiential resonance. According to G., the word *slope* brings about a spectrum of mental phenomena, including spontaneous associations and "seeing something" (a mental image of an angle), whereas derivative has almost no such effect. Thus, in spite of the fact that *slope* and *derivative* are mathematically indistinguishable and have exactly the same definition, the former is believed to be readily accessible to the student as a signifier–signified pair, whereas the latter is initially no more than an empty signifier. The emergence of these and other aspects of meaning is dealt with in the next section.

OBJECTS FROM SYMBOLS, ACT TWO: FILLING IN THE SEMANTIC SPACE

Object Mediation

In the templates-driven phase, the use of a new symbol may be quite effective and a person may have little difficulty communicating with others, but this ability is not accompanied by an awareness of the reasons why things work. Using Vygotsky's language (1987), one may say that in this phase, names and symbols are but "signs-for-others."[27] It is important to stress again that *templates-driven* does not mean meaningless, and that the period of templates-driven use may be extremely brief. When it comes to learning, it seems likely that the length of this period may be regulated by instructional intervention.

When employed in the templates-driven way, the signifier is not yet conceived by its user as standing for something else. In fact, the user may not even perceive the sign as a self-sustained entity. The basic meaningful units are all those more-or-less constant phrases within which the sign makes its appearances. It is usually only much later that the name or symbol gains independence. The liberation of the signifier from the confinement of constant phrases is usually accompanied by a reference to entities different from the signifier itself. Thus, for example, a student presented with an equation, $3(x + 1) - 2 = 3x + 5$, may transform it into $3x + 1 = 3x + 5$ and then say that "The equation has no solution because

---

[27]As opposed to "signs-in-themselves" and "signs-for-oneself." Vygotsky made this distinction when analyzing development of concepts.

the two sides represent linear functions the graphs of which do not cross each other." Here, the mediating entities are functions, which, according to the way the word *function* is used in the sentence, are independent objects that should not be identified with the signifiers ($3x + 1$, $3x + 5$, graph) themselves.

Let us take a closer look at the main characteristics of object mediation.

Flexibility and Generality of Use. As was just mentioned, the salient attribute of this new stage in the life of a structural sign is that its use becomes flexible. The sign gets life of its own, and the user is now able to incorporate the signifier into utterances that he or she has never heard before. This change may be compared to the transition from a mechanical use of a musical instrument, say, piano, to the use based on a knowledge of music. A person who has no musical education but who has learned to play a few melodies by memorizing the sequence of necessary key-strokes may be able to repeat these melodies at any time, and may even enjoy this greatly, but the person will probably not be able to play a new melody, even if that person can sing it. For such a person, finding the necessary keystrokes would be an uphill struggle. Others, who can de-compose melodies into basic elements, understand the principles of har-mony, and know how the elementary sounds may be produced by appro-priate actions, are able to compose, or at least reconstruct by themselves, melodies they have never played before. This ability to create novel uses is often regarded as an ultimate criterion of meaningfulness and under-standing. As Rotman (1994) put it while summarizing Wittgenstein's (1978) observations on meaning, "It is the move to new cases, and the subsequent use of the label [signifier] that constitutes its meaning" (p. 24).

The Symbol Starts Functioning as a Representation. Another salient phenomenon indicative of the phase of object mediation is a change in the role of a symbol: Rather than being the object of discourse (as, e.g., analytic expression in Euler's first definition of function), the symbol now becomes a representation of another entity. This new identity is conferred on the signifier by the way it is used. The "analytic expression," for instance, turns into a means of talking about a certain abstract object (e.g., *a set of ordered pairs*), which may also be represented with other symbols (e.g., a curve in the plane). From now on, if we wish to be precise, we should no longer say *This is a quadratic function* while pointing to the symbol x^2 or to a parabola; rather, now we should say that *This is an expression of (or a graph of) a quadratic function,* or *This expression (graph) represents a quadratic function.*

The distinction between "the object itself" and its representation is more difficult in the case of numbers, but it is still possible. Nowhere is the sense of the split made more evident than in the following statement by the French mathematician Alain Connes, who complains about people's frequent inability to see the "obvious" difference between a number and a numeral: "it would be wrong to attribute significance to the numerals that appear in the number. (Consider that very soon we will be celebrating the year 2000. The importance of this number is a purely cultural phenomenon: in mathematics, the number 2000 is utterly devoid of interest!) (Changeux & Connes, 1995, p. 13).[28]

As aptly expressed by Cassirer (1957), the developmental importance of the mental split between the signifier and the object signified can hardly be overestimated. The transition from signifier-as-an-object-in-itself to signifier-as-a-representation-of-another-object is a quantum leap in a subject's consciousness:

> The ontogenic development shows that wherever the function of representation stands out *as such*, where, instead of giving himself wholly to the actuality, [to] the simple presence of sensuous content, man succeeds in taking it as a representation of another, he has achieved an entirely new level of consciousness. . . .
>
> When the representative function of names has thus dawned on a child, his whole inner attitude toward reality has changed—a fundamentally new relation between subject and object has come into being. (pp. 112, 113)

In this context, it is important to stress two things. First, the change in the role of the symbol—from the-thing-in-itself to a representation—would usually not happen unless there are other symbols that can be regarded as signifying the same entity. The features that make us consider two symbols as referring to the same third object are discussed later. Second, once the symbol takes the role of representation, the whole discourse undergoes a modification. The old ways of expressing mathematical truths give way to new formulations. One glimpse into any old mathematical text would be enough to realize how far-reaching this change may be. Thus, the ongoing mathematical conversation, perhaps more than any other type of discourse, is similar to a living organism that incessantly grows and mutates without losing its identity.

The transition from signifier-as-an-object-in-itself to signifier-as-a-representation can be spurred by the teacher who insists on using language

---

[28]Our language does not always help in separating the number and the numeral the way Connes did. We say "78 is a two-digit number" whether we mean the signifier (which is sometimes called "numeral") or the number itself—the abstract object supposedly represented by this signifier. (A counterpart of this expression in AR discourse would sound rather funny; to say "78 is a two-digit number" is like saying that "Shakespeare is an eleven-letter person.") This difficulty in separating the signifier from the signified in speech and in writing is a permanent reminder that "referents" have no existence without symbols.

that underlines the separate existence of signifier and signified. Thus, rather than say, "Function x^2," the teacher would say, "Function *represented by x^2*." However, the awkwardness of such language, whose effectiveness is highly doubtful, may be too high a price to pay. The mental split between signifier and signified can hardly occur without a certain experience of the signified, and this experience is not a matter of language alone (see the later discussion of the experience of the signified).

The Symbol Is Often Inadvertently Exchanged With Other Signifiers. One of the most telling indications of semantic mediation is a phenomenon of a change in wording that may often be witnessed when people try to recapitulate a former statement or when they are asked to use a particular word or symbol in a sentence. For example, Dan (see the previous section), when requested to compose a sentence using the words "one and a half," replied: "Mother gave Yossi a shekel and a half."[29] In spite of the explicit request, the words *one and a half* did not appear in the utterance. Similarly, in another study, an 11-year-old boy who was asked to construct a sentence with the word *zero* said: "I gave all my apples to friends, so now I have nothing." The mechanism of semantic mediation is obvious here. In both cases, the students did not look at the words but rather through them, to the entities that these words seem to represent (the quantities one-and-a-half and zero, respectively). Without noticing, they then made a transition to different words that, for them, represented the same entities but for some reasons were more easily applicable within sentences. Incidentally, it is probably not by chance that in both of these cases the utterances constructed by the children came from AR discourse. The physical reality is the greatest provider of object mediation. It abounds in perceptually accessible objects that are ideal to think with and to use as signifieds.

Economy of Expression. As a result of object mediation, there is a substantial gain in the efficiency of discourse: Much more can be said now with one signifier. By assuming the role of a mere "representation," the given symbol becomes, in a sense, equivalent to other signifiers (think, e.g., about algebraic expressions and graphs), and thus, what until now had to be said twice—for each of the different signifiers separately—from now on may be said just once. Due to the mediation of an abstract object supposedly referred to by both of these symbols (function, in the case of the expression and graph), what is said with one signifier usually has meaning for the other.

---

[29]*Shekel* is an Israeli monetary unit.

Experience of the Signified (Abstract Object). One can hardly argue with the claim that there is more to "grasping a meaning" than can be found through purely structural linguistic analysis. We saw this in the discussion of *slope* and *derivative* reported earlier. In fact, convincing evidence for this can be found everywhere: from well-controlled clinical studies to field observations and to mathematicians' testimonies. Repeatedly, people report having vivid images of abstract objects, thinking without words, and having recourse to metaphorically transformed perceptual experiences (Hadamard, 1949; Johnson, 1987; Lakoff, 1987; Sfard, 1994a). As in a virtual reality game, the presence of mathematical objects may seem to a person to be real even if it is difficult for the person to communicate it to others. So it seems to be in Connes' case, judging from his statement on numbers and numerals given earlier. Indeed, the way he spoke shows that for him there is not much difference between numbers and physical objects when it comes to questions of existence: Both types of entities exist independently of human mind. To the psychologist, the experiential aspect of meaning seems too central to be neglected only because it does not yield easily to scientific investigation.

To summarize, the transition from templates-driven to object-mediated use of a symbol is a rich and multifaceted event. The remainder of this section is devoted to observations of how it happens. I have already mentioned two possible sources of object mediation. One of them is located within the closed system of mathematical discourse, and the other crosses its boundaries and reaches as far as AR discourse. We now take a closer look at each.

Intradiscursive Creation of Mathematical Objects

In this section I focus on the ways in which endogenous mathematical meaning is constructed. I show how the semantic space created by the introduction of a new signifier may be replenished with content coming from within the mathematical discourse itself.

As mentioned earlier, one typical indication of object mediation is the use of a number of signifiers as if they were but different representations of the same entity. All this begins with the awareness of some sort of "kinship" between signs. Such awareness may come about spontaneously or may be evoked by others (e.g., the teacher). It is important to stress that, more often than not, it is prior to any mention of an object ("referent"), and therefore may be viewed as a direct reason for its emergence. The already analyzed development of the notion of function is a good example.

There is also another type of kinship between symbols, one that expresses itself in an isomorphism of discursive formations built around these symbols. By *isomorphism of discourses* I mean a relations-preserving correspondence between the two discourses. This kind of relationship exists, for example, between a discourse that evolves around algebraic expressions with one variable and one that concerns two-dimensional curves. Indeed, any utterance about expressions (e.g., "$2x + 1 = 26 - 3x$ when $x = 5$") may be mapped onto an utterance about curves (e.g., "The straight lines with the slopes 2 and –3 and y-intercepts 1 and 26, respectively, cross each other at the point (5, 11)") in such a way that the logical relationships within each one of the two discursive formations are preserved. Once again, creation of an intermediate entity (function) that may be regarded as a common referent of the two symbols—the algebraic formula and the curve—is a feasible way to account for the isomorphism.

To summarize, endogenous semantic mediation in general, and mathematical objects in particular, arise between symbols as a result of an attempt to account for discursive equivalencies and isomorphisms. (The adjective *discursive* has been added to stress that these equivalencies and isomorphisms are phenomena that express themselves in the discursive use of signifiers.) It is noteworthy that the way we deal with linguistic equivalencies and isomorphisms in mathematical discourse is parallel to the manner in which these phenomena are accounted for in AR discourse. It is also worth mentioning, however, that the order of things seems to be reversed. In AR discourse perception of an object can sometimes be primary to any linguistic treatment, whereas the abstract objects of mathematics seem to be secondary to the awareness of discursive equivalence of a number of signifiers. This may be viewed as additional evidence of the perceptual sources of all human thinking and the metaphorical, embodied nature of imagination (Johnson, 1987; Lakoff, 1987; Sfard, 1994a, 1997).

As an illustration of the intra-discursive creation of object-mediation, I refer to another example from my study with Dan (see earlier discussion in this chapter). As the reader may recall, I presented Dan with new mathematical symbols—pairs of whole numbers on which some operations, called addition and multiplication, had been defined. Dan successfully constructed subtraction and division as reversals of these two operations. The resulting structure was that of rational numbers, but Dan had not been told that at any stage. Moreover, in spite of his intensive work with the pairs, he remained unaware of the isomorphism for the duration of the first meeting. By the end of the meeting, a problem appeared: Some of the divisions and subtractions yielded pairs of fractional, rather than whole, numbers (e.g., $(5,3):(1,4) = (5, ¾)$). According to the definition, these were not legitimate members of the new structure. After a brief discussion in which possible solutions were considered, the instructor suggested:

> How about the following idea: We will not distinguish anymore between all the possible pairs. We shall see some of them as equal. Some of them will be considered equivalent to each other. There will be pairs that, from our point of view, will be the same, even if they are written with different numbers. For example, (3,2) and (6,4) for us will be the same [writes: (3,2) = (6,4)].[30]

From this, Dan concluded that two pairs should be considered as equal if the relation between them could be presented in the following way:

> [1] the numbers [in the original pair] are multiplied . . . the two numbers are multiplied by the same number [and this is how the second pair is obtained].

This is a purely operational description: Dan identified the transformation that has to be performed on a pair in order to turn it into an equivalent pair. In the attempt to trace the subsequent transition to a structural definition, it is most enlightening to follow gradual changes in Dan's use of language. Even before the end of the first meeting Dan declared:

> [2] We can decide that pairs are equal according to the ratio . . . to the ratio of the two numbers.

The change with respect to utterance [1] is quite significant—and most telling. The transformation of a pair into an equivalent pair has been reified into a mathematical object called *ratio*. Rather than consider the two pairs alone (as in [1]), Dan helps himself with this third entity. This new object will be the touchstone of the equality between pairs. Dan's use of the words *according to* shows, however, that at this early stage, although it is obvious that the ratio is strongly related to the pairs, these pairs are not yet regarded as representations of the ratio.

During the second meeting, I could witness a gradual metamorphosis of the whole-number pairs from objects-in-themselves into representations

---

[30]As can be seen here, the idea of equivalence of symbols was suggested and then defined by the instructor rather than being intuitively raised by the learner himself. However, in spite of the lack of spontaneity in the opening move, I believe that the processes I was able to observe later were not much different from those that can be seen in more "natural" circumstances.

of some other objects. First, when recalling the decision made during the previous meeting, Dan told me:

[3] We said that some pairs of numbers will be equal because the ratio between the first and the second number is equal. . . .

This is but a repetition of [2]. However, a few moments later, the formulation changed. After I suggested that we may call the pairs *numbers* and asked Dan whether this proposal seemed to him acceptable, Dan replied:

[4] Yes, I think it is possible [to call the pairs "numbers"] because what really counts is the ratio between the two numbers in the pair, and I think that in fact we could write this [writes 8/5] instead of this [writes (8,5)]. We could write it as eight divided by five?

Here, for the first time, Dan identified the pairs with the ratio. This, however, was put in an interesting and telling way. Rather than say that a pair (8,5) *is* the ratio 8/5, he talked about replacement of the pair by the ratio. Thus, Dan pointed to a very close relationship between the pair and the ratio—so close that one may be replaced by the other. However, this still was not necessarily a relation of signifier–signified.

The transition to this relationship happened some time later, when on a certain occasion Dan unexpectedly declared:

[5] You just took numbers that I know and you represented them in a different way.

This time, Dan said explicitly that the pairs are representations of another entity. This other entity is a number already known to Dan from his past learning. This, incidentally, is how the chain of signification builds: the familiar numbers (of the form a/b), which once began their life as mere signifiers, are now fully fledged signs, which, in their turn, become signifieds of the new signifiers (the pairs (a,b)).

Several aspects of this story merit special attention. For Dan, the symbols 2/5, 11/5, and so on, are full of meaning. They bring with them a rich network of both intra- and interdiscursive relationships and a long history of abstract objects that evolved through the process of reification from the processes of division. (The symbol / within the rational number sign commemorates this history.) By assuming the role of "a representation" of rational numbers, the pairs (a,b) inherit all of this meaning. Above all, they become reconnected to the operational origins of the notion. Dan's later utterances make it quite clear that in his eyes the two symbols, a/b and (a,b), differed in their roles. Indeed, there could be little doubt that for him the pairs (a,b) acted as signifiers whereas the ratios a/b functioned as signifieds. When requested to perform any operation or investigation on the whole-number pairs, Dan invariantly switched to ratios. He did it even in a recall task, where he was asked to look at a series of pairs and recapitulate them later.

As may be seen from episode [6], which took place by the end of the second meeting, the bond between the signifier (the pair) and the signified (the rational number) soon became so strong that Dan would not distinguish between them anymore. The pair (a,b) and the rational number a/b were now referred to as the same (this is true at least in the case of the pairs of the form $(0, b)$ and the number 0).

[6] D: The moment I write zero comma something, $(0,b)$ for example, and I change it to $0/b$ which, according to what we said, is equal [to the pair $(0,b)$] then this is automatically equal to 0.

A: What does it tell you about the pairs?

D: That all the pairs with left component equal to 0 are equal.

A: Equal to each other?

D: Equal to 0.

To summarize, this example instantiates the process of intradiscursive construction of a mathematical object. Once certain signifiers were declared equivalent (equal), the need was created for an object that would give meaning to this equivalence. The object was eventually found,[31] and from then on the equivalent signifiers played the role of representations.

Interdiscursive Creation of Mathematical Objects: Connecting VR Discourse to AR Discourse

In the last section we saw how mathematical discourse produces its own meanings. One can hardly overestimate the importance of another process leading to the emergence of object mediation: metaphorical projection from one discourse to another. As noted before, AR discourse occupies a special position. I have already discussed some distinct structural similarities between AR and VR discourses. The focus in this section is on

---

[31]In this case, it was not built totally on its own because some previously constructed objects could be used as signifiers. When talking about *constructing objects*, I intend to say that the signifiers "referring" to these objects have already entered the phase of semantically mediated use, that is, the phase characterized by all the phenomena presented in a previous section (including the experiential aspects).

another kind of link between the two: the link created by names and symbols that are shared by both discourses. Such symbols are well known to all of us and can be found in abundance in everyday language. The names and symbols of positive integers and rational numbers, which are almost as common in everyday talk as they are in a classroom mathematical discourse, are the simplest examples.[32]

Naturally, mathematical signifiers are not always a shared property of AR and VR discourses. The existence of some of them, at least for some people, may be fully confined to mathematical discourse. This is certainly the case for such notions as matrix or complex number, provided the user knows nothing about their scientific applications. Some other mathematical signs are not mathematical at all for a person who is only able to use them within AR discourse. Much has been said lately about different brands of AR discursive formations that evolve around signifiers shared with mathematical discourse. There is talk about "everyday mathematics," "street mathematics," "market-place mathematics" and "ethno-mathematics" (Lave, 1988; Nunes, Schliemann, & Carraher, 1993; Saxe, 1988; Walkerdine, 1988). While marveling at Brazilian street vendors' ability to make appropriate calculations when selling their goods, and at similar skills displayed by uneducated women buying provisions for their families, the writers emphasize that the same people are usually stymied when faced with a requirement to make paper-and-pencil numerical manipulations. Clearly, for those who only know how to use numbers in everyday discourse, the number is not the same object as it is for the learner of mathematics in school. Although the same names appear in both discourses, these names lead to entirely different connotations and, thus, constitute different signs. Whereas a street seller thinks of numbers in terms (and images) of coins, school children identify numbers with written number symbols. To put it differently, if an abstract mathematical object that functions as a signified of, say, the term *five* is a totality of symbols, linguistic uses, and experiences related to this signifier, then the Brazilian vendor and the European pupil refer to completely different objects using the same number name.

For many people, a signifier—either mathematical or otherwise—must find its place in AR discourse in order to be meaningful. More than that, some researchers would claim that AR discourse is the only possible

---

[32]Of course, the uses of these signifiers may be quite different in the different discourses. Here is, for example, a sentence I read in the British Guardian (24.4.95), describing the celebrations of Shakespeare's birthday: "Six or 700 celebrants walked through the shrine in Henley Street." Here, 700 is used not as an indivisible number symbol, but as a shorthand for the words "seven hundred," so that each one of the two components has its own independent role within the sentence.

source of meaning for mathematics. This claim is usually supported with argument about the situatedness of learning (Brown, Collins, & Duguid, 1989; Lave, 1988; Lave & Wenger, 1991; Walkerdine, 1988).[33] In this chapter I have been trying to show that this position may be too extreme. Arguments have been brought forward to show that the intradiscursive production of mathematical meaning is not just possible; sometimes, it is the essence of mathematical creation. Nevertheless, it is now time to stress the importance of meaning that comes from outside mathematical discourse.

If a sign exists and functions in both AR and VR discourses, it is likely to be meaningful in the latter mainly due to the perceptual-world connotations it brings with it from the former. Thus, the symbols $\frac{2}{3}$ and 17 carry with them the metaphor of physical quantities (see Sfard, 1994b, 1997), and this metaphor is what mediates and regulates the uses of the signifiers both in AR and in VR discourses. If we take the ability to use a mathematical sign in AR discourse as a touchstone of understanding, then a small test I carried out recently among my university students has shown that not many of them could boast of having an object-mediated understanding of the concept of negative and irrational numbers. First, 18 students were asked to construct sentences with the numbers 1.5, $\frac{2}{3}$, and –3. Later, they were requested to compose questions, the answers to which could be $\frac{7}{9}$, –2, and $\sqrt{-2}$. In both cases, they were encouraged to look for utterances with "everyday content." Although both tasks—construction of everyday sentences and questions—proved easy in the case of the positive rational numbers 1.5, $\frac{2}{3}$, $\frac{7}{9}$ (see Fig. 3.11), for the rest of the numbers not many everyday utterances were provided. Students' responses were taken mostly from mathematical discourse itself. The few "everyday uses" of negative numbers were made solely in the context of temperature, latitude, and bank overdraft. In the first two examples, the number was applied as a label rather than as a measure of quantity. Most of the "everyday" questions to which the answer was supposed to be –2 suffered from out-of-focus syndrome; that is, although the negative quantity was somehow involved in the situation presented in the question, the actual answer to the question should be 2 rather than –2 (see the example in Fig. 3.11).

---

[33]In fact, the sweeping call to teach mathematics through solving real-life problems may be a product of a misinterpretation of the doctrine of situatedness. The whole point about this doctrine is that situations in which problems are being solved frame these problems in ways irreproducible in other situations. Thus, all those characteristics of a problem that are so helpful to its solving in a supermarket or at home are inevitably lost when the problem is transferred to school (cf. Lesh & Doerr's discussion of solving real-life problems, chap. 10, this volume). Moreover, nothing can be done about it since the loss is due to a fact that simply cannot be changed: that the school is not a supermarket.

Remark: the numbers in brackets show the percentage of students who constructed this type of example. In the second task, the students were encouraged to compose more than one question for each item, thus the percentages do not add to 100.

	AR discourse	VR discourse
SENTENCES		
1.5:	I drank a glass and a half of water (67%).	If one multiplies 1.5 by ⅔, one gets 1. (332%)
⅔:	Dan was hungry and he ate ⅔ of a pie. (75%).	⅔ is a rational number. (25%)
–3:	The temperature went down to –3. (42%)	–2 is greater than –3. (58%)
QUESTIONS		
7/9:	The pie was divided into 9 parts. I ate two of them. How much of the pie was left? (75%)	What is the result of ⅜ + ⅙? (92%)
–2:	label: temperature went down 12 degrees from 10 degrees. What is the temperature now? (42%) out of focus: How much money do you owe [sic!] to John? (25%)	What is the solution of the equation $3x + 9 = 3$? (100%)
$\sqrt{2}$:	What is the length of the hypotenuse in the right-angle triangle with sides equal 1? (25%)	What is the solution of the equation $x^2 = 2$? (75%) (16%—no response)

FIG. 3.11. Examples of sentences and questions composed by the students.

In my experiment with Dan, the request to compose sentences and questions with numbers of different kinds recurred several times. The student repeatedly stressed his difficulty with negative, irrational, and complex numbers (the latter were introduced to him beginning with the fourth meeting as pairs of real numbers and under the name "novel numbers"). He explicitly complained about his inability to compose "everyday" sentences and questions for these numbers. Here are representative samples of his utterances:

On complex number (2,3), meeting 7: I still don't know how to write (2,3) in a sentence. The two [real numbers] I can . . . I can say this as a mathematical sentence.

On –2, meeting 9: A question: "What is 1 minus 3?" [pause] . . . All I can think about is in a mathematical context.

On $\sqrt{2}$, meeting 9: A question: "Give an example of an irrational number" . . . [pause] I don't really have any question to ask.

Some other utterances have shown that the only link to AR discourse could come from the relation of order. Dan said this quite explicitly during the ninth meeting, while explaining the difficulty he experienced when trying to compose a sentence with $\sqrt{2}$ (Fig. 3.12).

Evidently, the symbol $\sqrt{\ }$ was for Dan still operational rather than structural and, in order to account for its structural use, Dan needed object mediation that could only come from AR discourse. His concept of number was inextricably tied to AR notions of quantity. This is why the numbers that could not be easily located between rational numbers (e.g., irrational, complex) did not count for Dan as "true" numbers. When I asked, during the ninth meeting, what the word *number* meant to him, the exchange presented in Fig. 3.13 took place.

The inability to incorporate negative, irrational, and complex numbers into AR discourse was for Dan an evidence that "these are not true numbers." Several times he made a distinction between the numbers that

---

[1]   A: Why do you smile?

[2]   D: Because I don't. . . . I have no sense of this number, I don't . . .

[3]   A: Try something . . .

[4]   D: "Dan ate $\sqrt{2}$ candies from the bag . . .

[5]   A: Great.

[6]   D: Not really.

[7]   A: Oh?

[8]   D: It's difficult to explain . . .

. . .

[35]   A: You have seen that there is a segment the length of which is $\sqrt{2}$. Doesn't it give you some sense of $\sqrt{2}$?

[36]   D: It helps a bit, but I still can't . . . I can't imagine a segment the length of which is $\sqrt{2}$.

[37]   A: What do you need to be able to imagine this?

[38]   D: I have to know what is $\sqrt{2}$. I have to present it as a rational number.

[39]   A: Why? What is the advantage of rationals over irrationals?

[40]   D: That you can grasp them. . . . That I can imagine without much difficulty what this number is . . . An example from real life . . . I have to see it as a number. π is easier for me because I can see it as 3.14, etc.

[41]   A: Does 3.14 give you anything which you don't have in the case of $\sqrt{2}$?

. . .

[51]   D: An exact measure of the number. 3.14 . . . I can now take a ruler, measure 3.14 and draw this interval . . . But even if I take the most precise ruler in the world, I can't draw a segment the length of which is $\sqrt{2}$.

FIG. 3.12. Numbers must have a precise magnitude.

[1]	D:	OK. Number is something we use for counting . . . We use them to assess quantity.
[2]	A:	The rational number can measure quantity?
[3]	D:	Yes, you can say . . .
[4]	A:	And the novel [complex] numbers can?
[5]	D:	The "left-hand numbers" [this is what we called the complex numbers of the form (a,0), which Dan has identified as "another representation" of "ordinary numbers"] can, but the others can't.
[6]	A:	So, are these numbers or not?
[7]	D:	[hesitates] . . . No . . .

FIG. 3.13. Numbers measure quantity.

"exist in the world" and those that are but man-made. During the eighth meeting, he tried to explain his inability to incorporate negative numbers into AR discourse, as presented in Fig. 3.14.

The claim about "unnaturalness" of irrational, negative, and complex numbers may be seen as an indication of Dan's uncertainty about the legitimacy and meaningfulness of these numbers. All of this means that Dan's sense of understanding numbers, like that of 17th- and 18th-century mathematicians, depended very strongly on his ability to use them in AR discourse. This example illustrates the point I am trying to make in this section. It shows that AR discourse is a very important, and sometimes irreplaceable, source of mathematical meaning. To put it differently, in certain circumstances transition to object mediation becomes possible only due to the "import" of signifieds from AR discourse.

[1]	D:	Minus is something that people invented. I mean . . . we don't have anything in the environment to show it. I can't think about anything like that.
[2]	A:	Is everything that regards numbers invented by people?
[3]	D:	No, not everything . . .
[4]	A:	For instance?
[5]	D:	For example, the basic operation of addition, one plus one [is two] and according to the logic of the world this cannot be otherwise.
[6]	A:	And half plus one-third equals five sixths. Does it depend on us, humans or . . .
[7]	D:	Not on us. You can show it in the world.
[8]	A:	I see . . . and 5 minus 8 equals –3. It's us or not us?
[9]	D:	It's us.
[10]	A:	Why?
[11]	D:	Because in our world there is no example for such a thing.

FIG. 3.14. Negative numbers are a human invention.

MAKING WORD FLESH—SOME DIDACTIC CONSIDERATIONS

Summary

In this chapter, mathematical discourse has been presented as an autopoietic system in which an intricate interplay of signifiers is a principal source of meaning. Although the discourse on numbers, functions, sets, and the like bears striking structural resemblance to the discourse on physical objects, there is no point in talking about objects of mathematics as entities existing independently of the discourse itself. In fact, the very idea of mathematical object is only metaphorical, and it refers to a particular use of signifiers. To be a fully fledged participant of mathematical discourse means, among others, to be able to use mathematical names and symbols with proficiency and with experiences similar to those that are characteristic of the use of structural signifiers in communication on material objects. However, because of a relative scarcity of perceptual support, the ability to make such an object-mediated use of mathematical names and symbols is not easy to attain.

In spite of the difficulty, new structural signifiers are being introduced to mathematical discourse all the time. The eventual gains of such additions are significant enough to recompense the effort necessary to develop object-mediated use of the new symbols. By changing the ontological status of focal mathematical notions from operational to structural (or from referring to processes to referring to objects), new signifiers enable turning the discourse onto itself; that is, they make it possible to initiate a higher level mathematical discourse—a discourse on the discursive procedures developed and practiced so far.

There is an inherent circularity in the process of construction of such a higher level mathematical discourse. On the one hand, introduction and use of the structural signifier have a constitutive role in establishing the objects of this discourse; on the other hand, participants' sense of existence of these objects is a condition for the effective use of the signifiers. This circularity is a source of additional difficulty, but is also the driving force behind the discursive growth: The lack of equilibrium between discursive practices and the participants' sense of the objects of the discourse is what impels this growth.

The way out of the circularity leads through the stage of templates-driven use of new signifiers, that is, use that is guided by old discursive habits and forms. The employment of new signifiers within previously established discursive templates is regulated through expectations and verifications. A former experience with signifiers deemed to be somehow analogous to the new ones engenders expectations about possible discursive uses of these new names or symbols. These expectations are then tested and, if confirmed, the given templates are added to the repertoire of the new signifier's possible uses; if refuted, the templates are deleted from the list. The confirmations and refutations are a product of either communicative interactions or deductive considerations. The object-mediated use will eventually develop endogenously, as a result of attempts to account for intradiscursive equivalencies and isomorphisms between symbolic systems, and exogenously, with the support of meanings developed by applying the signifier in other discourses.

Conclusions

After the detailed discussion of the mechanisms that underlie the growth of mathematical discourse, it is time to give some thought to the practical implication. Those who renounce the traditional vision of symbols as coming to capture ready-made meaning and to represent mind-independent intangible objects are likely to be critical also about traditional instructional practices.

As was mentioned before, it is widely believed these days that mathematical symbols should not be introduced before the concepts represented by these symbols are already understood, at least partially. However, if one accepts the thesis that there can be no talk about mathematical objects without mathematical symbols, then the request to prepare an easy, meaningful landing for symbolic newcomers seems inherently difficult—if not outright impossible. Thus, instead of asking "What comes first?" we would rather give thought to the question of how to orchestrate and facilitate the back-and-forth movement between symbols and meanings. This seems to be the only way to cope with the problem of circularity that is inherent in discourse that creates its own objects.

The roots of all language games people play go back to AR discourse. However, sequences of template transplants and chains of signification forged on the way from AR to VR discourse of mathematics may be so long that their AR sources are no longer visible from the distant VR end. They may be much too extensive to be fully reconstructed during 10 or 12 years of schooling. Indeed, as long as mathematical contents taught in today's high schools remain basically as they are, it seems hardly possible that the starting point of every instructional sequence is placed within AR discourse, or that the bridges between AR and VR discourses are constantly kept in sight when mathematical symbols are being manipulated. As I already mentioned, this is something that many mathematical educators find increasingly difficult to accept.[34] There can be little doubt that they have good reasons for their protests against mathematics for its own sake. As was shown in the last section, what seems natural and fully understandable for a mathematician brought up in a strict formalist tradition may be as inconceivable for the student as it was for the Medieval and Renaissance mathematicians who rejected the notions of negative and imaginary numbers because of the impossibility of incorporating them into AR discourse. Today's mathematicians may pay lip service to the requirement of AR usefulness by saying that AR applications "will be found one day." The necessity to postpone the relinking with AR discourse (possibly *ad infinitum*) does not affect their work and does not disturb their peace of mind. For the student, such a delay may be highly consequential.

The problem seems quite complex indeed: Only too often, linking VR and AR discourses is either too difficult to be feasible, or is simply impossible. However, two didactic avenues offer a certain promise. First, the bridging may sometimes be done in reverse order—something that may also save time and effort. Indeed, if we begin with purely mathematical discourse and then return to AR discourse already endowed with new mathematical signifiers, these new signifiers would often serve as looking glasses through which the tangible world would readily seem more orderly than before. As Miller (1991) put it, "We do not take signifiers as that which describes reality. We take signifiers as what enters the real to structure it" (p. 32). This, in fact, is to say that starting with mathematical signifiers may sometimes be the right thing to do. Not only abstract mathematical objects, but also real-world structures, do not come into existence by themselves, but rather have to be "symbolized into being." The claim that the structure is symbol independent, objective, and just waiting to be captured in symbols sounds as equally unconvincing as Michelangelo Buonarroti's modest assertion that his only role as a sculptor was to expose the forms that were "already there" in the stone.

For the sake of skeptics who doubt the possibility of meaningful activity with links to AR discourse temporarily suspended, let me remark that mathematical ideas that are firmly situated in mathematical context and are well connected to previously constructed concepts may appear as meaningful and relevant as those that grow from real-life situations. Here, the emphasis is, of course, on the issue of understanding and accepting

---

[34]The "extremists" would be most happy if the intramathematical creation of meaning was banned from schools altogether. However, rejecting endogenous mathematical meaning would be tantamount to the rejection of major portions of mathematics itself. Today's mathematicians might say that it would be banning all mathematics.

the rules of purely mathematical discourse—something that is quite difficult to attain and is, therefore, rarely found in schools. Another point to stress is the issue of context. Whether "real-life" or purely mathematical, it is the context that makes budding ideas meaningful and helps establish object mediation. If we recall how much was achieved by Dan in the clinically sterile situation in which the links to his former knowledge were deliberately withheld, we have every reason to assume that in a richer context his progress could be even more impressive.

Yet another argument in support of the possibility of learning mathematics intradiscursively has to do with the ways of incorporating new signifiers into mathematical discourse. Although in no situation should we expect the new mathematical objects to emerge without symbolical support, the symbols themselves do not have to be arbitrarily introduced. In the optimal case, within an appropriate context, they can be expected to grow as if "of themselves," just as in the late 16th century algebraic expressions emerged almost against mathematicians' better judgment out of the simple idea (which, nevertheless, required an exceptional ingenuity to be invented) of denoting unknown and given quantities with letters. The symbolic turnaround was triggered by the need to make the growingly complex discourse on numerical computations more manageable, integrated, and focused. Today's student may be similarly motivated while engaging in the activity of symbolizing.

The other promising direction is one that has opened up with the advent of computerized virtual reality. This special technological advance has brought an artificial extension to tangible reality. By rendering figments of human imagination perceptually real, it has increased dramatically the assortment of objects particularly well equipped to play the role of mediators within mathematical discourse. It seems quite plausible that great parts of mathematical reality, which until now could only be imagined, will soon materialize on the computer screen. If such a turn indeed takes place, its impact on students' ability to talk mathematics may be immense. Because of perceptual mediation, the learner will now be able to engage in VR discourse the way he or she conducts AR discourse. Giving mathematical objects "flesh" may be expected to substantially increase students' understanding of mathematics. This is what one can learn, for example, from the story told by Davis and Hersh (1981), on the impact of computer-generated images of "three-dimensional slices" of a four-dimensional cube. One of the authors reported that there was a quantum increase in his understanding when, after the images had been manipulated and explored for a while, "The hypercube leaped into palpable reality" (p. 404).

Whatever path we chose to usher young people into the world of mathematics, we may be better off if we think of this world as symbolized into being rather than merely represented with symbols. If we accept this, then one of the immediate conclusions will be almost identical with what may be learned from Shaw's "Pygmalion": If we wish our students to feel at ease in the virtual world of mathematics, we have to follow in Professor Higgins' footsteps and see to it that young people learn to speak mathematical language fluently and with a proper, "objected-mediated" accent.

ACKNOWLEDGMENT

The ongoing interchange between Paul Cobb and me was instrumental in bringing the ideas proposed in this chapter to their present form. I wish to thank Paul for his patient reading through several drafts, for his felicitous and ever-so-tactful criticism, and for his helpful suggestions.

REFERENCES

Bakhtin, M. M. (1986). *Speech genres and other late essays* (V. W. McGee, Trans.; C. Emerson & M. Holoquist, Eds.). Austin: University of Texas Press.

Bauman, Z. (1978). *Hermeneutics and social sciences*. London: Hutchison.

Bereiter, C. (1985). Towards a solution of the learning paradox. *Review of Educational Research, 55*, 201–226.

Blumer, H. (1969). *Symbolic interactionism: Perspectives and method.* Englewood Cliffs, NJ: Prentice Hall.

Brown, J. S., Collins, A., & Duguid, P. (1989). Situated cognition and the culture of learning. *Educational Researcher, 18*(1), 32–42.

Brown, R. W., & Berko, J. (1960). Word associations and the acquisition of grammar. *Child Development, 31*, 1–14.

Bruner, J. (1983). The acquisition of pragmatic commitments. In R. Golinkoff (Ed.), *The transition from prelinguistic to linguistic communication* (pp. 27–42). Hillsdale, NJ: Lawrence Erlbaum Associates.

Bruner, J. (1987). *In the search of mind. Essays in autobiography.* New York: Harper and Row.

Cassirer, E. (1957). *The philosophy of symbolic forms: Vol. 3. The phenomenology of knowledge.* New Haven, CT: Yale University Press.

Changeux, J.-P., & Connes, A. (1995). *Conversations on mind, matter, and mathematics.* Princeton, NJ: Princeton University Press.

Cobb, P. (1994). Where is the mind? Constructivist and sociocultural perspectives on mathematical development. *Educational Researcher, 23*(7), 13–20.

Cobb, P. (1995). Cultural tools and mathematical learning: A case study. *Journal for Research in Mathematics Education, 26*, 362–385.

Cobb, P., Gravemeijer, K., Yackel, E., McClain, K., & Whitenack, J. (1997). Mathematizing and symbolizing: The emergence of chains of signification in one first-grade classroom. In D. Kirshner & J. A. Whitson (Eds.), *Situated cognition: Social, semiotic, and psychological perspectives* (pp. 151–233). Mahwah, NJ: Lawrence Erlbaum Associates.

Cobb, P., Jaworski, B., & Presmeg, N. (1996). Emergent and sociocultural perspectives on mathematical activity. In P. Nesher, L. P. Steffe, P. Cobb, G. Goldin, & B. Greer (Eds.), *Theories of mathematical learning* (pp. 3–19). Mahwah, NJ: Lawrence Erlbaum Associates.

Davis, P., & Hersh, R. (1981). *The mathematical experience*. London: Penguin Books.

Demby, A. (1994). *Rozwoj procedur stosowanych przez uczniow klas V–VII przy przeksztalcaniu wyrazen algebraicznych* [Development of procedures applied by fifth- to seventh-grade students while transforming algebraic expressions]. Unpublished doctoral dissertation, Gdansk University, Gdansk, Poland.

Derrida, J. (1976). *Of grammatology* (G. C. Spivak, Trans.). Baltimore, MD: Johns Hopkins University Press. (Original work published 1967)

Dreyfus, H. D., & Rabinow, P. (1982). *Michael Foucault: Beyond structuralism and hermeneutics.* New York: Harvester Wheatsheaf.

Eco, U. (1976). *A theory of semiotics.* Bloomington: Indiana University Press.

Eco, U. (1990). Introduction. In Y. M. Lotman (Ed.), *Universe of mind* (pp. vii–xiii). London: I. B. Tauris.

Ervin, S. M. (1961). Changes with age in verbal determinants of word-association. *American Journal of Psychology, 74,* 361–372.

Foucault, M. (1972). *The archaeology of knowledge.* New York: Pantheon Books.

Foucault, M. (1973). *Madness and civilization: A history of insanity in the age of reason.* New York: Vintage/Random House.

Gottdiener, M. (1995). *Postmodern semiotics. Material culture and the forms of modern life.* Oxford, UK: Blackwell.

Gray, E., & Tall, D. O. (1994). Duality, ambiguity, and flexibility: A "proceptual" view of simple arithmetic. *Journal for Research in Mathematics Education, 25,* 116–140.

Hadamard, J. S. (1949). *The psychology of invention in the mathematics field.* Princeton, NJ: Princeton University Press.

Johnson, M. (1987). *The body in the mind: The bodily basis of reason and imagination.* Chicago: University of Chicago Press.

Kleiner, I. (1989). Evolution of the function concept: A brief survey. *College Mathematics Journal, 20,* 282–300.

Kline, M. (1980). *Mathematics: The loss of certainty.* New York: Oxford University Press.

Knorr, K. D. (1980). The scientist as analogical reasoner: A critique of the metaphor theory of innovation. In K. D. Knorr, R. Krohn, & B. Whitley (Eds.), *The social process of scientific investigation: Sociology of sciences* (Vol. 4, pp. 25–52). Dordrecht, The Netherlands: D. Reidel.

Lacan, J. (1977). *Ecrits: A selection.* London: Tavistock.

Lakatos, I. (1976). *Proofs and refutations.* New York: Cambridge University Press.

Lakoff, G. (1987). *Women, fire, and dangerous things: What categories reveal about the mind.* Chicago: University of Chicago Press.

Lakoff, G., & Johnson, M. (1980). *The metaphors we live by.* Chicago: University of Chicago Press.

Lampert, M. (1990). When the problem is not a question and the solution is not an answer: Mathematical knowing and teaching. *American Educational Research Journal, 27*(1), 29–63.

Lave, J. (1988). *Cognition in practice.* New York: Cambridge University Press.

Lave, J., & Wenger, E. (1991). *Situated learning: Legitimate peripheral participation.* New York: Cambridge University Press.

Mashler, M. (1976). *Algebra for seventh grade.* Tel Aviv, Israel: Hakibutz Hameuhad.

Maturana, H. R., & Varela, F. J. (1987). *The tree of knowledge.* Boston: Shambhala.

Miller, J.-A. (1991). Language: Much ado about what? In E. Ragland-Sullivan & M. Bracher (Eds.), *Lacan and the subject of language* (pp. 21–35). New York: Routledge.

Nunes, T., Schliemann, A., & Carraher, D. (1993). *Street mathematics and school mathematics.* New York: Cambridge University Press.

Palermo, D. S. (1963). Word associations and children's verbal behavior. In L. P. Lipsitt & C. C. Spiker (Eds.), *Advances in child development and behavior* (Vol. 1, pp. 31–68). New York: Academic Press.

Palermo, D. S., & Jenkins, J. J. (1963). *Word association norms: Grade school through college.* Minneapolis: University of Minnesota Press.

Peirce, C. (1931–1935). *Collected papers of Charles Sanders Peirce* (Vols. 1–6, C. Hartshorne, & P. Weiss, Eds.). Cambridge, MA: Harvard University Press.

Peirce, C. (1955). *Philosophical writings of Peirce.* New York: Dover Publications.

Poincaré, H. (1929). Science and method. In G. B. Halsted (Trans.), *The foundations of science* (pp. 359–546). New York: Science Press.

Reddy, M. (1979). The conduit metaphor—A case of frame conflict in our language and about language. In A. Ortony (Ed.), *Metaphor and thought* (pp. 284–324). New York: Cambridge University Press.

Rotman, B. (1994). Mathematical writing, thinking, and virtual reality. In P. Ernest (Ed.), *Mathematics, education, and philosophy: An international perspective* (pp. 76–86). London: Falmer Press.

Russell, B. (1904). Recent works on the principles of mathematics. *International Monthly, 4,* 84.

Ruthing, D. (1984). Some definitions of the concept of function from John Bernoulli to N. Bourbaki. *Mathematical Intelligencer, 6*(4), 72–77.

Saussure, F. de. (1986). *Course in general linguistics* (C. Bally & A. Sechehaye, with A. Reidlinger, Eds.; R. Harris, Trans.). La Salle, IL: Open Court. (Original work published 1916)

Saxe, G. B. (1988). Candy selling and math learning. *Educational Researcher, 17*(6), 14–21.

Sfard, A. (1991). On the dual nature of mathematical conceptions: Reflections on processes and objects as different sides of the same coin. *Educational Studies in Mathematics, 22,* 1–36.

Sfard, A. (1992). Operational origins of mathematical objects and the quandary of reification—The case of function. In E. Dubinsky & G. Harel (Eds.), The concept of function: Aspects of epistemology and pedagogy. *MAA Notes, 25,* 59–84.

Sfard, A. (1994a). Reification as the birth of metaphor. *For the Learning of Mathematics, 14*(1), 44–55.

Sfard, A. (1994b). Mathematical practices, anomalies and classroom communication problems. In P. Ernest (Ed.), *Constructing mathematical knowledge* (pp. 248–273). London: Falmer Press.

Sfard, A. (1997). Commentary: On metaphorical roots of conceptual growth. In L. English (Ed.), *Mathematical reasoning: Analogies, metaphors, and images* (pp. 339–371). Mahwah, NJ: Lawrence Erlbaum Associates.

Sfard, A., & Linchevski, L. (1994). The gains and the pitfalls of reification—The case of algebra. *Educational Studies in Mathematics, 26,* 191–228.

Tannen, D. (1993). *Framing in discourse.* New York: Oxford University Press.

Thompson, P., & Sfard, A. (1994). Problems of reification: Representations and mathematical objects. In D. Kirshner (Ed.), *Proceedings of Sixteenth Annual Meeting of the North American Chapter of the International Group for the Psychology of Mathematics Education* (pp. 3–34). Baton Rouge: Louisiana State University.

von Glasersfeld, E. (Ed.). (1991). *Radical constructivism in mathematics education.* Dordrecht: Kluwer Academic Press.

von Glasersfeld, E. (Ed.). (1995). *Radical constructivism. A way of knowing and learning.* London: Falmer Press.

Vygotsky, L. S. (1962). *Thought and language.* Cambridge, MA: MIT Press.

Vygotsky, L. S. (1978). *Mind in society. The development of higher psychological processes.* Cambridge, MA: Harvard University Press.

Vygotsky, L. S. (1987). Thinking and speech. In R. W. Rieber & A. S. Carton (Eds.), *The collected works of L. S. Vygotsky* (Vol. 1, pp. 39–285). New York: Plenum Press.

Walkerdine, V. (1988). *The mastery of reason.* London: Routledge.

Wittgenstein, L. (1953). *Philosophical investigations.* Oxford, UK: Blackwell.

Wittgenstein, L. (1978). *Remarks on the foundations of mathematics.* Oxford, UK: Blackwell.

Woodrow, H., & Lowell, F. (1916). Children's associations frequency table. *Psychological Monographs, 22*(5).

4

Means for Meaning

Willi Dörfler
University of Klagenfurt,
Klagenfurt, Austria

There are many different ways to use the term *meaning*. It is modified by such adjectives as subjective, objective, universal, referential, pragmatic, mathematical, context-bound, context-free, shared, and taken-as-shared, to name a few. Such modifying adjectives could lead one to suspect that the word *meaning* is not very meaningful or is even meaningless. From the Wittgensteinian (1977) standpoint, different meanings of *meaning* are connected to each other by a family resemblance, without their sharing any common core (such as in Wittgenstein's famous example of the concept of game). For my part, I take the position that it does not make sense, in a general way, to ask a question such as, "What is meaning?" One might ask for the meaning of a specific term, such as for the number *two*. But even that question quickly leads everywhere and nowhere, because for any answer that can be formulated finitely, one can surely point out some aspect that has not been included yet. And, even more important, any relevant answer will refer to many other words or concepts and their meaning(s).

Nevertheless, I find it unacceptable to be bound by these negative and limiting views. Because many individuals, laymen and scholars alike, use the word *meaning*, albeit in many different meanings, there must be some rationality to such widespread use. We are steadily confronted with the phenomenon that we can seemingly understand spoken and/or written utterances of other people and that we can make sense of our own writing and speaking. The term or concept of *meaning* postulates a quality or property of linguistic units that mediates between communicating people. If we know the meaning of the relevant words and sentences, we are able to understand. If we do not know, we do not understand. If we do not know the correct meaning, misunderstandings arise. This shows the close connection and relationship between the concepts of *meaning* and *understanding*. In fact, there is a strong interdependence or circularity between these two concepts. Understanding is the grasping of meaning, and because there is understanding, there must also be meaning associated with what we hear, read, speak, or write. Depending on our own philosophical or epistemological perspective, understanding depends on access to an objective meaning or on the individual construction of subjective, but socially mediated, meaning. Typical language use and also personal psychological experience lead to the view or the impression of an experiential reality in which meaning (of words, sentences, and terms) can be isolated, fixed, described, defined, and investigated, as though it were a physical property of material objects. Similarly, understanding is conceived of as a psychic or cognitive process comparable to a chemical process. (Perhaps meaning can almost be considered a type of catalyst.)

In explaining, that is, in developing theories for, human behavior beyond mere description, there is no choice other than to posit theoretical terms/concepts, such as *meaning* or *understanding*, and to develop perspectives about how human behavior is regulated by the corresponding entities or processes that are stipulated. This can be very productive, as the success of the natural sciences proves, but we should remain aware of the theoretical nature of the concepts involved. In addition, it is essential to take into account the empirical/ecological validity of the theories that are developed. These theories should be viable means for describing or modeling our experiences. And even without being able to substantiate such a claim here, I contend that many theories of meaning do not meet these criteria. Some of them make sense only for completely codified fields of knowledge, such as formal mathematical theories, and do not take into account related human activity.

Depending on the theoretical conception of *meaning*, different research questions will be asked. Certain meanings of *meaning* will exclude specific questions and research methods. The basic theoretical terms function like a lens or a prism through which we observe our experiences. What is describable, and thus observable, is highly determined by the theoretical conceptualizations that we bring to our experience. This certainly applies to the term *understanding* and the way it is operationalized in school. The basis for judging students' understanding depends heavily on the teacher's preconceptions of understanding and of the meaning of the subject matter in question. In addition, the teaching itself is strongly influenced, if not regulated, by those views held by the teacher. This clarifies the didactic impact of theories of meaning and understanding on the theory and practice of teaching and learning.

Despite this apparent untidiness about the ambiguous term *meaning*, we have to take a view on it. In this chapter, I take the following position. The only available and observable indicator that a subject has grasped the meaning—whatever this is—of a linguistic or symbolic entity is that the subject has a thorough command of its social use. Or, one could say, this is the way the word *meaning* is used. Thus, command of a discourse is taken to be based on meaning that the subject has constructed, that is, on subjective understanding. An analogy to physics might be useful here. When objects fall, such actions are taken to be indicators of gravitational force, which, as a theoretical term, is not observable. That is, we could have an adequate linguistic/discursive behavior corresponding to gravitation as that phenomenon that is driven by the meaning of the discursive elements. This analogy is supported by the everyday observation that all arguments concerning the meaning of a word or text are essentially arguments concerning usage. This is true even in those cases in which meaning is interpreted simply as the reference to a well-defined class of entities.

For me, a consequence of this position is that everything that enhances an individual's induction into a given discourse is taken as contributing to that person's construction of meaning. Further, it is only by participating in the discourse that individuals can receive enough feedback to assure themselves of having constructed the socially accepted meaning. (In the preceding sentences, I use the word *meaning* in the same way as I use *gravitational force*.) Thus, developing a theory of meaning is an attempt to explain how we can successfully participate in a discourse (cf. Sfard's emphasis on discursive activity, chap. 3, this volume). The title of this chapter, therefore, also could have been: "Means for Participation in a Discourse."

Throughout this chapter, I synthesize and extend ideas and notions that I have presented and developed previously. Also, several new ideas are offered. An essential feature of them is the network-like character of the means for meaning. Induction into a discourse is a complex, multidimensional process that demands many faculties of the individual. The reference list acknowledges references I used in my prior work. Not all of these references are made explicit in this chapter. However, I have included them to indicate to whom I owe much of the basic stance I take here as I substantiate and explicate my case of mathematics and mathematics learning (e.g., see Dörfler 1989a, 1991; Rotman, 1993).

The reader might ask what justifies the inclusion of my chapter into this volume on "Symbolizing, Communicating, and Mathematizing." Let me begin with communication. Any type of communication takes place within, and by the means of, discourse. Further, successful communication presupposes mutually compatible meanings on the part of its participants. Thus, the means for meaning discussed as follows are means for com-

munication as well. In this chapter, I elaborate on the notions of prototypes, protocols, and an as-if attitude. I argue that shared experiences
with prototypes or protocols will enhance the compatibility of these two
cognitive structures for individuals. On the other hand, communication,
even if deficient or fragmentary, is an important social framework of and
support for being introduced into a discourse and its means. Therefore,
I consider communication to be the social medium for the individual
construction of prototypes and protocols and also for the development
of what I call an "as-if attitude," even though I do not stress this point
explicitly in every case.

Similar remarks apply to symbols and their use. Specifically, many
prototypes in mathematics (or rather, their carriers, as explained later)
are based on symbolic structures (cf. Sfard's notion of templates-driven
use, chap. 3, this volume). These structures are frequently used tools for
constructing protocols as schematized records of actions and the results
of those actions. In other words, I make the case that the construction of
a protocol can be viewed as a special case of symbolizing or as a building
up of a model of the (mathematically) relevant traits of recorded actions.
More generally, any discourse makes extensive use of conventional symbolic means, and initiation into the discourse, in part, consists of appropriating those symbolic means. This is especially true for any mathematical discourse.

Mathematization, in my view, has so many different aspects and appears in so many different forms, for such a variety of purposes, that I
refrain from relating it to the topics in my chapter here. Nevertheless, we
could consider protocols as a special case of mathematization and we
could consider an as-if attitude as being a precondition for understanding
the role of mathematical models.

PROTOTYPES

In this section I elaborate my use of the word *prototype*, which, although
close to that found in the literature (e.g., refer to G. Lakoff, 1987), also
differs in several important ways. In the literature, prototypes are considered central elements in the category of referents of a word. Further,
the use of words in vernacular language is often regulated and monitored
by associating them with paradigmatic cases of their use. With the view
that meaning is a reference to objects of some kind, these cases are specific
examples of the potential referents of the respective word. They are
prototypes. For example, some birds are better exemplars of the concept
bird than others. They are prototypic birds. The decision to call an animal
a bird is made by its resemblance to the prototypic birds.

My use of the term *prototype* is broader because I admit situations, actions, systems of actions, symbol systems, and other entities as well. Further, the main aspect of a prototype is not the centrality in a category of referents, but is the capacity to guide activities of many kinds, not (just) linguistic use. For mathematics, such activities can be calculating, drawing, proving, arguing, or reading.

Initial Examples

The first example I present is the *number line,* which can serve as a prototype for the system Z of whole numbers. I emphasize that, in my view, the number line does not represent Z in an objective manner. However, the number line can be used to think "about" whole numbers and their operations and relations. The number line and other so-called "representations" make it possible to take part in the mathematical discourse "about Z." We also use the number line as a means of communicating purportedly about Z (cf. Sfard's discussion of the number line as a means to introduce negative numbers to students, chap. 3, this volume). Discourse about Z is essentially a discourse about the number line. And it is only in this sense that the number line represents Z.

As a second example, R^n can be a prototype for the concept of a (finite-dimensional) vector space. The sensible, or socially acceptable, use of vector space terminology is based on our experiences with R^n (or even with R^5). Here, I emphasize the word *experiences* strongly. Just as the adequate use of *bird* is based on socially guided experiences with birds, we need experiences with R^5 to be able to use it as a prototypic vector space. The latter requires the developing of a specific view on R^5 by such experiences as adding vectors, multiplying by scalars, determining subspaces or hulls, and determining linear dependence or independence. Although time-consuming, such activity can serve as an experiential basis for the learner in the difficult process of "constituting meaning." I do not say that the activity *is* the meaning. Instead, the activity of the individual that is meaningful in the eyes of others can be regulated by the prototype R^5. Thus, R^5 can be a means for thinking and talking in vector space theory. In the process, the prototype can even be refined and become further articulated. Conversely, having acquired the vector-space-theory discourse, one can become more independent of the prototype. That is, one knows how to use the terms. So, we might say one has constructed meaning.

As still another example, consider the concept of identity element with respect to an operation such as in group theory. Prototypes can be the number zero in the whole numbers with addition or the identity in any permutation group. As with our experiences concerning birds, experiences with various identity elements are the basis for adequately using the term *identity element.* We come to know when to apply the word *identity* in the same way that we come to know when to apply the word *bird*—through a socially guided learning process. There is even one advantage in the case of identity element. We can make all of the determining properties explicit in a formal definition. But again, the discursive use of that definition is, in principle, moderated by reference to the prototypes. Nevertheless, eventually one becomes inducted into the discourse around the term *identity* to such an extent that the discourse stands on its own and does not need support or guidance from the outside. Then one relies exclusively on the linguistic formulations, such as "$xoe = x$ for all x."

As a further example, take the term *operation* as it is used, for instance, in the definition of a group. One way to learn how to use it is to gain experiences with various kinds of operations. The latter acquire the status of a prototype for the learner through these experiences. There are many possible candidates for a group, including various types of numbers, matrices, and permutations. Then, by *operation* we designate something or everything that shows the same essential features as those experienced: We take one (symbolic) object and another, and by certain rules, derive or "calculate" a third object. To call something an operation, then, means just that. Similarly, one might learn the use of the word *tennis*—either by playing the game oneself or by observing others playing it. The latter is a possibility for learning how to use *operation* as well. Of course, as with any comparison, this one only grasps several features. Usually, for *tennis* there is no symbolic expression as there is for *operation* ($aob = c$).

Aspects of Prototypes

I now turn to listing various aspects that describe how I use the term *prototype* for this chapter. Although these aspects neither characterize nor define the term, a description of them is important to distinguish my idea of *prototype* from such related terms as *representation* or *model.*

First, a material object, including symbols, is not a prototype in itself, but gains that quality by virtue of a specific view an individual takes of it. This view primarily focuses on, or constructs, certain properties and relations, or executes actions. Thus, prototypes cannot be shown or perceived. They must be conceived of as a relationship to the respective object, as its carrier, which is expressed by a specific use or treatment. Strange as it may seem, this implies that the same objects can play different prototypic roles and that very different objects can be prototypic of the same concept.

As an illustrative example, consider the number line once again. By virtue of equidistant markings for the whole numbers, the line has the potential of being a prototype for (a finite segment of) Z. Here, we make use only of this subdivision of the line and various kinds of movements on it, thus leading to the arithmetic operations for Z. Thus, a prototype for Z emerges from this specific use of the number line and the operations on it. If we augment our use of the number line by arbitrarily finite subdivisions (which are idealized operations) of any interval, we are led to a prototype for the rational numbers Q. But we must keep in mind that this necessitates imposing a structure and specific operations on the number line. The rationals cannot be read off the line: They have to be read into it. This applies even more to the number line as the carrier of a prototype for the reals R. The irrationals are conceived of as the result of specific limit processes on the number line, starting from Q. That presupposes breaking the continuous line into single points. Therefore, the prototype arises as a conceptual structure from an intricate interplay between its material carrier and its user. This conceptual structure includes the executability of certain operations that are imposed on the prototype by the user.

As another example, consider the Cartesian graph of a real function. The graph can be the carrier of a prototype for function as a univalent correspondence. However, specific graphs can serve as prototypes for functional properties such as monotonic, oscillating, constant, and linear. Again, what the curve is a prototype of depends on the focus of attention of the user or the learner.

A second aspect of prototypes, related to the first, is that they are, of necessity, not universal. Instead, they are individual or even idiosyncratic, at least in the first phases of their development by the learner. To some extent, standardization and objectification occur in the process of social communication and negotiation. One agrees with others on certain prototypes, even though some degree of uncertainty may exist. In a broad sense, we can observe this in the common use of such words as *town* and *village* or *creek* and *river* and *stream*. In mathematics, however, this uncertainty is (almost) eliminated by the use of formal and symbolic definitions.

Third, to be more precise, *prototype* is a theoretical construct that designates a specified cognitive mechanism, by which one relies on one's experiences with specific objects and activities with them for the socially accepted use of linguistic terms. I should point out that linguistic terms and their use can gain the status of "objects" or carriers for prototypes (cf. Sfard's notion of *reification*, chap. 3, this volume). This rarely occurs in everyday language but is quite common in mathematics.

Fourth, the position developed here should be sharply separated from a representational view. I do not consider prototypic objects as representing the relevant abstract concept or abstract object. Rather, for me, an abstract concept or object is a specific way of talking about the prototypic objects based on experiences with them. Abstractness is better viewed as a manner of talking or as a quality of the respective discourse. The abstractness of the concept *bird* does not reside in an abstract object. Instead, it is a way of talking about birds as we experience them. Similarly, the abstract concept *identity element* does not refer to an esoteric object. Instead, it is a way of expressing experiences with various symbolic objects in a general manner. Formal definition should not be considered as creating an abstract entity but, rather, as an explicit rule for a correct discourse.

Fifth, in many cases, the prototype is a schema that is expressed by using symbols as variables. For instance, the formula for the identity element, $xoe = x$, for all x, might first arise as a symbolic description of a concrete case. By turning the referential symbols $(x, o, e, =)$ into variables that stand for themselves, we obtain a schema or a general type of formula that might be interpreted in a multitude of ways. This schema is a kind of symbolic prototype (discussed later in this chapter) for what is meant by being an identity element. Such a schema can also be viewed as a diagram, in the same way we use graphs of unspecified functions as diagrammatic prototypes for such functional properties as "increasing," "decreasing," "containing local maximum or minimum," and many others. My thesis is that these prototypes are used, to some extent, to monitor pertinent mathematical discourse, together with formal definitions and many other mathematical experiences.

The sixth aspect of prototypes that I wish to discuss relates to learning. In this case, prototypic exemplars should not be used only as a methodological means for teaching the relevant concepts with the verbal definition as an ultimate aim. Detaching a definition from its prototypes will reduce it to a purely linguistic formula. For example, forgetting what a bird is like will threaten the correct use of the word *bird*. However, recurring reference to the prototypes will greatly enhance adequate work with definitions. Perhaps the relevant concept could be viewed as the mutual relationship between symbolic description and prototypes, neither of which, by itself, suffices to regulate talking, thinking, writing, or understanding. Especially in advanced mathematics, I concede that there is a powerful possibility of purely verbal definitions that do not presuppose any reference to prototypical exemplars. This occurs in all those cases in which, by principle, entities that are not describable in finite terms are postulated by the definition. Examples include non-Lebesgue measurable sets in R and inaccessible sets in set theory. Yet, one could argue that the methods that constitute those mathematical entities, according to the accepted rules of formal mathematics, are a substitute for the non-available prototypes.

In the following sections, I further explicate the concept of prototypes by discussing these three classes: figurative, relational, and operative. In doing so, I clarify what it means when I state that a prototype has to be considered a specific relationship between the subject and the object.

Figurative Prototypes

I speak of a *figurative prototype* in those cases in which the physical/geometrical form and properties of the object are its constitutive aspects. There are no transforming actions. The relation to the object is restricted to perceptive activities. The external appearance is the determining feature. The perceptive activity is guided by salient properties of the form and structure of the relevant object. What counts as salient must be socially mediated and depends on the prior experiences of the individual. In any case, the prototypical objects lend themselves in a perspicuous way to adequate perceptive activity. The figurative prototype is best described as a specific way of seeing or, more generally, perceiving the relevant object. It is a schema of perception that can also be employed to produce copies of the object such as by drawing.

Examples. Examples abound in everyday language. In mathematics, geometric figures are associated with figurative prototypes. Focusing on the essential properties of a drawn square, such as four equal sides and four right angles, will give rise to a figurative prototype of *square*. Guiding the learner to avoid his or her inclusion of nonessential or irrelevant features is crucial. The prototype of *square* is not the marks on the paper but is one's way of perceiving these marks. That is, the prototype has to be developed or even constructed by the individual. Whether one's subjectively constructed prototype is adequate or not can only be checked by social communication and collaborative work.

Other examples of figurative prototypes are general graphs of functions (such as sinusoidal, linear, and exponential), in which what is of interest is the geometric shape. The geometric shape is related to such aspects as monotonicity, periodicity, and concavity. Of course, this figurative prototype is not sufficient for grasping the concept of function. However, it is one way of relating a holistic and qualitative view to the graph. Here again, the prototype develops through guided experience with graphs, by using, talking about, and thinking with them. I conceive of concept development as the socially regulated development of a variety of activities on and with the prototypic exemplars. To be specific, I could even say that the concept should be viewed as the network or system of those activities. Thus, *concept* is to be understood as a psychological term.

Although purely figurative prototypes are rare and extreme cases in mathematics (see other types discussed later), in some instances they present, nevertheless, certain relevant aspects. Geometrical features play a decisive role even in symbolic notation such as algebraic terms. To me, there is something like a figurative prototype of a polynomial or of a system of linear equations. This might be a specific polynomial or system, or an arbitrary one with variables as coefficients. In any case, the geometric structure is relevant for many pertinent cognitive functions, including memory, reproduction, recognition, and arguing.

Relational Prototypes

I return to the graph of functions to show the profound difference between relational and figurative prototypes. A graph in a Cartesian coordinate system expresses a relation of the x-values to the y-values in the usual but highly conventional way. Strictly speaking, this relation is not perceivable but must be constituted through the use of the graph. One way is to construct the graph pointwise, or to read the values of $f(x)$ for any given x. The graph is a type of carrier for the functional relationship. A graph can play this role for a specific function, whose graph it is, or for the concept of function in general. Again this depends on the focus of interest and attention. The prototype is not the marks on paper but is the specific use made of them. And the relevant relations emerge in the material and cognitive activities on, with, and through the graph (cf. Nemirovsky and Monk's discussion of Lin's activity with graphs, chap. 6, this volume).

For geometric concepts such as square, rectangle, circle, and ellipse, the figurative prototypes need to be complemented by relational proto-types that are based on the very same drawings as their carriers. This is necessary for advancing the mathematical treatment of those concepts because it is the constitutive relationships that are usually formalized in symbolic notation. Thus, a symbolic description of a circle with midpoint M as $\{X \mid d(X,M) = r\}$ reflects the relation of a constant distance between the midpoint M and the points X on the circumference. Of course, this defining relation cannot be read from the drawing but it must be inferred, for example, from the construction of the circle with compasses. In this view, the drawing changes from a figurative prototype to a relational one.

A similar transition occurs when one third of a disk is no longer viewed as a piece with a certain shape. Instead, the portion is viewed in relation to the whole disk, for example, when the former is copied three times to cover the latter. This action can be carried out or can be imagined. In this way, the prototype for the concept of *one third*, which, of course, has to be relational, emerges.

One important advantage of relational prototypes is their generalizabil-ity. A figurative one third of a disk is fairly fixed. But the relational view can be transferred to any whole, via the relevant action of dividing and combining. Mentally, the relation can be more easily detached from its carriers. With regard to the relational circle, one can detect the very same relation in the case of the sphere, or conceive of a square as a circle with respect to another measurement of distance.

Because most, if not all, mathematical concepts express relationships or even systems of them beyond some figurative aspect, the development of relational prototypes by the learner is an important process. This process has to be initiated, moderated, controlled, and corrected by social feedback from a teacher and from other learners. One has to offer appropriate carriers and activities with them in order to permit the relations to emerge for the learner. An important step, then, is their symbolic/linguistic description and focus, which, in turn, gain meaning partly from their prototypes. For their part, the symbolic notations can gain the status of prototypes themselves, if viewed appropriately. For instance, take the case of a system of linear equations viewed as a symbolic expression of a complex system of relations between the unknowns. One could even coin the term *symbolic prototype*, which is based on the conventions of how to read the symbols.

Operative Prototypes

Several times during the discussion of relational prototypes, I referred to actions that serve to exhibit the relations in question. For the actor, who is usually a learner, the potential carriers for a prototype have to admit the relevant actions or operations. An object is the carrier of an operative prototype if, in the view of the user, it lends itself to the execution of specific actions. Actions use the object, transform it or produce it. Then, the pertinent prototype is the schema of those actions rather than the carrier, even though the schema is associated with its carrier. Generally, the actions are applicable to different objects. At the same time, the different operative prototypes can be associated with the same object. It becomes clear that operative prototypes (more so than other kinds of prototypes) have to be learned, experienced, applied, and used, in order to become effective cognitive tools.

As a first example, take the number line again. To be rendered a prototype for Q, the line must be considered to admit arbitrarily finite subdivisions of any interval and to consist of separated points that result as the subdivision points. Similarly, this holds for the number line as the carrier for the real numbers. Or, as a more extreme case, consider an "extended" number line as it is used in nonstandard analysis as the carrier for the hyper real numbers. It is conceivable that some people might object to the executability of some actions or operations and, thereby, deny the sensibility of certain mathematical concepts (as in intuitionism or in constructive mathematics). Compare this with the section in this chapter that deals with an as-if attitude.

For other simple examples, consider geometric figures with their constructions viewed as operative prototypes. Also, specific transformations such as rotations or transformations of symmetry can constitute operative prototypes for those geometric concepts. For instance, rotating a circle, in itself, can have this status because its applicability is characteristic of a circle.

Small sets can be figurative prototypes for the relevant numbers. But the operative aspect is prominent for larger sets. A set of five elements becomes an operative prototype of the number five by applying a constituting counting action. Once again, I do not consider a set of five elements as a representation of the number *five*. For me, this is misleading terminology. Instead, the discursive object *five* is an abstracted way of speaking about our experiences with the various prototypes and their many uses. A set, being a representation of five, should only be seen as expressing the fact that certain (counting) actions are applicable to it.

To further illustrate what I mean by an operative prototype, consider the concept of *even number*. Arranging a finite set into two sets, so that their elements are paired, is an operative prototype for the concept *even number*. Analogous descriptions can be given for *odd number* and *prime number*.

Choosing r balls in sequence (without replacement) from an urn containing n different balls constitutes an operative prototype for r permutations of n objects. Noting their names in the given order produces another prototype of this concept (and this is a protocol of the prior action, as discussed in the next section).

The Cartesian graph is the carrier of a specific operative prototype by virtue of the action that exhibits the functional relation, of which the graph simultaneously is the relational prototype. Or, we might say that the graph is the result of noting the pairs $(x, f(x))$ that express the functional correspondence f. Here again, the carrier of an operative prototype is a kind of protocol of the results of the relevant actions, be they actual or imagined. This refers to the network character of the "means for meaning," which I am emphasizing in this chapter.

In all the examples and cases of prototypes mentioned so far, there is the specific issue of the cognitive construction of the prototype, based on adequate experiences with the various carriers. From a constructivist point of view, the carrier does not force the learner to focus attention on those features that will guide the development of the prototype. More often than not, such processes as trial and error and imitation will be involved and will sometimes lead to inadequate (cognitive) prototypes. This will only be detected in an intensive discourse, based on those protocols, when the learners find out that their prototypes and their discursive usage do not fit the socially accepted way of speaking (e.g., about the carriers). The other participants in the discourse, and especially the teacher, will have to point to such "misconceptions" and even look for them. Despite this absolutely necessary feedback and the potential of feasible prototype carriers that exclude many viewpoints, there will always remain a degree of uncertainty of the prototypes as constructed by the learner. However, the now broadly accepted notion of "taken-as-shared" (see Gravemeijer et al., chap. 7, this volume) aptly describes the state that is ultimately possible—namely, the state in which participants in the discourse have developed sufficiently compatible prototypes, enabling them to communicate with one another without contradictions. I should emphasize that a recourse to the prototype carriers, even in well-developed discourse, often offers great support. The carriers (via the possibly differing prototypes) are objects and means of the respective discourse. The same remarks and deliberations apply also to the topic of the next section, the protocols of action. But they are not repeated there.

To conclude this section on prototypes, I emphasize that, in most cases, for a successful concept development in the learning process, one has to rely on various prototypes taken from all of the types discussed here. This process is open-ended, showing that neither meaning nor understanding has fixed limits or has well-defined content or structure. Both meaning and understanding are better viewed as cognitive processes of an individual rather than as static properties. Further, I point to the important role played in this process by nonlinguistic objects as carriers of the various prototypes and, complementary to that, of the constitutive role of the activity of the learning individual (either in his or her perception or transforming actions). Meaning and understanding develop as a complex interplay between subject and object that must be socially mediated.

PROTOCOLS

Prototypes might be based on natural objects that we find in our surroundings. In many cases, however, artificially produced objects, such as symbols, serve as the carriers of prototypes for mathematical concepts. These artificial objects are, in many cases, a kind of record either of their construction or of the resulting outcome of this construction. Generally, this process of recording the essential stages, phases, and products of actions is one of the sources for mathematical notation, symbol systems, and concepts. I use the term *protocol* to designate the related cognitive process of focusing attention on those stages, phases, results, and products of one's actions and constructions, and of describing and notating them by some means.

Thus, protocols are part of the experiential world of the learning subject, either through the learner's own activity or by observation of the activity of others. Now my thesis is that protocols can be a supportive means for an individual to be inducted into the mathematical discourse about a concept using specific terms and phrases. Use of such terms and phrases can be based on the protocols and on pertinent experiences. Again, as with prototypes, those subjective experiences have to be socially guided and monitored, for example, by a teacher or by communication within a social group.

Initial Examples

As already indicated, many geometric figures can be viewed as the result of a construction process, which, in turn, gives rise to a protocol. For the circle and its construction by compasses, the protocol is based on the circular line obtained and on the constant distance of this line to the mid-point. The protocol can also be expressed verbally by describing the construction process and its main features and phases.

Similarly, a construction of a square in LOGO, by REPEAT 4[FW 100 RT 90], gives rise to, or even denotes, a protocol that is, of course, closely connected to the figure obtained. The latter, itself, can also serve as a protocol for the concept of square. From a mathematical point of view, both the protocol and the resulting figure can serve the purpose of analyzing the construction (that is, the action), and both exhibit the defining properties of a square. Other properties can be deduced from the protocol or its "trace" (i.e., the resulting marks on the paper or on the screen). Other LOGO procedures also provide good examples for protocols, either by themselves or by their trace on the screen.

Another illustrative example is the LOGO circle, which is the trace of walking and turning in a specific, regular manner, namely, that of constant curvature. It is an interesting (and not-so-rare) observation that different kinds of actions can give rise to the same carrier for a specific protocol. Thus, for the circle we have the LOGO procedure and the more common generation via compasses. The constitutive actions can be repeated on the trace or on the carrier of the protocol, with the latter functioning as a guide for the action.

As we know from LOGO research, the learner needs close guidance in developing protocols. This can be accomplished by drawing the learner's attention to the relevant steps, phases, and results of the action. Those experiences based on protocols, together with others, might provide the basis for participating in the pertinent discourse.

The Cartesian graph of a function provides another example of protocols. Assuming the availability of the Cartesian coordinate system as a cognitive tool for the learner, the pertinent action can be measuring values of $f(x)$ for various values of x. Marking the pair $(x, f(x))$ on the coordinate system, and thereby focusing attention on the correspondence of x to $f(x)$, produces the graph as a protocol of the measuring activity. The imagined execution of this action for all conceivable x leads to the common Cartesian graph of the relevant function f, which, in this sense, is the carrier of the protocol of an imagined action. The extension of this imagined action for an infinite number of values has to be stipulated as an ideal or as a thought experiment (cf. the next section). Thus, the graph of a function, considered as the (carrier of a) protocol, can be viewed as contributing to the development of the function concept by the learner and as supporting the learner's induction into the mathematical discourse about functions.

Various other ways of taking note of the correspondence of x to $f(x)$ are possible, all of which can play the role of a carrier for a related protocol; these include a table of function values, a list of pairs $(x, f(x))$, an arrow diagram, and a formula for producing $f(x)$ from x. Here we observe the phenomenon of having different protocols for the same type of action. Each kind of protocol permits the reconstruction of the essential steps of the action. Further, the various protocols can be transformed into one another. Note that, in this way, the (carriers of the) protocols do not appear as representations of an abstract concept for the learner. However, the abstract function concept is a way of talking about the protocols, which typically become schematized and generalized. One does not study the function concept, as such, but studies the properties suggested by the protocols (i.e., the common representations). Further, each of those protocols (or rather the schematic carrier of each) can serve as (the carrier of) a prototype for the notion of function. The whole field of these experiences can serve to monitor and guide the abstract discourse on functions. Talking about and using prototypes and protocols can also be a kind of initiation into that discourse, in the same way that common discourse is based on taken-to-be-shared experiences.

The central idea of the notion of a protocol, therefore, is the following. Epistemological analyses of mathematical concepts and symbolizations show that many of them are structurally and genetically related to certain systems of actions and their products (cf. Dörfler, 1984, 1989b). The specific form of this relationship depends on the relevant concept. The cognitive reconstruction and development of such a concept by the individual can start from his or her carrying out the pertinent actions, where these can be actual actions with concrete material objects, including symbols, or mental operations with imagined objects. The actual or imagined reproduction or observation of the actions of other people can serve the same purpose. Now, the concept is neither the action alone nor simply its schema. Nor does the action by itself suffice to reconstruct the relevant concept. The latter can only occur by reflecting on the action and its outcome. This reflection needs specific means. The protocol is suggested as a cognitive tool for that purpose. Supplying the student with opportunities for adequate actions and their protocols is, therefore, a didactic means for teaching and learning both mathematical concepts and the discourse based on and governed by them. This is in accordance with my view that meaning and understanding can be interpreted as the subjective, socially accepted and sensible way of talking, writing, and arguing through the use of relevant words. Further, this has to be based on adequate experience.

These examples show that an important precondition for the development of protocols by the individual is the availability of specific means as cognitive tools for the learner (cf. the use by Bransford et al. of a catalogue of SMART tools, chap. 8, this volume). Compasses, LOGO software, and the Cartesian coordinate system are examples. It cannot be expected that students in school invent these tools themselves. Instead, the teacher must provide them for the students. Through the use of these tools, the construction of protocols also leads to their apprehension by the learner. Material or cognitive tools need to be used in order to become effective means for acting and thinking. Generally speaking, a central aim and goal of schooling should be to introduce the student to a variety of socially provided tools and means, including basic mathematical concepts and methods. The provision of some tools, such as these, might lead to the development of others, via protocols.

Further Examples

At this point, the reader should bear in mind that the presentation of the following examples is sketchy due to space limitations. Further, I always presuppose that the necessary tools for establishing the protocol and taking the relevant notes are available. Such tools might be the result of prior developments by the students or they might simply be supplied by the teacher. Finally, the description of the examples does not purport to suggest a didactic program, although possibly one could be developed along such lines.

Sets. The formation of a finite set is a kind of bringing together of various objects, which then are viewed as forming a common whole. The action (material or imagined) of building up a set as a collection of objects (its elements) can give rise to many different protocols. Such actions include notating the names or images of these objects, verbally describing the collection, and giving a symbolic expression that generates the (names of the) objects. In this way, the conventional mathematical set notations arise as special cases of carriers for the protocols of the sets. The notion of a set appears as the protocol of the relevant action. Even in this simple case, different protocols and carriers are possible and sensible.

Natural Numbers. Here, the action clearly is any kind of counting activity. Protocols may be the verbal uttering of the number words, or the using of fingers or other representatives, such as tally marks, for the counted objects. All of these give a precise account of the main steps of the counting procedure with respect to the question of "How many?" On the other hand, those protocols (themselves) permit replication of these essential steps because the protocols are prototypes of (sets of) countable objects.

Decimal Numbers. Here again, a counting activity is the starting point. But now the activity is organized in a certain way by using counting symbols with the values of 1, 10, 100, 1000, and so on and by always changing to the next higher unit whenever possible. As in all of the examples, we assume that the learner is in a cognitive stage that enables the user to adequately carry out the actions. For instance, here the user must be able to mentally form higher order units, which can themselves be counted. That granted, the resulting protocol will be something equivalent to the decimal representation of the number of counted elements. Clearly, this representation reflects the main phases or steps of "decimal counting" and permits its replication in a very condensed form, if we assume that all of the higher order units have already been formed. A similar approach holds for other bases of the number system.

Decimal Fractions. Consider a measuring process by which one wants to exhaust a quantity of, say, less than one unit by tenths, hundredths, thousandths, and so on of the unit. This process naturally leads to a decimal fraction as its protocol and result. By reading this protocol, one can mentally reconstruct the process. First, take d_1 tenths, then take d_2 hundredths, and so on, until the whole quantity is obtained. Here, as in other cases, the protocol can further be used as an action plan to produce an object (a quantity) that will give rise to the protocol when the actions are carried out on it. Again, one can use different bases for the measuring process.

Fraction. A fraction can be viewed as a very curtailed or abridged protocol of a measuring process: m/n represents "m copies of quantity A are equal to n copies of quantity B," or "m copies of the nth part of quantity A yield the quantity B." Again, a wealth of different activities is possible concerning this relation of m/n to measuring processes from which, for instance, concepts such as equivalence of fractions, ratio of quantities, and addition of fractions can be derived. This example makes very clear that a pattern of signs has to be explicitly related to the actions that constitute (part of) the meaning of the signs (as an action protocol). In this specific case, the protocol m/n itself does not permit replication of the action. However, replication is possible if m and n are replaced by protocols (for the related counting processes). This corresponds to combining the counting and measuring processes. The number symbols can be viewed as names for the respective protocols or for the actions themselves. Then, m/n becomes a composed protocol. Still, this example makes clear that producing and reading a protocol relies heavily on the use of signs whose meaning is determined by convention.

Matrix. Consider two sets of elements (objects, properties, etc.) A and B and some way of measuring the "value" of a relation between elements of A and B. A protocol will very likely take the form of a matrix. Thus, a matrix can be viewed as a way of notating the values of (binary) relations. Further, the arrangement of its elements in rows and columns mirrors the stepwise process of determining these values. In this sense, a matrix then is not simply a static array of elements. Instead, it inherently has a dynamic structure or even several structures, such as, for example, the structure of scanning by rows or by columns. It is a schema of writing down symbols. Conversely, the idea of the matrix as the intended protocol determines the order of the steps in any measurement of this kind. Similarly, any type of table can be viewed, in a broad sense, as the protocol of some measuring.

Binary Operation. A binary operation on a set is usually defined as a mapping that maps every ordered pair of elements of the set onto an element of the set, with the latter being considered the result of the operation. In concrete (finite) cases of binary operations, one can easily record these results as a list or as a table with two entries. Then the protocols that arise and their carriers have the potential of exhibiting the feature which is captured in the static mathematical definition. I point to the subtle difference in how, for example, group tables are viewed here and how they are usually used. Here, the table results from completing all the single operations, and only the table leads to viewing the binary operation as an accomplished whole. In mathematics, the operation is considered to be given and the table is an illustration or representation of it. I think that cognitively this distinction makes a big difference.

Graph. Similarly, the act of drawing a combinatorial graph can be considered as recording a relation in a given set of elements. "Reading" this protocol gives a full account of the formal properties of the relation. A weighted graph even reports the strength of the relation between any two elements. As is well known, this type of protocol has become a topic of extensive mathematical investigation in the area of graph theory.

Binary Relation. In addition to a graph, there are many other ways of producing a protocol for binary relations, in which the action consists of checking whether two objects are related or not. Other carriers for protocols are as follows: a list of lists (indicating for each object to which objects it is related), a matrix, a list of pairs (of related objects), and a bipartite graph (especially for relations from a set M into a set N). All of these protocols make it possible to reenact the relation and to replay the steps of those actions that are essential for the relation. Further, it is possible to translate a protocol into any other protocol by noting the outcomes of the reenacted actions on the first by the second.

Angle. Typically, angles are viewed as static geometric objects that are defined in various ways. But angles can also be used as the protocol of a rotation (around the vertex of the angle): The first side is rotated into the position of the second. The very same protocol then results from angles that are considered to be equivalent. These equivalent angles (static or figurative) correspond to actions that everyone will naturally view as the same. Here again, the action can be replicated directly on the protocol or its replication can be easily imagined.

Algebraic Terms. These can be viewed as protocols that record some calculations or, better still, as the schema of the calculations. Conversely, an algebraic term tells me what calculations are to be made in which order (according to agreed-on conventions). Tree representations can play an equivalent role. In my opinion, an adequate understanding of elementary algebra would be facilitated if the concept of algebraic terms and their manipulations was based on the following understanding: Such terms are schematic protocols of (my own) calculations that I can use to give an account of them to myself or to others. As in all previous examples, an algebraic term viewed in this way makes it possible to reflect on the calculation (e.g., to study the influence of certain numbers on the outcome).

Permutations. If we draw r different numbers out of an urn with n numbers and we note the numbers in the order drawn, we obtain an r-permutation of the numbers $1, 2, \ldots, n$. This can be viewed as the (carrier of the) relevant protocol. Thus, the concept of r-permutation can be interpreted via an appropriate protocol. Similarly, r-combinations result when we disregard the order of the chosen numbers. Different kinds of protocols arise from various ways of notating rearrangements of objects in locations numbered from 1 to n. One way is to note, for each location, the number of the location to which its object is transferred. This can easily be done in the form of a table with two entries. This protocol, once again, is a record of an enacted rearrangement and also can be used as an indication of how to rearrange the objects. Another way is simply to note something such as 1 to 5, 5 to 7, 7 to 1, 2 to 3, and so on. Of course, this protocol of cycle presentation serves the same purpose.

Aspects of Protocols

In the following paragraphs, I discuss various aspects of the notion of a protocol in an arbitrary order because all of these aspects appear to be of equal relevance. However, not all of them apply to each individual case to the same extent.

A completed protocol, or rather its carrier, will be a static structure of signs forming a certain pattern that represents certain relationships between the signs. In a sense, this pattern can be treated as the resulting outcome of actions, or as a (rather symbolic) representation of it. However, just as good minutes of a meeting not only state the decisions made but also give an account of the discussions and deliberations leading to them, action protocols must make it possible to trace the stages of the process that lead to the final protocol. Thus, the protocol must reflect, in some way, a certain temporal pattern that is fundamental for the action as well as for the constituted mathematical concept. Very often, the temporal succession will be expressed by a spatial order in the protocol.

It might be appropriate here to emphasize that the related mathematical concept, in most cases, reflects only general and schematic aspects of the actions onto which the attention of the learner must be deliberately and consciously focused, for instance, by cues from the teacher. To "see" mathematical features in one's own actions is by no means trivial and further depends on the interests and the motivation of the learner. The problems related to this cannot be treated here, although they are very important for the didactic realization of the model presented.

In many cases, the (or a) mathematical structure that can be associated with actions of a certain type consists of transformations exerted on the objects on which the actions are carried out or of relationships between those objects that are induced by the actions. The protocol of the action, that is, the cognitive reconstruction of the concept, should reflect or make possible the reconstruction of these transformations and relationships. In this sense, the signs for the protocol play the role of objects on which those schematized actions that induce only the constitutive transformations and/or relationships can be instantiated. In other words, the protocol may be used to carry out by and on it just those steps of the actions that are the "germ" of the intended concept (and that have been recorded by the protocol). The protocol records or represents the (mathematically) essential features of the actions and makes it possible to replicate them.

The protocols (or, rather, their carriers) for natural numbers, as described earlier, demonstrate this feature very clearly. Each of them makes it possible to reenact or repeat the counting process that leads to the protocol itself. One way this can be done is by executing a counting process on the elements of the carrier itself (e.g., a list of tally marks). Alternatively, the symbols of the carrier of the protocol provide a prescription of how the counting is to be done (as in decimal notation). Of course, this presupposes that the user of the relevant carrier has constructed the related protocol as a cognitive tool. As another example, consider a square or a circle as a protocol of the related actions. Tracing the carriers (drawings) is a reenactment of such original actions that led to them, that is, a distinctive way of moving or walking. Similarly, the protocol of a permutation shows (to its cognitive owner) how to arrange the objects involved. In all of these cases, the importance of the transformation of the temporal succession (in the action) into a spatial order (in the protocol carrier) can be noticed. I presume for the learner that this reenactment of the constitutive actions or their distinctive steps and phases is a valuable way of developing the protocol itself as a stable cognitive structure. The translation between different protocols for the same mathematical notion might contribute to this. For instance, a different protocol can be used to record the relevant features of the reenactment of a specific protocol. Think of the various so-called representations of the function concept taken as the carriers for relevant protocols. The use of multirepresentational software is also related.

The intended reflection on the actions consists of recording the protocol that gives an account of the actions and their main goal. Because the protocol is a permanent record (in contrast to the transient action), it can be used repeatedly for analyzing the action by replicating it, for instance, in a schematized way on the protocol. It is very important for the individual cognitive process that the protocol is a record of the mathematical characteristics of one's own actions. The protocol should be a personal account of what one is interested in when carrying out the action. If the protocol is not experienced as an account of one's own actions, it cannot be really understood and will not be related to the actions in a meaningful way (cf. the use by Lehrer et al. of inscriptions with elementary school students, chap. 9, this volume).

In a didactic context, this means that the learner must be guided by the teacher to carry out the actions, to find out those objects and stages that are of essential relevance for the action, and to produce a protocol that represents those objects and stages. It should be emphasized that an action protocol is not uniquely determined by the actions. It will depend on how the learner structures and organizes his or her actions and, further, will depend on those means that are available for obtaining a protocol.

A protocol can be formulated by different media and in different sign systems. Perhaps one will begin with a verbal protocol, which, by using natural language, gives an account of those aspects in the flow of the action that are viewed to be the most important from a mathematical point of view. In some cases, it might be possible to translate this protocol into one that uses geometric or iconic objects. In other cases, it can be expressed in algebraic language. It might even be useful to produce several distinct protocols and to interpret the actions in all of them, thereby establishing a kind of translation from one protocol to another. One should never forget that the protocol receives its meaning, along with the rules for how to interpret and act on it, from the actions that it represents.

The protocol is potentially much more general than the action itself because, in most cases, it will be a schematic representation of certain aspects or features of the actions and their objects. This will often be reflected in that the signs used in the protocol have the character of variables or at least are considered as variables. In this way, the same protocol can be used as an account of many different actions, as long as these have the same "mathematical structure" as that expressed by the protocol and represented by the relevant mathematical concept. A didactic consequence is that the learner should experience this varied use of the protocol in as many different situations as possible. Thus, the protocol might also be used as a tool for structuring and planning concrete actions by substantiating the general schema (the protocol) in a given concrete context. In this regard, it is important to keep in mind that the protocol, by its very form and structure, makes it possible to carry out certain specific steps of the actions or at least to reproduce them. These are those steps that are constitutive for the related mathematical concept. This acting on the protocol or by the protocol, in a paradigmatic and prototypical way, exhibits the stages in the actions that are essential and the relationships that are important (from a certain point of view).

Usually, the carriers of the protocols are patterns of material signs and objects and, as such, can become the topic of further analysis and study. This is what might be called a mathematical analysis. Various properties of the protocols, possible transformations of and relations among protocols, and so on, can be devised and investigated through such analysis. Actions (material or imagined) that use the established protocols as objects to be acted on are most important. This can give rise to a new layer of concepts (and protocols), thus establishing a kind of hierarchy.

I do not pursue this topic any further here but simply give a few illustrative examples. In many cases, the protocol carriers can be combined in a specific way to obtain another carrier. Consider the arithmetic operations as instantiated on any of the aforementioned protocols for natural numbers. Or, consider the various operations with sets that give rise to appropriate operations with the protocol carriers, namely, union, inter-section, or difference. Other cases can simply be counting all possible protocol carriers (e.g., for permutations), or subjecting them to transfor-mation such as deleting or adding edges in a graph, transposing a matrix, and skewing a square. Structural properties of the protocol carriers are used to define properties of the related conceptual mathematical objects. Consider monotonic or convex real functions, periodic decimal fractions, prime, even, or odd numbers, or properties in graph theory (such as connectedness, tree, or path). In addition, I should mention that the remarks stated here also apply to prototypes.

Another important consideration is the introduction of names for the protocols. These names can be words from natural language or any other conventional signs. As the examples show, the naming of protocols makes it possible to establish compound protocols of more complex actions from simpler building blocks.

Because protocols by their very nature are based on actions (actual or imagined), their range of applicability is restricted to those concepts that are related to some kind of action or system of actions. This often implies some finite structure. In particular, the action must be finitely describable in principle, although we might imagine carrying it out infinitely many times, as, for example, in the case of the sine graph. For infinite or infinitesimal processes such as limits, derivatives, and integrals, we cannot devise a protocol whose structure reflects the structure of the intended mathematical concept. There is no conceivable symbolic structure that reflects the structure of, say, taking the derivative of $f(x)$ at x_0 with the same fidelity as we find in the examples given earlier in this chapter. This might be one explanation for the many problems with learning advanced calculus beyond a purely rule-driven approach. For instance, it is difficult to base the limit concept on experiences as they are provided by proto-types and protocols. In my view, these concepts depend very much on the prior development of very advanced discourse about the real numbers, about functions, and so on, permitting their introduction into the dis-course from the means provided by it. If one looks at the definitions for limit or derivative, this becomes fairly clear. These definitions can be illustrated and exemplified. However, in my view, none of these examples can be prototypic, in the sense of exhibiting what it means in that the limit or the derivative exists in general.

Allowing oneself to be inducted into a discourse and accepting it as a sensible attitude, such as that described in the next section, is of great help. Here, I only want to point out the limitations of the notion of protocols that show that, for "meaning and understanding" in mathematics, no single device is sufficient. In any case, a multitude of activities and attitudes appears to be a precondition for entering into mathematical discourse of any kind, if the goal is to genuinely participate in it.

In concluding this section on protocols, I emphasize that one of my purposes in stressing an action approach to finite mathematical concepts, via their protocols, is to counteract the prevailing static and figurative conception of school mathematics. In my view, the usual question of "What is the concept xy?" should be substituted, or at least complemented, by such questions as "Which actions can be recorded and/or guided by the concept xy?" This brings the mathematics closer to the individual and makes it part of his or her experience beyond the purely linguistic realm. Consequently, it is possible that the student then can experience the concepts and methods in question in a more personally sensible and meaningful way. On such a firm basis, then, access to advanced mathematics, in which approaches applicable to elementary mathematics are no longer viable, appears to be possible. As I discuss in the next section, sufficient confidence has to be acquired in order to indulge in the advanced discourse.

AS-IF ATTITUDE

As already has been discussed in the two previous sections, prototypes and protocols are conceived of as cognitive mechanisms that support an introduction into and a usage of (parts of) mathematical discourse. Both serve the purpose of supplying an experiential basis with concrete and perceivable objects that the discourse can be viewed as covering. Both are deeply rooted in the socially regulated activity of the individual. I have already pointed to major limitations of these mechanisms, inherent in the conception of many mathematical objects, that are constituted solely within conventional discourse.

My thesis in this section is that the conventions of mathematical discourse, beyond a cognitive understanding, need to be accepted and agreed on. Learners must indulge in the discourse, and this participation cannot be forced on them by cogent arguments. Indulgence in mathematical conventions and ways of speaking is partly an emotional willingness. And it proves sensible and justifiable only after hard, demanding work within the discourse and only after obeying its (often only) implicit rules (cf. Sfard's notion of templates-driven use, chap. 3, this volume). I assert that a specific view, called an *as-if attitude* (cf. Vaihinger, 1911/1986), can be of much support for accepting mathematical discourse.

This as-if attitude reflects an epistemological stance regarding quality and existence of mathematical objects. For me, mathematical objects (like any so-called abstract objects) are discursive objects. This means they come into existence exclusively by and within the discourse, even if this discourse ascribes to them existence and properties of an objective and independent character.

With respect to meaning and understanding, a consequence of this description is that meaning for mathematical concepts has to be partly ascribed or agreed on. In other words, there is nothing completely from the outside that could lend meaning to the discourse. But the discourse itself creates its meaning and sensibility (cf. Dörfler, 1993a, 1993b, 1995). This relates strongly to the Wittgensteinian position that the meaning of a term resides within its discursive use. I now try to explicate this general sketch with several examples.

Natural and Whole Numbers

Discourse about natural numbers at a somewhat advanced level (as in number theory) is about unique entities with names of 1, 2, 3, . . . and their properties, relations, and operations. According to this discourse, there is a specific mathematical object, say, 6, and to this object are attributed a great many properties and it is related to other objects of the same kind by many, often complex, relations: 6 is even, 6 is divisible by 2, 6 times 6 is 36, 6 is perfect, 6 is not a prime. Theorems in number theory, such as that there are infinitely many pairs of consecutive primes or the Prime Number Distribution Theorem, treat natural numbers as abstract objects. Similarly, in a notion as that leading from Z to Z_m, the integers must be considered as entities similar to material objects that enjoy distinctive properties, which can be combined, composed, or assembled. Consequently, the common names for integers are taken to refer to those abstract entities as their referents. The discursive creation of such objects as 3 and –4 is implicitly embedded in the discourse through such discursive elements as definitions, use of nouns, and the attribution of properties via adjectives. In a strict sense, these objects are not representable or imaginable. None of the common representations enjoys all of the properties we attribute to natural or whole numbers. For instance, a point on the number line is neither even nor odd. The purpose of the representations is, rather, to suggest properties and operations that, through discourse, are formulated as being properties and operations of the respective numbers. Evenness of a natural number can be read from a representation or, better still, from what is taken to be a representation (e.g., a prototype or protocol).

To make the point completely clear: The discourse flows as if there were uniquely determined entities (the numbers) with given properties and relations. These abstract entities can be materially represented in a faithful manner to determine their properties. In one sense, the discourse suggests that the abstract objects determine what counts as a representation. My position is quite the contrary. The system of representations and their mutual relationships determine the discourse about the abstract objects. Eventually, the discourse receives more independence and develops without directly referring to representations. New properties can then be introduced in a purely discursive manner, by basing them on those already known.

Developing Confidence

In the previous two sections, one can observe a progression in the development of mathematical discourse. It starts out as a discourse about relatively concrete and material activities, perceptions, and experiences about material objects and their properties and transformations. This discourse posits abstract objects and progresses to a discourse only about (and through the use of) them.

It should be clear that it is necessary to do more than just present representations, in order to understand this type of discourse and the concepts used by it. If metaphysical beliefs are excluded as a sensible basis, one viable way might be to assume the attitude described as follows. We speak as if there were those natural numbers with all of their properties and we speak as if we could use the representations to investigate them. We do this provisionally, as long as we do not detect contradictions or other shortcomings. We agree that this way of speaking and the methods developed for defining or deriving properties of the abstract objects are accepted as sensible. I emphasize that assuming an as-if attitude is the result of agreement, acceptance, indulgence, concession, and willingness on the part of the individual who trusts in others already fluent in the discourse. Most likely, after some experiences with the usefulness and power of the discourse, the individual develops more confidence and is prepared to be inducted into new realms of mathematical discourse. One could also view this process as a kind of progressive socialization or enculturation, both of which primarily are based on induction into a specific discourse.

Confidence in abstract objects might also be related to extensive experiences with their "representations." (Note that it is impossible to step out of the current discourse.) For instance, this applies to the extension of properties and operations to large or even to all natural numbers. Because everything works well with small numbers, we feel entitled to carry all that over to such discursive entities as 10^{1000} or even to all natural numbers. To speak about all natural numbers necessitates an as-if attitude because no one can convince us cognitively of any kind of existence of the set N as a completed whole. Positional notation systems and the number line might suggest that it is sensible to discursively extend the realm of numbers indefinitely. Experiences with their surveyable parts give enough legitimacy to say, "This can be continued arbitrarily in the given manner." But we have no means to force anyone to accept, for example, that any two natural numbers have a sum and a product. Consequently, arithmetic is a kind of thought experiment exploring the consequences of our as-if assumptions.

Although I cannot offer any empirical support, beyond personal experience and introspection, it is my thesis that understanding advanced mathematical discourse and experiencing it as meaningful also depend on some kind of as-if attitude. A consequence is that the teaching of mathematics must deliberately guide the development of this attitude and all the related processes. The goal should be a deliberate and conscious decision(!) on the part of the learner to accept the discourse as meaningful. Therefore, I view some of the commonly used teaching methods as inadequate because they attempt to lure the learner into the discourse by neglecting the inherent problems. In a sense, the discourse itself supports this by deceiving not only the learner, but possibly the teacher as well. The numbers and their operations exist in the ready-made discourse, making the problems of the transition to this stage no longer visible. Yet there is a great danger of learning only the surface features of the discourse in a rote manner. Such learning most likely leads to a parrot-like behavior, which is prone to mistakes and which impedes any further development and progress in the discourse.

In my view, the widely documented failures of manipulatives and other methodical means of teaching reside, to some extent, in the fact that learning mathematics and its discourse is not a purely cognitive constructive process. It is not sufficient just to build up imagination and mental models of representations for mathematical objects and concepts. Alone, this will not lead the learner to the discursively stipulated quality of the mathematical objects. There is a qualitative leap consisting of viewing the representations as representations of something that, of itself, is not accessible (and has no existence beyond the respective discourse).

Geometric Figures

I now turn to other examples. A very instructive one is the case of geometric figures, which we have also treated in the previous sections in relation to prototypes and protocols. The advanced geometric discourse of, say, Euclidean geometry has a quality similar to that of natural numbers. Drawings are viewed as representations of the actual geometric figure, which is an abstract object. This, of course, is not made explicit by the discourse. But to be understandable, the discourse presupposes this view or interpretation. For instance, it is clear that there is a unique square with a side of given length of which we have a multitude of more or less accurate drawings or sketches. The theorems of geometry, strictly speaking, are sensible assertions only for the abstract, ideal geometric figures. The Pythagorean Theorem holds only for mathematical right triangles and not for their empirical drawings. Generally, geometric discourse is two-sided. On the one hand, it is a discourse about empirical regularities of the drawings. On the other hand, it is about the mathematical objects. Very often these two functions are blended and not separated, which is both a strength and a weakness (cf. Nemirovsky & Monk's discussion of the notion of *fusion*, chap. 6, this volume). In fact, for the novice and the student it might be quite confusing and unsettling. Again, I assert that the conscious adoption of an as-if attitude might support understanding of and confidence in the geometric discourse. In that way, one can make the qualitative leap from using *triangle* as referring to the marks on paper to referring to a discursive object amenable to experience and reflection. This is connected with still another decisive change. First, the abstract concept is a way of talking about and expressing our geometric experiences with concrete drawings or other objects in a schematized and idealized manner. Later then, in a converse direction, the drawings are a means to talk about the abstract figures as mathematical objects. To determine the properties of the latter, one uses those of the former.

Various other as-if assumptions lurk beneath geometric discourse as follows: the infinite variety of figures; the infinite extension of the Euclidean plane; exact straightness of lines; exact flatness of planes in Euclidean space; and so forth. In the common discourse, all this appears completely unproblematic. Perhaps it is, as long as one remains inside the discourse. But these features might be severe obstacles for entering the discourse because, in principle, they are not, and cannot be, based on subjective experiences. As noted earlier, the concrete experiences and their reflection in the discourse can only serve to motivate and legitimate the extended discourse and support confidence in its sensibility. In the learning process, there will inevitably be a phase in which one has to trust and take a position such as, "Well, let's see what happens if we proceed in this manner." Meaning and understanding of a discourse reside to a large extent in its use and therefore cannot be provided beforehand from the outside. To learn and understand a discourse, one has to enter it and engage in it. This is a multifaceted process with cognitive, affective, emotional, and social components.

Complex Numbers

Another example, among many that are possible for substantiating my claims, is the field C of complex numbers. The pertaining discourse posits C as a unique construct comprising all uniquely determined abstract complex numbers. The theoretical discourse about C is based on and regulated by various "models" for C as follows: symbolic expressions $a + bi$, pairs of real numbers, 2×2 matrices, classes of polynomials modulo $(x^2 + 1)$, the Gaussian plane, and the Riemann sphere. The properties of, and operations with, the complex numbers are defined via these models. In principle, the abstract theory can be interpreted as a way of talking about the different models (which then would not be considered as models of C but possibly as models of each other). Yet, at some level, one has to take the view that there are abstract objects about which their taken-to-be models can provide relevant information. Consider sentences such as "Let z be a complex number" or "For all complex numbers z with. . . ." To feel comfortable with that kind of discourse presupposes assuming an appropriate as-if attitude with regard to complex numbers (cf. Sfard's discussion of Dan's uncertainty about the legitimacy of complex numbers, chap. 3, this volume).

For their common conception, the various potential models have to already be conceived of in a way that essentially transcends the realm of what can be presented concretely. For example, in the Gaussian plane we can show (also in imagination) only very finite portions with the relevant arrows, their sum, and their product. Extended experience with these finite portions gives rise to a kind of confidence or substantiated trust that one could carry out all the respective actions and operations also "far out" with very, very long arrows.

The finite portion can be treated as though it were a window, such as on a computer screen, that can be moved arbitrarily over the already taken-to-be infinite plane. Or, one can develop the view that takes finite drawings as a prototype, by focusing attention on the relevant relations and operations of the vector arrows. In any event, there must be some subjective experiential basis on which one can ground the as-if attitude, making it possible to accept an infinitely extended Gaussian plane and the unlimited executability of all the operations. Once more, I assert that this is a discursive process related to notions such as thought experiment or speech act, both of which can be motivated but not enforced. The acceptance of such as-if processes can be supported by relationships to construals that have already been proven to be sensible. Thus, if we have already taken as sensible the reals as a completed manifold, modeling C by pairs of real numbers might be quite convincing. In this way, as-if attitudes spread very quickly and eventually appear to be a natural position that cannot be doubted. By this point, one has been socialized as a mathematician. It is then difficult to step out of the discourse one is immersed in and think of a phase in which all that now is unquestionable, such as the infinity of C, was rather mysterious.

Real Function

Using still another example, I want to demonstrate that as-if attitudes must have a network-like character. A specific as-if view needs support from many others and, conversely, enhances legitimacy to others previously held. Each new success or progress lends more plausibility, credibility, or viability to the basic assumptions (e.g., about abstract objects as a sensible matter to talk about).

The example concerns real functions such as the sine function or exponential function. A great many as-if assumptions lurk beneath the common discourse about them and, according to the discourse, appear to be completely unproblematic. The relevant theory assures us that for every real number x, sine x and exponent x are well defined as numerical values. But for most, in fact for uncountably many, of those x, we cannot have a finite description and therefore can never get to know $f(x)$. Further, for those x in R that we can present finitely, we must apply an infinitely long procedure to evaluate $f(x)$, namely, the Taylor series. Again, this prevents us from ever knowing $f(x)$. Nevertheless, we speak about sine and exponent as though all this had been accomplished. We feel entitled to calculate approximations to the taken-to-exist exact values, for example, by a computer. We base the graphs of the functions, which again we take to present their exact behavior, on these calculations. And, of course, all of this extends to all of R based on an infinite number line. We group together all those inherently unknowable pairs $(x, f(x))$ and take them as a kind of new mathematical object to which we ascribe properties (continuity, differentiability, etc.) In addition, we can combine this new object with other such objects (e.g., consider the vector space of $C(R)$ of all functions continuous on all of R, which by necessity "contains" functions we will never conceive of).

Concluding Remarks

I do not criticize that kind of mathematics, but I want to exhibit to what degree it is based on acts of faith and is essentially of a discursive character. Neither the notion of material nor the notion of mental models makes sense or is applicable here. One has to rely on language and the conventional use of symbols. Similar observations that apply to previous examples are applicable to sine and exponential functions, too. At first, the abstract terms might serve the purpose of talking about a variety of concrete, even physical, experiences such as describing observations of growth processes or oscillations. This abstracted manner of talking then acquires some independence from the experiences and experiential phenomena referred to, so that the abstract objects gain discursive existence. First, the abstract description lends "meaning" to the experiences. Later, the abstract objects derive their "meaning" from their taken-to-be representations or applications.

One can justifiably ask why quite a few students accept, without hesitation, the sensibility of these kinds of mathematical constructs and their pertinent discourse, whereas other students never feel comfortable with, or may even refuse to accept, the necessary agreement. One theoretical explanation might be offered by the theory of image schemata that was developed by Lakoff (1987) and Johnson (1987). According to these authors, schematized bodily experiences are the sources for associating metaphorical meaning with words that are used in an abstracted context. For instance, our experiences with material objects are schematized in an image schema that is projected metaphorically to terms such as *abstract object* or *mathematical object*. Neither object is a palpable entity at all. But to each we ascribe properties that are experienced with concrete objects. For this to be possible, we do not even need mental imagery or the mental models that are now often encountered. Instead, the metaphoric use of terms is conceivable as a linguistic or discursive process, although starting from experientially constituted image schemas. At times, these image schemas might even be exteriorized by symbolic expressions that, in turn, can serve as generic terms. For instance, the general form of a decimal number or of an infinite decimal fraction can acquire this generic character for the student, thus serving as (the carrier of) the prototype for an arbitrary natural or real number. Generally, prototypes and protocols will have this generic character.

A cognitively oriented explanation for the failure to be inducted into the mathematical discourse is, therefore, the lack of image schemata on which to base the discursive extension and the many as-if attitudes. Again, this lack might result from an absence of pertinent experiences (which can be either quantitative or qualitative). Of course, there can be differences in the abilities of each individual to schematize his or her experiences and to make metaphoric use of words.

As already has been pointed out, there are mathematical notions that cannot be based on a generic prototype that is expressed by a symbolic schema. Although this holds for continuous functions, it holds even more for Lebesgue integrable functions because there is not a generic schema that describes an arbitrary member of these classes of functions. Yet we group all of them together to form sets, vector spaces, or Banach spaces.

I think that an as-if attitude certainly is required to make these groupings acceptable, if one wants to avoid metaphysical or Platonistic faith. Prior experiences with the success of these discursive processes provide a strong motivation for assuming such an attitude.

In this section, I have attempted to state that a didactic approach to mathematics, based on imagery, concrete experiences, prototypes, protocols, or on theories of representations and mental models, has to be complemented at least by both linguistic and affective/emotional aspects. Many mathematical construals can be interpreted only as part of a specific discourse, which cannot be forced on the student by purely rational arguments. A conscious decision to enter the discourse is necessary and can be supported, in my view, by the taking of an as-if attitude, for example, in regard to the existence of mathematical objects. This opens up a way of understanding advanced mathematics that does not look for (the principally impossible) mental models for abstract objects.

REFERENCES

Dörfler, W. (1984). Actions as a means for acquiring mathematical concepts. In B. Southwell, R. Eyland, M. Cooper, J. Conroy, & K. Collis (Eds.), *Proceedings of the Eighth International Conference for the Psychology of Mathematics Education* (pp. 172–180). Sydney, Australia: International Group for the Psychology of Mathematics Education.

Dörfler, W. (1989a). Prototypen und Protokolle als kognitive Mittel gegen Bedeutungslosigkeit und Entfremdung im Mathematikunterricht. In *Zukunft des Mathematikunterrichts* (pp. 102–109). Remscheid-Lennep, Germany: Soest.

Dörfler, W. (1989b). Protocols of action as a cognitive tool for knowledge construction. In G. Vergnaud, J. Rogalski, & M. Artigue (Eds.), *Proceedings of the Thirteenth Conference of the International Group for the Psychology of Mathematics Education* (Vol. 1, pp. 212–219). Paris: International Group for the Psychology of Mathematics Education.

Dörfler, W. (1991). Meaning: Image schemata and protocols. In F. Furinghetti (Ed.), *Proceedings of the Fifteenth Conference of the International Group for the Psychology of Mathematics Education* (Vol. 1, pp. 17–32). Assisi, Italy: Universita di Genova.

Dörfler, W. (1993a). Fluency in a discourse or manipulation of mental objects. In I. Hirabayashi, N. Nohda, K. Shigematsu, & F. Lin (Eds.), *Proceedings of the Seventeenth International Conference for the Psychology of Mathematics Education* (Vol. 2, pp. 145–152). Tsukuba, Japan: Program Committee of the 17th PME Conference.

Dörfler, W. (1993b). Haben wir Mathematik im Kopf. In G. Pickert & I. Weidig (Eds.), *Mathematik erfassen und lehren. Festband für Vollrath* (pp. 63–71). Stuttgart, Germany: Klett Verlag.

Dörfler, W. (1995). Mathematical objects, representations and imagery. In J. Mason & R. Sutherland (Eds.), *Exploiting mental imagery with computers in mathematics education* (pp. 82–94). NATO ASI Series F: Computer and System Series. Berlin-Heidelberg, Germany: Springer Verlag.

Johnson, M. (1987). *The body in the mind.* Chicago: University of Chicago Press.

Lakoff, G. (1987). *Women, fire and dangerous things.* Chicago: University of Chicago Press.

Rotman, B. (1993). *Ad infinitum. The ghost in Turing's machine.* Stanford, CA: Stanford University Press.

Vaihinger, H. (1986). *Die Philosophie des Als Ob.* Aalen, Germany: Scientia Verlag. (Original work published 1911)

Wittgenstein, L. (1977). *Philosophische Untersuchungen* [Philosophical investigations]. Frankfurt, Germany: Suhrkamp.

The Appropriation of Mathematical Symbols: A Psychosemiotic Approach to Mathematics Learning

Bert van Oers
Free University Amsterdam
Amsterdam, The Netherlands

There is probably no dispute about the importance of symbol use in mathematical thinking. Nevertheless, the appropriation of symbols remains one of the stumbling blocks in mathematics education for many pupils. In this chapter I discuss the appropriation of mathematical symbols from the perspective of action psychology, drawing to a large extent from the works of Vygotsky and his followers. The first part of the chapter gives a theoretical account of my psychological approach, putting it into a historical context and describing some of its core concepts. *Action*, *activity*, and *meaning* are key concepts in this approach. In the later sections of this chapter, I analyze mathematical symbol formation and mathematical concept learning from this psychosemiotic perspective. In addition to the psychosemiotic analysis, it is argued that a developmental approach to these learning processes is needed to fully understand the construction of mathematical meanings. In a last part of the chapter, I give some examples of how the promotion and development of symbol-meaning construction can be initiated during early education, laying a basis for the appropriation of mathematical symbols later on.

A DYNAMIC VIEW ON MATHEMATICAL THINKING

The conception of mathematics as a special type of human activity enjoys a growing popularity in modern thinking about mathematics education. Mathematics as a discipline is now generally conceived of as an activity in which constructive representation, with the help of symbols, plays a decisive role (Bishop, 1988; Freudenthal, 1973, 1991; Kaput, 1987). From the analysis of the historical context of mathematics education, it can be maintained that the connection between communication and knowing can only become imaginable by understanding symbolic means as means of the system of human activity, which is subjective as well as social (see for instance Otte, 1974). Elsewhere I have also argued for a conception of mathematics education that acknowledges the written-language characteristic of mathematics, thus emphasizing the importance of the symbol in the process of meaningful appropriation of mathematics as a cultural activity (van Oers, 1996b).

It is no wonder that this conception of mathematics is also reflected in modern discussions about mathematics education. Reading literature on the history of mathematics teaches us that problem solving and the use of symbolic technology always formed essential elements in the self-concept of mathematics. As Cassirer (1955, p. 75) put it: "Mathematics and physics were the first to gain a clear awareness of this symbolic character of their basic implements." These disciplines were the first to recognize the artificial nature of their instruments and to consider their results as mental constructions. By the same token, these disciplines traditionally tended to be as interested in the activity of doing mathematics as in mathematical results.

Not surprisingly, this approach to human thinking also spread to epistemology in general. The activity approach indeed gained much attention in the academic world during the past centuries. Since the 17th century, the approach was elaborated substantially in Europe, where Spinoza emphasized the constructive character of human thinking, and Leibnitz tried to overcome Cartesian dualism by proposing a monistic, active conception of human consciousness. Eventually this way of thinking also influenced educational thought. In the 17th century, Comenius put forward the idea that the best way of teaching an activity is to show it. As a general approach to learning, this view never lost its influence in European educational thought, although it was not dominant in educational practice for a long time. In the 19th century, von Humboldt tried to implement this view of knowledge and knowing into general education (in Germany) by emphasizing "activity" (*energeia*), rather than "product" (*ergon*). However, due to a variety of cultural circumstances (such as the urge to transmit the products of cultural history, rather than illuminate the strategies involved), this activity approach to school subjects did not become very popular in school practice until recently.

In one of his first substantial books on mathematics education, Freudenthal (1973) quoted Comenius's view on learning as follows: "The best way to teach an activity is to show it," or, as Freudenthal himself read this principle, "The best way to teach an activity is to perform it" (Freudenthal, 1973, p. 110). And this concept runs through all of his reflections on mathematics education. According to Freudenthal, mathematics is basically an activity of *mathematizing*: that is, organizing a (concrete empirical or abstract mental) domain, representing it with the help of symbols, finding problems, solving problems, and experimenting with symbolic means (as in a thought experiment), in order to become better acquainted with the properties of the domain under consideration (see also Gravemeijer, 1992; Gravemeijer, Cobb, Bowers, & Whitenack, chap. 7, this volume). In mathematics education, for Freudenthal, the "activity of structuring" is far more important than the mere mastering of fossilized mathematical structures (Freudenthal, 1979). In his approach to mathematics education, Freudenthal was clearly pursuing this old activity tradition with respect to education and learning (see also Freudenthal, 1991).

The same goes for the mathematics educationalist van Hiele (see, e.g., van Hiele, 1985). He was absolutely confident that it was possible to help students gain insight into mathematics if the teaching–learning process were adequately organized. His level theory about the organization of practices of mathematics education gained some influence in the movement for the innovation of mathematics (Gravemeijer, 1994; Hoffer, 1983).

More than Freudenthal, van Hiele was interested in the psychological aspects of mathematics education. He emphasized the importance of symbols in mathematics for grasping mathematical meaning. For him, symbols ideally become signals for relevant actions in a particular context, indicating those properties and relations in the situation that deserve special attention in the problem-solving process. According to van Hiele, appropriating the meaning of symbols is primarily a communicative process in a problem-solving context. However, in an educational setting this communication is not a straightforward transmission of information from the teacher to the pupils, because symbols may mean different things to different participants in the communication. Hence, the teacher and the pupils must come to a mutual understanding of the meaning of the symbols used. Only then can an attempt be made to bring these symbol-related meanings more into conformity with the mathematical conventions. Nowadays, this communicative process would be called *negotiation of meaning*.

With respect to his view on learning, van Hiele was clearly influenced by the Dutch learning psychologist van Parreren, who developed an action psychological theory of learning by elaborating on the ideas of Lewin.[1] I address this learning theory in a more detailed way in the next section.

---

[1]After the late 1960s, van Parreren broadened his theory by integrating the views of the Vygotskian cultural-historical approach. By doing so he and his colleague Carpay introduced Vygotsky into the Dutch academic discussions in the early seventies.

At this moment it is important to recognize that the general activity approach to human thinking influenced both mathematics education and learning psychology. It is not surprising then that the dynamic view on mathematics and the psychological theory of activity consistently go together and are, actually, interdependent with respect to the design of mathematics education (see also van Oers, 1990).

One of the core concepts in all dynamic views on mathematics is the concept of symbol. Symbols are indispensable as means for coding the results of thinking. More importantly, however, symbols also function as means for the regulation of the thinking process. They introduce new ways of organizing in the course of thinking, as argued by Vygotsky and his followers. Not surprisingly, mathematics educators starting out from a dynamic, activity-oriented view on mathematics also discovered the essential role of language-in-use as a fundamental symbol system for mathematical thinking (see, among others, Cobb, Wood, & Yackel, 1993; Ernest, 1991; Pimm, 1987). The invention, use, and improvement of appropriate symbols are characteristic features of the mathematical enterprise (see, e.g., Struik's 1990 magnificent description of the history of mathematics; see also Davis & Hersch, 1981).[2] Obviously, the efforts of the pupils to get a better grip on symbols in a meaningful way should be considered one of the core objectives of education, especially in the domain of mathematics.

In this chapter I focus on one contribution of an activity-theoretical approach to mathematics education, starting from this dynamic, activity-based view on mathematical thinking (mathematizing). In particular, I develop an activity-psychological view of the symbol, "the most significant of man's instrumentalities" (according to Werner & Kaplan, 1963, p. 11; see also Nemirovsky and Monk's discussion of Werner and Kaplan's work, chap. 6, this volume). From this perspective I deal with the *activity* of symbol formation and symbol use or, that is to say, with *symbolizing*. In the elaboration of this point of view, the basic psychological concepts are drawn from the works of Vygotsky, Leont'ev, Werner, and the Dutch psychologist van Parreren.

Acknowledging the importance of the symbol in the development of mathematical thinking is evidently consistent with recent empirical findings as well. According to empirical investigations of the development of

---

[2]This is not to suggest that mathematics is a once-defined, unchanging discipline. Nevertheless, the passion of mathematics, that is, the passion to comprehend things (such as music, measurement, space, number systems, ethics, eternity, solar systems, market economy, chaos, to name just a few) via analysis of orderly representations, remained the same existential precondition for mathematical activity throughout history. What changed, in accordance with the cultural-historically developing self-concept of mathematics, were the norms, rules, concepts, and conventions for how to accomplish this existential aim.

mathematical thinking in pupils, the failure of meaningful appropriation of mathematical symbols has turned out to be one of the main problems in mathematics learning (see, among others, Hughes, 1986; Walkerdine, 1988; see also research examining the relationship between dyslexia and mathematics, Miles & Miles, 1992).

The ultimate educational concern of this activity-oriented approach to (mathematics) education is to foster the development of autonomy in pupils with respect to their (mathematical) actions. Pupils must be educated to become responsible for their own mathematical actions, not by inventing their private mathematics but by collaboratively reconstructing "old" mathematical means and meanings and by discovering the relevance with respect to their current life activities.

At this moment, our understanding of this educational process is far from complete. In order to gain further insight into the processes involved and to enhance our educational abilities to foster the pupils' development, we will have to refine the core concepts, such as constructivity, activity, and symbolizing, as psychological phenomena. Mathematics educators show a tendency to get deeply involved in phenomenological analyses of subject matter (e.g., Freudenthal) or in curriculum and instructional problems (e.g., Howson, Keitel, & Kilpatrick, 1981; Malone & Taylor, 1993), without giving much attention to the psychological concepts they use.[3] Sometimes the psychological nature of these phenomena is taken for granted or simply overlooked. (See the critical review of recent developments in constructivism and socioconstructionism by Shotter, 1995.) In the next section, I briefly describe an action-psychological framework that might deepen our understanding of what it means to learn mathematics, especially with respect to the development of symbolizing in the mathematical domain.

TOWARD A PSYCHOLOGICAL FRAMEWORK FOR ANALYSIS

As a consequence of the general philosophical approach to the human mind and the act of knowing, the activity approach was a vital, although sometimes peripheral, paradigm in social science as well during the last few centuries in Europe. In the 20th century, the activity approach to learning and development was elaborated in the works of Werner, Lewin, Vygotsky, Leont'ev, van Parreren, and many others.[4] It was even exported

---

[3]As always, there are good exceptions to this. See Gravemeijer (1994).

[4]The works of Kurt Lewin and Heinz Werner substantively influenced both Vygotsky in Russia (see, e.g., van der Veer & Valsiner, 1991) and van Parreren in the Netherlands.

to the United States by the works of Dewey, Lewin, and Werner, but it did not have much influence there[5] until the last decade. Still, most of the recent elaborations of Vygotskian theory are biased toward linguistic, semiotic, and anthropological interpretations of Vygotsky, rather than being elaborations of the action-psychological aspects of the cultural-historical approach of Vygotsky, Leont'ev, and Lurija. The next three subsections give a brief account of an action-psychological approach to learning and the construction of meaning (see also van Oers, 1996b, 1996c). This frame of reference will be needed in my theoretical account of symbolizing and the appropriation of symbols later on.

General Tenets

The basic tenets of the activity approach to human behavior and development are most extensively formulated in the context of discussions concerned with Vygotsky's cultural-historical (sociocultural) theory. Thanks to publications of Wertsch (e.g., 1985), Cole (e.g., 1990), Moll (1990), Forman, Minick, and Stone (1993), and many others, there is no need at this moment for an extensive introduction into this approach (see, for a recent synopsis, Wertsch & Toma, 1995). Here, I describe only those issues that are important to understanding my further argument (see also van Oers, 1996c).

For Vygotsky, human behavior is essentially a cultural phenomenon. Current forms of behavior are the joint products of human biological equipment, the cultural history, and the characteristics of individual development. Adults are responsible for the development of the next generation in so far as they can actually influence the characteristics of individual developmental processes in a decisive way. By creating a zone of proximal development in his interaction with the child and by promoting learning processes within that zone, the adult can not only introduce culture into the child's life in a meaningful way, but can even promote the child's development as a cultural human being.

An important question now is how to define the *zone of proximal development*. Most Western interpretations of the zone of proximal development start from the definition given in the following English translation of Vygotsky's essay (1978) on the interaction between learning and development:

---

[5]We may have to make an exception for social psychology in the United States, and, undoubtedly, for Piaget, whose work is intrinsically connected to this European tradition. The position of Piaget vis-à-vis the activity approach (as conceived here) cannot be analyzed here. Michael Cole was one of the first in the United States to recognize the significance of activity theory. He still is one of the leading figures of this approach.

It is the distance between the actual developmental level as determined by independent problem solving and the level of potential development as determined through problem solving under adult guidance or in collaboration with more capable peers. (p. 86)

However, even though this translation is a correct rendition of what Vygotsky himself wrote about the zone, a narrow focus on this discrepancy formula of the zone leads to a distortion of the real meaning of the concept. As this working definition zooms in on the developmental state of an individual's performances, it leads to an individualistic and static interpretation of the zone, capitalizing on individual actions or functions. For Vygotsky, however, the zone is a dynamic concept referring to some culturally articulated context emerging in the interaction between adult and child (see Wertsch, 1985, pp. 67–76). Therefore, Vygotsky reiterated throughout his written work that *imitation* should be conceived of as the essential element in the definition of the zone of proximal development (see, e.g., Vygotsky, 1934/1982, p. 250). However, imitation is not to be interpreted as indiscriminate copying someone else's actions, but as a form of meaningful reenactment of some cultural activity, based on interactive reconstruction and on the reflexive exchange of meanings. By calling this process *imitation*, Vygotsky emphasized the important fact that human beings are always participating in preexisting cultural activities that they have not invented themselves, but that have been gradually developed in the foregoing cultural history. The zone of proximal development, then, should be conceived of primarily as a cultural activity in which children become involved with the help of adults (or with more capable peers). Within this activity, all individuals take part on the basis of the actions they have already mastered and that have a meaningful relation to the sociocultural activity. At least their actions need to be accepted by the other participants in the activity and ought to be consistent with the activity as a whole.

Vygotsky did not elaborate his concept of activity in great detail. From his use of the concept and from what he wrote about it, we can definitely infer that, for him, it is a sociocultural (metaindividual) phenomenon in which different individuals can take part and collaboratively perform their activity-related actions. Later on, Leont'ev elaborated a theory of activity in which he distinguished the conceptual difference between *activity* (as a meta-individual, cultural phenomenon) and *actions* (as particular individual performances). In his perspective, activity is an interpretative concept for the understanding of the cultural-historical dimension in the development of action systems. Basically, human behavior can only manifest itself through actions. It is only by interpretation that a person's individual actions can signify cultural activity. In general, activities are characterized by a motive and by their possible action-structures.

The structure of any particular realization of an activity is determined by its goal structure and its goal-directed actions at the individual level. Learning can only be based on the individual's own actions (as Vygotsky, 1991, wrote in his work concerning pedagogical psychology).

In the wake of Leont'ev, we can call this definition of activity (as distinct from actions) the qualitatively determined concept of activity. The already mentioned concept of activity refers to a culturally developed category of related actions held together by a motive. Obviously, not every possible action should be performed every time in every situation. Individuals have to make choices for the relevant actions, according to their goals in the given situation. They have some freedom with respect to the choice and the sequence of their activity-embedded goals and actions. But not just anything is allowed when one intends to accomplish a specific sort of cultural action. Take, for example, football playing as an activity. No one prescribes exactly how it is to be played. Actually, football actions are "chosen," by the player in the field, within the constraints of the rules and physical conditions of the game. Thus, every player has some degree of freedom as to the choice and sequence of his actions. But there are restrictions, such as that some actions (accidentally or deliberately) are not accepted as long as the players agree to play football, and these actions are sanctioned.[6] New football actions (such as heading, stopping a ball, jinking past someone, etc.) are to be learned within this activity, and (for the learner) they must have a meaningful relation to this activity. Indeed, the best way to learn an activity is to perform (or imitate) it.

As an aside, I have to add here that the qualitatively determined concept of activity must be strictly distinguished, according to Leont'ev, from a more quantitatively determined concept of activity that refers to the intensity of an activity, (i.e., the amount of effort on the part of an acting individual). This "activity" is the antithesis of "passivity" and indicates how much (mental) effort the individual invests in his actions. It is this latter interpretation of activity that is sometimes involved in discussions about the constructive character of human cognition. It must be distinguished from the qualitative version, which can be determined only by specifying the actions, motives and goals involved.[7]

---

[6]It would not be too difficult to develop a similar example about mathematics as an activity.

[7]There is a language problem here. Leont'ev used two different Russian words for the distinguished forms of activity: *dejatel'nost* and *aktivnost*, respectively. In many languages (such as in English, French, and Dutch), there is only one word available for the translation of both. In German both terms can be distinguished as *Tätigkeit* and *Aktivität*, respectively. In the other languages, there is often confusion about what exactly is meant (even in translation from Russian). When I use the term *activity*, I always refer to the qualitatively determined concept (*dejatel'nost'*; *Tätigkeit*).

The qualitatively construed concept of activity entails several very important educational implications. First of all, we must acknowledge that every activity has an individual form (the way it is realized in the situated, goal-directed actions of an individual) and a collective form. For mathematics education, this suggests that it is both necessary and useful for educational practices to characterize mathematics in terms of a reflexive relationship between an individual and a collective activity. This seems to be consistent with one of the conclusions of Cobb, Yackel, and Wood (1992) about the nature of mathematics education.

Another important consequence that I would like to point out here is that a participant in an activity can be considered the real agent of that activity only because he or she has social assistance. This assistance can be given by another human being or can be embodied in instruments (such as a calculator) or in other supportive systems (such as guidelines for actions, operating instructions, algorithms, a compiler program in a computer, etc.). The requirements for a realistic imitation (or personally meaningful reenactment) of a cultural activity are distributed, so to say, over different agents and means (cf. the Bransford et al. discussion of distributed support for knowing, chap. 8, this volume). As a result, no one needs to master all of the actions necessary to accomplish an activity. Neither is it necessary to carry out all of the required actions by oneself. By participating in a sociocultural activity, as well as by being allowed and able to use the various resources available, people can act as cultural agents. This explains, for instance, how a pupil can do mathematics without first having to become an expert mathematician.

As Lave and Wenger (1991) pointed out, such participation is peripheral in the beginning, but it may become more and more substantial if the participation lasts long enough. Lave and Wenger described many illuminating examples that show how a person grows into a practice. In a similar way, we can explain how a child grows into a speech practice just by being involved in communication and gradually developing abilities to participate actively in this communication. Likewise, the development of numeracy also follows this general pattern. For example, it is meaningless to ask whether children should have acquired prior knowledge of counting principles in order to learn counting. Both counting actions and the required rules need to be present in the same activity, although they need not be available in one and the same person. Expertise is not only the final measure that the pupils have to eventually achieve. But the expert is a collaborator in the activity from the beginning, bringing the future into the present (Cole, 1995). In other words, the structural endpoint of any mature activity needs to be present "in the interaction between child and adult as a precondition for this new structure to appear as an individual psychological function in the child" (Cole, 1995, p. 44;

see also Cole & Engeström, 1993). This is one crucial implication of Vygotsky's emphasis on imitation. By the same token, this also signifies an important requirement for any educational implementation of this concept of the zone of proximal development.

The importance of this cannot be overrated. In every activity, there is a distribution of functions among agents and means. (See Salomon, 1993, for further analyses of the idea of distributed cognition.) The nature of the social organization of the activity is eventually reflected in the style of intramental functioning (see van Oers, 1996b; Wertsch & Toma, 1995).

An Action Psychological View on Learning

The zone of proximal development defines the context for meaningful learning but does not account for learning itself. Learning, according to the action-psychological view, is always based on the situated manifestations of human behavior, that is, on actions. An action can be defined as follows: a goal-directed attempt to change an object, in order to make it (more) meaningful for some end (see Leont'ev, 1975; van Parreren, 1954, 1971, 1978). Examples are:

- *Tying* a shoelace (changing the shoelace into a form that will prevent one's shoes from falling from one's feet).
- *Peeling* an apple (changing the apple into an edible form).
- *Writing* a note (changing a piece of paper into a means of communication by putting graphic signs on it).
- *Counting* (changing a collection of objects into a particular quantity).
- *Calculating* 2 + 2 (changing the formula 2 + 2 into another form that suits the task at hand).

Every action is characterized by its object, its goal (the intended modification of the object), and its means for performance. According to the nature of the object, the goal, and the instrumental means, the performance of the action is structured in a particular way. Anyone who has ever written on a chalkboard knows that writing on a chalkboard is structurally different from writing on a piece of paper with a pencil. We can graphically represent an action as a relationship between a person (a pupil) and an object (P = pupil; O = object) as in Fig. 5.1.

But it is not only the object, the personal goals, or the means that determine the structure of an action. Actually, the structure of an action is, to a large extent, a result of learning how to handle an instrument for changing an object to some end and is often handed down to a child during his or her development. It should be noted here that the perform-

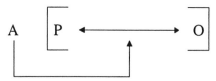

FIG. 5.1. An action as a relationship between a person (a pupil) and an object (P = pupil; O = object).

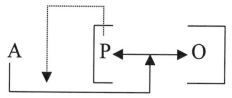

FIG. 5.2. The representation of the mediated action extended (A = adult, influencing a pupil's action).

FIG. 5.3. A process of qualitative change of an action, which depends on the object (O), the learner (P), and the social environment (A).

ance of an action not only refers to the process of carrying it out, but also to the mental reflections of preparing the action, making decisions, controlling and assessing it, and so on. In this broad sense, human actions are essentially culturally mediated actions. Hence, the representation of the mediated action must be extended as shown in Fig. 5.2 (A = adult, influencing a pupil's action). However, in reality this is not a one-way communication because the child gives some reaction (feedback) concerning the adult's attempts (action) to influence the child's object-oriented actions, shown in Fig. 5.3.

At this point, the learning process can be described as a process of qualitative change of an action. Referring to Fig. 5.3, we can see that this process depends upon the object (O), the learner (P), and the social environment (A). This theory of learning was developed and experimentally supported during the 1950s by Leont'ev, Gal'perin (see Haenen, 1996), and van Parreren. There can be changes with respect to the structure of an action, or with respect to the meaning of an action.

Changes in the structure of an action can be observed most clearly in actions involving motor manipulation. Picture someone using a typewriter for the first time. Then, compare this way of acting with how he performs after 6 months of practicing. There is a clear difference in the structure of his typewriting actions. The stages in the development of counting can also be construed as a succession of qualitatively changing actions. For instance, we see that concrete pointing to the objects is a vital aspect of the performance of the counting action. In later stages, this structural aspect of the action disappears or, to put it more appropriately, is transformed into a perceptual action of looking at the objects to be counted. Still later the material objects themselves are not even necessary; the counting action deals with the quantities per se (transforming them into other quantity representations). Of course, other changes occur as well, in the developmental process of the counting action, such as the growing fluency in the performance of the action, the generalization of the action to counting by composite units, and the gradual submission of the action to cultural rules of counting (e.g., the "how to count principles," Gelman & Gallistel, 1978).[8]

One very important aspect of the learning process must be described here in greater detail because it will be important in an action-psychological account of symbolizing. The qualitative transformation of an action can occur with respect to a variety of parameters (Gal'perin, 1969). One of them is the extensiveness of the action performance. At first the action is exploratory, tentative, hesitating (picture again the beginning typist!). But after a while, the action becomes abbreviated step by step, erasing the intermittent explorations and orientations. The actor needs to contemplate less and less during the actual performance, and doesn't have to ask himself such questions as "What's next?" or "How do I do it?" In fact, now the action will proceed more and more smoothly, be to the point, and become automatic. One could say that this action coalesces into one ephemeral operation.

This abbreviation process is essential for the development of recognition actions: that is, actions that aim at identifying situations, objects, or symbols, in order to find out what they mean. In the first stage of any recognition process, the action proceeds step by step, often checking critical features, working through a tree of decisions, and finally coming to a conclusion. Beginning bird watchers, for instance, need to check a whole series of features of the bird before they can conclude what bird it is that they see. After some practice, however, they immediately see what kind of bird it is. The extended identification process has been abbreviated into an "immediate" recognition.

Abbreviation processes are very important for all kinds of complex cognitive achievements. This is evident in the beginning reading process, but also in the mathematizing process (although this is often overlooked). The importance of this process of abbreviation for the historical and individual development of mathematical thinking has been shown clearly

---

[8]It is not, however, my intention here to develop an action-psychological account for the development of counting. Hence, I only refer to it sketchily now. There is much more to it than is pointed out here. See, for example, Steffe (1992).

by Sfard (chap. 3, this volume; also Sfard, 1991, 1992; Sfard & Linchevski, 1994). Sfard emphasizes the process–object duality in mathematical concepts. In the development of mathematical notions, the process-oriented conception of a mathematical symbol emerges first. However, this conception gradually becomes a structured object of mathematical thinking through a process of *reification*. To my mind, what Sfard identifies (at an epistemological level) as a reification process is parallel to the concept of abbreviation in my psychological analysis.

An additional argument for the importance of abbreviation in mathematical thinking was given by Bauersfeld (1995). He showed that the interpretation of a situation as a subtraction task (or some other mathematical operation) requires a process of identification in which a pupil has to "read" a situation (or a picture) as one that can be represented (e.g., $7 - 3$). Bauersfeld (1995, p. 146) stated, "The key operation of any problem solving is the mathematical modelling of all kinds of objects or situations, which may involve the selection and assignment of mathematical models." Acquiring proficiency in mathematical problem solving necessarily includes the abbreviation of this identification process, transforming this process from an extended exploratory form into some sort of more or less immediate (ephemeral) recognition of what is to be done in a particular situation. Of course, the decision might be mistaken, but that is no reason for denying the cognitive importance of abbreviation. Rather, this is a good reason for placing these abbreviated actions under permanent reflective control.

This process of abbreviation was studied experimentally by Gal'perin and his students. They demonstrated that verbalizing is an essential part of this process (Sabel'nikov, 1982). Eventually, the verbal symbol sort of "triggers" a process that immediately yields automatic actions, or even yields knowledge of action results. In terms of van Parreren's theory, we can say that the symbols acquire *action valency*. Just as the typewriter's keyboard acquires valency for a typist, and eventually controls the typist's actions corresponding to the words he or she has in mind, symbols also acquire a valency for particular actions. Ultimately, symbols suggest possible significant actions. According to van Hiele, symbol-related action valencies are also very important in the mathematizing process because they orient the person toward relevant actions in a problem situation.

In Gal'perin's system, the role of language is particularly important for the formation of abbreviated mental actions. Not only is language a means for regulating an action in accordance with some predetermined culturally preferred form, but it is also a means of representing an action and making it into a mental object (cf. Sfard's discussion of the history of negative numbers, chap. 3, this volume). Actually, in Gal'perin's theory, verbal representation of an action is the creation of a symbol for an action, which makes it possible to think of this action and its results without concretely performing it! The symbol eventually anticipates and represents the result of the action (Gal'perin, 1976).

To this point, we have only discussed some important structural changes of actions during the learning process. However, actions can change also with respect to their meaning. As the problem of meaning is rather complex (see van Oers, 1996b, 1996c; Wertsch, 1985), I cannot deal with it at full length here. In my definition of the action, I pointed out that the meaning of an action is related to the goal of the problem-solving task. It must be clear by now that the meaning of an action is not absolute. It can change when it is embedded in another problem-solving activity. Take again the example of the counting action. The initial action of touching and replacing objects is familiar to the young child. When the child becomes involved in counting activities, this "old" action acquires new meaning: counting. Or an even more illustrative example is the following: The action of counting on may acquire the new meaning of subtracting (e.g., when trying to find the difference between two numbers). Or the action of subtracting can acquire a new meaning of dividing. In the development of mathematical thinking, the attribution of new meanings to "old" actions is a very important kind of learning (cf. Sfard, chap. 3, this volume). In the next section, I deal more extensively with the activity of meaning making.

Semiotic Activity

Obviously, the problem of meaning and sign was a very important element in Vygotsky's thinking. He acknowledged that passing on culture to the younger generation is essential for the development of humanity, but he also realized that cultural meanings cannot be immutably transmitted to children in a ready-made form. Meanings develop, and they develop, in particular, in the learner during his or her interaction with other people. The learner is a crucial factor in this process. With the help of other people, the child has to figure out the meaning of cultural elements. While doing so, the child makes his or her own meaning, which usually (but not always) comes close to the culturally shared meanings. Sometimes it diverts. In any event, it is always the learner's own meaning. It takes special communicative efforts to find out to what extent meanings are indeed shared. We cannot do much more than assume that meanings are shared to some (a large?) extent. Actually, we would do better to speak of "taken-as-shared meanings" (see Cobb et al., 1993). As long as people can effectively communicate, there is a sound basis for the assumption that meanings are shared.

I refer to the sociocognitive endeavor of (re)making meaning and symbolic means (such as signs, symbols, diagrams, schemes, models, actions) as being *semiotic activity*. Semiotic activity is defined as the (inter- or intra-)mental activity of creating meanings and signs, by reflecting on the interrelationships between (changes in) signs and (changes in) their corresponding meanings, and of adjusting signs and meanings accordingly. A few examples may illustrate this kind of activity. From an early age, children are involved in some form of semiotic activity. When a child is trying to figure out the meaning of a word, he or she is often carrying out a semiotic activity, as the following example illustrates:

Pupil:	Is that a blackbird, miss?
Teacher:	Do you think it is a blackbird?
Pupil:	It is black, but its bill is not orange!
Teacher:	Well, maybe it is not a blackbird, then?
Pupil:	The bill must be orange. It can't be a blackbird! What is it, miss?
Teacher:	I think it is a jackdaw.
Pupil:	Must be a jackdaw.

In this example the pupil apparently reflects on the meaning of the symbol (blackbird) and notices a discrepancy between the meaning of his symbol *blackbird* and what he actually sees. Consequently, he changes his symbol.

A second example shows how young children count the number of buttons:

Child 1:	We got seven buttons.
Child 2:	No, it's eight. If it is seven, you have to take one away.

Child 2 obviously acknowledges the strict relationship between symbol and meaning. If we change the symbol (seven instead of eight), we have to change the situation to which it refers.

One nice example was given by Karmiloff-Smith (1995, p. 31), reporting a short segment of conversation between Yara (4 years old) and her mother:

Yara:	What's that?
Mother:	A typewriter.
Yara:	No, you're the typewriter. That's the typewrite.

Obviously, for this child the form of the symbol (*typewriter*) suggests a particular meaning (probably that a typewri*ter* refers to a person). If one wants to refer to the machine (i.e., evoke another meaning), one must use another symbol (*typewrite*).

Because this selection of examples might erroneously suggest that only young children are involved in semiotic activities, a final example with older children (about 12 years old) is given here:

Pupil 1: I do not understand what *pressure* means.

Pupil 2: Well, the book says it is "Force per area measure."

Pupil 1: I can read that, but I do not really understand. Do I weigh less when I lay down on the floor, instead of stand upright?

Pupil 2: What?

Pupil 1: Yeah. When I lay down, I'll occupy more area, so the pressure will be less, isn't it?

Pupil 2: . . . ah . . . ah . . . I think you're confusing "weight" and "force" (ah . . . or weight and pressure?). Look, the formula says, "Force per area measure," not weight per area measure.

Pupil 1: What's the difference. Can you explain me that?

Pupil 2: Let me think. Let's take a look in our book. What is the formula for "weight"?

The conversation goes on, showing how these pupils are reflectively trying to find out the meaning of the symbols P (pressure), W (weight), and F (force). They seem to start from the assumption that *different symbols must mean different things*. Then, they try to develop an understanding by comparatively switching from symbols to their respective meanings and by reflecting on the relationships between symbol and meaning.

Additional examples examples of semiotic activity in children will be given in the last part of this chapter.

I now want to emphasize, in the same way as Werner and Kaplan (1963) do, that both the construction (improvement; differentiation) of meaning and the constructive improvement of the symbol are constitutive in semiotic activity. Meanings and signs are inextricably linked and develop concurrently.

Up to now, Vygotsky and the Vygotskians have paid most of their attention to the problem of meaning. However, the concept of meaning still needs further elaboration. The definition of *meaning*, as that which signs refer to, is not really satisfactory. Do signs really refer to objects (situations, actions, other signs)? Objects can only be referred to as long as they already make sense to us. Hence, *meaning* is already included in the concept of the object itself and cannot be explained by reference to an object. For example, the symbol R, which can be seen sometimes next to a road, refers to *restaurant*. But this does not say anything unless I already know what *restaurant* means. And to know what *restaurant* means is to know what can be done at such a place: that is, what kind of special activity is to be carried out there. So ultimately, this symbol refers to a cultural *activity* (or, more specifically, to a pattern of context-bound desirable *actions*).

By attributing the symbol *restaurant* (or *R*) to a situation, we *predicate* the situation as something special (to be distinguished from other situations, such as a church or a warehouse). Following Vygotsky (1987, chap. 7), I assume that this process of predicating is essential to all activities dealing with meaning. *A sign (or symbol) always involves a form of predication, suggesting actions by which the referred-to object obtains its meaning.* Or, to put it more precisely, the symbol represents how an object (in our example, the house next to the road) was transformed (as a result of some action) and thus acquired its meaning. The description of the transformed object is actually *an utterance that reveals something new about the object and distinguishes it from other objects.* Linguistically speaking, this is what is generally called a *predicate* (see Hörmann, 1978; Leech, 1981). Reflection on the relation between some symbol and what it represents (or better, *predicates*) is a fundamental objective of semiotic activity.

Epistemologically, this approach to symbols/signs and meaning unavoidably forces us to abandon the idea of direct reference to objects. Basically, we can only refer to (identification) actions that produce a meaning of some object. Direct reference to objects now is exposed as an illusion, caused by the rapidity of an abbreviated identification action that, so to speak, "immediately" yields recognition.

Following a similar line of reasoning, we now can understand that the symbol 5 does not refer to some ideal object (see Dörfler's discussion of "as-if attitude" as it relates to natural numbers, chap. 4, this volume). Basically, it predicates a situation on the basis of, for example, a counting action. The meaning of this symbol can be construed as the result of this action. But in other situations, this same symbol may refer to a result of an ordering action, a summation, a subtraction, an extraction of a root, and so on. In all of these cases, we attribute the symbol 5 as being a predicate that will tell something new about a situation and make it distinct from other situations. The real meaning of this 5 depends on the action (such as $2 + 3$, $10 - 5$, etc.) by which it is produced. The rapidity of the abbreviated identification falsely suggests that the symbol immediately refers to the situation. Reflectively figuring out what this symbol means (i.e., identifying from what kind of action it results) is also a form of semiotic activity.

In his analysis of the phenomenon of meaning development, Vygotsky (1934/1982, chap. 7, section 4) already focused on the process of *predication* (see also Wertsch, 1985). I make use of this concept of predication in my further account of the symbol and symbolizing as I elaborate the concept of semiotic activity.[9] Predication is the process of attaching extra quality to an object of common attention (such as a situation, topic or theme) and, by doing so, making it distinct from others. The predicate offers new information about a shared object of attention. When you are among people waiting together for a red traffic light, it makes no sense to say, "This is a traffic light," but if you say aloud to them "Yes," you will notice a difference. All of these people share the notion of the red traffic light, as well as the related command to wait. What is new and informative for their common concern is the remark, "The traffic light turned green, so we can walk." Vygotsky noticed that most of the time there is no need to explicitly express the topic of shared attention in a communication with others, let alone with ourselves. We can abbreviate the sentence by just uttering the predicate in a simple (or even simplified) form (such as by saying "yes" when the traffic light turns green). At the social level, predicating is possible (and usual) when people share (presuppose) some topic of common concern. At the individual level, predicating is a regular psychological process that makes much of our thinking and communicating implicit. It is the psychological basis for the abbreviation and idiosyncratization of thought (Vygotsky, 1934/1982, 1987), which, in turn, is the real psychological cause for the fact that so much can be put together in one simple symbol.[10]

Basically, when people negotiate meanings, they (are supposed to) share a topic of mutual interest. Consequently, the process of negotiation can be interpreted as a social process of developing a topic, by pooling and probing predicates and by selecting socially agreed-on predicates. In other words, it is a struggle for shared meaning, a process of cooperatively figuring out what can be said validly about this topic.

Vygotskian scholars have not given as much attention to the sign as to the phenomenon of meaning. Sinha (1988) pointed out that most theories of meaning development (including Vygotskian theory) need to be supplemented by a theory of "materiality of representation."

As made clear by modern semiotic theories, signs differ in character. As Peirce pointed out, we can differentiate between signs by their functioning. In his opinion, we should make a distinction between *iconic signs*

---

[9]It is necessary to keep in mind that the term *predication* is used here in the psychological sense (as Vygotsky uses it), referring to the activity of constructing predicates, and relating judgments (see Hörmann, 1978). This is different from the linguistic (logical) use of the word, referring to "a common category shared by propositions, questions, commands, etc." (Leech, 1981, p. 124).

[10]Etymologically, the original meaning of symbol is the notion of "putting together" (because *symbol* derives from the Greek *sum-ballein* or "bring together," "mix," or also "combine," "conclude").

(referring to a referent on the basis of a perceptual similarity between sign and referent: $\Delta \rightarrow$ (triangle), *indexical signs* (referring to a referent on the basis of a real connection between sign and referent: smoke $\rightarrow$ _ fire), and *symbols* (referring to a referent on the basis of a conventional relationship between sign and referent: $\times \rightarrow$ multiplication).

However, Peirce's theory is a nondevelopmental theory of signs, indicating that material or graphic objects may fulfill their reference function in different ways. The same is true for a variety of other symbol classification systems (see also Pimm, 1987, p. 140ff). In their seminal work on symbol formation, Werner and Kaplan (1963) elaborated a theory about the ontogenetic development of symbolic activity. According to this theory, *symbolizing* is a "dynamic schematizing activity" (p. 17ff) in which symbolic vehicles are intentionally constructed and reconstructed in order to represent a given object. Through these vehicles, *symbolizing* enters directly into the construction of *cognitive objects*, determining how events are organized and what they mean (Werner & Kaplan, 1963, p. 15).

It is important to note that for Werner and Kaplan symbolizing is an evolving activity. In an individual's ontogeny, the first symbols are constructed on the basis of similarity to some referent. In the development of the activity of symbol formation during ontogeny, the symbols become emancipated from perceptual similarity. They refer to something else on the basis of inner theoretical relationships between symbol and referent. The necessity of a perceptual similarity now has disappeared. In this process, language plays a crucial role as a resource and a medium, contributing to development and emancipation of the symbols, and allowing a growing dissimilarity between the form of the referent and the form of the vehicle. Language provides the construction elements for new symbolic forms, such as word combinations, sentences, propositions, texts, and metaphors (see Pimm, 1987; Sfard, 1994, about the importance of metaphors as productive symbols in mathematical thinking!). An important tenet in these approaches is that symbols can never be meaningless; symbols always have meaning (although the basis for the association between symbol and meaning might be different, according to the developmental status of the subject). Development of symbolic activity always includes the change of both the symbol and the meaning.

In an earlier analysis of the symbol and semiotic activity, I ascribed three important functions to symbols (see van Oers, 1996b):

- Symbols refer to a particular group of actions.
- Symbols replace actions.
- Symbols provide the means for negotiation of meaning (a communicative function).

My present analysis still endorses this view, but adds a new dimension by explicitly relating meaning and action, and by emphasizing the predicative nature of symbols. According to the already described view of meaning and sign, now we can also conceive of words and word combinations (sentences, utterances, texts) as symbols referring to meaning: that is, as providing predicates that, presumably, can be attributed to topics of conversation. The symbolically represented predicate actually indicates how the object (topic) has changed into a new, distinct form, which more clearly indicates what I intend to say about the topic that I presupposedly share with my interlocutors. By taking these predicates as new objects for mental actions, we perform what Peirce called a "hypostatic abstraction" (see Parmentier, 1987, p. 30). This modified object then becomes a new symbol (cf. the Gravemeijer et al. discussion of chains of signification, chap. 7, this volume), suggesting new possible actions and providing a starting point for further development of the topic (the meaning involved). The comparison of symbolically represented predicates is the basic mechanism of dialogue and negotiation of meaning (see Markovà & Foppa, 1990).

However, it is not only purely linguistic means that function as symbols. There is another category of symbols that fulfills a predicative function, but with the help of perceptive structuring (such as diagrams, schemes or models). In the creative production of scientific knowledge, these symbolic devices remain important. In semiotic activity, the examination of the adequacy of symbols with respect to their referents, and the examination of meaning structures and the adjustments of symbols to these structures, are very important.

In the next section I illustrate how my view on semiotic activity and learning can contribute to the active promotion of symbolizing in the field of mathematics.

ASPECTS OF SYMBOLIZING
IN THE MATHEMATICAL DOMAIN

As pointed out in the preceding sections, semiotic activity is conceived of here as a general and fundamental activity of dealing with sign–meaning relationships. As such, it is broader than simply symbol use (or "sign-using activity" as Vygotsky, 1978, p. 46, would call it). Semiotic activity encompasses both the formation and modification of symbols and the (re)construction of meaning.

From the psychological point of view described earlier, mathematical activity (mathematizing) can be conceived of as a special type of semiotic activity. Reasoning from his dynamic conception of mathematizing, Freudenthal (1991), in my opinion, advocated a similar view when he wrote that mathematics is basically "an activity of discovering and organizing in *an interplay of content and form*" (p. 15; italics added). On the basis of the already described action-psychological theory of symbolizing, I contend here that symbols used in mathematics (i.e., *mathematical forms*) are also instruments for attributing meaning (new content) to presupposed mathematical objects (given and presupposed mathematical content). They suggest mathematical actions that can be performed in a given situation. Mathematizing can now be described, alternatively, as an activity of reflecting on the reflexive relationship of the new content (as suggested by the symbol used) and the old content (mathematical object and problem situation). Picture the somewhat boring situation of seven birds sitting on a roof, and two coming to join them. How many birds are there eventually on the roof? The operator-symbol + predicates the situation by suggesting that we have to add (rather than subtract, multiply, or whatever) to find the answer. However, adding in itself is not what makes this event an example of mathematizing. Mathematizing here consists of the reflection on the interrelationship between the situation, the mathematical objects given, and the actions, as well as on the conscious judgment that adding is adequate here.

Although mathematical symbols refer (abbreviatedly) to mathematically meaningful actions, they also may be called *reifications* of mathematical meanings associated with a term (compare again Sfard's notion of reification). The availability of such terms is necessary for both horizontal mathematizing (symbolizing situations in mathematical terms) and vertical mathematizing (symbolizing parts of mathematical structures and attributing new meanings, "predicates," to them). For further background information, see, for instance, Ernest (1991, pp. 75–79).

Mathematizing as a special form of semiotic activity is a complex process, consisting of many partial processes involved in meaning construction and symbol construction. Here, I cannot deal with mathematical semiotic activity in its entire complexity. I confine myself to the appropriation of mathematical symbols as means for mathematical symbolizing. I try to show how the construction of meaning can be conceived of with regard to those symbols. In this context, I furthermore give an account of the immediacy of symbol recognition as one important aspect of all complex cognitive functioning. However, it is not enough to master symbols and their meaning. It is equally important to be able to judge when a symbol can be appropriately used. Finally, in the wake of a Vygotskian approach to education, I also have to take developmental conditions into account as a factor in the improvement of mathematical thinking and symbolizing. As a result of this analysis, some conclusions can be drawn about the improvement of mathematical symbolizing through developmental education. I then dwell briefly on the issue of mathematics-inducing practices based on my own research in early education.

The Appropriation of Symbols and Their Meaning

A general theoretical description of the process of appropriation can be found in the theory of Gal'perin. Empirical investigations that he and his colleagues conducted show that the representation of an action and its result, in terms of symbols or verbal descriptions, is a very important stage in a learning process. This is not just a matter of coding the action. Above all, it provides a means for thinking of the action's result without having to actually perform that action.

The following example may help illustrate what might be taking place. Imagine a situation involving a collection of objects. Someone asks, "How many things are there?" A 3-year-old child starts counting, "One-two-three-four-five," although the questioner (let's say an adult) has already concluded that the number is five. (Maybe this is not the conclusion that the child will draw, so the adult will have to explain this to the child.) The adult continues by describing the situation as follows: "This is a lot of things and we would like to know how many of them are there. You counted 'one-two-three-four-five' and we then found out that taken to-gether" (the adult shows this "take-together action" by making a circling gesture around the assortment), "there are five" (writes down the symbol or shows a card: 5). By doing so, the child and the adult have transformed the amorphous collection of objects into a quantity. The "take-together action" is important to show the cardinal aspect of the counting action.

In terms of my present view on symbol, I can now analyze the rather ordinary event just described as follows. Psychologically, we can assume that the presence of the collection of objects, and even the act of counting, were evident for both the child and the adult. Actually, this was the topic they were talking about. The statement of the result (*it is five*) was new to the situation. By saying (and showing the symbol) *five*, the situation and the action were predicated. In fact, this predicate summarized the entire event. By systematically repeating this (or similar) events, we can eventually obtain the situation that this symbol (5) represents the *result of an abbreviated form of the counting action*. This is, then, the real meaning of this symbol thus far. Insight into the action meanings of the number symbol is an important basis for the further development of arithmetical and mathematical activity. It is probably impossible without the help of language. Indeed, Hitch, Cundick, Haughey, Pugh, and Wright (1987) found some evidence for the involvement of inner speech in the development of counting. As a result of this symbolization of the counting action, numeral use can become a flexible routine in more complex activities.

Such a strategy of abbreviating the counting action into a symbolized result was successfully implemented in Davydov's mathematics program for the early grades of a Russian primary school (see, among others, Davydov, 1957; Leusina, 1977). It also formed the basis of Davydov's strategy for the teaching of addition and subtraction (see a summary of this strategy in Gravemeijer, 1994). Davydov and Andronov (1979) experimentally could confirm the relevance of this strategy. They demonstrated experimentally that both the "take-together action" and the corresponding word/symbol were essential for the development of the abbreviated action of counting and adding.

In a recent study, Salmina (1995) summarized her research on mathematics teaching in primary school. She also emphasized the importance of the introduction of adequate symbols to represent mathematical actions and their results. Moreover, she stressed the importance of semiotic exploratory activity of children as one of the foundations of mathematical thinking. Pupils should be given the opportunity to experiment with symbols and meanings, and invent and explore their own forms of symbolization (by way of schemes, drawing, and diagrams) before they are led to the generally accepted mathematical symbols.

The educational importance of such action-suggesting symbols, such as models and schemes, has been demonstrated in several investigations (e.g., Talyzina, 1995). As a particularly interesting example, I would like to comment on symbolic representations as invented by the Dutch group of mathematics educators from the Freudenthal Institute. Gravemeijer (1994) gave many examples of such symbolizations. One of them is the so-called "empty number line" (a number line on which students initially mark only the numbers they need for their calculations), such as the one in Fig. 5.4 for calculating 65 − 38. According to Gravemeijer (1994, pp. 125–126), initial studies, involving this "empty number line" as a symbolic instrument of mathematical problem solving, have been encouraging. This is what we would have expected, on the basis of our symbol theory, because this diagram is indeed suggestive with respect to what actions to perform. With the help of this number line, the intermediate steps between 38 and 65 can be filled out in a convenient way to find the difference. In addition, this model articulates the result of the action and, most importantly for the abbreviation of the "number-line-based actions," allows the *anticipation* of future results of (intermediate) steps. The structure of the line can articulate some of the "footholds" of the steps to be carried out (marking 40 and 60). Thus, it supports the mental representation of the numbers to be added subsequentially (2, 20, 5). As experimentally shown by Sabel'nikov (1982), the exhortation to accomplish anticipatory mental actions definitely promotes and supports the abbre-

38   65

FIG. 5.4. An empty number line for calculating 65 − 38.

viation of an action. This anticipation of future action results is interpretable as a "predication" of the next step in the sequence of mental actions. This is impossible without the use of symbols.

What makes this model even more important as a symbolic device was beautifully illustrated by Gravemeijer when he demonstrated how this line can also help to show different strategies for action in an attempt to find the difference between 65 and 38. Figure 5.5 shows an illustration taken from Gravemeijer (1994, p. 121) that needs no further comment:

For subtraction (e.g. 65 – 38) two different approaches emerge (fig. 4.2a and b). One approach is to take away 38 from 65 (fig. 4.2a).

figure 4.2a: solving 65 – 38 as take away 38

A second approach is to compare 38 and 65, and then establish the difference (fig. 4.2b).

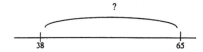

figure 4.2b: solving 65 – 38 by taking the difference between 38 and 65

The two approaches may be worked out in several different ways (fig. 4.2c).

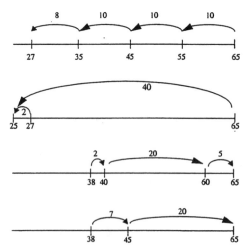

figure 4.2c: various strategies for solving 65 – 38

FIG. 5.5. Example of the empty number line from Gravemeijer (1994, p. 458). Reprinted with permission from the *Journal for Research in Mathematics Education.* Copyright © 1994 by the National Council of Teachers of Mathematics. All rights reserved.

As most of our cognitive results can be achieved in more than one way (by different actions), a symbol seldom represents just one action. This is an important consequence of our symbol theory. The appropriation of mathematical symbols should always include the appropriation of the multiplicity of meanings. However, traditionally, mathematical symbols (like number symbols, or =, etc.) are often (and mistakenly) introduced as referring to just one exactly described meaning. This restricts the meaning of the symbol and leads to a variety of problems, as has often been shown with respect to the interpretation of number symbols. Children who have learned the meaning of such symbols on the basis of counting often only see the ordinal aspect of this symbol. Not unexpectedly, they often appear to have difficulty with recognizing the cardinal aspect of it. Starting with another (e.g., cardinality-oriented) approach to number and its symbolization leads to another initial symbol content and to other problems as well (see Brissiaud, 1989). Recent discussions of the number concept show that there are different pathways to number (Bideau, Meljac, & Fischer, 1992). Mathematics education should clarify the multiplicity of meanings related to symbols by revealing the diversity of underpinning actions. Numerals should be demonstrated and explained to children as being symbols for a multiplicity of actions (such as for counting, adding, subtracting, etc.).

Returning to the empty number line, it is clear that this line, if used adequately by the teacher, can facilitate the discovery of the multiplicity of meaning, as well as support the abbreviation of addition and subtraction actions. In my opinion, this explains the success of this mediational means in the educational process. However, there is still one problem that I must address here. How do students know when this symbolic device is useful? How can they identify the situations in which this line is fruitfully applicable? I deal with such questions in the next subsection.

The Appropriateness of Symbols

It is not enough that pupils can use symbols and complex symbolic representations correctly. They should also be able to judge which symbols are relevant for a given problem situation. This brings us back to the kind of problems that we discussed earlier, referring to Bauersfeld (1995): namely, that most of the time it is not evident how to represent a situation in symbolic terms. Five birds sitting on a wire and three flying in the air can be represented as $5 + 3$, $x - 3 = 5$, or $5 - 3$ (among others), depending on what exactly we want to know, so the goal and the meaning of the situation must be clear. The possible representations must be evaluated by considering the meaning of the situation and by the objective of the original query. And even then it will not be obvious whether different representations are false or inadequate. If we suppose that the flying birds are flying away and we want to know how many birds there were on the wire in the first place, the situation could be identified as a counting situation (leading to a counting action of all the birds in the picture) or a calculation situation (leading to such representations as $x - 3 = 5$, or 5 + 3). In order to find out, the children must be able to comprehend the situation (or the text describing the situation and the goal), as well as be able to compare and assess different representations and their anticipated results.

This activity of reflecting on the relationship between a symbolic representation and the situation it refers to is a form of semiotic activity that is basic to all (horizontal) mathematizing. It has been revealed frequently that pupils have problems with comprehending a written assignment of a mathematical task. In a recent study, Desforges and Bristow (1994) found that most primary school children had problems attributing significant meaning to a text intended to give a hint on how to mathematize the task appropriately. The authors' conclusion that it might be better for children to read and discuss a mathematics question in the classroom is expressed by their statement, "It would seem that children need to be taught to read in mathematics" (Desforges & Bristow, 1994, p. 267).

Assessing the appropriateness of symbolic representations to the situation given is a result of a semiotic activity, in which different perspectives on the situation are symbolically represented and compared. As different perspectives are involved, the activity is essentially a social activity, even when someone is carrying out this activity mentally on his or her own (Kucinskij, 1983). The best way to learn this semiotic activity is through discursive means, examining and discussing different representations and their consequences for the achievement of the objective (cf. Dörfler, chap. 4, this volume; Sfard, chap. 3, this volume). Symbolic representations and models not only schematically represent the (supposedly) basic structure of the situation, but also regulate the discussion by focusing the attention of the participants on relevant and shared topics (see, e.g., Rubtsov, 1991). Again, symbols with their predicating capacity are indispensable.

Indeed, the social nature of the development of mathematical thinking is now generally accepted in modern theories of mathematics education. However, these theories, at best, often only suggest strategies for the organization of the social environment. There is also often an implicit assumption concerning the prerequisite abilities of the pupils for accomplishing this sociosemiotic activity. I tend to question the tenability of this assumption. From an early age, young children are already engaged in sociosemiotic activities. If semiotic activity is a fundamental precondition for meaningful symbolizing (and mathematizing), the improvement of this activity, by a developmental teaching approach that is introduced at an early age, might be an important contribution to the improvement of mathematics education. I will turn to this question in the next subsection.

The Development of Semiotic Activity

Because I interpret mathematical activity as a special form of semiotic activity, it is my assumption that mathematical activity emerges from semiotic activity in early-childhood play activities. Further, I assume that the development of mathematical thinking can be promoted and improved, therefore, by involving young children in sociosemiotic activities that are related to different kinds of symbolic representations involving reality or action patterns. The movement for improving mathematics education, then, may profit from a growing insight into the emergence of semiotic activity during children's development.

One of the fundamental methodological starting points for Vygotsky is that the study of human behavior should be conceived of primarily as the study of the *development* of behavior. Following this line of reasoning, I would say that we can only obtain deep insight into (mathematical) semiotic activity by *studying the development of semiotic activity.* Consequently, attempts to improve education should not be limited to merely optimizing the current organization of activities, but should also attempt to improve the development of these activities. This is a basic tenet of any Vygotskian approach to education. It is the fundamental aim of developmental teaching.

According to Vygotsky, semiotic activity (or "sign-using activity," as he calls it) is not a naturally given quality, but is a result of education. However, this "sign-using activity in children is neither simply invented nor passed down by adults" (Vygotsky, 1978, p. 46). Semiotic activity gradually evolves within the interaction between adults and children in the context of their shared sociocultural activities. As a developmentally new quality, this semiotic activity gains its psychological significance from its role in the overall functioning of the organism. By a series of transformations, the initially embedded semiotic actions eventually become differentiated from the original activity and can evolve into a more or less independent and conscious form of cognitive activity (cf. the Gravemeijer et al. discussion of the shift from *model of* to *model for*, chap. 7, this volume). This general description of the development of semiotic activity emerging from a more complex, miscellaneous practice is consistent with Werner's orthogenetic principle in development (see Werner & Kaplan, 1963).

From an early moment in development, children are drawn into activities in which meaning making and the dealing with (variances of) meanings prevail. For young children, these semiotic actions are still implicit in their current play activities. Basically, these semiotic actions can be seen as the embryonic states (to use a Vygotskian metaphor) of the later (discipline-bound) semiotic activities. By participating in these culturally determined play activities (and imitating adult activities—in the Vygotskian sense!), children and adults create a zone of proximal development. In such activities, the semiotic actions can be made explicit and can be learned, if adequately dealt with by the adult.

Many studies have already tried to reveal some of the details of young children's ways of dealing with meaning and representations. In their studies of the play-activities of young children (4 to 7 years old), Zaporožec and especially Venger have already shown that schematic representations (diagrams, drawings) can play a determining role in the child's transition from manipulative and role play to the stage of explicit and conscious learning activity (in the sense of Davydov, 1988). The study of semiotic activity in young children is intrinsically related to the construction and use of such iconic representations by young children. More in-depth studies must reveal whether and how these children can deal with iconic representations as symbolic representations of a part of their reality, whether they are able to reflect at all on the relationship between a representation and its referents, how a transition to more abstract symbolic representations takes place, and so on. (The Gravemeijer et al. investigation of the evolution of classroom practices in an elementary school classroom addresses this issue in chap. 7, this volume.) Although we still have a long way to go to achieve a detailed and full-scale picture of this developmental process, a few interesting findings can already be reported concerning this issue. In my opinion, these findings are also of relevance for the improvement of children's mathematical thinking.

In a long-term research program, Venger showed that iconic representations can indeed be inserted into play activities of young children during their regular activities at school (by schematizing stories, musical scores, making maps, and the like). Venger's empirical data indicate that these children, indeed, profit from this help with schematizing, as could be concluded from their relatively easy transition to learning activity in a later stage of their school career (Venger, 1986).

Several investigators have studied the semiotic activity in young children by interviewing and observing them during specially constructed tasks, in which the children's attention is drawn to the meaning of things and to the meaning of special signs referring to these things (among others, Glotova, 1990; Salmina, 1988; Sapogova, 1992, 1993). Most of the children in these investigations could make a distinction between an object and its corresponding symbol, and had some insight into the relationship between modifications of the symbols and changes in the situation referred to. It was important for these children that the symbols used are suggestive (i.e., that the symbols provide perceptual cues indicating the kind of action to be performed—see Sapogova).

In her study with 6- and 7-year-old children, Sapogova (1993) was able to establish evidence for the relationship between the ability to deal with simple symbolic representations (including the ability to reflect on the symbol–referent relationship) and the ability to experiment on a mental level with models and changes of models. (Sapogova called this mental experimenting a "thought experiment.") This finding is especially significant for a theory on the development of mathematical thinking because mental experimenting is an important element in mathematizing activity.

In our own studies, we could confirm these results in classroom settings. In one of these studies (see van Oers, 1994), we observed small groups of children in a classroom play activity during which the teacher had encouraged them to carry out a representational activity (making a diagram of the railway track they had built). We found that reflection on the correspondence between the diagram and the railway track was possible for the children. Moreover, it turned out that predicating was a vital link in this process. By predicating parts of the drawing ("this is a bridge"), they could verify whether there was really a bridge at a particular location on the real track.

Several other conditions that fostered the appearance of semiotic activity were revealed as well. One is that for the promotion and maintenance of semiotic activity, the semiotic actions must be meaningful for the children (e.g., the actions must have a clear communicative function). Furthermore, there must be a semiotically more capable person ("a participating semiotician," such as an adult or older child) involved in the children's activity, who promotes semiotic actions when they are relevant and who is in charge of the semiotic actions that the children cannot perform (independently) yet (see van Oers, 1995, 1997). In all of our studies, we emphasized the importance of play activity for the development of children of this age (following Elkonin's 1972 theory of development). Therefore, it was a permanently essential requirement for us that the attention for semiotic activity aspects did not disturb (and deteriorate) the quality of the play. Our research shows that focusing on the semiotic aspects of play does not disrupt the play activity if it can be integrated into the play in a functional way.

All of these studies converge, leading to the conclusion that although the children do not all perform equally well, semiotic activity is clearly within the range of these children's abilities. This provides a solid basis for the further study of early semiotic activity. In another study (van Oers, 1996a), we wanted to find out what mathematics-like actions occur in the context of a role play, and we wanted to see if these actions could be dealt with from our psychosemiotic point of view. The teachers we worked with constructed a shoe shop in a corner of the school where the children (ages 4 to 8 years old and in groups varying in number from four to nine children) could play, pretending they were in a shoe shop. The teacher was always a participant in the play activity. Most of the time she was a customer. But sometimes she was a shoe supplier, or sometimes she simply organized actions from a metalevel perspective (talking with children about their actions, asking questions, introducing problems, suggesting solutions, answering the children's questions, etc.). One of the most important roles of the teacher, from the investigator's point of view, was that of being the participating "semiotician." Moreover, the teacher gave careful attention to the quality of the play (making sure that semiotic interventions did not disturb its quality).

Eight sessions of the play activities of groups of children were video-taped for later analysis. It turned out that even in the youngest groups (A, B, C, and D in Table 5.1) many mathematics-like actions occurred (or

TABLE 5.1
Number of Teaching Opportunities in Each Session

Type of Opportunity for Groups	A	B	C	D	Total
Classification	1[a]	1[d]	—	2	
Seriation	—	—	—	—	
Conservation	—	—	—	—	
Counting	—	2	1	1	
One-to-one correspondence	2[b]	1[e]	—	—	
Measuring	14	1	1	4	
Estimating	1	—	—	—	
Solving number problems	—	—	—	1	
Simple arithmetic	—	1	—	—	
Quantitative concepts	11[c]	1	—	3	
Number words	6	—	1	1	
Space–time orientations	3	—	—	1	
Schematizing/notations	—	1[f]	2[g]	2	
Dealing with dimensions	4	—	—	—	
Dealing with money	—	3	1	—	
Number of events	42	11	6	15	74
Total duration of session	27 min	55 min	6 min	18 min	106 min

[a]This was an extended activity for more than 5 min in which the children sorted shoes according to color, size, and type. At times, even multiple classification was involved.

[b]Partly embedded in the classification task, when the children were looking for matching shoes (shoes that go together; shoes that are one pair); one-to-one corresponding also occurred when the children had to find a box for a pair of shoes or when they had to find the top that fit each box.

[c]Concepts such as more, less, the same, a pair, nothing, a lot, how much, and measure.

[d]Extended activity of more than 3 min in which the children sorted out mama shoes, papa shoes, child shoes, and baby shoes.

[e]Looking for a shoe that matched the one given/found.

[f]Symbolic reference (with letters) to different classes of shoes.

[g]Children made diagrams representing the piles of shoes, such as in a histogram or a bar graph.

actions that are generally considered to be important for the development of the number concept in children) without special encouragement from the teacher. The nature of the play situation was such that many of these actions occurred simultaneously. As a result, it was impossible for the teacher to deal with them on every occurrence. Sometimes the actions just happened. They could be registered at the time the tape was analyzed, but nothing could be done with them in the classroom setting. These events give some indication of the opportunities for teaching during a pretend (role) play activity. Table 5.1 gives a summary of the teaching opportunities in each session.

One event is described here in more detail. It shows how the teacher led the children into a semiotic activity requiring some kind of notation to be invented in order to refer to different categories of shoes. At first we see how children try to use perceptual indicators in their notational system to identify the shoes. Later, the children realize that these similarity notations are not very effective, so they start using additional symbols to indicate the shoes in the boxes. Throughout, a fundamental criterion for the children's actions and decisions was the experienced adequacy of the symbolic representation with respect to the intended meaning.

The setting started as an activity of establishing the shoe shop together. The teacher only provided the basic materials and paraphernalia (real shoes, boxes, a counter, a mirror, shoe advertisements, money, a shoe-measuring mat, a block note, an abacus, etc.). When the children started their play activity, there was a jumbled pile of shoes and a pile of boxes. The children first put most of the shoes in the boxes and then put them on the shelves of a rack. The teacher started questioning. (Notice that the children and teacher are constantly attributing and testing predicates within the situation at hand).[11] The activity proceeded as follows (T = teacher; p = pupil):

    (1) T: If someone wants to buy a shoe, and he wants a sandal, how can we quickly find the shoes we need?

    (2) P: Take all the shoes, look for it.

    (3) T: Well, that's a lot of work, isn't it?

---

[11]The translation of the protocol is somewhat stylized and abbreviated, in order to make it not too repetitious with respect to the children's utterances. Some utterances of the children could be understood only from the situation and their accompanying gestures and such. Literal translation would result in incomprehensible utterances. I record these utterances here in a somewhat improved version, but, of course, I preserve their meaning. Moreover, some of the children's remarks, interjections, half-completed or crumbled sentences, and so on, turn out to be intranslatable in a literal way, which would obscure their meaning. However, my adaptations of the children's utterances may have slightly affected the original flavor of the children's conversations.

[The pupils start looking in the boxes for a sandal.]

(4) P: Here it is!

(5) T: That's not my size.

(6) P: No, . . .

(7) T: Do you really have to check all the boxes?

[In the meantime the children keep looking for the desired shoe by opening boxes and looking into them.]

(8) T: This is a problem. How do they do it in a real shoe shop? Are there boxes in the racks?

(9) P: No, they put the shoes on the shelves.

(10) T: Yes, that's a good idea, then you can see immediately what kind of shoe it is.

[The children endorse the idea and start telling personal experiences.]

(11) T: Let's do it.

In the first phase of this activity (lines 1–11), the pupils and teacher are collaboratively interpreting the situation. The process can be characterized as a continuous chain of predications. In line 1 the teacher adds a predicate that actually defines the activity as a buying situation. This situation definition immediately generates a problem of finding the right shoe. Notice that evaluating the situation as a problem (1 and 8) actually is a predication, as well, suggesting that it requires hard thinking. No easy solution will be found (contrary to what one might think!). In order to solve this problem, one pupil adds another predicate (2), suggesting a special category of actions to be performed. However, the teacher encourages the pupils to reflect on the adequacy of this approach and this way of predicating the situation (7). Another predicate develops when a pupil says, "Put the shoes on the shelves" (9).

[Children start placing shoes on top of their boxes on the shelves of the rack until one child discovers a problem.]

(12) P: But how do we do it with the boxes at the bottom, then?

(13) T: Yes, what are we going to do with the shoes at the bottom?

(14) P: You can never reach them. . . .

(15) T: How about putting just one shoe on the shelf and leaving the other shoe in the box over here?

(16) P: Yes!

[The pupils immediately get to this work.]

(17) T: Now everyone who comes into our shop can see what shoes we have.

[The pupils are working while the teacher walks around.]

(18) T: Roy, which box matches with this shoe?

(19) P: This one.

(20) T: No, that one is gray. It is not the same.

[The pupil starts looking for the right shoe. The teacher continues asking children for shoes that go together. The pupils are very busy putting shoes on the shelves.] . . .

(21) T: Well, I think there is a problem here again. If someone wants to buy this shoe [teacher points to one shoe in the rack], how are we gonna find the other one?

[The pupils start opening the boxes and look for the matching shoe.]

(22) T: That's a lot of work! Is there no other way we can find to do this more quickly, finding the right shoe? We must be sure that we find the right shoe easily.

(23) P: We must leave the tops off the boxes!

Having contrived the situation definition as a "matching-shoe-finding situation," the children suggest different actions to solve this problem. In their matching activity, the children use means of showing or use verbal descriptions (e.g., 19, 20). Most of them are engaged in private actions, communicating the results to the teacher. The teacher again adds a new quality to the situation. She makes it a *public situation* (21: If someone wants to buy . . . [not just you or me] . . .). In doing so, she introduces *certainty*[12] as a new (public) norm. She hereby predicates the situation as one that requires certainty. With these predications the teacher evokes new communicative and reflective actions. As a result the pupils begin making public symbols.

(24) T: Yes, but then it is difficult to make piles. Maybe it is a good idea to make something on the outside of the box so that you can recognize what's inside?

(25) Ps: Yes, I know! [One pupil starts looking for a pencil or something to write with.] I know!

(26) T: Tell me what you are looking for.

(27) P: We're gonna put letters on them.

(28) T: Which letters?

---

[12]This requirement of *certainty* was assumed to be a basic condition for the beginning of mathematizing activity (see Freudenthal, 1991, p. 1). We had agreed with the teacher in advance that this quest for certainty would be introduced whenever possible and relevant. We assumed that this would encourage reflection on solutions and symbols (see lines 22, 34, 38). See van Oers (1996a).

The pupil points to numbers on a number table.

(29) T: Maybe we can make a drawing of the shoe in the box, to be sure we recognize them.

[The pupils start making labels to attach to the boxes.]

(30) T: [Asking children] Which shoe are you drawing? And you?

[One pupil shows his label with a drawing of a shoe on it.]

(31) P: Look, miss, this is for that shoe.

(32) T: Ah, you also put letters on it? Which shoe does it match to?

[The pupil points to a shoe.]

(33) T: But that one is already being done by Roy! You better take another one.

[All pupils are very busy making labels for a long time (about 5 minutes).]

(34) T: Are you doing this shoe? [The teacher clearly shows that she is not certain about that.] What can we add to it? What kind of shoes do we have?

(35) Ps: Women's shoes, boys' shoes, girls' shoes, gentlemen's shoes, . . .

[Roy shows a label he made.]

(36) T: What did you write on it?

(37) P: ??

(38) T: You cannot read it yourself? Do you think that you can find again which shoe is in which box? [The teacher is again prompting for certainty!]

(39) P: Yes.

(40) T: Well, then stick it onto your box.

The pupils are inventing symbols to refer to individual pairs of shoes (31–32), but later also to refer to categories of shoes (35). Predicating the situation as one that requires certainty, the teacher prompts reflection on the adequacy of the symbols for reference to shoes (38). By introducing categories, the teacher suggests a new way of predicating the shoes. This is not just a shoe. It is a baby shoe, a father shoe, and so on.

[The pupils are very busy making labels. They show them to the teacher. Some children show the following labels:]

(41) R D T I or R A I D

(42) Ps: What does it say?

(43) T: Raid. [Teacher reads: (raid)]

(44) T: Let's make a pile over here. One shoe in the rack, the other one in a box over there.

[The children are busy making labels with letters on them. The letters are supposed to suggest useful predications!]

(45) T: Maybe not everyone is able to read it. You can also make a drawing of the shoes.

(46) P: What does it say, Miss? [Pupil shows her label with letters MAAR.]

(47) T: It says, "Maar."

(48) P: [Repeats.] Mmmaar . . . these are mmmama-shoes.

(49) T: What a good idea of you to put an "M" on it for mama shoes! Do you think we could do that for all the mama shoes? Do you think you could do that, too? [To another pupil.]

(50) P: No.

(51) T: Well, if you cannot write the letter, you may stamp it. [Teacher offers a box with stamping materials.]

[The pupils take over this idea immediately and start making labels with stamped letter combinations, such as I D P B P B or R I T m.]

(52) T: If you have papa shoes, which letter will you put on it, then?

(53) Ps: P.

[The pupils are involved in the activity of making labels with the correct letter on each. After a while they start to stamp whole words (mama, papa, baby) on the label, sometimes asking the teacher first how to write the word. The scene ends with making piles of marked boxes that are sorted according to the symbols of the different categories they already had distinguished as mama shoes, papa shoes, children shoes, and baby shoes. After setting up these piles, the children start playing shoe shop.]

At first we see that the pupils are making mixed labels, using shoe drawings with arbitrary letters (41). But this does not seem very satisfactory (41–45). Then some pupils start transforming their symbols in accordance with the meaning they want to convey: M for mama shoes (46–53). Now the pupils can start predicating their shoes in an abbreviated form, saying, this is an M. They could use this form in their communications, as well as in their reflections on the adequacy of the use of symbols for particular shoes. This reflection on symbols and meaning, changing symbols, and adapting meanings is a genuine form of what we call semiotic activity.

Still later, with encouragement from the teacher, the children start a counting activity, using the piles of shoes. The children start counting the number of boxes in each pile. They make a drawing of each pile, matching the number of boxes in the representation and in the piles. The children are constantly switching between reality and the representation, matching both to each other. Actually, the children are reinventing the histogram. The drawing of a pile symbolized for the children a way of ordering the collection of shoes, as to category and number.

In the preceding example, we demonstrated how young children (5 or or 6 years old) were induced to participate in a mathematizing semiotic activity that was embedded in their pretend play. Here we clearly see how the shoe-shop activity was a mathematics-producing practice, not only because of the mathematics-like actions that emerged, but, more importantly, because of the way this community (pupils and teacher) acted in the quest for certainty with respect to the meaning of the symbols.

One additional remark might be in order here to further clarify the situation. It is clear that the children needed some assistance in order to carry out this semiotic activity. In this situation, the teacher had an important role to play. In some of the other role-playing activities, some older children (7-year-olds) were also involved. They could give assistance to the younger children, when the latter encountered problems of counting, of classifying, or involving money, and so on. This way of casting initial forms of sociosemiotic activity acknowledges the distributed character of semiotic activity. Presumably, in due time each pupil can learn to be in charge of a larger part of the semiotic activity.

These kinds of classroom activities (leading to situated mathematics, for example) are typical in the school in which we conducted this investigation. The results of this approach in the long run still are to be assessed. Our investigations make clear that it is possible to involve young children in semiotic activity and help them improve their ability to reflect on sign–meaning relationships, and to improve the signs (symbols) in order to make them more adequate for the intended meaning.

In another case study with a girl almost 4 years old (see van Oers, 1997), I found that she wanted to convey her meanings to another person very eagerly as she made drawings. When the girl felt that her meaning was not being properly communicated by her drawing, she started to add verbal comments (eventually telling a whole story) to supplement her drawing. By doing so (thus actually reconstructing her initial complex symbol), she constructed a new symbol that she supposed would be more adequate with respect to her intentions. In my interpretation, this provides a first glimpse of the transition from iconic signs to more abstract symbols. The children in the shoe shop were actually doing the same. They reconstructed symbols according to their intentions, gradually shifting to more abstract symbolizations.

I presume that the acquisition of some proficiency in such semiotic activity is a fertile basis for the meaningful appropriation of mathematical symbols and mathematizing. However, modern mathematics curricula seldom pay systematic attention to this aspect of the development of mathematical thinking. Certainly, some interesting beginnings have been made. Van den Brink (1989, 1991) organized classroom activities in which young children (from the age of about 6) were encouraged to invent and reflect on notational systems for simple additions and subtractions. Moreover, these children were successfully taught to use nonconventional, but suggestive, symbols such as arrows for symbolizing arithmetical operations. However, most of these examples begin with somewhat older children and, without exception, they begin exclusively in the domain of mathematics, unnecessarily (and presumably to the children's disadvantage) restricting semiotic activity to just one domain.

A STARTING POINT FOR A FUTURE
DEVELOPMENTAL PEDAGOGY OF MATHEMATICS

One of the shortcomings of most modern constructivist analyses of mathematics education is that construction as a cognitive process is conceived of as a nondevelopmental mechanism. When we conceive of construction as a developing activity of meaning construction with the help of symbols (as I have done here), then we can recognize that the character of constructing, itself, changes in the course of the child's development. The course of this development depends on the kind of practices and communicative interactions the child is brought into. Numeracy and (by all means) mathematical construction are produced by practices and sociocultural activities in which the child is involved (see also Walkerdine, 1988). An educationally relevant question then is as follows: Which kind of practices best produce the desired mathematical activities?

Obviously, one factor to consider is the educator or teacher. Quite to the point, Walkerdine contends that the "psychologist or teacher 'sees' mathematics or cognition *in* the activity in question. On the basis of this reading, the practice 'becomes' cognition or mathematics" (Walkerdine, 1988, p. 97). Everyday classroom practices may differ to a great extent, depending on what is seen as mathematically significant in the pupils' activity and, consequently, how the activity gives meaning to the pupils' actions (see Forman, 1996). Different practices probably produce radically different results, in terms of the type of mathematics and symbol appropriation that result from the educational process.

A fundamental factor in such "mathematics-producing practices" is the adult's attribution of mathematical meaning to the children's actions (including utterances). It is probable that this attribution process is accomplished differently at different stages of development. During children's play activity, it is important that the adult (teacher, mathematician) does not disrupt the activity as play (as this is the meaning that produces context for these young children). The adult must participate in the play and reveal how mathematizing can contribute to the play activity. By doing so, the significance of the mathematical actions may be revealed and examined.

By participating in the children's activity, the adult can treat some of the children's actions as "mathematical" and, consequently, try to introduce new means for performing these actions. Symbolizing, inventing notational systems, and exploring their meaning are obviously very important contributions to the children's role-playing activity. Moreover, our observations show that children really appreciate the interventions of the adult in their play, certainly when the children acknowledge the adult's contribution as an improvement of the reality of their imitation.

So initially, the adult's perception and predication of the situation determine which kind of actions (and goal structure) are seen as relevant to the situation and, by the same token, how mathematics becomes constituted into the situation (for illustrative analyses of the development of numeracy in social practices, see Saxe, Gearhart, & Guberman, 1984; see also Gravemeijer et al., chap. 7, this volume). Our observations in the shoe-shop play are clear illustrations of this process. Our research gives us reason to believe that the iconic form of the symbols and a narrative extension of these initial symbolizations (by verbal comments, which are eventually abbreviated into shorthand symbols) are fundamental elements in this process. At least these are the ingredients for meaningful semiotic activity during young children's play.

In the later stage of learning activity (from the age of about 7 years old), the roles are reversed. The teacher's/mathematician's role is now to put play into mathematics (rather than to put mathematics into play, as was the case in the previous stage). The pupils are now enticed to participate in a mathematical activity. When children are involved in mathematical activity, the way the teachers deal with the actions and solutions of the pupil is equally important. Of course, the mathematization then takes place cooperatively among adult, child, and peers, with everyone pooling and probing their interpretations of the situation, the task, the actions to be performed, and the symbols to be used. Similarly, the process of symbolizing and the appropriation of mathematical symbols are strongly dependent on how adults and children define that situation, as well as on the nature of the activity and the symbols used. The children are now "imitating" the mathematician's real activities of organizing, symbolizing, experimenting with mental models, and so on. This is what realistic mathematics education is about (see, e.g., Wood, Cobb, & Yackel, 1995).

In our tentative attempts to reveal some of the characteristics of semiotic activity and the process of symbolizing, we observed that there is usually an element of uncertainty with respect to the appropriateness of symbols and how they predicate the situation. Even young children try to reduce this uncertainty by refining their symbols and adding verbal comments (text). I assume that this is not different from what happens in later mathematizing, in which the negotiation of meaning is also embodied in symbol use and in explaining the meaning of symbols by constructing new (strings of) symbols.

The analysis of symbolizing in a mathematical context has led us to the realization that symbol use is intrinsically related to meaning, negotiation of meaning, and communication. Obviously, all communication requires a context (background) containing the implicit rules that make the meanings and symbols comprehensible (Hundeide, 1985), and that is the basis for the emergence of intersubjectivity (Rommetveit, 1985). Clearly, mathematical processes, such as learning and symbolizing, also need such a background. Symbolizing is embedded in mathematical practices that were invented before we (individually) came into existence and that thus preceded our personal lives. However, such preexisting mathematical practices are not abstract ideal entities but are human activities embodied in the actions and meanings of actual people who try to give voice to the cultural history, with the help of symbols and meanings, that they themselves have reconstructed from their legacy.

We still have a long way to go to gain a thorough insight into all of the details and complexities of this process. Until now, research for the improvement of mathematics education has primarily dealt only with negotiation of mathematical meanings and the automatization of mathematical operations. Indeed, there is no reason for playing down the educational significance of this research (see, e.g., Gravemeijer, 1994). However, these approaches often can be enhanced with the help of psychological know-how about learning and development, and by elaboration of the concept of constructivity and meaning making from a developmental perspective. Further improvement of mathematical education can be achieved by adopting a genetic approach, viewing mathematizing as a developing form of semiosis, rooted in early (nonmathematical) semiotic activity in young children's play.

A future theory of mathematical education should be conceived of as a developmental pedagogy for the appropriation of mathematizing, discursively creating a continuous series of practices that can produce realistic mathematical activities, in which pupils and teachers can cooperatively develop autonomy and responsibility for their own mathematical actions and symbolizations.

ACKNOWLEDGMENT

I am grateful to Paul Cobb, Koeno Gravemeijer, Anna Sfard, Erna Yackel, Rodney McNair and Sietske Roegholt for their thoughtful and stimulating comments on the first draft of this article.

REFERENCES

Bauersfeld, H. (1995). Structuring of the structures: Development and function of mathematizing as a social practice. In L. P. Steffe & J. Gale (Eds.), *Constructivism in education* (pp. 137–158). Mahwah, NJ: Lawrence Erlbaum Associates.

Bideau, J., Meljac, C., & Fischer, J.-P. (Eds.). (1992). *Pathways to number: Children's developing numerical abilities.* Hillsdale, NJ: Lawrence Erlbaum Associates.

Bishop, A. J. (1988). *Mathematical enculturation: A cultural perspective on mathematics education.* Dordrecht, The Netherlands: Kluwer Academic Press.

Brissiaud, R. (1989). *Comments les enfants apprennent à calculer. Au-delà de Piaget et de la théorie des ensembles.* Paris: Retz.

Cassirer, E. (1955). *The philosophy of symbolic forms. Vol. 1: Language.* New Haven, CT: Yale University Press.

Cobb, P., Wood, T., & Yackel, E. (1993). Discourse, mathematical thinking, and classroom practice. In E. A. Forman, N. Minick, & C. A. Stone (Eds.), *Contexts for learning: Sociocultural dynamics in children's development* (pp. 91–120). New York: Oxford University Press.

Cobb, P., Yackel, E., & Wood, T. (1992). A constructivist alternative to the representational view of mind in mathematics education. *Journal for Research in Mathematics Education, 23,* 2–33.

Cole, M. (1990). Cultural psychology: A once and future discipline? In J. J. Berman (Ed.), *Nebraska Symposium on Motivation: Vol. 37. Cross-cultural perspectives* (pp. 280–335). Lincoln: University of Nebraska Press.

Cole, M. (1995). Culture and cognitive development: From cross-cultural research to creating systems for cultural mediation. *Culture & Psychology, 1,* 25–55.

Cole, M., & Engeström, Y. (1993). A cultural-historical approach to distributed cognition. In G. Salomon (Ed.), *Distributed cognitions: Psychological and educational considerations* (pp. 1–47). New York: Cambridge University Press.

Davis, P. J., & Hersh, R. (1981). *The mathematical experience.* Boston: Birkhäuser.

Davydov, V. V. (1957). Obrazovanie nacal'nogo ponjatija o kolicestvo u detej [The formation of a basic concept of quantity in children]. *Voprosy Psichologii, 2,* 82–96.

Davydov, V. V. (1988). Problems of developmental teaching. *Soviet Education, 30*(8,9,10).

Davydov, V. V., & Andronov, V. P. (1979). Psichologičeskie uslovija proizchoždenija ideal'nich dejstvij [Psychological preconditions for the formation of ideal actions]. *Voprosy Psichologii, 5,* 40–54.

Desforges, C., & Bristow, S. (1994). Reading to learn mathematics: A report on primary school children's constructive activity in learning from text. In J. E. H. van Luit (Ed.), *Research on learning and instruction of mathematics in kindergarten and primary school* (pp. 251–268). Doetinchem, The Netherlands: Graviant.

Elkonin, D. B. (1972). Toward the problem of stages in the mental development of the child. *Soviet Psychology, 10,* 225–251.

Ernest, P. (1991). *The philosophy of mathematics education: Studies in mathematics education.* London: Falmer Press.

Forman, E. (1996). Learning mathematics as participation in classroom practice: Implications of sociocultural theory for educational reform. In P. Nesher, L. P. Steffe, P. Cobb, G. Goldin, & B. Greer (Eds.), *Theories of mathematical learning* (pp. 115–131). Mahwah, NJ: Lawrence Erlbaum Associates.

Forman, E., Minick, N., & Stone, C. A. (Eds.). (1993). *Contexts for learning: Sociocultural dynamics in children's development.* New York: Oxford University Press.

Freudenthal, H. F. (1973). *Mathematics as an educational task.* Dordrecht, The Netherlands: D. Reidel.

Freudenthal, H. F. (1979). Structuur der wiskunde en wiskundige structuren; Een onderwijskundige analyse [The structure of mathematics and mathematical structures; an educational analysis]. *Pedagogische Studiën, 56,* 51–61.

Freudenthal, H. F. (1991). *Revising mathematics education (China Lectures).* Dordrecht, The Netherlands: Kluwer Academic Press.

Gal'perin, P. J. (1969). Stages in the development of mental acts. In M. Cole & I. Maltzman (Eds.), *A handbook of contemporary Soviet psychology* (pp. 249–273). New York: Basic Books.

Gal'perin, P. J. (1976). *Vvedenie v psichologiju* [Introduction to psychology]. Moscow: Izd-vo Moskovskogo Universiteta.

Gelman, R., & Gallistel, C. R. (1978). *The child's understanding of number.* Cambridge, MA: Harvard University Press.

Glotova, G. A. (1990). *Celovek i znak. Semiotiko-psichologičeskie aspekty ontogeneza čeloveka* [Man and sign. Semiotic-psychological aspects of human ontogenesis]. Sverdlovsk, Russia: Izd-vo Ural'skogo Universiteta.

Gravemeijer, K. (1992). *Mathematics as mathematizing.* Paper for the Seventh International Conference on Mathematics Education (ICME-7). Québec, Canada.

Gravemeijer, K. P. E. (1994). *Developing realistic mathematics education.* Utrecht, The Netherlands: CD-β Press.

Haenen, J. (1996). *Piotr Gal'perin: Psychologist in Vygotsky's footsteps.* Commack, NY: Nova Science Publishers.

Hitch, G., Cundick, J., Haughey, M., Pugh, R., & Wright, H. (1987). Aspects of counting in children's arithmetic. In J. A Sloboda & D. Rogers (Eds.), *Cognitive processes in mathematics* (pp. 26–42). New York: Oxford University Press.

Hoffer, A. (1983). Van Hiele-based research. In R. Lesh & M. Landau (Eds.), *Acquisition of mathematics concepts and processes* (pp. 205–227). New York: Academic Press.

Hörmann, H. (1978). *Meinen und Verstehen: Grundzüge einer psychologischen Semantik* [To mean, to understand: Outlines of psychological semantics]. Frankfurt, Germany: Suhrkamp.

Howson, G., Keitel, C., & Kilpatrick, J. (1981). *Curriculum development in mathematics.* New York: Cambridge University Press.

Hughes, M. (1986). *Children and number: Difficulties in learning mathematics.* Oxford, UK: Blackwell.

Hundeide, K. (1985). The tacit background of children's judgments. In J. V. Wertsch (Ed.), *Culture, communication, and cognition* (pp. 306–323). New York: Cambridge University Press.

Kaput, J. J. (1987). Towards a theory of symbol use in mathematics. In C. Janvier (Ed.), *Problems of representation in the teaching and learning of mathematics* (pp. 159–195). Hillsdale, NJ: Lawrence Erlbaum Associates.

Karmiloff-Smith, A. (1995). *Beyond modularity: A developmental perspective on cognitive science* (2nd ed.). Cambridge, MA: MIT Press.

Kucinskij, G. M. (1983). *Dialog i myšlenie* [Dialogue and thinking]. Minsk, Belarus: Izd-vo BGU.

Lave, J., & Wenger, E. (1991). *Situated learning: Legitimate peripheral participation.* Cambridge, UK: Cambridge University Press.

Leech, G. (1981). *Semantics: The study of meaning* (2nd ed.). Harmondsworth, UK: Penguin.

Leont'ev, A. N. (1975). *Dejatel'nost', soznanie, ličnost'* [Activity, consciousness, personality]. Moscow: Politizdat.

Leusina, A. (1977). Wiskunde in de kleuterschool en de betekenis ervan voor de cognitieve ontwikkeling [Mathematics in early education and its relevance for cognitive development]. In C. F. van Parreren & J. M. C. Nelissen (Eds.), *Rekenen* (pp. 101–116). Groningen, The Netherlands: Wolters-Noordhoff. Translated from: *Doškol'noe Vospitanie*, nr. 9, 1969.

Malone, J. A., & Taylor, P. C. S. (Eds.). (1993). *Constructivist interpretations of teaching and learning mathematics*. Perth, Australia: Curtin University.

Markovà, I., & Foppa, K. (Eds.). (1990). *The dynamics of dialogue*. New York: Harvester Wheatsheaf.

Miles, T. R., & Miles, E. (Eds.). (1992). *Dyslexia and mathematics*. London: Routledge & Kegan Paul.

Moll, L. (Ed.). (1990). *Vygotsky and education: Instructional implications and applications of sociohistorical psychology*. Cambridge, UK: Cambridge University Press.

Otte, M. (Ed.). (1974). *Mathematiker über die Mathematik* [Mathematicians about mathematics]. Berlin: Springer.

Parmentier, R. J. (1987). Signs' place *in media res*: Peirce's concept of semiotic mediation. In E. Mertz & R. J. Parmentier (Eds.), *Semiotic mediation. Sociocultural and psychological perspectives* (pp. 23–48). Orlando, FL: Academic Press.

Pimm, D. (1987). *Speaking mathematically*. London: Routledge & Kegan Paul.

Rommetveit, R. (1985). Language acquisition as increasing linguistic structuring of experience and symbolic behavior control. In J. V. Wertsch (Ed.), *Culture, communication, and cognition* (pp. 183–205). Cambridge, UK: Cambridge University Press.

Rubtsov, V. V. (1991). *Learning in children: Organization and development of cooperative actions*. New York: Nova Science Publishers.

Sabel'nikov, V. K. (1982). *Formirovanie bystroj myšli. Psichologičeskie mechanizmy "neposredstvennogo" ponimanija ob-jektov* [The formation of fast thinking. Psychological mechanisms of "immediate" recognition of objects]. Mektep, Turkey: Alma-Ata.

Salmina, N. G. (1988). *Znak i simvol v obučenii* [Sign and symbol in education]. Moscow: Izd-vo Moskovskogo Universiteta.

Salmina, N. G. (1995). Obučenie matematike v načal'noj škole [Mathematics education in primary school]. In N. F. Talyzina (Ed.), *Formirovanie priëmov matematičeskogo myšlenija* (pp. 29–68). Moscow: Izd-vo Moskovskogo Universiteta.

Salomon, G. (Ed.). (1993). *Distributed cognitions: Psychological and educational considerations*. Cambridge, UK: Cambridge University Press.

Sapogova, E. E. (1992). Modelirovanie kak etap razvitija znakovo-simvoličeskoj dejatel'nosti doškol'nikov [Model formation as a stage in the development of the symbolic activity of young children]. *Voprosy psichologii, 5*, 26–30.

Sapogova, E. E. (1993). *Rebënok i znak* [Child and sign]. Tula, Russia: Priokskoe kniznoe izd-vo.

Saxe, G., Gearhart, M., & Guberman, S. (1984). The social organization of early number development. In B. Rogoff & J. Wertsch (Eds.), *Children learning in the zone of proximal development* (pp. 19–30). San Francisco: Jossey-Bass.

Sfard, A. (1991). On the dual nature of mathematical conceptions: Reflections on processes and objects as different sides of the same coin. *Educational Studies in Mathematics, 22*, 1–36.

Sfard, A. (1992). Operational origins of mathematical objects and the quandary of reification—The case of function. In G. Harel & E. Dubinsky (Eds.), *The concept of function: Aspects of epistemology and pedagogy* (MAA-Notes, Vol. 25, pp. 59–84). Washington, DC: Mathematical Association of America.

Sfard, A. (1994). Reification as the birth of metaphor. *For the Learning of Mathematics, 14*(1), 44–55.

Sfard, A., & Linchevski, L. (1994). The gains and pitfalls of reification—The case of algebra. *Educational Studies in Mathematics, 26,* 191–228.

Shotter, J. (1995). In dialogue: Social constructionism and radical constructivism. In L. P. Steffe & J. Gale (Eds.), *Constructivism in education* (pp. 41–56). Mahwah, NJ: Lawrence Erlbaum Associates.

Sinha, C. (1988). *Language and representation: A socio-naturalistic approach to human development.* New York: Harvester/Wheatsheaf.

Steffe, L. P. (1992). Learning stages in the construction of the number sequence. In J. Bideau, C. Meljac, & J.-P. Fischer (Eds.), *Pathways to number: Children's developing numerical abilities* (pp. 83–98). Hillsdale, NJ: Lawrence Erlbaum Associates.

Struik, D. J. (1990). *Geschiedenis van de wiskunde* [History of mathematics]. Utrecht, The Netherlands: Spectrum.

Talyzina, N. F. (Ed.). (1995). *Formirovanie priëmov matematičeskogo myšlenija* [The formation of methods of mathematical thinking]. Moscow: Izd-vo Moskovskogo Universiteta.

van den Brink, J. (1989). *Realistisch rekenonderwijs aan jonge kinderen* [Realistic arithmetic instruction for young children]. Groningen/Utrecht, The Netherlands: OW&OC.

van den Brink, J. (1991). Didactic constructivism. In E. von Glasersfeld (Ed.), *Radical constructivism in mathematics education* (pp. 195–227). Dordrecht, The Netherlands: Kluwer.

van der Veer, R., & Valsiner, J. (1991). *Understanding Vygotsky: A quest for synthesis.* Oxford, UK: Blackwell.

van Hiele, P. M. (1985). *Structure and insight: A theory of mathematics education.* Orlando, FL: Academic Press.

van Oers, B. (1990). The development of mathematical thinking in school: A comparison of the action-psychological and information-processing approaches. *International Journal of Educational Research, 14,* 51–66. Special Issue: B. Greer & L.Verschaffel (Eds.), Mathematics education as a proving-ground for information-processing theories.

van Oers, B. (1994). Semiotic activity of young children in play: The construction and use of schematic representations. *European Early Childhood Education Research Journal, 2*(1), 19–34.

van Oers, B. (1995, June). *Teaching opportunities in play.* Paper for the Third International Conference on Activity Theory and Social Practice, Moscow.

van Oers, B. (1996a). Are you sure? Stimulating mathematical thinking during young children's play. *European Early Childhood Education Research Journal, 4* (1), 71–88.

van Oers, B. (1996b). Learning mathematics as a meaningful activity. In P. Nesher, L. P. Steffe, P. Cobb, G. Goldin, & B. Greer (Eds.), *Theories of mathematical learning* (pp. 91–113). Mahwah, NJ: Lawrence Erlbaum Associates.

van Oers, B. (1996c). The dynamics of school learning. In J. Valsiner & G.-H. Voss (Eds.), *The structure of learning* (pp. 205–228). New York: Ablex.

van Oers, B. (1997). On the narrative nature of young children's iconic representations: Some evidence and implications. *International Journal of Early Years Education, 5,* 237–245.

van Parreren, C. F. (1954). A viewpoint in theory and experimentation on human learning and thinking. *Acta Psychologica, 10,* 351–380.

van Parreren, C. F. (1971). *Psychologie van het leren. Deel I.* [Psychology of learning. Vol. I]. Deventer, The Netherlands: Van Loghum Slaterus.

van Parreren, C. F. (1978). A building block model of cognitive learning. In A. M. Lesgold, J. W. Pellegrino, S. D. Fokkema, & R. Glaser (Eds.), *Cognitive psychology and instruction* (pp. 3–12). New York: Plenum Press.

Venger, L. A. (Ed.). (1986). *Razvitie poznavatel'nich sposobnostej v processe doškol'nogo vospitanija* [The development of cognitive abilities in early childhood education]. Moscow: Pedagogika.

Vygotsky, L. S. (1978). *Mind in society: The development of higher psychological processes.* Cambridge, MA: Harvard University Press.

Vygotsky, L. S. (1982). *Myšlenie i reč* [Thinking and speech]. In *Sobranie Socinenij II.* (Translation see Vygotsky, 1987). Moscow: Pedagogika. (Original work published in 1934)

Vygotsky, L. S. (1987). *Thinking and speech.* New York: Plenum Press. (Translation of Vygotsky, 1982).

Vygotsky, L. S. (1991). *Pedagogičeskaja psichologija* [Pedagogical psychology]. Moscow: Pedagogika.

Walkerdine, V. (1988). *The mastery of reason: Cognitive development and the production of rationality.* London: Routledge.

Werner, H., & Kaplan, B. (1963). *Symbol formation: An organismic-developmental approach to language and the expression of thought.* New York: John Wiley & Sons.

Wertsch, J. V. (1985). *Vygotsky and the social formation of mind.* Cambridge, MA: Harvard University Press.

Wertsch, J. V., & Toma, C. (1995). Discourse and learning in the classroom. In L. P. Steffe & J. Gale (Eds.), *Constructivism in education* (pp. 159–175). Mahwah, NJ: Lawrence Erlbaum Associates.

Wood, T., Cobb, P., & Yackel, E. (1995). Reflections on learning and teaching mathematics in elementary school. In L. P. Steffe & J. Gale (Eds.), *Constructivism in education* (pp. 401–423). Mahwah, NJ: Lawrence Erlbaum Associates.

"If You Look at It the Other Way ... ": An Exploration Into the Nature of Symbolizing

Ricardo Nemirovsky
Stephen Monk
TERC, Cambridge, Massachusetts

> *Symbolize: Unite elements or substances of similar qualities.*
> (The Barnhart Dictionary of Etymology, 1988)

Imagine a child playing with other children and using a stick as a horse: The child jumps around his friends, goes places, feeds the horse, claims that the horse is lazy, and so forth. In creating this make-believe play, the child is making present a horse, a horse that otherwise would be absent in this child's life. Furthermore, he is not only making the horse present but doing things with it. We say that the horse is *ready at hand* to convey this idea that the horse is made to participate in the child's playful activities. This scene exemplifies what we call symbolizing: a creation of a space in which the absent is made present and ready at hand.

It is important to understand that when we talk about "making the absent present" we refer to the ways in which symbolizing is *experienced* by the symbol user. This is not a statement about a realistic correspondence between an entity that is objectively absent and that is brought to actual presence (e.g., an actual horse that lives somewhere and that the child brings to his play). Instead, it is an attempt to describe the symbolizer's imaginative sense that something is metaphorically present around him, and his immersion into the pretend that what is experienced as presently there can be changed by handling symbols.

Conceiving of symbolizing as the creation of a space in which the absent is made present and ready at hand elicits at least two major issues: (a) the nature of such a space, and (b) the ways in which the absent is made present and ready at hand. Regarding the first one, we have characterized this space—a space populated by symbols and metaphoric presence—elsewhere[1] as a *lived-in space*. The expression *lived-in* highlights the notion that this is not a space in which being near or far is distance to be measured by a ruler, but instead by what the symbolizer experiences as being close or far away. For instance, it is similar to someone, talking on the phone with a close friend who is oceans away, feeling that her friend is closer to her than her next-door neighbor.[2] We can talk about her experience by saying that in her lived-in space her friend *is* closer to her than her next door neighbor.

Through an analysis of a conversation with Lin, a 10-year-old girl, we explore the two issues just raised: the nature of the space in which the absent is made present, and the ways in which such a process occurs. We focus this exploration on two notions: fusion and trail-making. By using the previously mentioned scene of children's play, we exemplify fusion as a child's acting, talking, and gesturing without distinguishing between the horse and the stick: that is, treating the stick *as if* it were a horse even though he knows that it is not. Trail-making, on the other hand, relates to how the play is enacted by the child without following a script. In other words, the play is an ongoing creation in which actions and words, rather than stemming from a planned sequence, emerge from the activity itself in open-ended ways.

The section entitled "Fusion" proposes that fusion is a central quality of symbol-use. Throughout the chapter, the relationship between symbolizing and children's play is a guiding connection. Children's play is not simply an analogy to symbol use. It has long been recognized that our play as children is a crucial activity through which each one of us has practiced and learned to symbolize (Piaget, 1962; Slade & Wolf, 1994; Winnicott, 1971/1992). Fusion and trail-making are qualities common to both symbol use and children's play.

Our overall perspective in undertaking this exploration can be described by the following statement from Werner and Kaplan (1963):

> Our thesis is thus opposed to the widespread view which treats symbolic vehicles and referents as two fully formed entities that are externally linked to each other through continuous pairing and reinforcement. If one accepts

---

[1]For an analysis of what we mean by "lived-in space," see Nemirovsky, Tierney, and Wright (1998).

[2]Heidegger (1927/1962) elaborated on how the experience of something being more or less far expresses one's interest in "making the remoteness of that something disappear, in bringing it close" (p. 139): "When, for instance, a man wears a pair of spectacles which are so close to him distantly that they are 'sitting on his nose,' they are environmentally more remote to him than the picture on the opposite wall" (p. 141).

this latter view, one implicitly denies to symbolization (including language) any creative role in the cognitive organization of experience and thought: symbolic vehicles then become reduced to a complex system of markers, useful merely for routine indication of referents and for communication about preformed judgments and concepts. (p. 15)

Through the analysis of a conversation between Lin and our colleague, Tracey Wright, we attempt to elucidate the nature of symbol-use as an ongoing, joint and open-ended creation of meaning and communication.

THE STUDY

The interview with Lin that we discuss in this chapter was part of a teaching experiment conducted in a fifth-grade class at an elementary school in East Boston. This teaching experiment was also a pilot trial for a curricular unit subsequently published (Tierney, Nemirovsky, & Noble, 1995). The unit includes 4 weeks of classroom activities focused on the interplay between ways of moving, graphs and number tables. All the classroom sessions were videotaped. When the students worked in groups, we videotaped a small team of four students, of which Lin was part. In addition, we conducted individual interviews with the members of this subgroup. The researchers and teachers involved regularly discussed the design of the activities as they were tried out in the classroom.[3]

This chapter is an analysis of three selected episodes, the first of which took place in the classroom:

Episode 1: Does This Description Match This Graph? (Duration: 1 min.)

The other two episodes are successive segments from Tracey Wright's individual interview with Lin which took place a week later:

Episode 2: Two Bears Racing and Graph 3 Revisited. (Duration: 4 min.)

Episode 3: Making a Step Graph of the Speeds. (Duration: 2 min.)

Episode 2 is the main excerpt for the section on fusion, and Episode 3 is the center of our discussion on trail-making. Each one of these two sections includes an introduction that presents the main ideas to the reader, the annotated transcript, and a final discussion. We end the chapter with a

---

[3]The participants in this process were the following members of the "Math of Change" group at TERC: David Carraher, Steve Monk, Ricardo Nemirovsky, Tracy Noble, Analucia Schliemann, Cornelia Tierney, Paul Wagoner, and Tracey Wright; and two fifth-grade teachers from the Boston area: Barbara Fox and Jo Ann Pepicelli.

short essay about how these views on the nature of symbolizing relate to curricular design.

FUSION

> Fusion: The figurative sense of a blending together of different things. (The Barnhart Dictionary of Etymology, 1988)

The most common assertion about how one makes sense of symbols is that one must understand what they *stand for*. Symbols are often defined as something that stand for something other than themselves. This definition implies that grasping a symbol as a symbol necessarily involves recognizing the thing "other than itself" being shown by it. So, for example, one shows that one grasps the meaning of the word *milk* by being able to refer to instances of that white liquid that is "the other" that the word *milk* stands for. This characterization of symbol use seems to be naturally connected to the view that thinking is a matter of associations, such as associations between the word *milk* and instances or qualities of milk.[4] According to this view, the meaning of a symbol emerges through the associative process.

Associationism has an ancient history in philosophy and psychology dating back to Aristotle. It has evolved into many sophisticated ideas and studies. The questions raised by associationism are far from trivial. How is it, for example, that a baby learns to recognize what the word *milk* stands for? Or what rules of association may enable someone to understand that *rabbit* refers to an animal and not to the white color of its skin?

If grasping a symbol as a symbol is based on the associations elicited by the symbolizer, how can we describe the experience of *not* seeing a symbol as a symbol? The question is not about correct or incorrect associations. For someone who is learning English, for instance, the word *rabbit* could be mistakenly associated with mice, but still, she is taking the word *rabbit* as a symbol, because she perceives it as standing for something other than itself. Neither is the question about what is meaningful or meaningless. If one does not know Hebrew, say, and is shown a text in Hebrew, one still could see it as a symbol (e.g., of the person who is showing us the text or as a title of a book) even though its linguistic

---

[4]Suppose that someone asks someone else, while pointing at a photo, "Who is this person?" and the response is, "He is George." One might be inclined to say that such a response invites the inquirer to associate the image on the photo with the word "George" and the word "George" with a known person whose name is George, so that, as a result, the inquirer is likely to recognize such a person in the photo.

meaning is unavailable to us. The experience of *not* seeing a symbol as a symbol has been studied by anthropologists and psychologists in its many forms: fetishism, animism, magic, and so on. In many of these practices, the symbol does not stand for something other than itself, but it *is* that "something other." A clay reproduction of an animal, for example, can be a fetish if it is treated as *being* the animal itself rather than as standing for the animal.

We maintain that associationism and fetishism are two opposed and extreme ways to use symbols that do not capture the vast majority of situations in which people symbolize. Our intent in introducing the notion of fusion is to open up a broad horizon of possibilities—in between associations and fetishes—which, we believe, encompasses most actual experiences of symbol use.

Consider, for example, two girls playing with stuffed animals. They act as if the stuffed animals were their pets looking for something to eat. When the girls talk, they adopt the voices their pets are supposed to have and enact their imaginary pets' shifting moods, such as being upset or excited. In this common scenario, the girls bring in many types of associations, such as the stuffed animals standing for pets, a pillow representing food, or a stick representing a tree. However, saying that the girls are establishing associations is an extremely impoverished and incomplete description of their play. Suppose that all the girls do is establish associations, so that they say to each other "This is a bear," "This is my cat," and so forth. In such cases, we (and the girls) would *not* say that they are playing at all. They are playing only when they *act, talk, and gesture* as if the stuffed animals were their pets looking for food. In the course of their play, they might elicit changing uses, often without "announcing" them (e.g., acting as if a pillow were food may be enough to use it as such). However, the essence of their play is the ongoing creation of an experiential and active world that has its own coherence and evolution, and in which the pillow is actively used as food, the stuffed animals are actively made to behave as their pets, and so forth. At the same time it is important to acknowledge that, as they play, the girls are aware that the stuffed animals are not real pets: That is, they know that if they get bored or have something else to do, they won't have to take care of their imaginary pets. This awareness is what makes their activity play; for the girls, the stuffed animals are not fetishes.

We see the girls' play as a symbolizing activity: that is, as a creation of a lived-in space in which the absent is made present and ready at hand. The absent, in this case, is all those things that the girls act on and talk about in spite of their not being there: their pets, food, the tree, and so forth. The absent is not only made present (e.g., they may comment on how delicious the food-pillow is), but is ready at hand—that is, they can *do things* with it. (For example, they may decide to hide the food-pillow from their pets.) As we have pointed out before, associationism, with its emphasis on absence (the girls talk about imaginary pets that are not presently with them), and fetishism, with its emphasis on presence (the stuffed animals are their pets which are presently there), are two extreme forms of using symbols that do not capture the nature of the girls' symbolizing.

How can we understand this illusory presence? We characterize the girls' play with the stuffed animals as a fusion experience. We define fusion as acting, talking, and gesturing without distinguishing between symbols and referents (e.g., acting as if the pillow were food), while being aware of the illusion (e.g., knowing that the pillow is not really food). Fusion experiences are pervasive in everyday life and can adopt infinite forms: from discussing directions on a map to commenting on a photograph; from drawing a face to gesturing the shape of an object. As such, it is impossible to make progress in our understanding of fusion unless we focus on concrete examples. This section is about qualities of fusion experiences with mathematical symbols as they emerge from an interview episode with Lin. Specifically, we elaborate on five aspects of fusion.

First, it is well known that ambiguity is inherent in talk because whatever is being said is always susceptible to many interpretations and meanings. A conversation involves the management of ambiguity, not its elimination; in many circumstances (e.g., telling jokes) ambiguity is actually pursued. We give examples of how, in the context of a fusion experience, ambiguity can be purposeful and expressive. Second, a common characterization of how symbols become understood describes them as being *transparent* to the symbol user. We illustrate why the metaphor of fusion is more appropriate to symbolizing than the metaphor of transparency. Third, we explore the linguistic expressions of fusion. To this end, our commentaries focus on Lin's and Tracey's ambivalent uses of the words *here* and *path*. Fourth, we clarify how the experience of fusion is different and unrelated to the experience of confusion. And fifth, our analysis reveals how fusion involves taking perspectives. Fusion is introduced as an adoption of points of view toward the visual qualities of the graph and the current and past events portrayed by the graph, as well as toward the actions and intentions of the symbolizers themselves.

Episode 1: Does This Description Match This Graph?

This vignette took place in the classroom. It was a short and inconclusive interaction between Lin and Tracey. Lin discussed the graph that, a week later, would become the central theme during the interview.

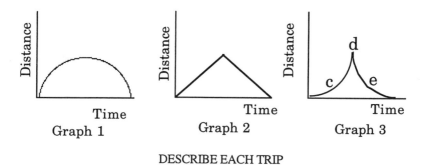

DESCRIBE EACH TRIP

FIG. 6.1. Graphs shown on student "motion stories" activity sheet.

Lin called Tracey and showed her the activity sheet of Fig. 6.1 on which each student was writing three "motion stories" corresponding to the graphs. Lin referred to Graph 3.

(1) Lin: Tracey, do you think this description [written on her student sheet] matches this [Graph 3]?

(2) Tracey: You said [reading Lin's description] "it goes faster and faster and then it goes the same speed again, but it goes down instead of up." OK, so the line goes down instead of up. [Lin: Yeah.] Um hmm, and the trip you said goes faster and faster [section c]. [Lin: Um hm.] And, then, when the line goes down [e], you said the trip is going the same speed. As what?

(3) Lin: As, the other side [c]?

(4) Tracey: As the other side, OK. And so, so this speed, for the trip the person was going faster and faster [c]. And then what happened here [d]? What did he [a person they are imagining took the trip] do?

(5) Lin: He turned around.

(6) Tracey: And then how was he traveling here [top of e]?

(7) Lin: He was s–l–ow.

(8) Tracey: And then [bottom of e]?

(9) Lin: And then fast, only in reverse.

(10) Tracey: He went in reverse—

Lin's interpretation of Graph 3 did not resurface during the subsequent group and classroom discussion. Tracey and Lin were both left with questions about it—questions that would become an essential part of their conversation a week later.

Episode 2: Two Bears Racing and Graph 3 Revisited

This 4-min episode took place a week after Episode 1, during an individual interview after the daily math class. Earlier in the interview, Lin and Tracey had been using a plastic bear to show ways of moving at different speeds. They moved the plastic bear up and down along a vertical scale by pulling a string tied to the bear. Their activity consisted of creating number tables and graphs to show how to move the bear. They had taken turns creating these representations individually, so that the other one would interpret the graph and try to reproduce the original motion. During Episode 2, Tracey and Lin talked about graphs of two "bears" racing.

The graph used by Tracey and Lin in this episode are all position versus time graphs. The hand-drawn graph changed during the episode. At the end, it looked like Fig. 6.2. The grid that appears behind the graph represents 1-inch squares printed on the paper. That paper was used only because it was the only paper readily available. Except for tracing the axis, Tracey drew the graphs without paying attention to the grid. For clarity of exposition, we distinguish, within the graph, three "lines" that we label A, B, and C, as in Fig. 6.3.

Through the classroom activities, a convention had become established in which position versus time graphs were represented as line graphs and step size versus time graphs were represented as bar graphs. Given

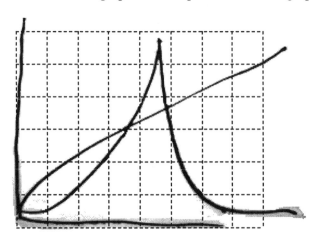

FIG. 6.2.   Final version of Tracey and Lin's position versus time graph for Episode 2.

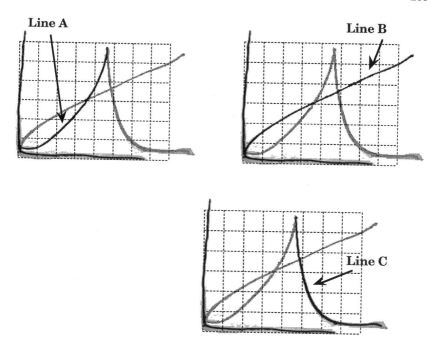

FIG. 6.3. Labels for the three "lines" on Tracey and Lin's position versus time graph for Episode 2.

that lines A, B, and C were line graphs, Lin and Tracey treated them as the type of graphs that depict positions over time in spite of the fact that the axes were not labeled.

Annotated Transcript. See Fig. 6.4.

(16) Tracey: [Finishes drawing Graph 4.] So, let's say these are two bears. And, they're having a race. And this [Graph 4] is the position of the bears. Which bear do you think would win the race?

(17) Lin: That one [pointing to top of A].

Tracey began to describe Graph 4 by saying, "Let's say these are two bears." In saying so, she made present their previous use of a plastic bear in which they pulled a string tied to the bear to move it up and down along a vertical scale. There was only one actual plastic bear used previously, but a strength of making present the absent is that two bears are as easy to conjure up as one. Note Tracey's use of the word "these": "these" indicated two lines on paper as well as two bears having a race. The word "these" referred simultaneously to both the lines and the plastic bears. This referential ambiguity was important to Tracey's ex-

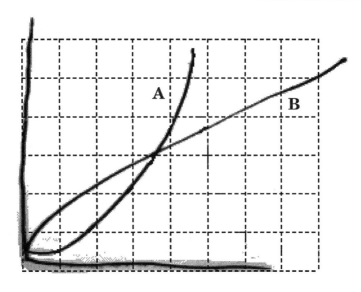

FIG. 6.4.   Graph 4.

pression. In other words, she meant that "these" are simultaneously both. Some readers may perceive in her statement a lack of precision and definition. They may even prescribe that she "should" have said something like "these two curves represent two bears having a race along two parallel lines."

In our view this typical criticism misses the point, which is that ambiguity is an inherent aspect of talk and gesture, and that in the course of a conversation ambiguity is sometimes an impediment and, at other times, a meaningful and purposeful contribution. Ambiguity is intrinsic to what conversants deal with in making sense of each other. Had Lin responded with a question such as "where are they racing?" it is likely that Tracey would have made clarifying remarks specifying the racing track. Two comments are pertinent here: (a) One does not participate in a conversation dispelling every possible unintended interpretation, which would make the talk unbearably redundant and scholarly (cf. Sfard, chap. 3, this volume). Rather, a conversant is always implicitly assessing what is relevant to dispel, given what she knows about and expects from the other conversants. (b) Often ambiguity is intended. For example, with the words, "say these are two bears" (16), Tracey was not only inviting Lin to associate Graph 4 with their previous activities with the plastic bear, but inviting her to make them actively present in their talk and gestures about Graph 4. Lin's immediate response suggests intended ambiguity in conversation when she says "that one" because the "one" might have been simultaneously line A, the bear shown by it, and the location of the end of the race.

(18) Tracey: How come?

(19) Lin: 'Cause it's curved like that [tracing A]. It goes faster and
                    faster [pointing to top of A]. And this one [B] is kind
                    of curved like, right here [bottom of B], then it goes kind
                    of straight [tracing top of B] so it kind of goes slower
                    and slower at first, then it goes steadily. This one's [A]
                    going to go faster and faster, and this one's [A] in the
                    lead so far, so I think this one [A] will win.

*Note Lin's use of "it" (19) in her analysis of Graph 4: "Then it goes kind of
straight [tracing top of B] so it kind of goes slower and slower at first, then it
goes steadily." Going straight and going steadily are both qualities of "it." "It"
fuses curvature of the graph line with speed of the bear's motion. Lin's utterances
in (19) suggest why we think that the nature of symbolizing is better grasped
by the metaphor of fusion than by the metaphor of transparency. Often it is
stated that to understand a symbolic expression is to perceive it as "transparent,"
as if its meaning becomes available by "seeing through" it (cf. Cobb, chap. 2,
this volume; Sfard, chap. 3, this volume). However, the metaphor of transparency
implies that symbols are meaningful when they come to be invisible. Imagine a
wall that becomes transparent so that we can see through it; to say that a wall
becomes transparent is equivalent, at least from the visual point of view, to saying
that the wall disappears, that it becomes nonexistent to us. This is the implication
that we find misleading in the metaphor of transparency. It is not the case that
Graph 4 was transparent to Lin in (19). The visual attributes of Graph 4 remained
in the foreground of her interpretation. What she expressed was a fusion of the
curved aspects of Graph 4, with the speed aspects of the bears' motion, by creating
an "it" that "goes" more or less straight as well as more or less fast.[5]*

*Another clarification that emerges to us from (19) is that saying that Lin
fused curvature and speed in the "it" that "goes" does not imply that she became
unable to distinguish the curvature of the graph from the speed of the imaginary
bear. Moreover, we can trace her account along separate descriptions of curvature
and speed in Fig. 6.5.*

*In sum, this commentary intends to suggest through the example that fusion
is neither a transparent "seeing through" that is blind to the specific traits of
the graph, nor a "mixing up" that loses sight of how a graph can be different
from two bears racing; instead, it is a way of using the graph in which curvature*

---

[5]It is important to note that by the metaphors of transparency and fusion we refer to
the common experiences with transparency and fusion: A glass window, by virtue of being
transparent, enables us to see what we might see in the absence of the glass. On the other
hand, some authors use the term *transparency* in more elaborate ways. Wenger (1990) defined
transparency as a relational balance between visibility and invisibility, so that a graph might
open up certain "fields" of visibility and invisibility, which could encompass simultaneous
attributes of the graph and the represented situation. This particular use of the word
transparency seems to be more akin to what we mean by *fusion*.

the Curvature is:	so . . . the Speed is:
And this one [B] is kind of curved like, right here [bottom of [B],	it kind of goes slower and slower at first
then it goes kind of straight [tracing top of B]	then it goes steadily.

FIG. 6.5. Tracey and Lin's account along the descriptions of curvature and speed.

makes present the bears' speed, so that an "it" is created, gestured, and talked about that "goes" at once according to certain curvatures and to certain speeds. Some readers may argue that this is an overinterpretation of Lin's utterances and that each one of her "its" refers to different entities, sometimes to the graph and some other times to the imaginary bear.

To make the case that the latter is a superficial interpretation, our following two commentaries illustrate how Tracey's and Lin's linguistic and gestural expressions reveal more than words with separate references. The examples focus on their use of the words "here" and "path."

(20) Tracey: Huhn. So, he's in the lead here [top of A]? [Lin: Uh hunh.] How about like, here [a point just beyond the start]? Who was in the lead, here [a point just beyond the start]?

(21) Lin: Here—this one [B] was in the lead.

(22) Tracey: How come?

(23) Lin: 'Cause this [B] is above [A]. 'Cause it's closer to the finish [tracing an imaginary horizontal line at the top].

Let us explore the significance of Tracey's and Lin's talk and gestures regarding the word "here." Lin had already used "here" in (19) when she said, "is kind of curved like, right here*." We have described the notion of symbolizing as a creation of a lived-in space. We think of the "here" in (19), (20), and (21) as a discursive articulation of the lived-in space that Tracey and Lin were creating. The "here" was simultaneously a certain place on the paper, a certain time in the story of the bears' race, and a certain closeness to the "finish." In a general sense this is not different from the phenomenon of someone pointing at a map and saying "I live here," when it is obvious to the conversants that this person does not live on a piece of paper; the "here" that is pointed out is at once on the map and on a certain street that is far from the map. On the other hand, the lived-in space that Tracey and Lin invoke in the "here" of Graph 4 is not map-like because it includes a temporal sequence before–after, suggested by the past tense of Tracey's "Who was in the lead." It is structured around the idea of being in the lead, and a path on Graph 4 was not viewed by them as a path on the race track. The graphical space that Lin talked about in (23) is marked by the special* *significance of the "finish," a region that she demarcated at the top of the graph so that being in the lead was an index of relative closeness to that critical place.*

(24) Tracey: Un hun. So, if it's more above then he's more in the lead? [Lin: Yeah. Hmmm.] And how about here [point where A and B cross in Graph 4]? What happened when they were cross?

(25) Lin: They cross each other's paths, so at this part it's kind of like a tie, 'cause it's together.

(26) Tracey: Un hun. So, here's [crossing point] where they were tied in their race? [Lin: Yeah.] Hmm. [Pause.]

Lin completed the description of the crossing point on Graph 4 by saying, "They cross each other's path." In the ordinary usage of English, one would not describe the situation of two racers being next to one another as "crossing each other's path." Some readers will take this utterance as an indication that Lin saw Graph 4 as a depiction of the trajectory of the race, so that the bears' paths crossed each other at that point. It is always possible to isolate something said by a student and, out of context, diagnose this utterance as a known mistake. This is a frequent approach among those identifying misconceptions. However, by paying attention to the context of this conversation, we can see that this is not an appropriate interpretation. Tracey and Lin had always played out motion along a linear path, which was also true of all the previous classroom activities. In addition, if Graph 4 had portrayed the bears' trajectory for Lin, it would not make sense that being "above is being more in the lead," that going straight is going steady, or that the curvature indicates going faster or slower. According to our interpretation, "They cross each other's path" is a meaningful expression of fusion. The word "path" means literally a way along which one can walk or move. But, as we all know, in figurative speech "path" is used in a much broader sense. It is appropriate to talk about the paths of the bears on the graph without implying that the bears actually follow them as a physical trajectory. Not only that, if we recognize Lin's experience of fusion between Graph 4 and the bears' race, it is a natural and expressive use of the word "path." Tracey, in response, found it natural to interpret Lin's "crossing each other's path" as meaning that at that time the bears were at the same place in their race.

(26) Tracey: Um, the other day we were looking at graphs in the classroom and one of them went like this [tracing A] and then it went kind of like this [drawing C] . . . Remember that? [Lin: Yeah.] What—could you tell the story of this bear's trip [tracing A and C]? [Refer to Fig. 6.6.]

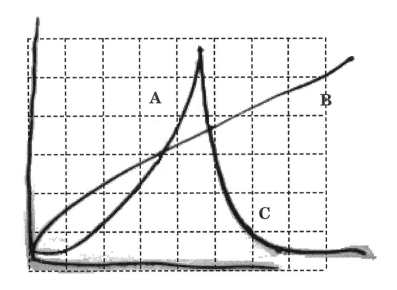

FIG. 6.6. Graph 5.

(27) Lin: [Tracing A.] It went faster and faster to here [top of A]
               and then it went also faster and faster [tracing C].

(28) Tracey: So, he got faster and faster as he was [tracing C] coming
               back to the beginning of the race [the starting position]?
               [Lin: Yeah.] And um, how can you tell? What are you
               looking at?

(29) Lin: 'Cause, the curve [C]. 'Cause if you look at it like this
               way [shows with hands, rotated 90 degrees clockwise],
               it's kind of like slow here [top of C]. [Tracey: Yep.] And
               then it goes like straight up, almost straight up right here
               [bottom of C]. 'Cause it goes fast right here [bottom of C].

(30) Tracey: So, so straight, so straight means fast [pointing to bottom
               of C]?

*Lin interpreted the lines A and C as each telling the same speed story: that
is, going faster and faster, but in different directions. In (28), Tracey rephrased
Lin's account, while wondering about how Lin had come to this conclusion:
"What are you looking at?" This question suggests how fusion does not prevent
Tracey and Lin from being able to separate signifier and signified whenever they
feel that they are not understanding each other. Tracey's question shifted their
talk from signified (e.g., "It went faster and faster" in (27)) to signifier ("'Cause,
the curve" in (29)), marking an "associationist" turn in their conversation; that*

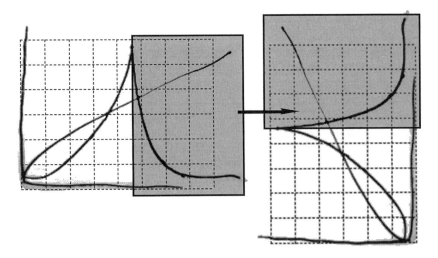

FIG. 6.7. Figure showing how Lin turned Graph 5 to look at line C.

is, associationist in the sense that they tried to make explicit which visual feature of the graph was associated with which motion of the bear. It may be that these associationist turns are typical of conversational moments in which the participants feel that they are failing to communicate and need to step back.[6] Lin explained how she was looking at Graph 5. The following figure shows how Lin "turned" her view of Graph 5 to look at the line C, so that it was perceived by her as a speeding up similar to line A (Fig. 6.7).

The interpretation of Graph 5 that Lin described in (29) and in the subsequent dialogue was not understood by Tracey, nor by any of us on the research team, at the time of the interview. Only after reviewing the videotape a number of times did we come to the interpretation given here. We can recall the group meeting in which we reacted with surprise when one of the participants said, "Oh, she seems to be looking at the graph sideways!" It might be appropriate to say that at the time of the interview, Tracey and her colleagues felt "confused" by Lin's reiteration of the idea that she had expressed in the classroom a week earlier. This observation creates an opportunity for us to clarify the term "confusion" and how it differs from our notion of fusion.

Confusion is used in common speech in at least two senses: as an experience and as a diagnosis. As an experience, confusion indicates a state of not-knowing. It can range from a very well-defined set of alternatives that one is incapable of deciding on (e.g., "I'm confused—I don't know whether I want to do this or that."), to a state of total bewilderment in which nothing seems to be in place

---

[6]We thank Paul Cobb for his observation about this "associationist" turn and its relationship to conversational breakdowns.

(e.g., "I'm confused. What is he talking about?"). As a diagnosis, on the other hand, it implies that someone is taking one thing for another or not distinguishing between two different things. This diagnosis type of confusion can itself occur as taking one thing for another (e.g., "She confused me with my brother"), or as a disordered mixing up (e.g., "He confuses birds. He cannot tell a parrot from a sparrow—they are all the same to him."). Note that confusion as an experience and confusion as a diagnosis can be independent. For example, someone who confuses one person with another may not feel confused at all. For her this person is the other one, so she does not perceive herself to be in a state of confusion. We are interested in commenting on confusion not as a diagnosis but as an experience.[7]

In reaction to (29), Tracey probably experienced confusion. Why was Lin seeing both lines A and C as speeding up? The issue that we want to address in this commentary is that Tracey's "confusion" is unrelated to the ongoing "fusion" between Graph 4 and the racing bears. Their fusion experience was such that for Lin line C made present a bear going faster and faster, whereas for Tracey it made present a bear going slower and slower. On the other hand, not knowing why Lin was seeing line C as a speeding up was likely to elicit a feeling of confusion in Tracey. Distinguishing between fusion and confusion is similar to distinguishing between color and shape: They are qualitatively different from each other. Any color can go with any shape and vice versa. In other words, fusion neither prevents nor stimulates confusion.

(30) Tracey: So, so straight, so straight means fast [pointing to bottom of C]?

(31) Lin: No, it was str-, if straight up [bottom of C] is fast, [Tracey: Uh hun.] really fast, it . . . And if it's like, a straight line like this [the portion of C to the right (almost horizontal)] it's kind of like stopped, [Tracey: Right.] if you look at it this way [normally] . . . But if you look at it the other way . . . [rotated 90 degrees].

(32) Tracey: So, like, up to here [marking off a section near the bottom of C] he's like stopped?

(33) Lin: Umm, 'cause [tracing C]. Yeah, but, if you turn around [rotated counterclockwise 90 degrees], like, the way that the bear's facing, I guess this [bottom of C] would go fast [Tracey: Yep.] and then right here [top of C] is kind of stopped, maybe.

---

[7]We think that, in education, confusion as a diagnosis is vastly overused and is often used as a way to express and deny one's own experience of confusion. For example, it is common that, in feeling confused about what a student is saying, one tends to sanction that "the student is confused" and so immediately ceases to listen to the student and proceeds to articulate an explanation, striving to have the student eliminate "her" confusion.

(34) Tracey: This [top point] is kind of like stopped?

(35) Lin: Like it goes sl-, slow at first [tracing C from top down] and then it goes faster and faster.

(36) Tracey: Uh huh. Because he's turning around?

(37) Lin: Yeah.

(38) Tracey: What if we were to make a step graph of the speeds here [tracing A and C] of this bear's trip?

In (31), Lin distinguished between two different ways of looking at the graph. On the one hand, one can look at the graph in "this way," which meant taking the upper part of the graphical space as being upward and the lower part as being downward. But one can also "look at it the other way"—that is, look at the graph sideways (rotate counterclockwise 90 degrees) so that the portion of the shaded area that was to the right of C is now above C and the portion that was to the left of C is now below C. Adopting the former point of view, the bottom of C indicates "stopping," whereas from the latter one it indicates "going fast." Note how, by adopting the rotated view, Lin pointed out the horizontal bottom of C as she said, "if straight up is fast." Responding to Tracey's puzzlement, Lin explained her ideas further in (33). There, in order to illustrate why the bottom piece of C can be seen as fast, Lin added a new element: "Yeah, but if you turn around [rotated counterclockwise 90 degrees], like, the way that the bear's facing, I guess this [bottom of C] would go fast . . ."

The main theme that we want to highlight in this commentary is that a fusion experience involves the adoption of a point of view. Fusion involves perspective-taking. To clarify this idea, it may help to recall the analogy with children's play. When, for example, a child is pretending that a stuffed animal is a dog, she is not making present "any" dog. Rather, it is a dog with a specific character, distinct needs, and typical ways of being. It may be, for instance, a dog who gets upsets very easily, whose name is Marty, and who barks loudly. One way to describe this acting with the stuffed animal according to a certain pattern of individual proclivities is to say that the child is adopting certain points of view that form what could be called "Marty's perspective." From this perspective, it could be, for instance, that chasing cats is entertaining, candies are unpalatable, and water is scary. This is a perspective that, during the play, she is ascribing to both the dog and herself.

Similarly, Lin's use of the graph involved adopting points of view that she ascribed to both the bear and herself. In order to account for the sharp peak in the graph, Lin found it natural to adopt different points of view for looking at the sections "before" and "after" the peak. The peak signaled for her a "turning around" of the bear and of herself. At the peak, the bear turned around (from going up to going down), and she turned sideways (from up toward the top of the page to up toward the right of the page). This does not reflect a "confusion" between the bear's motion and the graph, but reflects Lin's taking up an organized

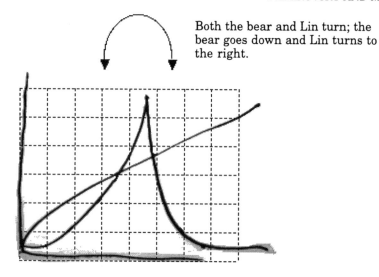

Both the bear and Lin turn; the bear goes down and Lin turns to the right.

FIG. 6.8.   Lin's account of the peak in the graph.

(although mistaken) point of view about the graphical nature of the peak and how it reflected the motion of the bear (Fig. 6.8).

What is being fused encompasses the visual qualities of the graph (e.g., the peak), the motion of the bear (e.g., its turn around), and oneself (e.g., "but if you look at it the other way."). We hope that this commentary will help to make clear that a fusion experience is not a disorganized "mixup" of symbols and referents. A fusion experience, far from constituting a disordered mixture of ideas, comes to be integrated into an overall perspective from which a symbolizer, such as Lin or Tracey, talks, gestures, and interprets according to patterns that encompass the symbolizer and the symbolized.

Discussion

We use the term symbol when we wish to emphasize a fusion or indissolubility of form and meaning. (Werner & Kaplan, 1963, p. 15)

Through our commentaries, we have stressed five points. First, ambiguity is an inherent quality of human interaction that can serve purposefully and expressively in fusion experiences. In these contexts, ambiguity is not merely vagueness, but is a creative effort to highlight connectedness and to build a whole. Second, fusion is a more appropriate metaphor for the nature of symbolizing than the metaphor of transparency. Although transparency suggests the image of "seeing through" symbols, fusion is closer to the idea of "seeing in" symbols. It makes the symbolizer's activity of merging symbolic expressions, which are full of idiosyncrasies, more salient with a horizon of experiential events, stories, and intentions. Third, fusion experiences can be recognized in the qualities of linguistic expression. We exemplified this point by examining Lin's and Tracey's uses of the words *here* and *path*. Instead of diagnosing "false" mistakes, our analysis helped us notice the fruitful ambiguity of their utterances. Fourth, fusion and confusion are different kinds of experiences. They do not necessarily evoke each other. Fusion is rooted in make-believe imagination. It is unrelated to feeling disoriented or to being unable to distinguish symbols and referents. And fifth, fusion is an engagement with the here-and-now of the symbolizer that involves adopting points of view: In other words, the symbol user points out events and qualities of her lived-in space and, in this way, takes up a distinct perspective—a perspective ambiguously ascribed to herself and to the tools at hand.

In order to broaden this discussion, we next explore the connections between and points of departure of our previous comments and those of Werner and Kaplan in their *Symbol Formation* (1963), which is a classic work in the literature on the psychology of symbol-use (cf. van Oers, chap. 5, this volume). In tracing the process of symbol formation, Werner and Kaplan often used terms such as *fusion, indissolubility, unity of meaning and form*, and others. They use these terms in two different ways. The first one, which is akin to the use we make in our analysis, appears when they focus on the general nature of symbol-use:

> Consider the non-linguistic gestural expressions of such attitudes as doubt, puzzlement, contempt, or haughtiness. . . . Since such gestures are characteristically culture-bound and yet, attain the appearance of "naturalness," one can see in such instances how material patterns (for example, body movements) become infused with meaning—infused to the extent that one cannot separate the pattern and its meaning: the gesture is the indissoluble unity of form and content. (p. 20)

Although this former statement is cognate to our analysis, their second sense of *fusion*, tied to their developmental analysis, is not. From a developmental perspective, Werner and Kaplan used *fusion* to describe the child's inability to differentiate between symbols and referents, things and actions, objects and contexts of use, and so on. Fusion and partial fusion are, in this case, used as markers of primitive stages of development. This second sense of fusion is *not* like ours. We want to stress this point because, through our experience of discussing the idea of fusion, we have noticed a very strong tendency to interpret fusion as a childish attitude or as an ephemeral approach of beginners, which expertise dissipates. Elsewhere (Nemirovsky, Tierney, & Wright, 1998), we argued that the difference between children and adult experts is not the presence or absence of fusion but that which they bring to their fusion experiences.

An expert mathematician may, for instance, recognize unusual geometric properties in shapes described by a set of complex equations, in the same way that a musician may "hear" a piece of music described by a musical score. Fusion is not the province of children and "concrete" materials. Rather, it is a pervasive quality of symbol use found at any age level.

Werner and Kaplan's developmental theory seems to express the perception of fusion as an immature phase—a view that we have found to be widespread. They identify progress in development through the growth of a function that they call *distancing*, through which the child becomes able to differentiate, thus allowing fusion to disappear. For instance:

> Still another example concerns the vocable *door* applied by Hilde [an 11-month-old girl] to such diverse things as the *food tray of her high-chair, cork*, and *door*. This vocabulary clearly referred to "obstacle standing in her way of getting out of, or at, something." . . . These illustrations suggest that the early names do not depict stable, circumscribed things but rather refer to global events in which things and the agent's (the speaker's) action upon things are intimately fused. (p. 118)

According to Werner and Kaplan, this type of fusion or lack of differentiation can also happen among adults who regress to "a more primitive" (p. 398) type of representation (e.g., a verbal description that is represented with line drawings).[8] In our opinion, even if one accepts the idea that very young children cannot distinguish between symbols, referents, and contexts of use, this does *not* indicate a general developmental trend, from fusion to distancing, that can be used to say that a symbolic expression is primitive or advanced.

Returning to our analysis in this chapter, there is nothing primitive in what Lin and Tracey are talking about and acting on. Our developmental distinction between children and adults as symbol users (between Lin and Tracey, say) is not marked by the presence or absence of fusion, but by what they, as individuals, bring to their fusion experiences. When needed, Lin and Tracey did distinguish between symbols and referents. Moreover, we conceive of fusion not as an inability to separate symbols and referents, but as an engagement into the world of make-believe that animates symbols and makes them meaningful.

---

[8]Werner and Kaplan extended this argument to the analysis of cultures by arguing that the languages of illiterate peoples tend to be more fused and undifferentiated than those of civilized cultures. They ended the book with the following quote from Meillet: "The trend [in the advance of civilization] has been to eliminate the concrete and expressive categories of values and to assign to the abstract categories a role of ever-increasing importance" (p. 503).

TRAIL-MAKING

Caminante, no hay camino
Se hace camino al andar
Caminante, no hay camino
Solo estelas en la mar[9]
  —Antonio Machado

In this section we explore ways of using symbols in dealing with unfamiliar situations. We examine another episode in the conversation between Lin and Tracey (which took place immediately following the one described in the previous section), characterizing the qualitative aspects of their activity as they, in dealing with the motion graphs, made present and ready at hand their past experiences and expectations. We begin with an analogy that will help us to introduce a notion central to our analysis: the distinction between path-following and trail-making. Consider the familiar problem of finding a way to go to a previously unknown place. We describe two contrasting scenarios.

First, suppose that a friend is explaining to you how to get to her house. It is likely that she will describe a sequence of "directions." Each direction is an instruction for what to do whenever an action has to take place ("get off at so-and-so subway station"), or whenever several options become available ("when you get to the fork, take the right path"). Your friend will set the directions in relation to the type of landmarks that will be noticeable and to places that will offer several possible alternatives. Getting to the friend's house by following such a sequence of directions exemplifies what we call *path-following*.

Path-following is an extremely common and useful way to go to an unknown place. It is efficient, requires minimal or no familiarity with the area, and, if the directions are "good," provides us with a high degree of success in arriving at the place. Path-following has drawbacks as well. Unless we practice the directions frequently, we are likely to forget them, or when something goes wrong (e.g., we miss a certain landmark or the road is closed), the chances of getting lost are considerable. A more profound deficiency of path-following is that, by centering our attention onto the "next" marker or turning point, we tend to ignore the broader surroundings and disregard the overall significance and idiosyncrasy of each place we go through. Path-following tends to elicit a sort of tunnel vision focused on detecting the next landmark or looking at the odometer to detect how far we have traveled.

---

[9]Walker, there is no path/ The path is made by walking/ Walker, there is no path/ Only wakes on the sea.

Let us now imagine a different scenario. You are hiking through the woods in order to reach the peak of a hill. At times you encounter trails that you walk along because they go in the "right" direction, but at other times you have to make trails. Even though you cannot see the peak that you are approaching, it is critical to preserve a general sense of its location. Some tools can be crucial for maintaining this orientation (e.g., a compass, a map, or a procedure to derive the orientation from the position of the sun). The terrain or the vegetation may force you to temporarily detour in a direction different from the one in which you want to go. You keep in mind how long you have been hiking and the proximity of nightfall. You try to interpret your surroundings, searching for clues about where you are, for foreseeable obstacles, or for surprising butterflies. This type of going to a place is what we call *trail-making*. Trail-making can be difficult, time-consuming, and sometimes risky. On the other hand, it enables us to go to places that otherwise are unreachable and it makes possible a close understanding of the area we go through.

We have described these two contrasting scenarios as a means to clarify ideas. Path-following and trail-making are experiential modes of going to an unfamiliar place. As such, it is not difficult to imagine conditions under which each of them can take place either in the city or in the wild. Their different qualities are what matter to us: In path-following, one is centered in the execution of a sequence of directions, whereas in trail-making, one is constantly assessing how to deal with the local circumstances in order to get closer to the final destination. Further, trail-making has an irreducible component of improvisation in response to unexpected situations. In sum, in path-following, our interaction with the area we pass through tends to be restricted to scanning the next landmark, whereas in trail-making there is an openness as to what is going to happen next and how to cope with it.

We use the analogy of going places to illustrate different approaches to solving mathematical problems. Solving mathematical problems in the manner of path-following is all too common in school mathematics. It amounts to following a sequence of "directions" that are often described in textbooks (e.g., the sequence of steps to solve a pair of linear equations). In mathematical problem solving, as in the world of going places, path-following can be an efficient and helpful means to arrive at a "correct" solution. But it has also similar drawbacks in both situations as well: It is easy to forget, there is the likelihood of getting "lost" when the expected marks do not show up, and there is a narrow "tunnel vision" that overlooks alternative possibilities and approaches. We need to stress that, although the distinction between trail-making and path-following is useful to clarify ideas, in the actual experience of going to a new place, or in solving a new mathematical problem, we often combine both or shift from one to the other in response to shifting needs and purposes.

Thus far, we have a sense of what trail-making is like in terms of going to unfamiliar places. What would it be in the areas of mathematical problem solving and symbolizing? This is the question that we explore in this section.

At the end of Episode 2, Tracey suggested in (38): "What if we were to make a step graph of the speeds here [tracing A and C] of this bear's trip?" An important component of the classroom activities had been the interplay between graphs of position versus time and "step graphs," which meant bar graphs displaying the size of the steps taken by the one walking. Figure 6.9 an example of a corresponding pair of position and step graphs. One can imagine the creation of a step graph from a given graph of position versus time, in terms of following a sequence of directions such as these: (a) Partition the position versus time graph into regular intervals, (b) mark the height of the graph at the end of each interval, and (c) translate each difference between successive heights to the step graph, and so on. However, we are going to see how Lin's creation of the step graph was neither for her nor for Tracey a straightforward enactment of a sequence of directions. Lin came to create the step graph with several expectations as to what it should show (e.g., going from slow to fast, and then slow to fast again). As Lin added bars to the step graph,

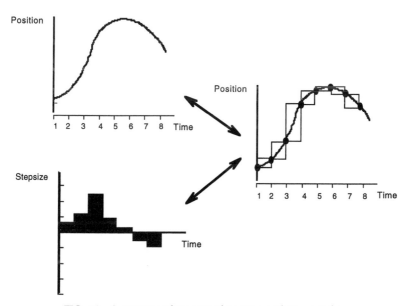

FIG. 6.9. A corresponding pair of position and step graphs.

she encountered puzzling aspects that led her to revise her ideas and to approach the task in different ways. This episode is an occasion to exemplify our notion of trail-making.

Our commentaries highlight three aspects of trail-making—that is, highlight three qualities of making present and ready at hand that further characterize trail-making. First, any symbol use entails a limitless background of features, unintended attributes, and resources, all of which have latent possibilities that are potentially significant (cf. Dörfler, chap. 4, this volume; Sfard, chap. 3, this volume). We comment on how moving these ignored "details" to the foreground is a pervasive quality of trail-making. Second, we highlight how, in the process of trail-making, making present and ready at hand is, to a large extent, something that *happens* to the symbol user. And third, we describe how trail-making entails an open-ended interplay between enacting plans and coping with local circumstances.

Episode 3: What If We Were to Make a Step Graph?

Annotated Transcript.   Refer to Figs. 6.10 and 6.11.

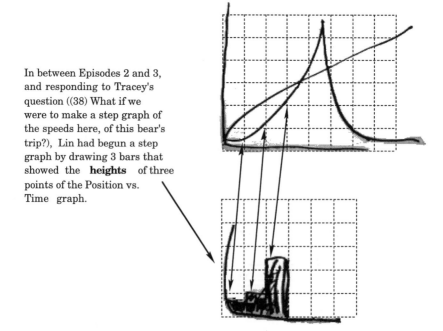

In between Episodes 2 and 3, and responding to Tracey's question ((38) What if we were to make a step graph of the speeds here, of this bear's trip?), Lin had begun a step graph by drawing 3 bars that showed the **heights** of three points of the Position vs. Time graph.

FIG. 6.10. Step graph showing heights of three points of the position versus time graph.

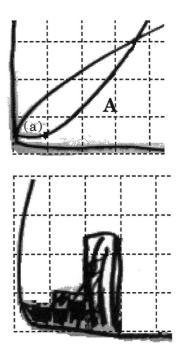

FIG. 6.11. Making a step graph.

(39) Tracey: [Can you] put dots [pointing to line A] to show which pieces [pointing to the step graph] you're, you know, or break up this [line A] so I know which . . . ?

(40) Lin: Half [drawing dot (a)].

Even though Tracey's original drawing of the graph marked the axis along the lines of the paper's grid, the grid had not been an outstanding element for her in the tracing of the graph itself. Moreover, she had used a paper with a grid because it was the only paper available to her. When Tracey drew the graph, she did not plan to situate the peak in between the grid's vertical lines, nor did she intend that the crossing points between the graph and the grid follow a particular pattern. However, as soon as Lin started to develop the step graph, the grid became crucial and shaped all of the ensuing transactions. The centrality of the grid was unintended by Tracey.

The shifting role of the grid exemplifies how, in any symbol use, there is always a background of features, forgotten purposes, ignored resources and idiosyncrasies, which configure a wide terrain of latent possibilities: that is, a background that is open-ended and packed with the unintended. This commentary aims to illustrate how making present and ready at hand often involves trans-forming aspects of the "background noise" into prominence and realizing the dormant possibilities of the unintended. Furthermore, we suggest that this is an important quality of what we have called "trail-making," which is a type of making present and ready at hand For the next segment, refer to Fig. 6.12.

(41) Tracey: OK, so that's [dot (a)] half, [Lin draws dot (b).] that's [dot (b)] one.

(42) Lin: [Lin draws dot (c).] This [dot (c)] is one. [She draws the added horizontal line at a height of two on the step graph.]

(43) Tracey: OK, so that's . . .

(44) Lin: Yeah. And that's, oops. I messed up on that one [crossing out the step graph]. I messed up [drawing a new set of axes].

(45) Tracey: What messed up? What didn't you like?

Refer to Fig. 6.13.

(46) Lin: 'Cause this is a step graph, I thought it was a . . . 'Cause at this one [pointing to dots (b) and (c)] it only goes one but I did [gesturing 1,2,3 on the third bar of the step graph] three by mistake.

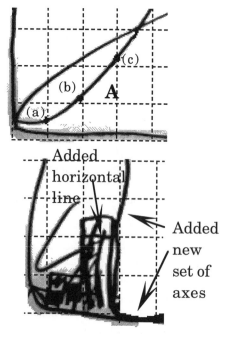

FIG. 6.12. Continuing the step graph.

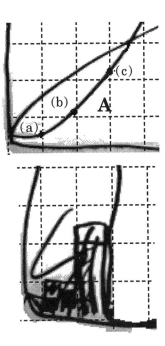

FIG. 6.13. Intermediate step graph.

(47) Tracey: He only goes at a speed of one [pointing to dots (b) and (c)].

(48) Lin: Yeah, right here [gesturing in between dots (b) and (c)], see?

(49) Tracey: Un, huh. From here to here [in between dots (b) and (c)] you mean?

(50) Lin: Yeah.

(51) Tracey: Uh hun.

Lin was explaining to Tracey how she was making the bar graph; she was doing it by marking the points in which line A crossed the vertical lines of the grid, and was stating their heights as indicated by the grid's unit. However, in (42) something remarkable took place. As soon as Lin drew the point (c), she commented about it: "This is one." She found herself noticing something disturbing. At that particular moment, Lin's former practice of creating step graphs in the classroom—step graphs that showed increments, not heights, of position versus time graphs—became present to her. The main point of this commentary is that making present and ready at hand is, to a large extent, something that happens to the symbol user. There had been no concerted plan by either Tracey or Lin to notice and question that dot (c) "was one." Instead, as Lin drew dot (c), a way to create and talk about step graphs that she had practiced in the classroom came to her. First, Lin tried to account for the "one" by adjusting the overall height of the third bar to the grid. However, very soon she concluded that "I messed up" and crossed out the whole bar graph. Lin went from creating and explicating her bar graph to seeing it as a mistake. Recognizing the "one" of point (c), Lin shifted her attention from being immersed in creating something (the step graph) to reflecting on it as a particular manner of doing things (an erroneous one).[10] This event exemplifies what we mean when we say that making present and ready at hand in the manner of trail-making is, to a large extent, an experience that "happens" to the symbol user. Symbolizing is making possible the sudden and unanticipated encounter with past experiences that can radically transform the "here and now" of the symbolizer.

Refer to Fig. 6.14 for the next segment.

(52) Lin: One [drawing bar (a)] and another half [drawing bar (b)], then one whole [drawing bar (c)], then, [drawing dot (cc)] no . . . Wait, it doesn't stop right there [crossing out dot (cc)], it stops right here [dot (d)]. About two [draws bar (d)]. Two, then about um . . . This [point (e)] is only half the second.

(53) Tracey: Yeah.

(54) Lin: So, four maybe [draws bar (e)].

(55) Tracey: Oh, OK.

Now refer to Fig. 6.15.

(56) Tracey: So, the four [bar (e)] showed which piece of that [gesturing the area of the peak around dot (e)]? Could you put a dot to show which piece [of the upper graph] the four [bar (e)] shows?

(57) Lin: Yeah, 'cause it's [dot (e)] only half [halfway between the vertical lines]. [Tracey: Un huh.] This one [dot (d)] to here [dot (e)] is only like half of it; [and the height between dots (d) and (e)] is two, so I decided to double it so it's [bar (e)] four.

(58) Tracey: OK.

---

[10]This type of looking back at what one has done and *seeing* it *as* something is an attitude that several philosophers have called "seeing as" (Heidegger, 1927/1962; Wittgenstein, 1953). Such a shift is ever-present in human activity (e.g., from being engaged in a specific conversation to seeing the conversation as surprising, boring or intriguing).

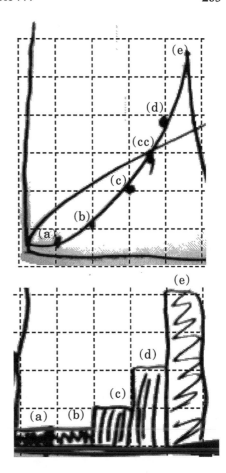

FIG. 6.14. A further stage of the step graph.

(59) Lin: OK, now this one [dot (e)] to here [drawing dot (f)], another four? [She begins a new bar on the negative side.] Maybe?[11]

At this time the overall graph that Tracey and Lin had drawn was the one shown in Fig. 6.16.

---

[11]The rest of the interview is fascinating but too long to be included in this chapter. To preserve her sense that after the peak the bear sped up, Lin tried to parcel the steps after the peak by evenly dividing the *vertical* axis, so that right after the peak the step size was small and it increased over time. After several questions by Tracey, Lin changed her mind and thought that the curve after the peak showed that the bear was slowing down. Subsequently, she created a "correct" step graph.

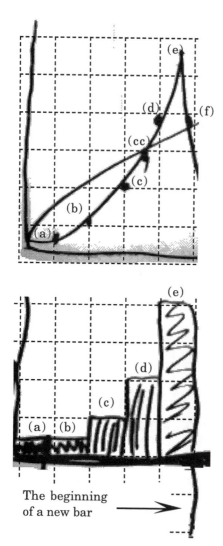

FIG. 6.15. Adding another bar to the step graph.

The beginning of a new bar ⟶

The overall goal that Lin pursued in these exchanges was the creation of a step graph based on the position versus time graph. In (52) Lin initiated a new "trail" focusing on successive increments. However, in approaching this overarching goal, Lin had to cope with the local circumstances of each increment. Figuring out how to deal with the particulars of each increment involved her facing unexpected issues and questions. This experience resonates with the notion that Suchman (1987) described as the interplay between "plans and situated actions." Suchman argued that human activity is neither a follow-up of well-defined plans, nor the uncoordinated response to each local situation, but a complex dynamic in which plans are

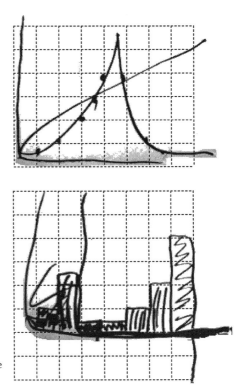

FIG. 6.16. Final version of the step graph.

no more than resources contributing to how people act with regard to their local situations and purposes. Often plans are retrospective constructions: that is, organized descriptions of one's past actions. But throughout our activities and our pressing toward the future, situated actions always have the potential to alter plans in unexpected ways. There are three instances in which Lin copes with the local circumstances of each increment that we will discuss.

First, Lin drew (52) the dot (cc), and then said: "no . . . Wait, it doesn't stop right there [crossing out dot (cc)], it stops right here [dot (d)]." Note that as Lin marked the sequence of dots intersecting the grid with line A, from dot (a) onward, this was the first time that the graph intersected with a horizontal line of the grid between successive dots. Probably her initial impulse in drawing dot (cc) was to mark it because it was an intersection between the grid and the graph. However, she quickly noted that dot (cc) did not belong to the sequence, stressing that to develop a step graph one has to "stop" at the vertical lines. The idea of where one has to "stop" was significant from her previous classroom activities. During the initial part of the interview, Tracey and Lin had actually moved the bear in discrete steps, stopping after each step and marking its position at regular intervals on the graph. We interpret this moment as a subtle movement from marking intersections on a grid/graph to "stopping" at the vertical lines. Lin dealt with her first encounter with the grid's horizontal lines by making present the action of stopping at regular intervals and so refining her overall emerging plan for the creation of the step graph.

Second, by the end of (52), Lin arrived at the peak of the graph. Given her sense that one has to stop at the vertical lines, the peak posed a problem to her: "then about um . . . This [point (e)] is only half the second." She solved the problem by doubling the height of the bar so that she could imaginatively reach the next "stop." Note that this solution was in harmony with her overall expectation that the bear, traveling according to line A, moved faster and faster. This moment is perhaps emblematic of Suchman's notion of "plans and situated actions." From the beginning of (52), Lin was enacting an approach that, at least retrospectively, can be described as a plan infused with goals and expectations. However, the local circumstances of the point (e) posed a new challenge—one without a ready-to-use solution. She then took a turn in her "trail" that was neither an enactment of a stipulated move nor a fortuitous reaction to the peculiarity of the peak. Instead, it was a creative response that adjusted her plan, preserved her expectations, and accounted for the singularity of the peak.

Third, in (59) as Lin strove to figure out the increment between dots (e) and (f), she encountered another troublesome situation: "another four? [She begins a new bar on the negative side.] Maybe?" Her "Maybe?" expressed hesitation. Her initial suggestion of "another four" might have been stimulated by the symmetry between the segment (d) ↔ (e) and (e) ↔ (f). On the other hand, there are several aspects that might have caused part of her hesitation. The most central one is that she may have expected a "slow" speed for the bear right after the peak. Another aspect is that her process of stopping at the vertical lines did not require her to double the increment (e) → (f), because dot (f) was already on a vertical line. Lin then decided to set a negative bar of "two." This was the beginning of a conversation through which she changed her overall interpretation of the second half of the position versus time graph, concluding that it described a bear going from fast to slow. It is in this sense that her situated action toward the increment (e) → (f) initiated a new "trail" along which she radically changed her original plans and expectations.

In sum, the heart of this commentary is that the open-ended interplay between plans and situated actions are a central aspect of trail-making. In this type of symbol use, making present and ready at hand bursts from the creative interweave between envisioning plans and coping with the local circumstances.

Discussion

Episode 3 exemplifies a manner of symbolizing that we have called *trail-making*. Our notes identify three inherent qualities of trail-making: moving idiosyncratic and unintended "details" into the foreground, making the absent present and ready at hand as something that "happens" to the symbolizer, and noting the interplay between plans and circumstances. Trail-making is a type of symbol use in which the background details are an open-ended supply of possibilities and latent meanings that can be revealed by the symbolizer; in which insights "come" to the symbol user; and in which plans and goals are useful resources to be revised, dismissed, or made up according to the local circumstances.

We distinguish trail-making from path-following. The prevalent image in path-following is that of a symbol user who has a goal and a plan that consist of a sequence of actions and choices, interacting with an environment containing symbols to be encountered. The symbol user enacts the plan in response to the symbols that the user encounters. Sometimes, the subject's plan comes from a teacher or a textbook. Other times it is devised in advance by the subject.

The distinction between trail-making and path-following should not be misunderstood as a clear-cut dichotomy with "positive" and "negative" values attached to each. Each refers to ways in which symbol use is experienced as we deal with novel or unfamiliar situations. In other words, each does not describe types of behavior but describes experiences of the symbolizer. Often, we enter into trail-making or path-following regardless of what we have been instructed to do. In mathematics education, it is not unusual that a lesson intended by the teacher to be oriented toward trail-making (e.g., investigating the uses and properties of Pascal's triangle) is experienced by some students as a set of directions to follow in the manner of path-following (e.g., a procedure to calculate the coefficients of polynomial expansion). On the other hand, the practice of following fixed procedures to solve a problem triggers, at times, students' experiences of trail-making.

Not only do we frequently combine or move flexibly from one approach to the other, but both manners of meeting the new and unfamiliar have their own legitimacy and importance. Path-following is generally prevalent when one is aiming solely for the achievement of a final result (e.g., to get somewhere, to fix an instrument, etc.), whereas trail-making reflects an attitude of exploration, openness to the unexpected, and fascination toward a horizon of unanticipated possibilities. Comparatively speaking, as a human experience, path-following is a confined and restricted form of trail-making because of its rigidity, fragility, and narrowness. But in many contexts of life these are precisely the qualities that one wants in order to quickly achieve an unfamiliar goal and to minimize the time and energy invested.

Some readers may deem that the metaphors of trail-making and path-following are not applicable to mathematical activity because neither trail-makers nor path-followers create the landscape through which they move; in other words, seemingly in solving a mathematical problem there is no equivalent to the terrain or path one goes through. However, one does not need to assume a platonic reality of mathematical ideas to recognize that in approaching a mathematical situation one experiences the encounter of contraints, unexpected patterns, promising clues, and so forth, not unlike what one finds in making a trail or following a path. Lin's encounter of the peak being in between successive points on the grid, or the puzzling symmetry between the segments before and after the peak, had experiential qualities that resemble facing an out-of-place landmark on a street or the appearance of alternative and unanticipated trails.

Observations related to the dynamics of trail-making and path-following have been made by other researchers who focus on the careful analysis of students who deal with symbolic expressions (Magidson, 1992; Meira, 1995) or on the nature of mathematics teaching (Lampert, 1990; Simon, 1995). Magidson, for example, analyzed how 12 pairs of students defined linear functions, using graphing software to create a star burst—that is, lines radiating in all directions from a center point. She analyzed "instances in which students set unexpected goals or in which seemingly arbitrary aspects of the problem or computer program have a profound effect on the resulting activity" (p. 67). An example of the latter was that the star burst shown on the student sheet and the predefined setting in the software both displayed an 8×8 grid. To Magidson's surprise, many students used the 8×8 grid as a point of departure, leading them to explore ideas that would not have arisen from a grid of a different size.

One type of conclusion that we are invited to draw from these observations, a conclusion pointed out by Magidson, is that when symbols are used in a trail-making fashion we can never totally anticipate how students will deal with a problem. We cannot fully know in advance what the problem is going to be in the students' eyes. However, the fact that anticipation is not completely realizable is only a portion of a larger set of issues involved in the question: How does planning relate to play and fortuitousness? Many of the ideas we have described, such as the productive use of ambiguity, the unpredictable shift of background details to the foreground, or the provisional role of plans, may seem to some readers to devalue the activities of planning and curricular design, or even to question their plausibility. Highlighting the limitations of anticipation and predictability can be superficially understood as an argument for abandoning planning and embracing complete improvisation. However, this is not the reading that we intend.

To elaborate on this theme, we focus the discussion on the apparent contradictions between common notions of planning and design on the one hand, and the phenomena of play and fortuitousness on the other. We find it productive to explore these issues by examining the relationship between designers (e.g., curriculum designers) and users of the design (e.g., teachers and students). We argue that both designers and users cope with uncertainty and create what the design becomes. However, the designer's uncertainty and creativity are different from those of the user. The following paragraphs describe these differences.

First, there is the uncertainty of the designer and the creativity of the user. The creation of environments for a future that cannot be fully anticipated is the core task of design. In essence, curricular design poses the same challenges as designing a house, a public policy, or a newspaper. One can only conjecture how the house, the public policy, or the newspaper will be lived in, used, or read. One has to envision the inherent multiplicity of circumstances, people, and needs that will come into contact with the design, transforming it into something that is different and often unintended by the designer. An architect, for example, can define the layout of a house, its structure and functionality, but no design can determine what the house will mean to its dwellers: that is, the memories, feelings, activities, and images of which the house is going to be part. In other words, the house as a lived-in space is a creation of those who live in the house, who actively merge the house's design with their own life experience.

Second, there are the creativity of the designer and the uncertainty of the user. We describe the designer's activity as a creation of continuities and discontinuities within the broader culture. For example, an architect's design of a house expresses certain styles (e.g., colonial, classic, etc.), relationships to the environment (e.g., standing within the landscape), emphasis of material textures (e.g., wood, glass, metal, etc.), historical conventions (e.g., choice of color and form), and so forth. The design of the house incorporates many cultural traditions and, at the same time, rejects others. The user who comes to live in the house enters into contact with those traditions, often without being aware of doing so. The uncertainty that the user experiences may be expressed by questions such as: Why was the house designed in this way? Where does the design come from? What kind of lived-in world originated such a house? The design of the house, like an old text or song, has hidden roots that embrace the dwellers' existence.

From this point of view, a design—in any of its infinite forms: that is, a song, a game, a play, a device, and so forth—is an attempt to participate in someone else's creation of his or her lived-in spaces and is an attempt to cope with the fact that one cannot fully anticipate the nature of this participation (cf. Sfard, chap. 3, this volume). In addition, it involves the creation of cultural breakdowns and continuities that the user, although unsure about its origins, comes in contact with.

Such is also the case with curricular design. Our design of the classroom activities that we piloted in Lin's class, for example, was our attempt to participate in fifth-grade students' experimentation with position and step graphs and with their use of these graphs to symbolize number patterns and motion patterns (e.g., "speeding up," "moving steadily," etc.). However, we could not foresee that Lin would create a way of looking at graphs in which she would see shapes according to her changing point of view. Nor could we anticipate the many experiences that other students developed from the same activities. Lin created an unintended perspective on how number patterns and motion patterns relate to each other. At the same time, she and her classmates practiced some ways of using discrete mathematical methods (e.g., partitioning time at regular intervals) that have a long and important history and, although Lin remained unaware of their historical roots, she came into contact with those cultural artifacts that were factors in our curricular design.

The subtle and complex dynamics relating to designers and users—both contributing to what the design comes to mean and coping with uncertainties—are reflected in the conversation between Tracey and Lin, as the following paragraphs demonstrate.

First, both participants contribute. When Tracey and her colleagues designed the interview, they did not plan that the grid would be used as a pivotal element. Even though the grid—that is, the equally spaced vertical and horizontal lines—was on the paper before Lin and Tracey started to talk about step graphs, what it came to mean to them, the way it punctuated their conversation and its shift into the foreground, was their creation.

Second, both participants cope with uncertainties. In (39) when Tracey asked, "[Can you] put dots [pointing to line A] to show which pieces [pointing to step graph] you're, you know, or break up this [line A] so I know which . . . ?", she simply wanted to understand what Lin was doing. But, at the same time, her request brought to the foreground issues involved in making a continuous curve discrete. As she drew the point (c) in (42), Lin's comment that "This is one" was not the result of Tracey saying, "Look, this is one," but of Tracey's effort to dispel her own uncertainty about Lin's actions. As Lin marked discrete points on the continuous curve, she found herself noticing something disturbing. At that particular moment, Lin's former practice of creating step graphs in the classroom—step graphs that showed increments, not heights, of position versus time graphs—became present to her. Lin's experience in (42) was one of disclosing, to Tracey and *to herself*, that she had not been dealing with the bar graph as a step graph even though she had been thinking that she had. The idea "came" to her. That insights "come" or "happen" to us is a way of saying that we often experience what we become as surprising and unexpected. After (42) Lin was in a different place: that is, different because she brought back the classroom practice of seeing a step graph as a sequence of increments, developed a sense that she had "messed up," expressed her intent to start all over, and so forth.

The design—a blueprint, a script, or, in general, any artifact—brings into being a point of encounter between users and cultural threads woven by the designer. Artifacts make possible encounters across time, geography, language, history, and sensibilities. Even though what these encounters come to mean to the users often emerges anew, they manifest shifting streams of cultural continuity and discontinuity. The ending segment of the conversation between Tracey and Lin illustrates this artifact/encounter dialectic. The artifact was the graph that Tracey had drawn on the square paper. On this artifact Lin reencountered the idea—rooted in old mathematical traditions—of steps made at regular intervals of time. She encountered it anew because preserving the regularity of the intervals was problematic to her. In all of the transactions after (52), all the ideas that Lin put into practice were interpretations of what "making a step graph" had meant to her in the classroom activities and were a recognition of possible actions at hand. For example, in (52) Lin encountered the fact that the peak was "only half the second." On the one hand, her sense was that each bar in a step graph had to span the same unit ("the second"). On the other hand, she could not pass over the peak because it was too remarkable. All these sensibilities nurtured in her classroom experience perplexed her. Lin solved her puzzlement by recognizing a possible course of action grounded in the idiosyncrasy of the peak: that is, given that it was more or less in the middle of two successive seconds, she decided to double the corresponding step, somehow forcing the peak to reach the next second.

These interpretations suggest that the artifacts of curricular design, like the documentation of a game or a song, are to be "played" by others who will encounter in them meanings and ideas that we can only partially foresee, and by others who will enter into contact with cultural practices and conventions of remote origins. In this discussion, we have analyzed curricular design in its relationships to design in general. The next section focuses on some specifics of curricular design that make it different from other types of design activities.

ABOUT CURRICULAR DESIGN

In this chapter, we have attempted to articulate a conception of symbolizing as a creation of a lived-in space in which the absent is made present and ready at hand. In this lived-in space, the symbolizer fuses the present with the absent, as well as the symbols with the referents. In the second part, we argued that the lived-in space in which the symbolizing takes place is not controlled by deterministic forces (i.e., the use of certain symbols does not impose meaning on the symbolizer), but is pregnant with open trajectories that can be realized by trail-making—a manner of symbolizing that overlaps the experiential qualities of uncertainty and creativity. Finally, we described design as a creation of artifacts that develop as tacit points of contact between individuals and the cultural perspectives adopted and rejected by the designer. Curriculum design, in particular, involves the creation of artifacts (i.e., description of activities, documentation of students' ideas, manipulatives, software environments, etc.) intended to open up domains of contact between teachers, students and practices that are historically situated within the broad culture (cf. Bransford et al., chap. 8, this volume; Lehrer, Schauble, Carpenter, & Penner, chap. 9, this volume).

This section is informed by our own work in curriculum design, particularly in the Investigations Project (mathematics curriculum for grades K–5), which included the pilot-teaching experiment conducted in Lin's classroom. We use situations that occurred in Lin's classroom as examples. The theme we intended students to explore with this curricular unit was the interplay between graphs, number tables, and motion stories. We wanted fifth-grade students to learn about position and step graphs, and to use these graphs to express verbal descriptions of motion (e.g., "speeding up," "going at a constant speed," etc.) and number patterns.

It follows from the main theses of this chapter that the curricular artifacts do not control or determine, by themselves, what they will mean to the students. This is because of two factors:

1. The lived-in space in which the absent is brought to presence and readiness to hand is constituted—fused—by the symbolizer, that is, the main source of what comes to dwell in these lived-in spaces is the symbolizer's life experience.
2. Symbol use in the manner of trail-making involves the creation anew of continuities and discontinuities with the cultural perspectives that originated the artifacts.

This lack of artifact-driven determinism shifts the role of the teacher to the foreground. It is the teacher who deals with the unexpected and unintended approaches emerging in the midst of students' symbolizing. The teacher, like a sailor piloting a boat, makes decisions in response to both the issues coming forth in the classroom and her own sense of direction and priorities. We call the teacher's sense of direction and priorities her "agenda."

Consequently, to the extent that we care about the outcomes of education, the most central aim of curriculum design is to support, enrich, and influence teachers' agendas. This priority is increasingly advocated in the field (Ball & Cohen, 1996), and is at the core of the curricular materials created by the Investigations project (Russell, 1997), whose audience is the teacher. A teacher's agenda emerges from his or her complex, largely implicit background of views about the nature of mathematics, mathematics education, teaching and learning, social values, and so on, as well as from a background of concrete experiences with the use of classroom logistics and with ways of seizing fleeting events. Accordingly, as is the case with the Investigations Curriculum, important components of the curriculum materials should be (a) reflections on the nature of mathematics learning, and (b) vignettes of actual classroom episodes and students' work. However, in order to avoid fragmenting curriculum design into theoretical discussions and practical logistics, it is important to articulate an intermediate and unifying level of design encompassing both—in other words, a way of shaping the curriculum, as the teacher must necessarily do, so that it merges into a whole the overall perspectives on mathematics education with classroom actions.

To describe our notions about these unifying aspects, we consider three aspects: the design of resources, of boundaries, and of encounters. These three aspects can be recognized in many types of design. For instance, designing a house involves designing resources (e.g., resources for cooking), boundaries (e.g., walls separating internal and external spaces), and encounters (e.g., areas to meet visitors). The following examples, chosen from our pilot experience in Lin's classroom, include resources for students' conceptualization of discrete motion, boundaries setting constraints to students' activities, and encounters with mathematical ideas.

Designing Resources

Several classroom sessions in Lin's class involved the use of a computer simulation displaying a Girl and a Boy running along parallel tracks.[12] Their motion is defined by a set of commands with which students can set the Boy's and the Girl's step sizes, starting positions and many other parameters. Graphs and number tables describing the Boy's and the Girl's motion appear on the computer screen as they run. Before working in Lin's classroom, we conducted a pilot trial in another school. In this earlier trial, we asked students, after they had set the parameters for the Boy's and the Girl's run, "Who is going to win the race?" We noticed that some students responded to the question only after looking very attentively at the Boy and the Girl running on the computer screen, as if the only way to know the answer was to observe carefully their apparent motion. We realized that

---

[12]The software is called Trips. It has been jointly developed by Douglas Clemets and Julie Sarama and is published together with the curriculum.

these students were treating the software simulation as a system whose behavior has to be ascertained empirically, rather than grappling with it as a programmable environment—that is, as an environment in which setting the parameters determines in advance the motion of the Boy and of the Girl. These students did not envision the Boy's and the Girl's movement as events determined by the original commands.

Our sense was that the issue was not how to infer the result of a race from its parameters (e.g., they already knew that if runners start together, the winner is the one who runs fastest), but from the nature of the computer simulation: that is, what the software was actually doing. In response to this realization, we decided to design a resource: that is, an entry point into the inner workings of the simulation. To this end, we designed a new series of activities that students developed in parallel with the computer simulation. In these activities, students used Cuisenaire rods and a meter stick. Each side of the meter stick was a "track" and the Cuisenaire rods represented the step size of the Boy and the Girl. Students marked each step by discretely advancing each Cuisenaire rod. They generated number tables by recording the locations of the end of the Cuisenaire rods on the meter stick. The students solved different problems (e.g., what set of parameters can generate this motion story: "The Girl started way behind but she got to the end sooner than the Boy") either with the computer simulation or with the Cuisenaire rods.

We tried these activities in Lin's classroom. Students moved fluently between the simulation and the Cuisenaire rods, seeming to grasp their equivalence. At times, the students used the software to "test" whether their number tables in which they recorded the successive locations of the Cuisenaire rods were correct. We see these activities as an attempt to provide a resource for students, just as we might provide a map or a rope to someone who is going to explore the woods. The sense in which resources are valuable to students is something that grows out of conducting teaching experiments. The process of curricular design has many of the qualities that we have described as part of trail-making. We could not have known in advance that the activities with Cuisenaire rods would be useful to students. Moreover, there may be many other resources that could have been helpful to students, and it is likely that by trying the curricular activities in other classrooms we could have identified some of them. Designing curricular activities is a never-ending activity (Russell, 1997). The question is not when the design is finished, but when it is adequate.

Designing Boundaries

Teachers face the necessity of deciding which aspects of the stream of students' activities to include and which to omit. These often-tacit decisions draw an intangible and mobile boundary. On occasion, as curricular designers we have a clear sense of a certain boundary that we want to preserve, even though how to convey this to the students is uncertain. In the early development of the "Patterns of Change" unit, for example, we wanted to focus on the speed with which we can walk along a line, and not on ways of walking (e.g., jumping, tiptoeing, walking backward, etc.). Simply asking students for different ways to go from one place to another along a straight line elicits an enormous range of possibilities. How can we deal with them? If we state a criteria for what "counts," will it be perceived as an arbitrary judgment? Does it matter? To stress the centrality of speed in this curricular unit, we decided to require that walks be described in terms of variations of speed. This constraint is an example of curricular overspecification intended to orient students' activities toward the unit's mathematical content.

In other circumstances, we were initially unaware of highly significant boundaries that we were setting. For instance, several activities in our unit involved the creation of number tables describing successive positions of a student walking along a 10-m tape measure at regular intervals of time. Individual students walked along the tape measure, dropping small bean bags every 2 sec (assisted by another student who said "drop" every 2 sec). Students discussed the different patterns of bean bags on the tape measure, how they corresponded to different ways of walking, and how number tables could indicate those patterns. We decided in advance that 2 sec is a good interval because it gives enough time to drop the bean bag and because the resulting separation of successive bean bags on the floor is suitable for revealing the range of speeds within which we usually walk.

However, in our initial thinking, we did not question our idea of dropping bean bags at regular intervals of time. After a few classroom sessions, we came to realize that the notion of marking positions at regular intervals of time (every 2 sec), no matter how natural it seemed to us, is a very particular way to proceed. Sometimes students tended to mark where the speed had changed (e.g., "from this bean bag to that one, go at two steps per second"). Others used the bean bags to indicate step size, so that each step indicated the distance between two successive bean bags. These approaches led us to make crucial changes in the curricular design. We realized that step size is an extremely useful variable because it unifies time and space; that is, the bean bags marking steps given at a regular interval of time (e.g., every two seconds) indicate simultaneously the "when" and the "where" of the walk. Step size became central, to the point that, as we have seen in the episodes with Lin, students discussed "step graphs" instead of "speed graphs."

The new design (tried out in Lin's classroom) was still firm on the issue of "every two seconds." In part, this was because it seemed to us that the classroom logistics posed serious difficulties for "lifting" this boundary and, in part, because at that time we still had not grasped the value and origins of some of the students' alternatives. The classroom observations made us aware that we had set a rigid boundary—marks at regular intervals of time—that might have prevented us and the students from seeing other possibilities. In our ongoing analysis of the videotaped classroom sessions, we are still grappling with and learning about how students used the bean bags and number tables to communicate motion stories.

Designing Encounters

It is often said that curricular activities should provide students with opportunities to encounter mathematical ideas, profound insights of the past thinkers, and the diversity of cultural practices. The notion of "encounter" elicits the analogy with encountering a person. Suppose that one wants a friend to meet a colleague. One might design an encounter, including its time and location, its context (e.g., informal but with a specific issue to talk about), the surrounding expectations, and so forth. The design of the encounter influences, but does not determine, what our friend will make of the colleague. It is never superfluous to inquire, after the meeting, what each thought of the other, and in doing so one may expect surprising answers. The same is true of students encountering mathematical ideas in the classroom.

One of the most critical encounters that we have designed in the "Patterns of Change" unit involves the relationship between distance and step graphs. This relationship, which we know to be intimately connected to the fundamental ideas of calculus, was discussed, practiced, and used by the students in the contexts of walking along a straight line, making patterns with blocks, and interpreting number tables. A crucial activity to "set the stage" for the students' encounter with mathematical ideas is, we believe, the students' invention of mathematical representations (Bednarz, Dufour-Janvier, Poirier, & Bacon, 1993; diSessa, Hammer, Sherin, & Kolpakowski, 1991). We have found these activities important not because we would expect students to necessarily develop the mathematical ideas in question spontaneously and independently, but because these inventing activities can generate a context that allows a meaningful encounter with them. For example, in Lin's classroom we organized activities in which the students invented ways to represent how to walk along a straight line. Figure 6.17 shows a drawing by Lin and her partner, Tyra, that they gave to another pair of students for their interpretation and walk during the first session of the "Patterns of Change" unit.

Lin and Tyra broke down the trip into five segments: (a) three baby steps, (b) stop for 5 sec, (c) 4 big steps, (d) stop for 3 sec, and (e) 15 baby steps. They showed step size by pictures of large and small shoes, stopping

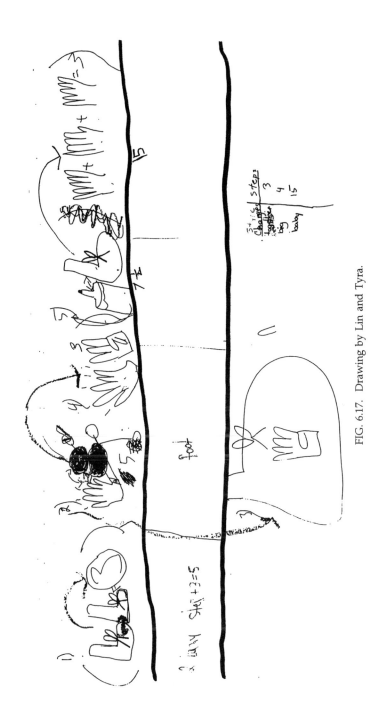

FIG. 6.17. Drawing by Lin and Tyra.

with a full hand, and time with a certain number of fingers up and numbers written near them. We can easily recognize that their representation is not immediately related to distance or step graphs. However, there are important elements in it that are central to distance and step graphs, including the size of the steps and how the step size changes over time and space. Asking students to invent representations has been an important part of our efforts to create contexts for their encounters with mathematical ideas—contexts that incorporate their own questions and proposals. In addition, through this inventing, students are likely to generate alternative approaches that we might not have conceived of, creating in us wonder and inspiration.

We have described three aspects of curriculum design that can unify the discussion of theoretical perspectives and classroom actions: the design of resources, of boundaries, and of encounters. We see curriculum design as fully embedded in the conduct and documentation of teaching experiments (cf. Gravemeijer et al., chap. 7, this volume). It is from these teaching experiments that we can select illustrative stories and examples to serve as a basis for future assessment. To a large extent, we see curriculum design as a struggle with the need to make explicit the resources, boundaries, and encounters that the designers intend, so that they can relate to teachers' agendas. By stressing that a teacher's agenda is a key to his or her fruitful use of play and fortuitousness, we have attempted to clarify that having such an agenda is consistent with an image of symbol use in which some of its qualities are productively ambiguous, unintended, and unpredictable.

ACKNOWLEDGMENTS

This research has been partially supported by National Science Foundation grant MDR-9155746. All opinions and analysis expressed herein do not necessarily reflect the views of the funding agency. Part of the work reported herein was supported under the Educational Research and Development Centers Program, PR/award R305A60007, as administered by the Office of Educational Research and Improvement, U.S. Department of Education. However, the contents do not necessarily represent the position or the policies of the National Institute on Student Achievement, Curriculum, and Assessment, the Office of Educational Research and Improvement, or the U.S. Department of Education.

REFERENCES

Ball, D. L., & Cohen, D. C. (1996). Reform by the book: What is—Or might be—The role of curriculum materials in teacher learning and instructional reform? *Educational Researcher, 25*, 6–8, 14.

Bednarz, N., Dufour-Janvier, B., Poirier, L., & Bacon, L. (1993). Socioconstructivist viewpoint on the use of symbolism in mathematics education. *Alberta Journal of Educational Research, 39*, 41–58.

diSessa, A., Hammer, D., Sherin, B., & Kolpakowski, T. (1991). Inventing graphing: Meta-representational expertise in children. *Journal of Mathematical Behavior, 10*, 117–160.

Heidegger, M. (1962). *Being and time.* New York: Harper & Row. (Original work published 1927)

Lampert, M. (1990). When the question is not the problem and the answer is not the solution. *American Educational Research Journal, 27*, 29–63.

Magidson, S. (1992). What's in a problem? Explore slope using computer graphing software. In W. Geeslin & K. Graham (Eds.), *Proceedings of the Sixteenth Annual Conference of the International Group for the Psychology of Mathematics Education* (Vol. 2, pp. 64–71). Durham: University of New Hampshire.

Meira, L. (1995). The microevolution of mathematical representations in children's activity. *Cognition and Instruction, 13*, 269–313.

Nemirovsky, R., Tierney, C., & Wright, T. (1998). Body motion and graphing. *Cognition and Instruction, 16*(2), 119–172.

Piaget, J. (1962). *Play, dreams and imitation in childhood.* New York: W. W. Norton.

Russell, S. J. (1997). The role of curriculum in teacher development. In S. N. Friel & G. W. Bright (Eds.), *Reflecting on our work: NSF teacher enhancement in K–6 mathematics* (pp. 247–254). Lanham, MD: University Press of America.

Simon, M. A. (1995). Reconstructing mathematics pedagogy from a constructivist perspective. *Journal For Research in Mathematics Education, 26*, 114–145.

Slade, A., & Wolf, D. P. (Eds.). (1994) *Children at play.* New York: Oxford University Press.

Suchman, L. A. (1987). *Plans and situated actions: The problem of human–machine communication.* New York: Cambridge University Press.

Tierney, C., Nemirovsky, R., & Noble, T. (1995). *Patterns of change: Tables and graphs.* Palo Alto, CA: Dale Seymour.

Wenger, E. (1990). *Toward a theory of cultural transparency: Elements of a social discourse of the visible and the invisible.* Palo Alto, CA: Institute for Research on Learning.

Werner, H., & Kaplan, B. (1963). *Symbol formation: An organismic developmental approach to language and the expression of thought.* New York: Wiley.

Winnicott, D. W. (1992). *Playing and reality.* London: Tavistock/Routledge. (Original work published 1971)

Wittgenstein, L. (1953). *Philosophical investigations.* New York: Macmillan.

INSTRUCTIONAL DESIGN ISSUES RELATED TO SYMBOLIZING, COMMUNICATING, AND MATHEMATIZING

7

Symbolizing, Modeling, and Instructional Design

Koeno Gravemeijer
Freudenthal Institute, The Netherlands
Vanderbilt University

Paul Cobb
Vanderbilt University

Janet Bowers
San Diego State University

Joy Whitenack
University of Missouri

Recent trends in mathematics education indicate a shift toward a view of mathematics learning as an inherently social and cultural activity (Brown, Collins, & Duguid, 1989; Cobb & Yackel, 1996; Greeno, 1991; Schoenfeld, 1987; Sfard, 1994). This shift has implications for theories of instructional design, the majority of which have a primarily individualistic focus. For example, constructivism offers an orienting framework within which to address pedagogical and design issues. However, as a psychological theory, it does not support designers' efforts to envision the social setting within which students might be acting (cf. Bransford et al., chap. 8, this volume). The task for the instructional designer, in our view, is to create sequences of instructional activities that take account of both the evolving mathematical practices of the classroom community and the development of individual students as they participate in those practices.

The shift from focusing exclusively on individual development to seeing mathematical learning as occurring in social context is consistent with current instructional recommendations. In particular, many current reform recommendations suggest that the starting points for mathematics instruction should consist of settings in which students can immediately engage in informal, personally meaningful mathematical problem solving.

From this reform perspective, the challenge is to support individual students' transition to forms of mathematical activity in which the use of conventional symbols carries the significance of acting on experientially real mathematical entities. If this individual developmental process is placed in social context, the challenge for the designer becomes that of supporting the collective learning of the classroom community, during which taken-as-shared mathematical meanings emerge as the teacher and students negotiate interpretations and solutions.

Both this situated approach and its individualistic counterpart can be contrasted with the traditional transmission view of instruction in which mathematical symbols are treated as referring unambiguously to fixed, given referents. The teacher's role in this traditional scheme is typically cast as that of explaining what symbols mean and how they are to be used by linking them to referents. Frequently, this involves the use of concrete materials or visual models designed to ensure that students learn mathematics meaningfully. Implicit in this approach is the assumption that such models embody the mathematical concepts and relationships to be learned. However, from our perspective, the explanatory power of such didactic models can be seen "only in the eye of the beholder." That is, although adults can recognize mathematical relationships in the models as a consequence of their prior mathematical enculturation, the students might only see the concrete material. As a result, the taken-as-shared meanings that emerge as the teacher and students negotiate their interpretations of the materials might well differ markedly from those intended.

In this chapter, we consider several approaches to instructional design as we focus on the question of how to support the development of both collective mathematical meanings and the understandings of individual students who contribute to their emergence. In addressing this question, we attempt to move the discussion of instructional design beyond that of simply taking traditional (transmission) approaches as a strawperson against which to propose an alternative. Instead, we take several innovative approaches that are currently being proposed as our contrast set. In the first part of the chapter, we clarify the underlying assumptions of these approaches by extending Doerr's (1995) distinction between expressive and exploratory models. In the second part of the chapter, we outline a third approach to instructional design that has been developed within the tradition of Realistic Mathematics Education (RME). This approach incorporates aspects of both the expressive and exploratory approaches by beginning with students' expressive models while aiming to proactively support the emergence of increasingly sophisticated ways of symbolizing and understanding. The critical aspect that distinguishes this approach from the other two is that the design process involves the explicit formulation of hypothetical learning trajectories (Simon, 1995). To this end, the designer conducts an anticipatory thought experiment by envisioning both how proposed instructional activities might be realized in interaction in the classroom, and what students might learn as they participate in them. In the final part of the chapter, we acknowledge that the approach based on RME involves an inherent tension between individual students' expressive creativity and their enculturation into established mathematical ways of knowing.

ALTERNATIVES TO THE TRANSMISSION APPROACH

Doerr's (1995) distinction between expressive and exploratory computer-based designs provides a useful starting point from which to consider innovative approaches to instructional design. According to Doerr, exploratory computer-based models are designed with a specific, scientific endpoint in mind. The goal when designing these models is to create, in essence, microworlds (cf. Papert, 1980) in which objects follow specific sets of rules. One example is a microworld in which balls fall in accordance with Newtonian laws of motion (cf. White, 1993). Students explore this model by developing hypotheses and then varying input parameters to investigate how well their conjectures align with the model. Similarly, in the realm of mathematical modeling, Kaput's (1994) MathCars program contains a microworld in which students explore the linkage between mathematical symbol systems and the authentic everyday experience of driving in a car. In contrast to exploratory models, Doerr stated that expressive models are developed by students themselves to explain phenomena using a variety of software tools. Here, students invent models that express their developing interpretations of the phenomena in question. Doerr (1995) clarified that this model-building approach begins with students' informal understandings and progressively builds on them. In this approach, students' development of mature scientific understanding occurs through incremental reformulations of commonsense knowledge.

We first consider the exploratory modeling approach and take Kaput's (1994) and Nemirovsky's (1994) work as paradigmatic cases. The instructional intent in each case was to help students bridge the gap between formal mathematical activity and authentic experience. The instructional design approach is one of helping students appropriate mature mathematical symbolizations through investigation. We are particularly interested in Kaput's and Nemirovsky's conjectures about how students might develop relatively sophisticated understandings that, for the adult, are inherent in the exploratory models. We suggest that although intended instructional endpoints are readily apparent, the possible learning routes by which students might develop these understandings are not fully elaborated.

To highlight the contrast with the exploratory approach, we next present two examples of the expressive approach by discussing studies reported by Bednarz (Bednarz, Dufour-Janvier, Poirier, & Bacon, 1993) and diSessa (diSessa, Hammer, Sherin, & Kolpakowski, 1991). These two studies both describe experiments in which students invented increasingly sophisticated symbolizations with limited guidance. In presenting their analyses, Bednarz et al. and diSessa et al. both describe the actual developmental route by which the students progressed. However, as both authors acknowledge, no distinct mathematical endpoints were elaborated prior to instruction.

The Exploratory Approach

Exploring Graphing. The defining characteristic of exploratory approaches is that students explore conventional mathematical symbolizations in experientially real settings. The instructional intent is usually well defined in approaches of this type and typically involves students' development of the mathematical understandings inherent in the mature use of symbolizations. One example of such an approach is Kaput's (1994) MathCars.

In discussing the rationale for MathCars, Kaput argued that one of the core instructional problems in algebra instruction is that closed algebraic forms do not correspond to real-life phenomena. To illustrate this point, he described current mathematical instruction as moving around on an "island of mathematical symbolizations" that are separated from students' authentic experience. To further explicate this point, Kaput noted that most mathematical software is also confined to the island of mathematics. For example, in terms of this island metaphor, both algebraic functions and graphs of algebraic functions are located on the island. The implication is that mathematizing a situation, such as a car trip in which the car moves at a constant speed with a linear distance–time graph, does not support students' attempts to bridge the gap between the mainland of authentic experience and the mathematical island of symbolizatons because both the graph and the story belong on the mathematical island. Kaput's point is that the situation was developed to conform to the symbolization, whereas in authentic trips, cars do not move at a constant speed.

Kaput's contention that students do not view driving at a constant speed as an authentic experience can be illustrated by an anecdote from a seventh-grade classroom (Gravemeijer, 1990). A teacher/researcher asked a group of seventh graders the following question: *A car drives at a speed of 50 kilometers per hour. How long would it take to travel 500 meters?*

The students argued that they could not answer the question because they did not know how fast the car was going. This response indicates that, for them, the formal concept of a car's constant speed did not fit with their real-life experiences. So they interpreted the given speed as the average speed over a 1-hr trip, which made it impossible to say anything about the time spent on an arbitrary part of 500 meters.

Kaput's (1994) proposal is to bridge the gap between the island of formal mathematics and the mainland of authentic experience through the use of computer-based linked representation systems. Thus, rather than confronting students with ready-made graphs of time and distance, Kaput looked for settings where the students can maximally exploit their own authentic experience to investigate and understand these means of symbolizing. One such setting is driving a car. MathCars provides a computer-simulated driving experience that involves a windshield view, a configurable dashboard display, clocks, and odometers. When a student clicks on a button, the computer creates distance–time graphs, velocity–time graphs, and data tables of the simulated trip. The power of this system is that these various mathematical symbolizations are linked to the dashboard display. In this way, the everyday experience of motion in a vehicle can be linked to the formal graphical representations. Kaput suggested that an explicit connection can be made as students monitor a trip in, for example, a school bus. This activity would include having students keep a log of time and distance at constant intervals when riding on a real bus and then reenacting the bus ride with the MathCars software.

Kaput suggested that students' learning may be facilitated by supporting their efforts to explore the physical linkages between the mathematical symbolizations and their own experiences, reflect on their own experiences, and generate new hypotheses. He argued that "as the model develops ... the mental model based in the mathematical representations comes to relate more directly to conceptualizations of the setting" (Kaput, 1994, p. 390). Ideally, this mental model should integrate various mathematical symbolizations such as graphs, tables, and algebraic expressions on a more abstract level. Kaput took care to underscore that his approach is not yet fully elaborated:

> Of course a major question is whether the strongly situated forms of these activities can yield widely applicable knowledge, whether the horizontal linkages of actions ... at the physical level can yield flexible structures at the mental level. The current work of the author assumes that this will not come easily, but will need to be built systematically through combinations of careful variations of the simulations themselves and physical activities distinct from simulations. (Kaput, 1994, p. 394)

We concur with Kaput that this approach to instructional design holds considerable promise that warrants further investigations. Kaput's comments indicate the need to formulate hypothetical learning trajectories that involve specific conjectures about both the process of students' mathematical development and the way in which acting with the MathCars system constitutes a means of supporting it. We would also note that the computer can be viewed as a social mediator (cf. Newman, Griffin, & Cole, 1989; Pea, 1993; Teasley & Roschelle, 1993). This indicates the importance of locating students' activity with the MathCars system in social context. Only then is it possible to describe the process by which students appropriate graphing and other ways of symbolizing. This issue of appropriation is addressed directly by Nemirovsky (1994) (see also van Oers, chap. 5, Sfard, chap. 3, and Dörfler, chap. 4, this volume).

Appropriating Ways of Symbolizing. A second example of the exploratory approach to instructional design is provided by Nemirovsky (1994). His account, like that of Kaput, focuses on the ways in which students might appropriate mathematical meanings as they explore linkages between physical activity and graphical symbolizations. As is the case with Kaput's MathCars system, formal symbolizations such as distance-time graphs are introduced at the outset. However, in contrast to Kaput's primarily psychological perspective on individual mathematical development, Nemirovsky based his rationale on a sociocultural view of learning as a process of appropriation. Building on the theoretical perspective of Bakhtin (1986), Nemirovsky distinguished between symbol systems and symbol use. He argued that a symbol system is an object that is typically analyzed apart from activity. In contrast, symbol use is a meaningful, situated activity. For example, a Cartesian graph can be viewed as an example of a symbol system in and of itself. Symbol use, on the other hand, involves the process of reasoning about functional relationships with Cartesian graphs (see also Lesh & Doerr, chap. 10, this volume for a contrast between models and modeling).

Although Nemirovsky, together with Monk, recently elaborated his theoretical perspective by drawing on phenomenology, his use of Bakhtin's ideas is helpful in clarifying aspects of the exploratory approach to instructional design. For example, the distinction between symbol systems and symbol use serves to counter the long and unfruitful tradition of striving to reduce symbolizing to a rule-governed activity. By illustrating that ready-made symbol systems are the result of abstractions from lived utterances, Nemirovsky demonstrated that the process of learning to reason with symbolizations such as graphs is not merely a matter of learning rules for producing and using those symbolizations. Instead, this learning involves developing meaning by reconceptualizing the situation symbolized by the graph.

In line with his emphasis on symbolizing as an activity, Nemirovsky described a computer-based device that links observable physical activity with coordinate graphs. In one analysis, Nemirovsky (1994) described the process by which a student, Laura, appropriated graphical symbolizations displayed on the computer screen. The experimental setup involved a motion detector connected to a computer that could generate real-time graphs of moving objects on a computer screen. Nemirovsky's intent in developing this set up was to investigate what is involved in using graphical symbolizations to reason about physical change. When Laura placed the motion detector on a toy car and moved it along a straight path toward and away from the computer, the computer generated a distance–time, speed–time, or speed–distance graph. Nemirovsky's consequent analysis, which focused on the way in which Laura attempted to make sense of, among other things, the meaning of a negative velocity graph, documented her actual learning trajectory. This documented learning trajectory is significant in that it chronicles the process involved in experimenting with and reflecting on the relation between the actual motion of the toy car and real-time symbolizations in the form of coordinate graphs. Of particular interest are the "Aha" experiences that supported Laura's continued exploration and reinterpretation of both the symbolizations and physical motion as she appropriated the symbolization to her own use.

Discussion of the Exploratory Approach. The two cases we have considered indicate that an exploratory approach to design does not typically involve formulating a hypothetical learning trajectory in advance (Simon, 1995). These proposals do not contain a set of anticipatory learning conjectures regarding students' learning process and the means for supporting its development. Instead, systems that might constitute productive learning environments are developed. In addition, the focus in this approach is typically on the activity of individual students. Nemirovsky, for example, drew on sociocultural theory when developing the rationale for his motion-detector system. However, although he interacted with Laura throughout her exploration, this interpersonal communication is not itself made the object of analysis. A further similarity between the two cases is that they both reflect the island metaphor in that ways of symbolizing such as graphing are seen as initially separated from students' authentic experiences. In each case, computer-based linkages are used to mediate the dualism between the mathematical island and the mainland of authentic experience. This approach can be contrasted with the expressive approach, in which students' ways of symbolizing are taken as the starting point.

The Expressive Approach

Inventing Symbolizations. Bednarz et al. (1993) called their perspective an invention approach. They developed the rationale for this approach by challenging the widely accepted view that mathematical learning involves the construction of internal representations that reflect the mathematical characteristics of predefined external representations. Instead of presenting symbolizations as external representations of preexisting mathematical relationships, they argued that symbolizations should come to the fore as tools constructed by the students themselves. Additionally, they contended that this symbolizing activity has both an individual and collective aspect in that mathematics can be seen as a continually evolving human social construction. In their view, symbolizing is integral to the creation of new mathematical entities and thus to knowledge construction.

For Bednarz et al., the instructional starting point should be communicative situations in which students symbolize their mathematical understandings. This can be contrasted with exploratory approaches, in which formal mathematical symbolizations are introduced at the outset. The Bednarz et al. initial goal is to involve students in activities in which they are asked to produce a description of some real-world situation in order to communicate their understandings to someone else. They reported an experiment conducted in a first-grade classroom that followed this approach. The starting point is a story about a city bus (or a school bus) with passengers entering and getting off. The story is simulated with the help of a Fisher Price bus and toy figures. In the communicative setting that is established, one of the students has to find a way to keep track of a sequence of events in such a way that another student who has neither seen or heard what happened could deduce the story from the first student's invented symbolizations. Thus, the symbolization must inform the outsider about both the number of passengers who get on or off at each stop and the final number of passengers on the bus at the end of the story.

With regard to issues of instructional design, the Bednarz et al. analysis indicates that students can invent a variety of symbolizations. For example, the students combined several conventional symbols with which they were already familiar (such as arrows and numerals) with stylistic images of buses. According to the authors, these ways of symbolizing emerged because the students were invited to be critical and reflective about the notations they produced. The focus was therefore not on predefined symbolizations, but instead on developing ways of symbolizing that were adequate for communicative purposes. The Bednarz et al. case study serves to illustrate the plausibility of both involving students in the process of developing symbolizations, and of taking communicative settings in which students perceive the need to express their understandings as starting points. However, the question of how conventional ways of symbolizing might eventually emerge remains unanswered as the proactive support provided both the teacher and the instructional designer is not discussed. In this regard, it is significant that Bednarz et al. did not appear to develop a hypothesized learning trajectory in advance. We would note, however, that their analysis of the first-graders' learning could inform the formulation of a learning trajectory that takes account of social context. The second example of the expressive approach that we consider does take account of the role of the teacher. This analysis was reported by diSessa et al. (1991) and focused on six instructional sessions in which students "invented graphing."

Inventing Graphing. diSessa et al. clarified that the invention process they documented was more or less incidental to their investigations. That is, they did not set out, a priori, to support students' efforts to "invent" graphing. The diSessa et al. original goal was to prepare a group of eight bright, sixth-grade students for the introduction of distance–time and speed–time graphs by supporting their development of metarepresentational knowledge.[1] Consequently, although they did not define a hypothetical learning trajectory in advance, their analysis illustrates that the teacher's and the students' roles as members of a classroom community could, in principle, be incorporated into a hypothetical learning trajectory aimed at supporting the emergence of metarepresentational knowledge.

In the first of the lessons that diSessa et al. analyze, the students were asked to describe, with some type of symbolization, the motion in the following scenario: A person drives a car, then stops, then drives away slowly. This was initially an open situation in which the teacher guided the discussion by asking questions about the students' symbolizations such as: Which is the simplest? Which shows the stop? Which shows the duration of the stop? The teacher's role in supporting the students' learning therefore appears to be pivotal (see also Lesh & Doerr, chap. 10, and Bransford et al., chap. 8, this volume, for discussion of the role of the teacher). In this regard, the diSessa et al. analysis differs from the three previous cases we have discussed. In the course of a series of discussions, the students shifted from symbolizing motion with slanted lines to drawing a continuous line that symbolized position. The main point to note is that the norms for determining whether a new graphical representation was preferred over a former one was based on the students' evolving metarepresentational knowledge. Further, as diSessa et al. pointed out,

---

[1]On our reading, diSessa et al. define metarepresentational knowledge as knowledge arising from conversations about the benefits and drawbacks of various representations that can support the emergence of taken-as-shared views regarding the conventions of widely accepted representations and symbolizations such as graphs of motion.

the teacher played an essential role in supporting both this developmental process and the invention of ways symbolizing.

In summary, this case study documents how a teacher took a group of students' self-developed symbolizations as the starting point and guided the development of culturally accepted ways of symbolizing through a process of social negotiation. From an instructional design perspective, the critical aspect of this case study is the focus on the teacher's role as she continually guided the evolution of both classroom norms and taken-as-shared goals. diSessa et al. noted, for example, that the teacher set tasks, provided criteria, suppressed some of the students' symbolizations, provided a conceptual focus, revisited problematic issues, and, perhaps most importantly, kept track of long-term goals. Thus, although diSessa et al. did not outline a specific learning trajectory in advance or offer specific suggestions for the development of an instructional design theory, their description provides a paradigm case that can inform further design and pedagogical efforts. In particular, their analysis can guide the development of hypothesized learning trajectories by helping designers anticipate both criteria that should be established and the specific problems and issues that might arise as students discuss their invented ways of symbolizing motion. In addition, their analysis helps clarify the proactive role of the teacher in supporting this process.

Discussion of the Expressive Approach. Bednarz et al. and diSessa et al. both described the social settings within which students developed increasingly sophisticated ways of symbolizing. Thus, they both offer an alternative to the exploratory approach in which students develop meanings for conventional ways of symbolizing that are introduced at the beginning of an instructional sequence. In general, the expressive approach might be described as bottom-up in that the starting point is students' ways of symbolizing. This contrasts with the exploratory approach, which might be described as top-down in that mature ways of symbolizing are introduced at the outset. In many ways, the two approaches instantiate the perennial distinction between instruction that emphasizes invention and that instruction emphasizes discovery.

As we have noted, the diSessa et al. initial intent was not to develop a sequence of instructional activities that would lead to the invention of graphing. Their original intent was to focus was on metarepresentational competence, the emergence of which is demonstrated in their analysis. From our point of view, their report describes the process by which inventing graphing emerged in an instructional setting. In addition, the work of diSessa et al. is helpful in focusing on the role of the teacher. However, we note that the teacher had to intervene on an ad hoc basis because diSessa et al. did not develop a hypothetical learning trajectory in advance. The teacher could only plan locally and had to capitalize on students' contributions by relying on her intuitions about of conventional graphing. A similar comment about the absence of hypothesized learning trajectories also applies to the other three cases we have considered. Innovative approaches to instructional design that aim to support reform in mathematics education rarely involve the formulation of conjectures about either the course of students' mathematical development or the means that might be used to support it. Instead, like the diSessa et al. teacher, design often proceeds on an ad hoc basis in which local decisions are not informed by a longer-range view of the instructional process. In the third approach, we consider that the formulation of tentative, potentially revisable learning trajectories is integral to instructional design.

ORIENTATION: AN ACTIVITY-ORIENTED VIEW OF SYMBOLIZING

Meira (1995) noted that analyses of mathematical activity often separate cognitive processes (labeled as *internal*) from the manipulation of symbolizations or inscriptions (labeled as *external*). He argued that this separation tends to downplay the role of symbolizing in mathematical development. To overcome this limitation, he proposed

> an activity-oriented view that takes cultural conventions, such as notational systems, to shape in fundamental ways the very activities from which they emerge, at the same time that their meanings are continuously transformed as learners produce and reproduce them in activity. (p. 270)

Meira's emphasis on the "dialectical relation between notations-in-use and mathematical sense making" (Meira, 1995, p. 270) can be seen in both the exploratory and expressive approaches. In the case of the exploratory approach, Nemirovsky (1994) noted that the appropriation of ways of symbolizing involves the creation of meanings that are continually transformed while investigating both symbolizations and what they symbolize. For their part, proponents of the expressive approach describe the ways in which students' mathematical understandings evolve as they develop and revise their ways of symbolizing. This concern for the critical role that notations-in-use play in mathematical development is also prominent in theories of distributed intelligences (Dörfler, 1993; Pea, 1993).

Following Meira, we would argue that alternatives to the traditional transmission approach should take account of both the reflexive relation between symbolizing and sense making, and the dynamic character of this relation. It is while actually engaging in the activity of symbolizing that symbolizations emerge and develop meaning within the social setting of the classroom. The approach we discuss in the following pages incorporates this activity-oriented view while simultaneously capitalizing on the strengths of both the exploratory and expressive approaches. On the one hand, the dialectical relation between symbolizing and mathematical sense-making indicates the value of student initiative. On the other hand, the eventual goal of enabling students to reason powerfully with conventional symbolizations points to the need to introduce symbolizations developed in advance by the designer. These two aspects of design are central to the theory of Realistic Mathematics Education on which the third approach is based.

Realistic Mathematics Education

RME is rooted in Freudenthal's (1971, 1973) interpretation of mathematics as an activity that involves solving problems, looking for problems, and organizing a subject matter resulting from prior mathematizations or from reality. The designer's overall goal is to support the development of these mathematical activities by envisioning shifts or changes as they might occur within the social context of the classroom. According to Freudenthal, emphasis should be placed on the activity of organizing or mathematizing—as it is called in later publications (cf. Gravemeijer, 1994b; Treffers, 1987). Students engage in mathematizing for several reasons. These include goals for:

- Generality: generalizing (looking for analogies, classifying, structuring).
- Certainty: reflecting, justifying, proving (using a systematic approach, elaborating and testing conjectures, etc.).
- Exactness: modeling, symbolizing, defining (limiting interpretations and validity).
- Brevity: symbolizing and schematizing (developing standard procedures and notations).

These characteristics suggest that, for Freudenthal, the process of learning mathematics involved creativity and active construction of models to generalize conjectures. This envisioned process stands in sharp contrast with students' efforts in traditional instructional settings to master mathematical procedures through memorization. Freudenthal views mathematizing as the key process in mathematics education for two reasons. First, mathematizing is not only the major activity of mathematicians; it also familiarizes students with a mathematical approach to everyday settings. Because mathematizing fosters applicability, in which personal experience is seen as critical, RME is consistent with some aspects of the exploratory approach. Second, mathematizing relates to the idea of reinvention, a process by which students formalize their informal understandings and intuitions. This process may be seen as paralleling the intentions of an expressive approach. Freudenthal in fact argued that mature, conventional symbolizations should not be taken as the instructional starting point. He was particularly critical of this practice and called it an antididactic inversion in that the process by which the mathematicians developed mathematics is turned upside down (Freudenthal, 1973). In his view, the goal for mathematics education should be to support a process of guided reinvention in which students can participate in negotiation processes that parallel (to some extent) the deliberations surrounding the historical development of mathematics itself.

The heart of this reinvention process involves mathematizing activity in problem situations that are experientially real to students.[2] It is important to note that reinvention is a collective as well as an individual activity in which whole-class discussions centering on conjecture, explanation, and justification play a crucial role. These discussions bear some resemblance to the discourse of professional mathematicians in that students' deliberations involve reflecting on mathematical interpretations and solutions. However, it should be stressed that idealized mathematical discourse represents the practice of a mathematical research community, whereas the mathematical activity in realistic mathematics education is closer to the practices of applied mathematicians. Additionally, we acknowledge that the social structure of the classroom, with its institutionalized power imbalance between the role of the teacher and that of the students, may preclude argumentation as it is realized in mathematics research communities. In our view, these power structures have a positive aspect in that the teacher can express his or her authority in action by initiating reflective shifts in discourse such that what is said and done in action subsequently becomes an explicit topic of discussion (cf. Cobb, Boufi, McClain, & Whitenack, 1997).

Reinvention Through Progressive Mathematization. We contend that an instructional approach in which the teacher builds proactively on students' contributions is only possible if the sequence of instructional activities consists of problems that give rise to interpretations and solutions that can advance the instructional agenda. By proactive, we mean that the teacher attempts to planfully attempt to capitalize on students' rea-

---

[2]Experientially real problems often involve everyday life settings or fictitious scenarios, but not necessarily so; for the more advanced students, a growing part of mathematics itself will become experientially real.

soning to achieve her pedagogical agenda. These continual negotiations between the teacher and students support the emergence of taken-as-shared meanings when certain social and sociomathematical norms are in place (Cobb & Yackel, 1996; Yackel & Cobb, 1996). In our work in reform classrooms, one of the major goals has been to promote the negotiation of classroom norms that support collective mathematizing. Ultimately, conversations in which students discuss the adequacy of their mathematical interpretations and solutions can serve as situations in which they might reflect on their own and others' mathematical reasoning (cf. Lehrer et al., chap. 9, this volume). In this regard, Bednarz et al. and diSessa et al. both observed that the students in their studies initially developed sketchy, self-invented ways of symbolizing that did not resemble commonly accepted mathematical language. These initial ways of symbolizing evolved as the teachers and students in both studies negotiated their meaning and significance. Both studies therefore illustrate a process of progressive mathematization in which students' ways of symbolizing and reasoning are subject to explicit negotiation.

Given the importance we attribute to mathematical discourse, we find it useful to focus on the mathematical development of the classroom community as well as that of individual students. Further, we have come to the view that hypothesized learning trajectories involve anticipations about possible developmental routes of the classroom community rather than of any particular student. In addition, our comments about the crucial role of classroom norms indicate that the design process should take account of the classroom microculture. In particular, an envisioned learning trajectory necessarily involves assumptions about the classroom social environment. Within a microculture that supports and encourages productive mathematical discourse, the reinvention process involves two aspects, *horizontal mathematizing* and *vertical mathematizing* (Treffers, 1987). In the case of horizontal mathematization, the classroom community develops informal, taken-as-shared ways of speaking, symbolizing, and reasoning as the students attempt to mathematize starting-point problems. By way of contrast, when these ways of describing become the subject of further mathematization, Treffers spoke of vertical mathematization. It is during the interplay of these two processes that symbolizations and symbol use are reinvented. In other words, symbol reinvention emerges as students engage in instructional activities in which they formalize their informal interpretations and solutions. The challenge for the designer (and the teacher) is to anticipate a developmental route for the classroom community that culminates with the powerful use of conventional symbolizations.

As an illustration, we may refer to the ways in which students may "invent" the long division algorithm (Gravemeijer, 1994b). On the one hand, students mathematize realistic scenarios involving "ratio division."

These initial activities are described in terms of horizontal mathematization. As students reflect on their solution methods, they engage in vertical mathematization. During this process, they generalize their interpretations of successive subtractions. As a consquence of these reflections, they formalize the division algorithm.

Realistic Mathematics Education in Terms of Heuristics. The preceding discussion of horizontal and vertical mathematization gives some indication of how reinvention through progressive mathematization might take place in the social setting of the classroom, but it does not explicate specific heuristics that guide the design of instructional sequences. We first comment on the nature of RME as an instructional theory and then delineate three core heuristics.

It is important to appreciate that RME was not contrived as a formal, finished, instructional theory. Instead, the developers of RME view it as a theory in progress. In fact, Freudenthal's philosophy of "mathematics as a human activity" has sparked several decades of developmental research (Gravemeijer, 1994a, 1994b) and continues to guide current work. The aim of this research is to develop and analyze instructional sequences that fit with Freudenthal's orienting philosophy. In this process, RME theory has been developed by reconstructing the domain-specific instruction theory underlying the local theories implicit in these instructional sequences (Treffers, 1987). As a consequence, RME consists of an interrelated series of instructional activities, instructional sequences, local instruction theories, and more general tenets. The general tenets that stem from generalizations of local theories can be viewed as heuristics for instructional design (see also Gravemeijer, 1998).

The first of these heuristics, the reinvention principle, involves looking at the history of mathematics to see how certain mathematical practices developed over time. This heuristic guides the designer's efforts to construct a learning trajectory and also highlights potential barriers, dead ends, and breakthroughs. Given these insights, the developer asks whether students might develop mathematical understanding by following similar developmental paths. A second aspect of the reinvention principle suggests ways in which students' informal interpretations and solutions might "anticipate" more formal mathematical practices. For this reason, students' initially informal reasoning can be used as a starting point for the reinvention process (Gravemeijer, 1994b; Streefland, 1990). Consequently, in this approach to design, the developer takes both the history of mathematics and students' informal interpretations as sources of inspiration and tries to formulate a tentative, potentially revisable learning trajectory along which collective reinvention (as a process of progressive mathematization) might be supported.

One of the most challenging aspects of this approach is finding problem situations that might support progressive mathematization. A second heuristic, that of didactical phenomenology, plays an important role in guiding the development of these problems. The word *phenomenological* as used by Freudenthal (1983) refers to a phenomenology of mathematics. In this phenomenology, the focus is on how mathematical interpretations make phenomena accessible for reasoning and calculation. In other words, the concern is with how the "thought-thing" (nomenon) describes and analyzes the "phenomenon." In a didactical phenomenology, this relation is analyzed from a didactical point of view.

We view didactical phenomenology as a design heuristic because it suggests ways of identifying possible instructional activities that might support individual activity and whole-class discussions in which the students engage in progressive mathematization (Gravemeijer, 1994b). If we consider mathematics as a product of communal activity rooted in attempts to solve practical problems in increasingly effective ways, it is reasonable to expect to find present-day situations that could accommodate a variety of mathematical interpretations. In other words, we can imagine that formal mathematics came into being as a process of generalizing and formalizing situation-specific problem-solving interpretations and solutions. Thus, the goal of the phenomenological investigation is to create settings in which students can collectively renegotiate increasingly sophisticated solutions to experientially real problems. These initial settings can then be taken as starting points for horizontal mathematization in a classroom culture that supports further vertical mathematization.

Emergent Models. RME's third heuristic for instructional design focuses on the role that emergent models play in individual students' learning and in the collective mathematical development of the classroom community. The term *model* as it is used here can refer to a task setting or to a verbal description as well as to ways of symbolizing and notating. Thus, although we speak of models and symbolizations interchangeably, there is a slight difference. In Realistic Mathematics Education, the term *model* is understood in a dynamic, holistic sense. As a consequence, the symbolizations that are embedded in the process of modeling and that constitute the model can change over time.

Modeling as it is conceptualized in RME shares some commonalities with both the expressive and exploratory approaches to design. For example, like the expressive approach, the overall intent is to capitalize on students' creativity. However, we view students' creations as being situated within the classroom microculture and as contributing to the development of taken-as-shared ways of symbolizing. This focus on taken-as-shared models that emerge through negotiation is consistent with our approach of formulating hypothetical learning trajectories for the class-room community rather than for any particular student. The notion of emergent models also encompasses some aspects of the exploratory ap-proach in that both aim to make it possible for students to eventually use conventional symbolizations in powerful ways. However, in the explora-tory approach, dynamic computer-based symbol systems are often pre-sented at the outset. The goal is that individual students (or groups of students working at a computer) will recreate the accepted ways of rea-soning with these symbolizations. In contrast, an approach consistent with RME attempts to build up from students' initial informal activities to conventional ways of symbolizing. This approach of proactively support-ing the emergence of taken-as-shared models involves both the judicious selection of instructional activities and the negotiation of the ways of symbolizing that students create as they participate in communal class-room practices. In this process, the teacher attempts to achieve his or her instructional agenda by capitalizing on students' contributions and by introducing ways of symbolizing that fit with their reasoning. Students are still encouraged to develop their own models, but in situations that are chosen to support the realization of a proposed learning trajectory. In addition, attention is given to negotiation and to collective reflection as well as to individual creation. In this scheme, the proposed learning trajectory provides a vision of various ways of symbolizing that could be capitalized on in whole-class discussions to support the process of col-lective mathematization and reinvention.

Our description of the process of collective mathematization, in which informal, self-developed models evolve into more sophisticated models, is purposely left open ended for several reasons. First, it would be naive to expect or claim that any proposed learning trajectory could predict the exact route through which any classroom community would pass. In practice, the conjectured learning trajectory is continually adjusted and modified in response to observations of students' activity (cf. Simon, 1995). Second, in contrast to the claims of developers who aim to bridge the gap between informal and conventional ways of symbolizing by assimilating the latter directly to the former, our goal is to support an emergence of meaningful symbolizations that arise during collective negotiations in which students attempt to revise their present ways of notating in order to describe a situation more effectively or efficiently. These caveats ac-knowledged, it is possible in our view for the designer to lay out a proposed developmental route for the classroom community in which students first model situations in an informal way (this is called a *model of* the situation) and then mathematize their informal modeling activity (this produces a *model for* mathematical reasoning). For example, referring again to the earlier example of the emergence of long division, students may create a model *of* a situation in which they find the number of buses needed to transport a certain number of supporters through repeated subtraction. Later, the class may discuss ways to use multiples of the number of seats in a bus to determine the number of buses needed. At this point, the discussions have shifted from explicitly talking about a situation, to talking about repeated subtraction as a model *for* reasoning about the mathematical relations involved. A hypothesized trajectory of this type involves the conjecture that the model, which emerges as students formalize their reasoning, will gradually take on a "life of its own" independent of situation-specific imagery. The benefit of such a trajectory is that it outlines both a learning agenda and a possible means for attaining it. In this way, it can serve as a resource for the teacher attempting to proactively support the collective development of taken-as-shared symbolizations and meanings.

The transition from a model of to a model for is generally consistent with Sfard's (1991) historical analysis of the process of reification. Sfard argued that the history of mathematics is characterized by repeated processes of reification in which understandings that initially existed only in action were objectified, thus creating mathematical entities that were experienced as existing independently of activity.[3] For example, she traced the origin of the notion of function to calculational actions that produce an output for a given input. Functions were subsequently defined as a set of ordered number pairs that could be produced by calculating. Later, functions emerged as full-fledged entities with certain properties. It was then possible to compare linear and quadratic functions or continuous and discontinuous functions. Without making claims about the role of models in the history of mathematics, we would argue that emergent models can be employed in mathematics education, to foster similar transitions.

Note that the objective of fostering the reification of mathematical activity implies that what is reified in the model-of to model-for transition is the process of acting and reasoning with the model, not the symbolization itself. This emphasis on activity differentiates approaches based on RME from approaches that involve a modeling point of view (e.g., Lehrer et al., chap. 9, and Lesh & Doerr, chap. 10, this volume). In these latter approaches, a model is considered to capture mathematical structures or relationships implicit in starting-point situations. In contrast, a model as we have characterized it originates from students' ways of acting and reasoning in the starting-point situations. Although this distinction is subtle, it has implications for design in that our focus when formulating learning trajectories is on students' anticipated interpretations and solutions rather than on the starting-point situation per se.

---

[3]A similar discussion of the role of reification can be found in Ernst's (1991) analysis of the theoretical reconstruction of informal knowledge.

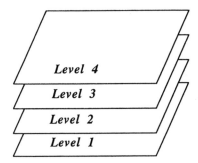

Level 1: Activity in the task setting, in which interpretations and solutions depend on understanding of how to act in the setting (often out of school settings)

Level 2: Referential activity, in which models-of refer to activity in the setting described in instructional activities (posed mostly in school)

Level 3: General activity, in which models-for make possible a focus on interpretations and solutions independently of situation-specific imagery

Level 4: Reasoning with conventional symbolizations, which is no longer dependent on the support of models-for mathematical activity

FIG. 7.1. Levels of activity.

The model-of/model-for distinction can be elaborated by identifying four general types of activity as shown in Fig. 7.1. Although the four types of activity clearly involve a developmental progression, we would reject the implication that they involve a strictly ordered hierarchy. In practice, discussions of general activity and of reasoning with conventional symbols frequently fold back to referential activity or even to activity in the setting (McClain & Cobb, 1998). The development both of collective mathematical practices and of the understandings of individual students who participate in them appears to be a recursive, multilevel process (Pirie & Kieren, 1994).

Our goal in describing the four levels of activity is to illustrate that models are initially tied to activity in specific settings and involve situation-specific imagery. At the referential level, models are grounded in students' understandings of paradigmatic, experientially real settings. In whole-class discussions, these models are integral to explanations in which students describe how they interpreted and solved tasks centering on the starting point settings. General activity begins to emerge as students' reasoning loses its dependency on situation-specific imagery, and the role of models gradually changes as they take on a life of their own. This transition can be seen as a process of reification wherein the students begin to collectively reflect on their referential activity. In the process, the model becomes an entity in its own right and serves more as a means of mathematical reasoning than as a way of symbolizing mathematical activity grounded in particular settings.

THE STRUCTURING NUMBERS INSTRUCTIONAL SEQUENCE

In order to further elaborate the notion of a learning trajectory in general and the transition from a model of to model for in particular, we describe the evolution of classroom mathematical practices during a recent teaching experiment conducted in a first-grade classroom in a southeastern suburban setting. The goal of this teaching experiment was to support students' development of general number sense for numbers less than 20. That is, our instructional goal was to support the emergence of what Greeno (1991) described as a sense of knowing one's way around a mathematical environment. We first discuss the design heuristics of mathematization and reinvention, didactical phenomenology, and emergent models by describing the Structuring Numbers instructional sequence and the conjectured learning trajectory. We then describe the classroom teaching experiment by first documenting the norms for participation that were established in the first-grade classroom. Next, we trace the mathematical practices that emerged as the teacher and students negotiated their interpretations and understandings, and compare this actualized learning trajectory to the conjectured learning trajectory. Finally, we step back to focus specifically on the role of symbolizing in the actual learning trajectory.

Design Heuristics in Relation to the Structuring Numbers Sequence

Mathematization and Reinvention in Relation to the Structuring Numbers Sequence. The arithmetic rack sequence was created to support flexible quantitative reasoning with numbers up to 20.[4] In terms of Greeno's (1991) environmental metaphor, the intent was that students would come to act in a quantitative environment structured by relationships between numbers up to 20. Observationally, this would be indicated by their flexible use of thinking or derived fact strategies to solve a wide

---

[4]Working in the domain of numbers up to 20 may misleadingly be identified with the notion of basic skills. It is therefore essential that we explain our position on basic skills before we describe the instructional sequence. The label *basic skills* is heavily value laden and brings to mind a traditional stance that is reductionist with regard to both mathematics and student activity. However, rejection of the reductionist view on learning and instruction does not imply that we can dispense with the notion of skills. It does, however, imply that we need to reconceptualize them. Instead of talking about skills as consisting of automated subskills, we would prefer to speak of skilled activity. This reconceptualization also bears on the relation between skills and understanding. In the traditional view, skills stand in opposition to understanding—each is the antithesis of the other. In the view we endorse, understanding is an integral, inseparable aspect of skilled activity.

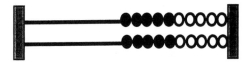

FIG. 7.2.   The arithmetic rack.

range of tasks. For example, the students might solve a task interpreted as $14 - \_ = 6$ by reasoning that $14 - 4 = 10$, and $10 - 4 = 6$, so the answer is 8. Alternatively, they might reason that $7 + 7 = 14$, so $14 - 7 = 7$, and $14 - 6 = 8$. Our global intent was that the numerical relationships implicit in these and other observable strategies would be ready-to-hand for the students. In other words, they would not have to figure out appropriate strategies to use. Instead, our goal was that the students would come to have the experience of directly perceiving relationships as they interpreted and solved arithmetical problem situations. Needless to say, coming to act in such an environment is a major intellectual achievement that requires proactive developmental support and is profoundly influenced by the material and symbolic tools that students use. The challenge for design was therefore to conjecture a learning trajectory and the means of supporting it that culminated with this intellectual achievement.

One source of guidance for design was provided by research that documents students' informal solution strategies. Findings have consistently revealed that some students frequently develop strategies that use the doubles (and multiples) of five as points of reference. In explaining these findings, van den Berg and van Eerde (1985) noted that the spontaneous use of 5 and 10 as reference points is related to the creation of finger patterns that embody the results of counting.[5] Treffers (1991) also suggested that strategies centering on the doubles and on 5 and 10 as reference points reflect numerical relationships implicit in common finger patterns. For example, a student might show 8 as 5 fingers on one hand and 3 on the other, or as 4 fingers on each hand. These patterns can themselves be curtailments of counting on the fingers by one. In Steffe, Cobb, and von Glasersfeld's (1988) terms, the finger patterns embody the results of counting.

Based on these finding, Treffers (1991) designed a device called the arithmetic rack whose use would support the development of numerical reasoning in which five, ten, and doubles can emerge as points of reference. This device consists of two parallel rods each containing 10 beads. As shown in Fig. 7.2, the first 5 beads on the left of each rod are red, and

---

[5]The idea of supporting the development of five as a reference point is not new. We note Hatano's (1982) use of 5-tiles, Fletcher's (1988) 5-frames, Wirtz's (1980) 10-frames, and the numerical images in older approaches to arithmetic (Radatz & Schipper, 1983). In RME, however, the focus is on students' reasoning, whereas the preceding examples tend to rely on a rather scripted use of manipulatives.

the second 5 beads are white. Students use the rack by moving all the beads to the right and then creating various configurations by sliding beads to the left. For example, if a student wants to show 8, she might move 5 beads on the top rod and 3 on the bottom, or she might move 4 beads on each rod. These ways of acting with the rack reflect relationships implicit in finger patterns and, from the observer's perspective, appear to involve taking five and doubles respectively as points of reference. In the hypothetical learning trajectory that we outline, the instructional activities involved using the rack to solve a range of additive tasks.

Didactical Phenomenology in Relation to the Structuring Numbers Sequence. As a design heuristic, didactical phenomenology involves finding phenomenologically appropriate situations from which models might emerge in the course of classroom activities and discussions. In the case of the Structuring Numbers sequence, one type of situation identified involved a scenario about a double-decker bus. We planned to introduce the arithmetic rack once students had explored this situation. Our intent was that beads on the top and bottom rods would be used to show the number of passengers on the top and bottom decks of the bus, and that moving beads would signify the number of passengers getting on or off the bus. It is important to note that most of the students might never have seen a double-decker bus, let alone ridden on one. We therefore anticipated that the teacher and students would discuss the scenario at some length and perhaps act out riding a bus so that it would become an experientially real situation. The heuristic of didactical phenomenology does not therefore imply that initial, starting-point settings should be authentic in the sense that they fit with students' actual, lived out-of-school experiences. Instead, the intent is to identify situations that can become experientially real for students relatively quickly and that these situations constitute settings from which mathematically significant models might emerge. Thus, this approach to design involves taking account of the potential endpoints of the instructional sequence even when choosing starting point situations. To paraphrase Ball (1993), it is an approach that involves keeping one eye on the mathematical horizon and the other on students' current understandings, concerns, and interests.

Emergent Models in the Structuring Numbers Sequence. It is important to emphasize that the learning trajectory we envisioned when developing the instructional sequence necessarily involved assumptions about the nature of the classroom microculture. For example, we anticipated that the students would engage in conversations in which they not only described how they had acted with the arithmetic rack, but also explained how they had interpreted tasks and thus why they had used the rack in particular ways. Further, the teacher would proactively support the emergence of different and increasingly efficient solutions. These comments again underscore the importance of giving explicit attention to the classroom social context.

The first instructional activities that we planned for the structuring numbers sequence were those involving the double-decker bus scenario. We intended to build on a prior instructional sequence called Patterning and Partitioning that emphasized partitioning collections of up to 10 items by first asking the students to generate different ways in which a given number of passengers could sit on the two decks of a double-decker bus. van den Brink (1989), the developer of the bus scenario, conjectured that the need to partition arises naturally once a distinction is made between the passengers on the upper and lower decks. Further, in this situation, solutions such as 6 and 2, and 2 and 6 count as different in that they signify different arrangements of people on the bus. Once the practice of generating different partitionings had emerged, we planned to introduce the arithmetic rack as a means of showing the number of passengers on each deck. Thus, in the conjectured learning trajectory, the rack would initially function as a model *of* the number of passengers on the two decks.[6]

The first planned instructional activities in which the children used the rack involved generating configurations (e.g., "How could you show 15 people on the bus?") and evaluating given configurations. We conjectured that ways of reasoning that involved grouping, particularly by taking 5, 10, and doubles as points of reference, might emerge as a mathematical practice. To the extent that this occurred, the arithmetic rack would gradually be constituted by the classroom community as a numerically structured device in line with its designer's intentions. The interpretation of, for example, 5 red beads and 1 white bead on both rods as 10 and 2 would then be self-evident and beyond justification.

The next set of instructional activities that we outlined before the teaching experiment began dealt with situations in which passengers got on and off the bus. For example, after the students had shown nine passengers on the bus, the teacher might ask, "How many passengers would be on the bus when seven more get on?" We anticipated that, for the sample task, some students might first move nine beads on the top rod and then add seven more by moving the remaining bead on the top rod and six on the bottom rod (see Fig. 7.3a). *From the observer's perspective*, a going-through-ten strategy is *implicit* in this solution (i.e., $9 + 1 = 10$, $10 + 6 =$

---

[6]It should be noted that the anticipated relation between the beads and the passengers was fairly normal. We reasoned that, from the students' perspective, the beads signified the number of passengers, not the passengers themselves. We therefore conjectured that it would not matter which bead was shifted when a passenger got off the bus, as long as the total decreased by one.

(a)

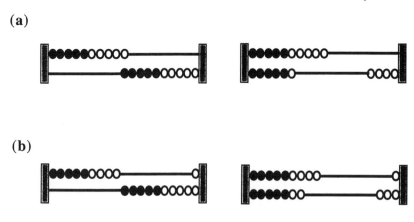

(b)

FIG. 7.3. Two ways of acting with the arithmetic rack to solve 9 + 7 = __:
(a) going-through-ten and (b) doubles.

16). We also anticipated that other students might first move nine on the
top rod as before but then move seven on the bottom rod and then
recognize the resulting configuration as 7 and 7 is 14, and 2 more is 16
(see Fig. 7.3b). In this case, a doubles strategy is implicit in the students'
solution. At this point in the conjectured trajectory, the arithmetic rack
would function as a model of a wider range of events in the bus scenario.

The intent of the next set of planned tasks was to support the emergence
of the numerical relationships implicit in students' use of the rack as
explicit topics of conversation. We conjectured that this would make it
possible for the rack to gradually become a model *for* numerical reasoning.
To this end, we envisioned a scenario in which the teacher and students
might discuss the need to develop ways of notating their reasoning with
the rack so that they could communicate it to others. Subsequent activities
would then involve developing and negotiating symbolizations, the key
criterion being that other children in the class could understand how the
task had been solved. This anticipated development follows diSessa et al.
(1991) in acknowledging the importance of metarepresentational knowledge. In addition, we imagined that the teacher would play a proactive
role that might involve introducing ways of symbolizing that fit with
students' activity. For example, the ways of reasoning with rack shown
in Figs. 7.3a and 7.3b might be symbolized as shown in Fig. 7.4.

Clearly, the teacher's envisioned role of both supporting the development of students' ways of symbolizing and introducing conventional
ways of symbolizing that fit with their activity involves an inherent
tension. In the planned activity as we imagined it, the teacher's symbolizations would constitute offers but without the implication that students
should merely imitate them. In the analysis reported by Bednarz et al.
(1993), the symbolizations that the students developed combined various

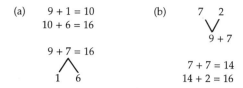

FIG. 7.4. Possible ways of notating the solutions to $9 + 7 = \_$ shown in Figs. 7.3a and 7.3b.

conventional symbols (e.g., arrows, numerals) with other invented symbols to communicate their methods. Similarly, in the RME model, one hopes that the ways of symbolizing introduced by the teacher might serve as a resource that students could adapt to their purposes. In the case of the Structuring Numbers sequence, for example, the overall intent was that students would eventually come to reason with symbolizations that were independent of the arithmetic rack itself. In our view, such a goal could only be attained if the mathematical practices established in the classroom involved using thinking strategies flexibly to solve a range of additive tasks.

This description of the hypothesized learning trajectory in terms of an anticipated sequence of classroom mathematical practices traces a route through the four types of activity summarized in Fig. 7.1. For example, the planned starting point for the hypothetical trajectory involved activity in the setting of the double-decker bus scenario. We anticipated that reasoning with the arithmetic rack would first serve as a model of activity in this setting (i.e., referential activity), but that it would subsequently take on a life of its own and become a model for numerical reasoning (i.e., general activity). We conjectured that the development of ways of notating would play a crucial role in this transition. In the conjectured trajectory, the final type of activity shown in Fig. 7.1 would emerge as reasoning with number relations took on a life of its own.

The design heuristic we have illustrated, that of emergent models, involves the transition from acting with the arithmetic rack as a model *of* a phenomenologically appropriate scenario to acting with the arithmetic rack as a model *for* more sophisticated mathematical reasoning. We would acknowledge that this general heuristic provides a relatively crude description of a complex process. However, we contend that it suffices to provide an orientation for the design of instructional sequences. It is also important to stress that a conjectured learning trajectory is just that, a conjecture. Although it provides a sense of direction for instruction, it is tentative and potentially revisable. Following Simon (1995), we have argued that the relation between the conjectured learning trajectory and the local judgments made in the classroom while enacting a sequence is reflexive (Cobb, 1996; Gravemeijer, 1996). On the one hand, the trajectory constitutes the broad, encompassing backdrop against which local judgments are made. On the other hand, the conjectured trajectory itself evolves as a consequence of those local decisions and judgments. As a consequence, the actual learning trajectories realized in classrooms are "inextricably linked to histories that are lived, much like paths that exist only as they are laid down by walking" (Varela, Thompson, & Rosch, 1991, p. 205). In other words, although there is an overall instructional intent and a conjectured developmental route at any point, both are open to revision as the actual learning trajectory is realized in interaction in the classroom. In this regard, the process of enacting an instructional sequence illustrates the process of trail making discussed by Nemirovsky and Monk (chap. 6, this volume).

As a final observation, we again emphasize that the conjectured learning trajectory we have outlined is cast in the collectivist terms of classroom mathematical practices. In this regard, the focus is on the mathematical development of the classroom community rather than on that of any particular student. Of course, this does not imply that the students will all learn in lockstep. Instead, students make a range of qualitatively distinct mathematical interpretations even as they participate in the same classroom mathematical practices (cf. Cobb & Yackel, 1996). We should therefore stress that observations of individual students' activity inform the process of revising the conjectured learning trajectory as an instructional sequence is enacted in the classroom (Simon, 1995). Further, individual students' actual learning trajectories can be delineated by analyzing the development of their reasoning as they participate in the evolving classroom mathematical practices. In simultaneously viewing individual students' mathematical activity as acts of participation, the analysis necessarily locates their learning in the social context of the classroom.

The Structuring Numbers Classroom Teaching Experiment

The Structuring Numbers sequence was one of two instructional sequences enacted during a 3-month teaching experiment conducted in a first-grade classroom. The class consisted of 7 boys and 11 girls, most of whom were from middle- or upper-middle-class families. The teacher with whom we collaborated, Ms. Smith, valued her students' reasoning and wanted to further develop an instructional approach that capitalized on their contributions. The data corpus generated during the experiment comprised videotaped individual interviews conducted with all 18 children in September, December, and January; video recordings of additional interviews conducted with 10 children in November; video recordings of 47 mathematics lessons; copies of all the students' written work; and three sets of daily field notes.

The first instructional sequence enacted in the teaching experiment was called Patterning and Partitioning. The rationale for this sequence is based on research indicating that using an arithmetic rack by grouping beads rather than by counting beads by one is itself a developmental achievement for young children. The instructional activities in the Patterning and Partitioning sequence focused on using finger patterns flexibly, on evaluating configurations of up to 10 items without counting (i.e., by patterning), and on generating different partitions of collections of up to 10 items (e.g., a picture collection of 8 items viewed as 7 and 1, 6 and 2, etc.). This latter type of instructional activity served as a precursor for the double-decker bus activity that was the starting point for the Structuring Numbers sequence.

A detailed analysis of the teaching experiment (Whitenack, 1995) indicated that the majority of the 18 students did come to act in an environment that was structured by relationships between numbers up to 20. We draw on this analysis first to document the classroom social and sociomathematical norms and then to describe the actual learning trajectory realized in the classroom.

Social and Sociomathematical Norms

Classroom social and sociomathematical norms are central aspects of the classroom microculture within which instructional sequences are enacted. The microculture established in Ms. Smith's classroom was one in which alternative interpretations were valued and respected. The general social norms she negotiated with her students included expectations that:

1. The students would explain and justify their thinking when contributing to whole-class discussions.
2. The students would listen to contributions made by their classmates.
3. The students would indicate when they did not understand a classmate's explanation or contribution and ask clarifying questions.

As these three norms indicate, the classroom microculture emphasized active participation and attempting to understand on the part of all students. In contrast to these general classroom social norms, sociomathematical norms are specific to normative aspects of students' mathematical activity (Yackel & Cobb, 1996). A sociomathematical norm that was renegotiated throughout the teaching experiment was that of what counted as a different mathematical solution. Ms. Smith responded differentially to students' contributions, indicating that she particularly valued noncounting solutions that she and the students came to call "grouping ways." A detailed analysis of Ms. Smith's role in proactively supporting her students' mathematical learning indicates that this was an important aspect of her effectiveness as a reform teacher (McClain, 1995). In particular, the sociomathematical norms established by Ms. Smith and her students enabled the students to become aware of more sophisticated forms of mathematical reasoning, thereby making it possible for their problem solving efforts to have a sense of directionality (cf. Voigt, 1995). In accomplishing this, however, Ms. Smith continued to accept and actively solicit counting solutions from students whom she judged were not yet able to develop grouping solutions. This ensured that all students had ways to actively participate in the evolving classroom mathematical practices.

As a consequence of Ms. Smith's role in guiding the development of sociomathematical norms, various types of counting solutions that researchers would judge as different (e.g., counting all vs. counting on) were not judged as different in this classroom. In contrast, Ms. Smith and the students did differentiate between various types of grouping or thinking strategy solutions. These solutions were judged as different if they involved either (a) different quantitative interpretations (e.g., a task interpreted as $6 + \_ = 14$ rather than $14 - 6 = \_$), or (b) different calculational processes such that numerical entities were decomposed and recomposed in different ways (e.g., solutions that used doubles and 10 as a point of reference were to be judged as different). As has been argued elsewhere, what counts as a different mathematical explanation can differ markedly from one classroom to another and can profoundly influence the mathematical understandings that students develop (Yackel & Cobb, 1996).

Documenting the Actual Learning Trajectory:
The Evolution of Mathematical Practices

Our goal in describing the evolution of classroom mathematical practices is to document both the instructional sequence as it was realized in the classroom and the learning of the classroom community. In general, classroom mathematical practices evolve as the teacher and students discuss problems and solutions, and involve means of symbolizing, arguing, and validating in specific task situations (cf. Balacheff, 1990). The analysis of the Structuring Number sequence teaching experiment involved delineating the following five practices:

1. Making configurations on the arithmetic rack.
2. Describing configurations in terms of fives, tens, and doubles.
3. Reasoning in terms of groups while solving addition and subtraction tasks.
4. Reasoning in terms of number relations to make and evaluation configurations.
5. Reasoning numerically to solve addition and subtraction tasks.

Mathematical Practice 1: Making Configurations on the Arithmetic Rack. Students participated in the initial mathematical practice by either counting beads by one or moving groups of beads to show a given number of people on the double-decker bus. During discussions of their solutions, an increasing number of students began to describe the resulting configurations in terms of groups. For example, students who had counted, say, seven individual beads on one rod sometimes explained that they had moved five and then two more beads, or that they had moved a group of seven beads. In these instances, the students appeared to reconceptualize their prior activity when they referred to beads to explain what they had done. As might be expected, some students continued to describe their solutions in terms of counting by ones. Although Ms. Smith accepted these explanations as well as those that involved grouping, she and the students implicitly negotiated that grouping solutions were more efficient and were therefore particularly valued.

An important aspect of these initial discussions was that, rather than asking the students to explain how they had actually made configurations, Ms. Smith asked them to describe the configurations that were shown on their racks. In doing so, she initiated exchanges that focused on ways of interpreting activity with the rack rather than on the specific sequences of actions that the students had carried out. This served to guard against the possibility that the use of the rack might become proceduralized.

One exchange that occurred during the second week of the sequence and on the second day that the students used the arithmetic rack illustrates the variety of their solutions. During this particular episode, Ms. Smith and the students discussed how one could show eight people sitting on the double-decker bus. The discussion began as Ms. Smith called on one of the students, Amy, who explained that the configuration she had made was "four and four." In redescribing Amy's solution, Ms. Smith spoke as though Amy had intentionally made two groups of four.

> Amy said that she showed a group of four on the top and a group of four on the bottom because a group of four and another group of four to make eight altogether on the bus. Raise your hand if you showed it the same way that Amy did. [Several students raise their hand]. Okay you can put your hands down.

Following this exchange, another student, Casey, offered a different solution in which he showed eight as five and three on the bottom rod. He explained, "Five plus three . . . okay you have five [makes finger-pattern for five] six, seven and eight [counts on as he raises three fingers on his other hand]." Ms. Smith then redescribed Casey's explanation:

Casey thought of it as having all eight on the bottom but he looked at it as a group of five and a group of three [points to the five beads and then to the three beads on the bottom rod of a rack projected onto the whiteboard.]

In redescribing Casey's explanation, Ms. Smith seemed to imply that he thought of eight as five and three before he made the configuration. Similar to the previous exchange with Amy, Ms. Smith appeared to interpret Casey's solution as one that involved grouping. In contrast, when other students explained that they had counted by ones, she did not redescribe their solutions in terms of prior anticipations.

Through discussions such as these, Ms. Smith and the students negotiated that grouping solutions were particularly valued and that these solutions involved moving groups of beads rather than counting individual beads. Further, the way in which Ms. Smith attributed intentionality to the students' explanations supported the development of these types of solutions and serves to illustrate her proactive role in this classroom. However, we should stress that students were not obliged to solve tasks in this manner. Ms. Smith encouraged students to participate in ways that made sense to them and continued to accept counting solutions. We saw no indications that students were merely attempting to mimic more sophisticated forms of reasoning.

Mathematical Practice 2: Describing Configurations in Terms of Fives, Tens, and Doubles. As Ms. Smith and the students continued to discuss solutions that involved making or evaluating configurations, explanations in which the students referred to groups of five and ten and, occasionally, to doubles emerged as a distinct mathematical practice. Although we had anticipated this transition when we formulated the hypothesized learning trajectory, we did not specify the diverse ways in which students might participate in this practice. For example, during an activity called Rack Bingo some students counted all the beads in a configuration shown to them by the teacher. They could recognize five beads of one color as "five" after they had counted, but this seemed to signify a specific figural pattern of beads rather than a numerical quantity. In contrast, other students first counted five beads of one color and then reasoned in terms of groups to evaluate the entire configuration. For these students, the result of counting appeared to be a numerical quantity rather than a figural pattern. Finally, the remaining students did not count at all but instead reasoned in terms of groups, sometimes describing their solutions in terms of imagining the activity of creating groups of five from beads of different colors (e.g., three red and two white on different rods).

The following episode, which took place during the fourth week of the instructional sequence, further illustrates the different ways in which students explained their reasoning. As the episode began, Ms. Smith briefly showed a configuration of five beads on the top rod and eight on the bottom rod. She then called on one of the students, Donald:

Donald:　I saw thirteen because I saw five plus five and I know that makes ten.

T:　　　　Yeah.

Donald:　... and add three more. When I got ten I just put it all, and I added the other numbers to make like one, two, three [makes a horizontal motion with his hand] and I got up to thirteen.

T:　　　　Okay, Donald said he saw thirteen but he grouped them, he did group them. He grouped five and five to make ten and then he saw three more so that made it up to thirteen.

Grouping explanations of this type appeared to be readily comprehensible to most students and did not need further justification. By this point in the teaching experiment, it was fairly common for students to explain that five and five made ten, or that ten and so many more made n-teen. This is not to say that all the students interpreted the configurations in the same way. As we have indicated, although these ways of describing configurations had become a form of classroom practice, the students made a range of qualitatively different interpretations as they participated in this practice. We therefore emphasize that the mathematical practices we have identified focus on the mathematical development of the classroom community by documenting the evolving taken-as-shared basis for communication. One of the challenges when analyzing the actual learning trajectory of a classroom community is to document the different ways in which individual students participated in the practices.

Thus far, we have indicated that the practice of making configurations on the rack evolved into the practice of describing configurations in terms of fives, tens, and doubles. In this transition, aspects of students' activity that were implicit when they participated in the first practice subsequently became explicit in the second practice. That is, reasoning in terms of groups emerged from the students' initial activity of making configurations on the rack. In accounting for this transition, we have indicated the crucial supportive role of both the teacher and of the instructional activities. The rack bingo game was particularly important in supporting the shift from counting to grouping solutions in that efficient ways of enumerating configurations emerged as useful for the task at hand—namely, filling up their bingo cards.

Mathematical Practice 3: Reasoning in Terms of Groups While Solving Addition and Subtraction Tasks. As we have seen, the second mathematical practice involved reasoning in terms of groups to evaluate a given configuration. The third mathematical practice emerged as a natural extension when the students solved addition and subtraction tasks presented in the setting of the double-decker bus scenario. In the case of addition tasks, the third practice involved first showing the initial number of passengers and then the additional passengers who got on the bus by moving beads on the top and bottom rods, respectively. Most students then reasoned in terms of fives, tens, and doubles to evaluate the resulting configuration. For example, when asked to find how many people were on the bus if there were initially eight passengers and seven more got on, many students moved eight beads on the top rod and seven on the bottom rod. Some then evaluated this configuration by reasoning that 8 and 2 (from the 7) made 10, and 5 more was 15. Others explained that two fives (one on the top and one on the bottom) made 10, and 5 more made 15. Although this practice did not constitute a major advance over the second practice, its significance becomes apparent when we discuss the emergence of the subsequent practices.

Mathematical Practice 4: Reasoning in Terms of Number Relations to Make and Evaluate Configurations. The fourth mathematical practice emerged as the students continued to solve addition and subtraction tasks posed in the setting of the double-decker bus scenario. It involved a shift from moving beads on the top and bottom rods and then evaluating the resulting configuration to creating configurations flexibly by making groupings that facilitated the enumeration. In other words, although students had participated in the third mathematical practice by reasoning in terms of groups that they happened to have established, they participated in the fourth practice by proactively anticipating bead configurations in ways that would facilitate enumerating the collection. Further, although groups had previously been ready-to-hand when *evaluating* configurations, numerical relationships now emerged as ready-to-hand as when *making* configurations. For example, instead of solving the task corresponding to 8 + 7 by moving eight beads on the top rod and seven on the bottom, some students moved eight and two more on the top and then five on the bottom because they anticpated that this would be easier to evaluate. From our perspective as observers, these students' activity with the rack appeared to involve an anticipatory going-through-ten strategy. As we see later, the way in which Ms. Smith notated the students' reasoning played an important role in supporting the emergence of this fourth mathematical practice.

To clarify this shift in mathematical practice, consider an episode that occurred during the fifth week of the Structuring Numbers sequence. In this episode, Ms. Smith wrote the number sentence 6 + 7 = _ on the whiteboard and asked the students to determine the number of people on the bus. Most students used arithmetic racks to solve this task. In the subsequent discussion, one student, Kendra, explained her answer of 13 as follows:

> Because I know that six plus six is twelve and I know that, I know that seven plus seven is fourteen and thirteen is in the middle between . . . between twelve and fourteen so I think it would be thirteen.

Kendra did not appear to refer to her actions with the arithmetic rack as she gave this explanation. However, when Ms. Smith redescribed Kendra's explanation, she turned on the overhead projector and used an overhead version of the arithmetic rack to show a configuration of six beads on the top rod and seven on the bottom rod and then continued:

> Kendra thought about something she knows, six plus six . . . a group of six and six is twelve [moves one bead off the bottom rod to show six and six] and she knows that a group of seven and seven is fourteen [moves one bead onto both the top and bottom rods to make seven beads on each] and fourteen, so she had six and seven and that would be thirteen [moves one bead off the top rod].

As she spoke, Ms. Smith notated her actions with the arithmetic rack, writing 6 + 6 = 12, then 7 + 7 = 14 below, and finally 6 + 7 = 13 between the first two sentences (see Fig. 7.5a).

As the discussion continued, two other students explained that they had solved the task differently. The first student, Leigh, explained that she moved six on the top rod and seven on the bottom rod and then evaluated the resulting configurations to arrive at an answer of 13.

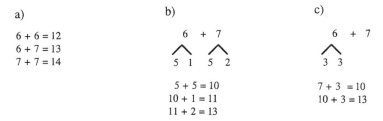

FIG. 7.5. Ways of notating (a) Kendra's, (b) Leigh's, and (c) Donald's solutions to 6 + 7.

And I saw that [it would] make ten [referring to the two fives on the top and bottom rods] and one would make eleven [referring to the white bead on the top rod] so these two [two white beads on the bottom rod] would make thirteen.

Although Ms. Smith redescribed this solution by using the overhead arithmetic rack, she did not notate it by writing number sentences. Significantly, as Leigh had first made a configuration and then evaluated it rather than anticipating a configuration, her solution would have been cumbersome to notate (a possible way of notating this solution is shown in Fig. 7.5b). Thus, in differentially notating some solutions but not others, Ms. Smith supported the development of anticipatory solutions and implicitly indicated that these solutions were particularly valued. In addition, her notating encouraged the students to interpret their activity with the rack in terms of numerical relations rather than groupings of beads.

The third student who gave an explanation, Donald, did not refer to the rack but instead said, "I think it's 13 because um, because um, I [went] up to seven and I took [three] out of the six and it left me with three so I know that um ten plus three is um 13." Ms. Smith notated his solution as shown in Fig. 7.5c. In contrast to Leigh, Donald described his activity with the rack in terms of numerical relationships that appeared to be ready-to-hand for him. In notating his solution, Ms. Smith made it possible for the going-through-ten strategy implicit in his reasoning to become an explicit topic of conversation.

In summary, as the fourth mathematical practice emerged, the focus of discussions shifted from evaluating already established configurations to describing anticipatory ways of acting with the rack in terms of numerical relationships. Thus, although most of the students had previously thought of six as five and one more, this and other relationships were now ready to hand as they solved tasks.

Mathematical Practice 5: Reasoning Numerically to Solve Addition and Subtraction Tasks. Although students spoke of numerical relationships as they participated in the fourth mathematical practice, imagery of acting with the rack appeared to be implicit in many of their explanations. In contrast, students no longer relied on this imagery to support their reasoning when they participated in the fifth mathematical practice. The numerical relationships that they had previously anticipated when making configurations on the rack had now taken on lives of their own when the students solved tasks posed in a variety of different scenarios by reasoning with written notations.

We illustrate this final shift in mathematical practices by examining an episode that occurred at the end of the instructional sequence. In this episode, Ms. Smith posed a task corresponding to $8 + 9 = \_$. First, Jordan

(a) $8 + 9$

$\bigwedge$

$1 \quad 7$

$9 + 1 = 10$
$10 + 7 = 17$

(b) $8 + 8 = 16$
$\quad 8 + 9 = 17$

(c) $9 + 9 = 18$
$\quad 8 + 9 = 17$

(d) $8 + 8 = 16$
$\quad 8 + 9 = 17$
$\quad 9 + 9 = 18$

(e) $8 + 9$

$\bigwedge$

$2 \quad 7$

$8 + 2 = 10$
$10 + 7 = 17$

FIG. 7.6. Ms. Smith's notations for (a) Bob's, (b) Karen's, (c) Amy's, (d) Leigh's, and (e) Joseph's solutions.

explained that he had counted on two fours from nine. Several other students then explained their solutions, which Ms. Smith redescribed and notated as shown in Fig. 7.6.

T: Okay. Thank you. Jordan said he did it by counting ... Did someone else figure it out a different way? Bob?

Bob: I knew if you took one, if you had nine and then ... plus eight and then you took one away from the eight and put it with the nine and you would have seven left and that would make seventeen [notates as shown in Fig. 7.6a].

T: Did you understand what Bob said? Did that make sense? Did someone do it a different way? Karen?

Karen: I knew that if eight plus eight was sixteen and you have one more it would be seventeen [notates as shown in Fig. 7.6b].

These explanations indicate that Karen had used a doubles as a reference whereas Bob had used ten as a reference point. The discussion continued as follows:

T: Ah, Amy, another way?

Amy: I thought about nine plus nine be eighteen and if I had eight plus nine then that would be seventeen [notates as shown in Fig. 7.6c].

T: [Redescribes Amy's solution method] Another way, Leigh?

Leigh: I thought about eight plus eight equals sixteen and nine plus nine equals eighteen so um I thought about it, it should be in the middle so nine plus eight should be seventeen [notates as shown in Fig. 7.6d].

Jos: Um I had like ah, I took the nine away. I mean I take, I took like two away from the nine and put it with the eight and that would make ten and I had about seven more [inaudible] [notates as shown in Fig. 7.6e].

T: Okay. Joseph was still making it up to ten, he broke up the nine instead of the eight. He broke up the nine and used the two to go with the eight to make eight and two is ten, and ten plus the seven he had left over to make seventeen [points to the notation on the board recording Joseph's solution method].

The fact that none of the students reiterated a solution that had already been explained indicates that the subtle differences between the various solution methods were taken-as-shared. Further, to avoid repetition, the students must have been monitoring the contributions of their classmates and differentiating them from their own solutions (cf. Yackel & Cobb, 1996). Ms. Smith's notating supported this process by providing records of previously explained solutions.

To investigate the ways of notating that the students had developed as they participated in exchanges such as those illustrated in the sample episodes, Ms. Smith asked them to make records of their thinking when they solved tasks individually so that other students could understand their reasoning. The challenge of symbolizing their thinking proved to be relatively unproblematic for most students. Four students' symbolizations to a task corresponding to 8 + 6 are shown in Fig. 7.7. As can be seen, only the first child's way of notating is entirely consistent with that of the teacher. The other three students had adapted aspects of Ms. Smith's notation in original ways. This suggests that although the students understood Ms. Smith's redescriptions of their solutions, they were not obliged to mimic her way of notating but could instead devise notations that both supported and expressed their reasoning.

Our analysis of this fifth mathematical practice reflects the claim that reasoning with numerical quantities had become institutionalized in the teaching experiment classroom by the end of the instructional sequence.

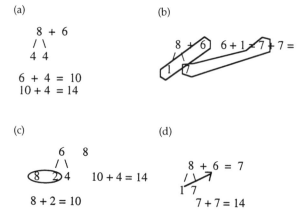

FIG. 7.7. Students' symbolizations of their reasoning when solving a task corresponding to 8 + 6.

This, of course, is not to say that the students interpreted and solved tasks in identical ways. Although reasoning numerically was routine for the majority of the students, some participated in the fifth practice by using the arithmetic rack as necessary or by counting. The exchange with Jordan in the sample episode indicates that Ms. Smith continued to accept a wide range of explanations while indicating that thinking strategy solutions were particularly valued. Thus, the students participated in and contributed to the evolution of the mathematical practices that constituted the social situation of their development in diverse and personally meaningful ways.

Reflection: Symbolizing and the Emergence of a Mathematical Environment

The analysis of the classroom mathematical practices indicates that many of the conjectures we formulated when outlining the hypothesized learning trajectory proved to be viable when we conducted the teaching experiment in collaboration with Ms. Smith. However, the analysis clarifies both the diversity of individual students' mathematical reasoning and the *process* of the classroom community's collective mathematical development. With regard to this latter issue, the analysis also illustrates the four levels of activity shown in Fig. 7.1. Initially, the students acted in the task setting when they and the teacher acted out riding on a double-deck bus. In contrast, the first three mathematical practices involved referential activity in that using the arithmetic rack was institutionalized as a *model of* activity in the double-decker bus scenario. The fourth mathematical practice involved general activity in that use of the rack was institutionalized as a *model for* numerical reasoning. Finally, the fifth mathematical practice involved reasoning with numerical relations without the support of the rack.

This actual learning trajectory exemplifies Freudenthal's (1991) contention that "mathematics should start and stay within common sense." Freudenthal intended this adage to be interpreted dynamically and argued that common sense is not static. He noted, for example, that what is common sense for a mathematician differs significantly from what is common sense for a layperson. In addition, he emphasized that common sense evolves in the course of learning. Thus, in the first phase of the actual learning trajectory, riding a double-decker bus scenario was established as a commonsense activity. By the end of the teaching experiment, acting in an environment structured in terms of numerical relations had become common sense. Freudenthal further clarified his position by substituting the term *reality* for common sense: "I prefer to apply the term 'reality' to that which at a certain stage common sense experiences as real" (Freudenthal, 1991, p. 17). This use of the term *reality* in Realistic

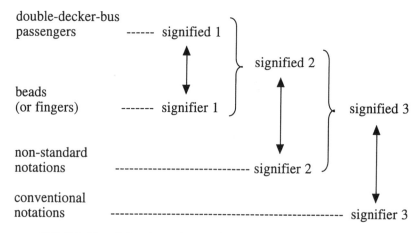

FIG. 7.8. The chain of signification that emerged during the teaching experiment.

Mathematics Education (RME) is highly compatible with Greeno's (1991) environmental metaphor and emphasizes that the overall goal of instructional design is to support the gradual emergence of a taken-as-shared mathematical reality in the classroom.

Throughout the analysis, we have emphasized the crucial role that symbolizing played in the evolution of the classroom mathematical practices and thus in the emergence of a mathematical reality. The ways of symbolizing that Ms. Smith and the students established in fact constituted a chain of signification (Cobb, Gravemeijer, Yackel, McClain, & Whitenack, 1997; Walkerdine, 1988; Whitson, 1997). The basic component of a chain of signification is a sign, where a sign is thought of as a semantic relation between a signifier and a signified. A new link in the chain is established when a sign itself becomes the signified for a new signifier. The chain of signification established during the teaching experiment is shown in Fig. 7.8.[7]

In Fig. 7.8, sign 1 consists of the semantic relation between signified 1 (the distribution of passengers on the double-decker bus) and signifier 1 (the beads on the two rods of the rack). This sign subsequently became the signified 2 for the nonstandard notations that Ms. Smith initially introduced (signifier 2), and the semantic relation between them constituted sign 2. We can also envision that sign 2 might itself become the signified 3 for more conventional ways of notating (signifier 3).

---

[7]This chain of signification is somewhat simplified in that it does not take account of the semantic relations established during the Patterning and Partitioning sequence that immediately preceded the Structuring Numbers sequence. In addition, the chain is drawn linearly and does not show variations in task settings.

It is important to stress that this chain of signification emerged as the classroom mathematical practices evolved. As Walkerdine (1988) noted, signifiers such as the arithmetic rack and informal notations were initially established as substitutes for preceding terms, with the assumption that the meaning of those terms would be preserved through the links of the chain. However, Walkerdine went on to argue that an original sign combination (i.e., distribution of passengers on the double-decker bus/beads on the two rods of the rack) is not merely concealed behind succeeding signifiers. Instead, the meaning of the sign evolves as the chain is constituted. Walkerdine's fundamental contention was that a sign combination that originates in a particular practice slides under succeeding signifiers that originate in other practices motivated by different concerns and interests. In the case of the Structuring Numbers sequence, sign 1 was initially constituted within a narrative about people riding a double-decker bus. The concerns and interests in the first mathematical practice were those of using the arithmetic rack to show how passengers could be seated on the bus. Later, as the students participated in the fifth mathematical practice, the concerns and interests were primarily mathematical and involved reasoning in terms of numerical relationships.

This account of signs sliding under succeeding signifiers provides a semiotic analysis of the process of mathematization that occurred during the teaching experiment. The crucial aspect of this analysis for our purposes is that the process of a sign sliding under a signifier corresponds to the model-of/model-for transition that is central to RME. This correspondence illustrates that RME is a design theory that proactively exploits the constitution of semiotic processes as a means of supporting students' mathematical development. Further, Walkerdine's (1988) perspective enriches the design theory. For example, we have seen that formulating a conjectured learning trajectory when planning an instructional sequence involves, in part, specifying possible model-of/model-for transitions. Walkerdine's work emphasizes the importance of locating these transitions in social context by considering the possible practices within which acts of signification or modeling might originate.

In summary, our intent in describing the evolution of mathematical practices in one classroom has been to document the mathematical development of a classroom community over an extended period of time. In reflecting on the analysis, we have brought semiotic processes of symbolizing and modeling to the fore. Viewed in this way, the negotiation of ways of modeling did not stand apart from classroom mathematical practices but was instead a central aspect of their evolution. We therefore follow Meira (1995) in emphasizing that the meaning of symbolizations cannot be separated from the activity of symbolizing (cf. Lesh & Doerr, chap. 10, and Nemirovsky & Monk, chap. 6, this volume). In the next section of this chapter, we address the question of how collective symbolic meanings evolve in more general terms by examining cases from the history of mathematics.

A BROADER PERSPECTIVE ON SYMBOLIZING AND MEANING

As the discussion of the Structuring Numbers sequence makes clear, symbolizing is not restricted to reasoning with conventional mathematical symbolizations, but also includes inventing (and, in some cases, reinventing) alternative symbol systems. In the history of mathematics, the development of these two types of symbolizations can be seen as two aspects of a single process. On the one hand, conventional symbolizations were established as culturally accepted ways to communicate mathematical ideas. On the other hand, newly invented symbolizations arose as mathematicians struggled to develop new ideas and understandings. These new ways, in turn, often called into question prevailing ways of reasoning and symbolizing. As a consequence, standard ways of symbolizing frequently became subject to a process of analysis, reflection, and mathematization. Two broad phases can be discerned in this process of mathematization. First, the meanings of the newly invented symbolizations were intimately connected with the settings from which they were derived. Later, this connection gradually moved into the background and the new symbolizations began to be interpreted apart from their original settings. As a consequence, the symbols began to develop meanings within the broader context of mathematical activity. As Bednarz et al. (1993) noted, Descartes and Leibniz each stressed one of these two general phases in the mathematization process.

For Descartes, the connection between symbolizations and the setting from which they derived was critical. In his view, the value of symbolizations was to "keep track of reasoning in a succinct fashion" (Bednarz et al., 1993). Leibnitz, on the other hand, stressed the use of symbolizations that were detached from their origin. For him, the function associated with symbolic writing "not only helps the reasoning, it replaces it. In fact, it dispenses the mind from 'thinking' the concepts it handles, by substituting calculation for reasoning, the sign for the thing signified" (Corturat, cited by Bednarz et al., 1993). This view highlights the value of using standard, well-established symbolizations that make it possible to perform computations routinely and efficiently without having to attend consciously to their meaning. We may infer, however, that Leibnitz also valued the fact that the substitution of signifiers for signifieds could lead to the creation of new mathematical environments.[8] His emphasis on the role of signification in the development of mathematical ideas is consistent with Sfard's (1991) discussion of the process of reification wherein actions with symbols that signify mathematical entities subsequently themselves become mathematical entities. We can further clarify this process by taking the historical development of the use of letters as symbols in algebra as an example. In doing so, we interpret the shift from one source of meaning to the other in terms of RME design theory.

According to Harper (1987), one can identify three broad phases of the historical development of algebra: pre-Diophantes, from Diophantes through Vièta, and post Vièta. Major steps in this development included Diophantes' introduction of letters to denote unknown quantities, and Vièta's use of letters for known quantities. Vièta's extension of the use of letters from unknown to known quantities was critical in that it created opportunities for generalization. This sequence of developments can be interpreted in terms of the four levels of activity that characterize model-of/model-for transitions as shown in Fig. 7.1. In Diophantes' approach, although the unknown quantities were truly unknown, they were also fixed. This was because Diophantes' algebraic description mathematized a specific setting. In other words, his use of letters was comparable with what we have called a model *of* the specific setting, in the sense that we can situate this use of letters at the level of referential activity. The letters derive their meaning from the specific setting they refer to. Vièta's approach was more general in that the "known" quantities could be filled in afterward. As a consequence, the unknowns were not fixed, and thus not tied to a specific question. Vièta's approach can therefore be situated at the level of general activity in that algebraic expressions were used by him to express and support reasoning about relations between variables. The development from Diophantes' to Vièta's approach can therefore be seen to involve a model-of/model-for transition in the course of which letters or, better, variables took on a life of their own and became entities in their own right. Before this shift occurred, the meaning of letters was tied closely to the setting that was symbolized, as Descartes suggested. After the shift occurred, a variable could be treated as an independent symbol as Leibniz suggested.

This transition was not, of course, the final chapter in the development of algebra. Instead, the activity of using algebraic symbols came to be viewed as a system that could itself be investigated and analyzed. As an example, consider procedures for simplifying equations. At first, algebraic expressions were interpreted as descriptions of arithmetical calculations.

---

[8]Bednarz et al. (1993) noted that, in Leibnitz's view, "the organization of the words/signs contributes and precedes the organization of ideas."

Later, attention shifted to the structure of expressions. As a consequence, experienced mathematicians were able to interpret an expression as composed of "chunks" more complex than a simple variable. In grasping the structure of an expression in this direct manner, they are acting in a mathematical environment in which algebraic relations are ready-to-hand for them in much the same manner that numerical relations were ready-to-hand for the first graders in the teaching experiment classroom. For example, a mathematician might view an expression such as $5(\sin x - 2)^2 + 3(\sin x - 2) = 7$ as a quadratic equation in $(\sin x - 2)$. On the other hand, the expression $5(\sin x - 2)^2 + 3(\sin \pi/4 - 2) = 7$ might be seen as an addition that can be turned into a subtraction—$5(\sin x - 2)^2 = 7 - 3(\sin \pi/4 - 2)$—in order to solve for x. In this regard, Wenger (1987) spoke of a "global substitution principle" wherein the expression $5(\sin x - 2)^2 + 3(\sin \pi/4 - 2) = 7$ is thought of as $A + B = C$, and can therefore be immediately transformed into $A = C - B$.

In reflecting on this process of algebraization, we may note that for the mathematician, the activity of reasoning with algebraic relations eventually takes the character of acting in an algebraic environment—when we may borrow Greeno's (1991) metaphor of an environment. In terms of the RME design theory, we may situate this activity at the level of formal mathematical reasoning, while at the same time denoting "formal mathematical reasoning" as a form of reasoning that builds on arguments that are located in such a newly formed mathematical reality. Thus, in this account of the history of algebra, we see the gradual emergence of new mathematical reality. Further, we contend that the two sources of meaning for symbolizations emphasized by Descartes and by Leibniz are equally important in this process; they are, so to say, two sides of the same coin. Against this background, we question the common characterization of shifts in the level of activity as abstractions in the sense that the connections with the settings in which the symbolizations originated are severed. Instead, we see greater value in descriptions that are cast in terms of reification (Sfard, 1991). Described in this way, mathematization is not a destructive process of cutting ties to underlying phenomena, but is instead a constructive process of creating a new reality in which the meanings of underlying phenomena evolve as they are mathematized. Accounts of this type fit with the view of mathematics inherent in RME design theory as it is summarized by Freudenthal's notion of mathematics as a human activity.

Note that a similar constructive process of creating a new reality can be discerned in the development of number. Here, the children start out with number words that first play a nominative role in the activity of counting. For instance, when a student is asked to find out how many candies are pictured, the student may solve the task by counting the candies with number words. Over time, the result of this process becomes reified such that the number becomes a referent for a quantity. As students engage in further activities involving the structuring of quantities, they develop number relations and, at the same time, further develop the notion of a quantity as an object-like entity in and of itself. In this process, the explicit references to the objects that constitute the quantity gradually drop out of the student's description. One reason for this is that, when reasoning with the rack, which objects are referred to becomes self-evident for the student. Another reason is that a second shift is taking place in which the student's view of numbers makes a transition from characterizations of sets of objects (e.g., eight beads, eight bus passengers, etc.) to numbers as mathematical entities. Crudely stated, this shift can be seen as a transition from viewing numbers as adjectives ("eight beads") to viewing numbers as nouns ("eight"). For the student, a number viewed as a mathematical entity still has quantitative meaning, but this meaning is no longer dependent on its connection with an identifiable quantity. In the student's experienced world, numbers viewed as mathematical entities derive their meaning from their place in a network of number relations. Such a network may include relations such as $8 = 5 + 3; 8 = 4 + 4;$ or $8 = 10 - 2$. For our purposes, the critical aspect of this network is that the students' understanding of these relations transcends the context of beads, bus passengers, or other countable objects. That is, when students form notions of mathematical entities, they view these relations as holding for *any* eight objects.

In our view, this shift from numbers as referents to numbers as mathematical entities—in the enactment of the sequence—is reflexively related to the model-of to model-for transition described earlier. On the one hand, the students' activity of structuring quantities as they act with the rack fosters the constitution of a framework of number relations. On the other hand, through the students' development of this framework of number relations, the students' activity with the rack can take on its role as a model *for* mathematical reasoning.

In sum, we may remark that we see clear parallels between the history of algebra and the process of the first graders' mathematical development both as it was conceptualized when formulating a hypothetical learning trajectory and as it was analyzed when delineating the actual learning trajectory. At the risk of using a much abused term, that of *authenticity*, we contend that RME design theory offers an authentic description of both the process of mathematization and the means of enabling students to participate in it. In using the term *authentic* in this manner, we are not focusing on observable features of instructional tasks such as whether they fit with students' out-of-school experiences. Nor are we focusing on specific characteristics of what is traditionally called mathematical content. For example, our focus on the historical development of algebra does not imply either that manipulating algebraic expressions is the only authentic form of algebraic activity or that it should be the primary instructional goal in school. Instead, we use the term *authentic* to refer to the process by which mathematical realities are created. Instructional sequences developed in line with RME are authentic in the sense that they involve a conjectured process of mathematization by which students might come to act in a mathematical environment.

CLOSING ARGUMENTS

In the first part of this chapter, we contrasted two alternative approaches to instructional design, the exploratory and the expressive approaches. Against this background, we then discussed a third approach in some detail, that of RME, by taking the Structuring Numbers sequence as a paradigmatic example. These three approaches share several points in common that serve to differentiate them from traditional approaches to instructional design. For example, each approach takes what is experientially real to students as the starting point for the learning process. Further, all three have similar endpoints in mind, namely, that students will come to act in a mathematical environment in powerful ways. In addition, proponents of all three approaches emphasize the critical role of symbolizing in mathematical development and challenge the traditional dichotomy between internal concepts and external symbolizations. Instead, in each approach, symbolizing is seen to be a central aspect of mathematical reasoning.

Differences between the approaches concern the way in which each attempts to support students' mathematical development by capitalizing on their constructive activities. We saw that in the expressive approach, the intent is to encourage students to develop their own ways of symbolizing with limited guidance from the teacher. However, an issue that remains to be addressed by proponents of this approach is that of coping with the tension between accepting the symbolizations that students invent and attaining the instructional goal of enabling students to reason with culturally accepted symbolizations in powerful ways. Proponents of the exploratory approach address this tension by introducing conventional ways of symbolizing from the outset and attempting to link them to students' everyday experiences or actions. As we saw, this linkage is typically effected by using computer systems that enable students to test their developing interpretations of conventional symbolizations.

A key issue that differentiates RME design theory from both the expressive and the exploratory approaches is the emphasis that it places on the formulation of conjectured learning trajectories as part of the design process. For example, we noted that the analysis of instruction consistent with the expressive approach can inform the development of such trajectories. However, proponents of this approach do not typically outline a hypothetical trajectory from students' initial, informal ways of symbolizing and reasoning to more sophisticated ways of reasoning that involve the use of conventional symbolizations. Similarly, proponents of the exploratory approach discuss the value of linkages between students' personally meaningful activity and conventional ways of symbolizing, but do not typically propose a learning trajectory by which students might come to reason with those symbolizations in powerful ways. As a consequence, the teacher is offered little guidance in terms of either the types of instructional activities to use or the kinds of questions to pose.

In presenting the example of the Structuring Numbers sequence, we illustrated how RME's heuristics of reinvention, didactical phenomenology, and emergent models serve to guide the development of hypothetical learning trajectories that can be investigated and revised while experimenting in the classroom. This example also illustrates that the RME approach to design is consistent with aspects of both the expressive and the exploratory approaches. In line with the expressive approach, the intent of the Structuring Numbers sequence was to support the gradual emergence of increasingly sophisticated ways of reasoning and symbolizing. However, we also saw that the teacher introduced particular ways of symbolizing at certain points in the instructional sequence. This is reminiscent of the exploratory approach in that the students were expected to develop personally meaningful ways of reasoning with these symbolizations. In this regard, designers who follow the RME approach have to cope with the inevitable tension between the expressive ideal of building on students' contributions and deciding in advance which symbolizations students might come to use. The aspect of RME theory that makes this tension tractable is that the selected ways of symbolizing are designed to fit with the ways of reasoning that students have developed at particular points in the instructional sequence. For example, we described how, against the background of the prior Patterning and Partitioning sequence, students' activity with the arithmetic rack was designed to fit with ways of reasoning documented in the research literature. Later, we described how the teacher used nonstandard symbolizations to record the students' solutions. The analysis indicates that these ways of symbolizing did fit with students' activity and that they played a crucial role in supporting the students' development. Nonetheless, in reflecting back on the teaching experiment, we have come to question the relatively limited role of students' contributions and therefore question the direct way in which the symbolizations were introduced. As a consequence, one of the revisions we are making to the Structuring Numbers sequence is to develop instructional activities in which the need to develop ways of symbolizing might itself become an explicit topic of discussion. This would then support students' development of metarepresentational knowledge (diSessa et al., 1991). Further, students might then view conventional ways of symbolizing as a means of resolving a problem.

A second fundamental issue that differentiates RME from the expressive and exploratory approaches is the manner in which it takes account both of the collective mathematical development of the classroom community and of the mathematical learning of the individual students who participate in it. For example, we illustrated that hypothetical learning trajectories embody conjectures about the possible learning route of the classroom community and involve expectations about the social and sociomathematical norms. Further, we discussed how collective mathematical development can be analyzed in terms of the evolution of classroom mathematical practices. In doing so, we also indicated the diverse ways in which the individual students participated in the mathematical practices we identified. In our view, this dual focus on communal norms and practices and on individual students' socially situated mathematical understandings is a major strength of RME design theory. In particular, RME is aligned with recent theoretical developments in mathematics education that emphasize the socially and culturally situated nature of mathematical activity.

In conclusion, it is important to stress that RME is not a prescriptive theory whose application will ensure that a particular vision of mathematics education will be achieved. RME is instead a theory that has emerged from and continues to be grounded in the practical activity of designing. Its contribution lies in the guidance it offers as we develop conjectures of possible ways of supporting students' mathematical development and investigate those conjectures while experimenting in classrooms. The example of the Structuring Numbers sequence documents a case in which that guidance proved to be of great value.

ACKNOWLEDGMENTS

The general theoretical analysis reported in this paper was supported by the Office of Educational Research and Improvement under grant R305A60007. The analysis of the sample instructional sequence was supported by the National Science Foundation under grant RED-9353587. The opinions expressed do not necessarily reflect the views of either the National Science Foundation or OERI.

REFERENCES

Bakhtin, M. M. (1986). *Speech genres and other late essays*. Austin: University of Texas Press.
Balacheff, N. (1990). Towards a problematique for research on mathematics teaching. *Journal for Research in Mathematics Education, 21*, 258–272.

Ball, D. (1993). With an eye on the mathematical horizon: Dilemmas of teaching elementary school mathematics. *Elementary School Journal, 93,* 373–397.

Bednarz, N., Dufour-Janvier, B., Poirier, L., & Bacon, L. (1993). Socioconstructivist viewpoint on the use of symbolism in mathematics education. *Alberta Journal of Educational Research, 39,* 41–58.

Brown, J. S., Collins, A., & Duguid, P. (1989). Situated cognition and the culture of learning. *Educational Researcher, 18*(1), 32–42.

Cobb, P. (1996, December). *Instructional design and reform: A plea for developmental research in context.* Paper presented at the Meeting on the Role of Contexts and Models in Mathematical Learning, Leiden, The Netherlands.

Cobb, P., Boufi, A., McClain, K., & Whitenack, J. (1997). Reflective discourse and collective reflection. *Journal for Research in Mathematics Education, 28,* 258–277.

Cobb, P., Gravemeijer, K., Yackel, E., McClain, K., & Whitenack, J. (1997). Mathematizing and symbolizing: The emergence of chains of signification in one first-grade classroom. In D. Kirschner & J. A. Whitson (Eds.), *Situated cognition theory: Social, semiotic, and neurological perspectives* (pp. 151–233). Mahwah, NJ: Lawrence Erlbaum Associates.

Cobb, P., & Yackel, E. (1996). Constructivist, emergent, and sociocultural perspectives in the context of developmental research. *Educational Psychologist, 31,* 175–190.

diSessa, A. A., Hammer, D., Sherin, B., & Kolpakowski, T. (1991). Inventing graphing: Meta-representational expertise in children. *Journal of Mathematical Behavior, 10,* 117–160.

Doerr, H. M. (1995, April). *An integrated approach to mathematical modeling: A classroom study.* Paper presented at the annual meeting of the American Educational Research Association, San Francisco.

Dörfler, W. (1993). Computer use and views of the mind. In C. Keitel & K. Ruthven (Eds.), *Learning from computers: Mathematics education and technology* (pp. 159–186). New York: Springer-Verlag.

Ernest, P. (1991). *The philosophy of mathematics education.* London: Falmer Press.

Fletcher, R. J. (1988). The power of five: The step before the power of ten. *Arithmetic Teacher, 34,* 5–10.

Freudenthal, H. (1971). Geometry between the devil and the deep sea. *Educational Studies in Mathematics, 3,* 413–435.

Freudenthal, H. (1973). *Mathematics as an educational task.* Dordrecht, The Netherlands: Reidel.

Freudenthal, H. (1983). *Didactical phenomenology of mathematical structures.* Dordrecht, The Netherlands: Reidel.

Freudenthal, H. (1991). *Revisiting mathematics education.* Dordrecht, The Netherlands: Kluwer.

Gravemeijer, K. (1990). Context problems and realistic mathematics instruction. In K. P. E. Gravemeijer, M. van den Heuvel, & L. Streefland (Eds.), *Contexts, free productions, tests and geometry in mathematics education* (pp. 10–32). Utrecht, The Netherlands: OW&OC.

Gravemeijer, K. (1994a). Educational development and educational research in mathematics education. *Journal for Research in Mathematics Education, 25,* 443–471.

Gravemeijer, K. P. E. (1994b). *Developing realistic mathematics education.* Utrecht, The Netherlands: CD-β Press.

Gravemeijer, K. (1996, December). *Instructional design for reform in mathematics education.* Paper presented at the Meeting on the Role of Contexts and Models in Mathematical Learning, Leiden, The Netherlands.

Gravemeijer, K. (1998). Developmental research as a research method. In J. Kilpatrick & A. Sierpinska (Eds.), *Mathematics Education as a Research Domain: A Search for Identity (ICMI Study Publication)* (Book 2, pp. 277–295). Dordrecht, The Netherlands: Kluwer.

Greeno, J. G. (1991). Number sense as situated knowing in a conceptual domain. *Journal for Research in Mathematics Education, 22,* 170–218.

Harper, E. (1987). Ghost of Diophantes. *Educational Studies in Mathematics, 18,* 75–90.

Hatano, G. (1982). Learning to add and subtract: a Japanese perspective. In J. P. Carpenter, J. M. Moser, & T. A. Romberg (Eds.), *Addition and subtraction: A cognitive perspective* (pp. 211–224). Hillsdale, NJ: Lawrence Erlbaum Associates.

Kaput, J. J. (1994). The representational roles of technology in connecting mathematics with authentic experience. In R. Biehler, R. W. Scholz, R. Sträßer, & B. Winkelmann (Eds.), *Didactics of mathematics as a scientific discipline* (pp. 379–397). Dordrecht, The Netherlands: Kluwer.

McClain, K. (1995). *An analysis of the teacher's proactive role in supporting students' mathematical development.* Unpublished doctoral dissertation, Vanderbilt University, Nashville, TN.

McClain, K., & Cobb, P. (1998). The role of imagery and discourse in supporting students' mathematical development. In M. Lampert & M. Blunk (Eds.), *Mathematical talk and school learning: Where, what, and how* (pp. 56–81). New York: Cambridge University Press.

Meira, L. (1995). The microevolution of mathematical representations in children's activity. *Cognition and Instruction, 13,* 269–313.

Nemirovsky, R. (1994). On ways of symbolizing: The case of Laura and velocity sign. *Journal of Mathematical Behavior, 13,* 389–422.

Newman, D., Griffin, P., & Cole, M. (1989). *The construction zone: Working for cognitive change in school.* New York: Cambridge University Press.

Papert, S. (1980). *Mindstorms: Children, computers, and powerful ideas.* New York: Basic Books.

Pea, R. D. (1993). Practices of distributed intelligence and designs for education. In G. Solomon (Ed.), *Distributed cognitions* (pp. 47–87). New York: Cambridge University Press.

Pirie, S., & Kieren, T. (1994). Growth in mathematical understanding: How can we characterize it and how can we represent it? *Educational Studies in Mathematics, 26,* 61–86.

Radatz, H., & Schipper, W. (1983). *Handbuch für den Mathematikunterricht an Grundschulen.* Hannover, Germany: Schroedel.

Schoenfeld, A. H. (1987). What's all the fuss about metacognition? In A. H. Schoenfeld (Ed.), *Cognitive science and mathematics education* (pp. 189–216). Hillsdale, NJ: Lawrence Erlbaum Associates.

Sfard, A. (1991). On the dual nature of mathematical conceptions: Reflections on processes and objects as different sides of the same coin. *Educational Studies in Mathematics, 22,* 1–36.

Sfard, A. (1994, September). *The development of the concept of concept development: From God's eye view to what can be seen with the mind's eye.* Paper presented at the Symposium on Trends and Perspectives in Mathematics Education, Klagenfurt, Austria.

Simon, M. A. (1995). Reconstructing mathematics pedagogy from a constructivist perspective. *Journal for Research in Mathematics Education, 26,* 114–145.

Steffe, L. P., Cobb, P., & von Glasersfeld, E. (1988). *Construction of arithmetical meanings and strategies.* New York: Springer-Verlag.

Streefland, L. (1990). *Fractions in realistic mathematics education, a paradigm of developmental research.* Dordrecht, The Netherlands: Kluwer.

Teasley, S., & Roschelle, J. (1993). Constructing a joint problem space: The computer as a tool for sharing knowledge. In S. Lajoie & S. Derry (Eds.), *Computers as cognitive tools* (pp. 229–260). Hillsdale, NJ: Lawrence Erlbaum Associates.

Treffers, A. (1987). *Three dimensions. A model of goal and theory description in mathematics education: The Wiskobas Project.* Dordrecht, The Netherlands: Reidel.

Treffers, A. (1991). Het rekenrek 1&2 [The arithmetic rack]. *Willem Bartjens, 8*(3), 151–153; *8*(4), 199–200.

van den Berg, W., & van Eerde, D. (1985). *Kwantiwijzer* [Number diagnostics]. Rotterdam, The Netherlands: SVO/Erasmus University.

van den Brink, F. J. (1989). *Realistisch rekenonderwijs aan jonge kinderen* [Realistic mathematics education for young children]. Utrecht, The Netherlands: OW&OC.

Varela, F. J., Thompson, E., & Rosch, E. (1991). *The embedded mind: Cognitive science and human experience.* Cambridge, MA: MIT Press.

Voigt, J. (1995). Thematic patterns of interaction and sociomathematical norms. In P. Cobb & H. Bauersfeld (Eds.), *Emergence of mathematical meaning: Interaction in classroom cultures* (pp. 163–201). Mahwah, NJ: Lawrence Erlbaum Associates.

Walkerdine, V. (1988). *The mastery of reason.* London: Routledge.

Wenger, R. H. (1987). Cognitive science and algebra learning. In A. H. Schoenfeld (Ed.), *Cognitive science and mathematics education* (pp. 218–251). Hillsdale, NJ: Lawrence Erlbaum Associates.

White, B. (1993). Thinker tools: Causal models, conceptual change, and science education. *Cognition and Instruction, 10*(1), 1–100.

Whitenack, J. W. (1995). *Modeling, mathematizing, and mathematical learning as it is situated in the classroom microculture.* Unpublished doctoral dissertation, Vanderbilt University, Nashville, TN.

Whitson, J. A. (1997). Cognition as a semiosic process: From situated mediation to critical reflective transcendence. In D. Kirschner & J. A. Whitson (Eds.), *Situated cognition theory: Social, semiotic, and neurological perspectives* (pp. 97–149). Mahwah, NJ: Lawrence Erlbaum Associates.

Wirtz, R. (1980). *New beginnings, a guide to the think, talk, read math center for beginners.* Monterey, CA: Curriculum Development Associates.

Yackel, E., & Cobb, P. (1996). Sociomath norms, argumentation, and autonomy in mathematics. *Journal for Research in Mathematics Education, 27,* 458–477.

8

Designs for Environments That Invite and Sustain Mathematical Thinking

John Bransford
Linda Zech
Daniel Schwartz
Brigid Barron
Nancy Vye
and the Cognition and Technology Group (CTGV)
Vanderbilt University

In this chapter we discuss a set of theoretical principles that guide our attempts to design environments that invite and sustain mathematical thinking (see Nemirovsky & Monk, chap. 6, this volume). The particular environments that we describe are intended for students from fifth grade to adult, and are organized around the Jasper Woodbury Problem Solving Series—a series of 12 videodisc- and CD ROM-based adventures that focus on areas such as rate (in the context of trip planning), statistics, geometry, and algebra (see Cognition and Technology Group at Vanderbilt [CTGV], 1997). However, the design principles that we discuss go beyond Jasper and apply to a wide variety of mathematical curricula.

In the first section of this chapter we discuss several theoretical analyses of understanding and social environments that provide the foundation for our thinking about instruction. In the second section we illustrate how different sets of principles can be combined to create different kinds of learning environments. We begin by describing environments that incorporate only a few of the principles discussed in the first section and end by describing environments that incorporate all of them. This gradual incorporation of principles parallels changes in our group's thinking about design, and we illustrate these changes. In many ways, these changes in thinking reflect our attempts to synthesize insights from two different literatures: the "regular" cognitive literature and the "situative" cognition literature (e.g., see Anderson, Reder, & Simon, 1996; Cobb, 1994; Greeno, 1997; Lave, 1988; Moore et al., 1996; Rogoff, 1990). Changes in our thinking also reflect the degree to which the cognitive psychologists in our group have paid increasing attention to the mathematics literature. We say more about these literatures as the discussion proceeds.

In the third section of this chapter we provide a detailed description of an instructional environment that embodies our most recent thinking about design, and we discuss some of our initial findings about how it has played out in classrooms. We end with a brief summary and a discussion of possible "next steps" in our work.

THEORETICAL PRINCIPLES THAT PROVIDE THE FOUNDATION FOR OUR THINKING ABOUT INSTRUCTIONAL DESIGN

Our goal in this section is to discuss a set of theoretical principles that guide our approach to instruction. We assume that a major goal of education must be to help students understand the meaning or significance of new information rather than merely memorize it as a set of facts or procedures. We also assume that there are basic processes of learning and understanding that are common to all disciplines, but that attention must be paid to the unique characteristics of particular disciplines such as history, science, and mathematics. Our research group concerns itself with cross-disciplinary as well as within-disciplinary learning because we believe that each discipline can be approached in ways that strengthens learning in the other areas, and vice versa (e.g., CTGV, 1993, in press). In fact, it is possible that the entire set of standards suggested by different organizations and disciplines (e.g., AAAS, 1989; NAS, 1996; NCTM, 1996; New Standards, 1995) cannot be achieved unless educators explicitly search for cross-disciplinary connections that create synergies with respect to learning. The focus in this chapter is primarily on mathematics learning, but our goal as a research group is ultimately to link mathematical inquiry and understanding with the exploration of other disciplines.

Understanding "Meaningfulness" or "Significance"

Our attempts to make information meaningful have been strongly influenced by theorists such as Dewey (1933), Buhler (cf. Blumenthal, 1970), Hanson (1970), and others. For example, in *How We Think*, Dewey provided an insightful discussion of differences between "brute things" and meaningful events and objects. He stated:

> To grasp the meaning of a thing, an event or a situation is to see it in its
> relations to other things; to note how it operates or functions, what conse-

quences follow from it; what causes it, what uses it can be put to. In contrast, what we have called the brute thing, the thing without meaning to us, is something whose relations are not grasped. (Dewey, 1933, p. 135)

The objects represented in Fig. 8.1 can be used to clarify Dewey's ideas about meaning (cf. Bransford & McCarrell, 1974). To many people, these objects are basically "brute things." Everyone assumes that each is some sort of tool, but the exact function of each tool is often difficult to grasp without more information. The information provided in Fig. 8.2 should help transform each "brute thing" into something more meaningful. When tools such as these become meaningful, they become richly connected with other aspects of people's lives.

In the area of mathematics, many concepts and their visual and symbolic representations are meaningful to experts but essentially "brute

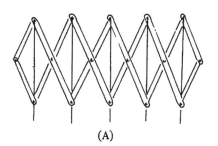

(A)

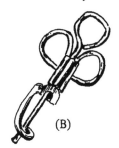

(B)

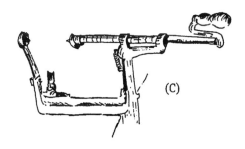

(C)

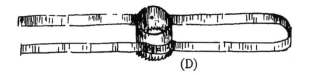

(D)

FIG. 8.1. An example of "brute things."

(A)   A "parallel line drawer-marker"
(not pictured)

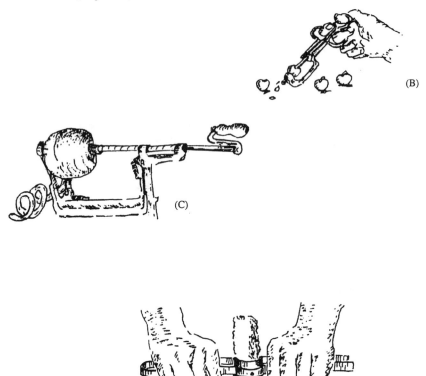

(B)

(C)

(D)

FIG. 8.2. Contexts that make "brute things" into meaningful objects.

things" to novices. The object illustrated in Fig. 8.3 provides an example.
A person is using this object to estimate the height of a tall tree. College
students we have interviewed knew that this was a triangle and even a
"right triangle." A few knew that it was an isosceles right triangle. However, none understood the special properties of isosceles right triangles
for measurement, namely, that the height of an object sighted at an angle
of 45 degrees will equal the distance one is standing from the base of the
object. Mathematics experts understand the object in Fig. 8.3 at a very
different level from novices.

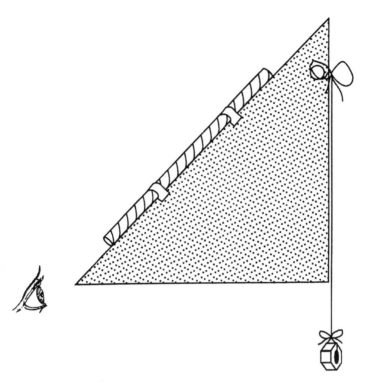

FIG. 8.3. Tool to measure heights.

Dewey's analysis of meaningfulness versus brute things also applies to symbolic expressions such as $Y = 2^n$. To a mathematician, this expression represents a function with special properties. To a novice the significance of $Y = 2^n$ is much more limited. For many college freshmen we have interviewed it is often viewed as "a formula we studied when I was taking math."

An important design principle that has helped us create environments that support understanding rather than mere memorization involves the creation of teams that pair experts in particular disciplines with what we call "accomplished novices." The latter are people who are knowledgeable about some area (e.g., psychology), but who do not have expertise in the particular area that is the focus of the research and development project (e.g., mathematics). The job of accomplished novices is to relentlessly pester the content area experts until they are able to understand concepts that the experts are discussing. This helps overcome a common problem of expertise, namely, that things become so intuitively obvious that one forgets the difficulties that novices have in grasping new ideas (e.g., Chi, Glaser, & Farr, 1991). Elsewhere, we describe how development of the Jasper series (see Fig. 8.4) has been influenced through collaboration

The Adventures of Jasper Woodbury

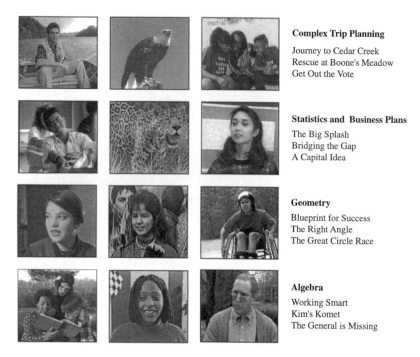

Complex Trip Planning
Journey to Cedar Creek
Rescue at Boone's Meadow
Get Out the Vote

Statistics and Business Plans
The Big Splash
Bridging the Gap
A Capital Idea

Geometry
Blueprint for Success
The Right Angle
The Great Circle Race

Algebra
Working Smart
Kim's Komet
The General is Missing

FIG. 8.4. The Jasper Series.

between mathematics experts and other "accomplished novices" on the design team (Bransford et al., 1996).

Advantages of Attempting to Understand What Makes Things Meaningful

One reason for helping students understand the meaningfulness or significance of information is that they invariably want to know, "What's this for?" or "Where will I ever use this information?" Seeing the potential usefulness of information motivates students to learn. In the area of geometry, for example, we have asked people (including college freshmen and middle school math teachers) to explain what they understood about uses of geometry. Except for "to measure area and volume," they had very few ideas (Zech et al., 1994). Nearly all of these individuals were very excited when we helped them discover uses of geometry for "measuring the earth" (Zech et al., 1994). Some became angry that they had never been helped to realize this before.

A second reason for helping students understand the significance of new information is that it helps overcome the "inert knowledge" problem. Whitehead discussed this problem in 1929; he argued that much of schooling produced knowledge that remained "inert" and was not useful for problem solving. In the last 15 years, research has provided insights into why and when knowledge remains inert (e.g., see Adams et al., 1988; Bransford et al., 1989; Gick & Holyoak, 1980, 1983; Lockhart, Lamon, & Gick, 1988).

In a classic paper on problem solving and education, Simon (1980) clarified why the knowledge underlying competent performance in any domain cannot be based on simple facts or verbal propositions but must instead be based on something more similar to production systems. Productions involve "condition–action pairs that specify that if a certain state occurs . . . , then particular mental (and possibly physical) actions should take place" (Anderson, 1987, p. 193). Productions thus provide information about the critical features of problem situations that make particular actions relevant.

For our purposes, it is the notion of specifying the contexts in which actions are appropriate (the notion of "conditionalizing" one's knowledge) that we find most valuable about Simon's argument. (One can accept the importance of conditionalized knowledge without necessarily agreeing that production systems are the best or only way to represent useful knowledge.) Theorists such as Simon (1980) and Anderson (1982, 1987) provide important insights into the need to help people conditionalize their knowledge—to acquire knowledge in the form of condition–action pairs mediated by appropriate goal-oriented hierarchies rather than as isolated facts.

Simon echoed Whitehead (1929) and Gragg (1940) in noting that many forms of instruction do not help students conditionalize their knowledge. For example, he argued that "textbooks are much more explicit in enunciating the laws of mathematics or of nature than in saying anything about when these laws may be useful in solving problems" (p. 92). It is left largely to the student to generate the condition–action pairs required for solving novel problems.

Franks and colleagues (Franks, Bransford, Brailey, & Purdon, 1991) noted that one of their favorite examples of the lack of explicit emphasis on conditionalizing one's knowledge comes from a textbook on experimental design. On page 195 of the book was a section entitled "Which Test Do I Use?" It stated: "How to choose a statistical test was postponed until now so that various aspects of data analysis could be presented." The text then included a discussion of the uses of various statistics. The entire discussion totaled 13 sentences in length. Anyone who has taught statistics knows that a major challenge for students is to learn when, why and how to use particular approaches to statistical analysis such as *t*-tests, *F*-tests, nonparametric tests, and so forth. A mere memorized list of tests and their formulas does students little good.

At a general level the idea of conditionalizing one's knowledge is related to the ability to understand why, when, where, and how particular types of knowledge are useful. This understanding allows people to use knowledge as a tool to solve important problems. Our ability to use physical tools requires a similar type of understanding. Consider the knowledge necessary to know when, where, how, and why to use a particular type of scissors. Examples of different types of scissors, and some of their contexts of usage, are provided in Fig. 8.5 (cf. Bransford & McCarrell, 1974). If you could recognize different examples of scissors but had no idea about the contexts in which each was used most appropriately, your knowledge would not be "conditionalized."

Challenges of Communication. The ease of helping people understand objects, symbols, and events depends strongly on the knowledge currently available to them. Buhler's theory is very helpful in this context (cf. Blumenthal, 1970; Bransford & Johnson, 1973):

> Buhler's field concept was most important. Given two speakers of the same language, no matter how well one structures a sentence his utterance will fail if both parties do not share the same field to some degree. . . . There are inner aspects of the field, such as an area of knowledge, or outer aspects, such as objects in the environment. Indeed, the field can be analyzed into many aspects. The total field (Umfeld) consists not only of the practical situation (Ziegfeld) in which an utterance occurs, but also the symbol field (Symbolfeld) which is the context of language segments preceding the segment under consideration. . . . The structure of any particular language is largely field-independent, being determined by its own particular conventional rules, but the field determines how the rules are applied. . . . With a "rich" external field less needs to be specified in the sentence. (p. 56)

Mismatches between information in a message and the semantic field of learners can result in several different types of experiences. One is that messages may be incomprehensible to novices because they lack, or fail to activate, relevant background knowledge (e.g., Bransford & Johnson, 1972, 1973). A second and even more problematic situation is one in which learners think they understand but do so at only a surface level because they miss distinctions that seem obvious to experts yet often remain tacit (Schwartz & Bransford, in press). For example, consider a statement such as "The dressmaker used the scissors to cut the cloth for the dress." This statement is understandable to most people; they can easily imagine a person using a pair of scissors to cut some cloth. However, what will

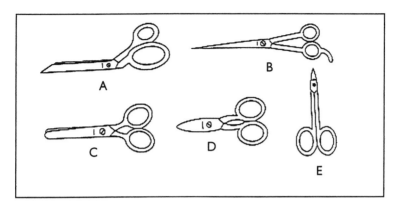

Structure

Function

a. Dressmaker's shears
Heavy
One hole larger than other

Blades off-center and alligned with
finger-hole edge

Because of heavy use.
Two or three fingers will fit in larger hole
— allows greater steadiness as one cuts
cloth on flat surface.
Blade can rest on table surface as cloth is
cut — again, greater steadiness.

b. Barber's shears
Very sharp
Pointed

Hook on finger hole

To cut thin material; for example, hair.
Permits blades to snip close to scalp and to
snip very small strands of hair.
A rest for one finger, which allows scissors to
be supported when held at various angles —
hence, greater maneuverability.

c. Pocket or children's scissors
Blunt ends

Short blades

Scissors can be carried in pocket without cutting
through cloth; children can handle without poking
themselves or others.

Allow greater control by the gross motor movements of the child just learning to cut.

d. Nail scissors
Wide and thick at pivot point

Slightly curved blades

To withstand pressure from cutting thick and rigid
materials; that is, nails.
To cut slightly curved nails.

e. Cuticle scissors
Very sharp blade

Small, curved blades

Long extension from finger holes to
joint

To cut semielastic materials; for example, skin of
cuticles.
to allow maneuverability necessary to cut small
curved area.
As compensation for short blades, necessary for
holding.

FIG. 8.5. Varieties of scissors and their functions.

detailed images of the dressmaker's scissors look like? A scissors expert, or a dressmaker, will have a much more differentiated concept of scissors than most casual comprehenders. The experts understand that there are many different types of scissors, and that each is adapted for different purposes (see Fig. 8.5). If asked to order a new pair of scissors for the dressmaker, experts would know to look for the relevant features whereas novices might not. Several studies show how people's understanding and representation of concepts such as "scissors" is affected by the contexts of usage and listeners' expertise (e.g., see Anderson & Ortony, 1975; Barclay, Bransford, Franks, McCarrell, & Nitsch, 1974).

As another example of the importance of well-differentiated concepts, consider students' attempts to comprehend a statement such as "The developmental psychologist showed first graders, fifth graders and college students a set of 30 pictures and found that their memory for the pictures was equivalent" (Schwartz & Bransford, in press). Novices can understand this statement at some level, but chances are that their understanding of "memory" will be relatively undifferentiated. In contrast, an expert will assume that this experiment must have involved recognition memory rather than free or cued recall—unless the pictures were carefully chosen to map very explicitly into a domain of organized knowledge (e.g., dinosaurs) where the children had more expertise than the adults (e.g., Chi & Koeske, 1983; Lindberg, 1980). In short, the expert can construct a number of well-differentiated scenarios, whereas the novice understands only superficially.

Developing Well-Differentiated Knowledge

The challenge of helping students develop well-differentiated knowledge is informed by theories of perceptual learning (e.g., Bransford, Franks, Vye, & Sherwood, 1989; Gagné & Gibson, 1947; Garner, 1974; Gibson & Gibson, 1955). These theories point toward the importance of contrasting cases as guides to noticing and differentiation. A focus on contrasting cases emphasizes that meaning cannot be captured and represented by looking at objects and ideas in isolation, or by assuming that the meaning of symbols is given solely by their referents. Instead, meaning depends on an object or symbol's "place in a system of relationships" or broader "knowledge field."

As an illustration of the importance of knowledge fields, consider a demonstration from Garner (1974). He asked readers to look at the stimulus in Fig. 8.6 and asked: "How would you describe the figure?" Garner noted that most people described it as a circle or a circle with two lines. Some described it as two concentric circles.

Garner continued his demonstration by considering the same figure (we call it the standard figure) in the context illustrated in Fig. 8.7. This

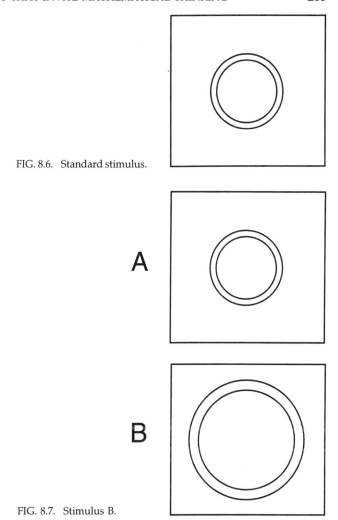

FIG. 8.6. Standard stimulus.

FIG. 8.7. Stimulus B.

time the standard is in the context of Stimulus B. Now features such as the size of the circle become relevant. When people see the standard in isolation, they generally fail to mention anything about size.

Garner continued his demonstration by considering the standard in a new context such as Stimuli C and B in Fig. 8.8. Now features such as the location of the circles within the border become salient.

Garner noted that one could continue indefinitely so that additional features become salient—features such as the thickness of the lines, the fact that the lines are solid rather than broken, the color of the ink. Garner's conclusion from his demonstration was that the meaning of a single stimulus depends on its position in a *field* of alternatives. These *fields of*

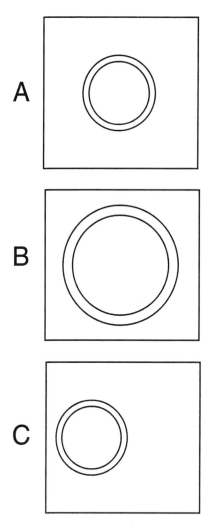

FIG. 8.8. The Standard Stimulus
and additional examples.

contrasting cases affect the features that we notice about particular objects
and events.

Noticing, Contrasting Cases, and Meaningfulness. Both J. Gibson and
Gibson (1955) and Garner (1974) focused primarily on perceptual learning
and differentiation. We noted earlier that theorists such as Dewey (1933)
and Buhler (e.g., see Bransford & McCarrell, 1974) focused on issues of
understanding by considering how an object's place in a system of relationships determines its meaningfulness. People's understanding of the
meaning of objects and events affects what they learn from contrasting
cases.

As an illustration, consider the set of grids shown in Fig. 8.9. Each differs from the others on a number of important dimensions. As a group, the grids illustrate a set of contrasting cases that are related through some sense of family resemblance involving "gridness." Without knowledge about the functions of the grids, it is difficult to decide which dimensions of similarity and difference count and which do not.

To illustrate, Grid 1 occurs in two different sizes: 1 by 1 ft and 5 by 5 ft. Grids 4 and 5 are 1 by 1 ft and 2 by 2 in, respectively. These examples provide contrasting cases involving sizes. Are the size differences important? Without more information, it is difficult to know.

Gerri's Grids

1. The ORIGINAL Grid

*Simple, elegant; the original Grid.
Order yours today.*

Approximately 1 ft. x 1 ft.

2. A 5 ft. x 5 ft. Version of the Original!

*Bigger and better.
And amazingly, the
same price as the Original.*

Approximately 5 ft. x 5 ft.

3. The Rounded Grid

*Aesthetically pleasing.
Be the envy of all your friends.*

Approximately 1 ft. x 1 ft.

4. "Intricate Designs"

*Slightly more expensive,
but worth the price.*

Approximately 1 ft. x 1 ft.

5. A 2 in x 2 in Version of "Intricate Designs"

*Easy to carry.
A great personal gift.*

Approximately 2 in. x 2 in.

6. "Precision Personified"

*Intricate & exacting.
Just the qualities you
want in a grid.*

Approximately 1 ft. x 1 ft.

7. The Random Grid

*Limited quantities.
Fun and challenging.*

Approximately 1ft. x 1 ft.

FIG. 8.9. Grids.

Particular dimensions of contrast become relevant when one is told that the grids are for T-shirts designed for the "backscratchers' society." They are used for purposes of communication between "scratchees" and "scratchers." Under these conditions, the relevance of the sizes become clearer. The 5 by 5 ft size is much too large for a T-shirt, and the "2 by 2" version is much too small.

The grid example illustrates the importance of viewing objects and events from the perspective of a "bigger picture" that includes knowledge of the social environments in which grids are useful. Without this knowledge, the grids are more like Dewey's "brute things."

Cycles of Action, Feedback, Revision, and Reflection. It is relatively easy to understand someone's description of backscratchers and their usefulness because most people have experienced itching and know the difficulty of reaching their backs in order to scratch. In Buhler's terms, speakers and listeners share a common "semantic field" (cf. Blumenthal, 1970). Even in the case of backscratchers, however, simply listening to someone's description does not guarantee a well-differentiated understanding. Imagine, for example, that one wanted to design one's own backscratcher T-shirts. What is the exact shape of a grid that best fits most backs? How far up or down on the T-shirt should the grid be placed? How does one adapt the grid for smaller and larger sizes of people and T-shirts? Are all areas of the back equally likely to have itches, or should backscratching targets be focused on particular areas and ignore others?

It would be difficult to develop in-depth understanding of these issues without frequent chances to design grids, test them, and revise them as needed (cf. Lesh & Doerr, chap. 10, this volume). Over time, it is probable that opportunities to test and revise would result in the design of different grids for different purposes—for people of different sizes, for backs with different types of "itching zones," for people with different kinds of aesthetic preferences, and so forth. (This is analogous to the invention and refinement of different kinds of scissors illustrated in Fig. 8.4.) In short, cycles of action, feedback, and revision would be necessary even for the domain of backscratching, where most people share a rich semantic field.

In most academic areas such as mathematics, science, and history, there is much less likelihood that experts and novices share a semantic field that is as rich as the backscratching situation. As noted earlier, this semantic field is necessary in order to assess the adequacy of one's current level of understanding. For example, most adults feel that their understanding of the concept "gold" is adequate because they can differentiate things like gold paint and gold watches from silver paint and silver watches. However, if placed in a situation where they need to differentiate fool's gold from real gold, they soon discover that they need a much more technical understanding of gold (cf. Bransford, 1979). In addition, we noted earlier that experts in an area often do not realize how much of their own understanding is based on well-differentiated knowledge derived from years of experience. As a result, challenges of communicating about most academic areas are much greater than the challenges involved in exploring backscratching grids.

It is instructive in this context to note Norman's (1993) discussion of Plato's concerns about the need to actively test and revise one's understanding in order to ensure adequate understanding.

> Socrates, Plato tells us, argued that books would destroy thought. How could this be? After all, books, reading, and writing are considered to be the very essence of the educated, intellectual citizen. How could one of the foremost thinkers of civilization deny their importance? (Norman, 1993, p. 44)

Norman explained that Socrates was worried about the fact that dialogue is interactive whereas books simply present information.

> When the idea is presented by a person, the audience can interrupt, ask questions, probe to get at the underlying assumptions. But the author doesn't come along with a book, so how could the book be questioned if it couldn't answer back? This is what bothered Socrates. (p. 45)

Discussions about texts are important because they can create interactive conditions that help people test their current levels of comprehension and revise their ideas.

Reflection and Representation

Acts of testing one's understanding and revising are often accompanied by acts of reflection, which can affect how people represent their experiences. A number of studies suggest that people's representations of situations have strong effects on the degree to which they will transfer their knowledge to new settings (e.g., Anderson, Reder, & Simon, 1996; Bransford & Stein, 1993; Bransford, Vye, Adams, & Perfetto, 1989; Brown, Bransford, Ferrara, & Campione, 1983). If people simply learn a set of procedures without an understanding of what they are doing, why they are doing it, and how it relates to more general principles, chances are that there will be little initial transfer to new situations. However, if people are helped to represent their experiences at more general levels, the probability of transfer is improved.

As an illustration, consider once again the experience of first seeing the grids in Fig. 8.9 as "brute things," and then being told that they are for backscratcher T-shirts. This experience could be represented at a number of different levels. One is simply the episodic representation of understanding at Time 1 (before being told the function of the grids) and Time 2. Another level of representation could involve the understanding that this experience represents an example of how the activation of relevant knowledge can affect one's abilities to learn from contrasting cases. A third level of representation could involve the realization that backscratcher grids represent one of many possible examples of how people have invented tools that allow them to accomplish various activities that would otherwise be difficult or impossible (e.g., Bacon, 1620; Bransford & Stein, 1993; Norman, 1993).

Clearly, there are many ways to represent a particular set of experiences. We assume that representations are affected by ways in which people reflect on their experiences, and that these representations affect the probability that any particular experience will support one's adaptation to new problems and situations (e.g., see Anderson, Reder & Simon, 1996; Bransford, Vye, Adams, & Perfetto, 1989).

Analyses of Social Environments

During the past several years, our research group has become increasingly aware of the need to move beyond an exclusive focus on the individual and pay careful attention to the assumption that all human endeavors are socially situated (cf. van Oers, chap. 5, this volume). A number of theorists in the "situated cognition" literature have helped us see the importance of this kind of analysis (e.g., Brown & Campione, 1994; Brown, Collins, & Duguid, 1989; Cobb, Wood, Yackel, & McNeal, 1992; Cobb, Yackel, & Wood, 1992; Greeno, 1997; Lave, 1988; McLaughlin & Talbert, 1993; Rogoff, 1990). One way to characterize the impact of this work is to conclude that "culture is not an option." Classroom, school, and community cultures are always present, irrespective of whether they are explicitly analyzed.

The situated cognition literature has helped us see that teachers and their students are always embedded in sociocultural environments that have powerful effects on learning. This literature has also prompted us to analyze the culture and organization of our Learning Technology Center (LTC) because all of us felt that it was an excellent example of a learning community and we wanted to better understand such communities (Barron et al., 1995; CTGV, 1997). This analysis has been very helpful to us in thinking about the social organization of classrooms. For example, we discovered that the role of outsiders (visitors, journal audiences, grant review boards) is extremely important for our center. This helped us notice that some classrooms are relatively "self-contained" whereas others are organized around opportunities to interact with "outsiders," who often present challenges that unite the teachers and their students. Thinking about these issues has prompted us to include "social structures" as an important part of our design principles. For example, we have designed special SMART (Special Multimedia Arenas for Refining Thinking) Challenge Programs to provide some of the advantages of outside audiences to students and teachers in classrooms (e.g., Barron et al., 1995, in press; CTGV, 1997; Vye et al., 1998).

Thanks to opportunities to collaborate with McLaughlin and Talbert (1993), we have also come to appreciate the importance of viewing organizations such as classrooms as embedded in other organizational structures such as teacher communities, school communities, and the broader community of administrators, parents, business leaders, and others. We say more about the importance of embedded contexts later on.

Distributed Support for Knowing

An additional principle that is highly relevant to the design of instructional environments involves what we call *distributed support for knowing*. Analyses of people's functioning in everyday contexts shows clearly that "expertise" (in the sense of the ability to perform some task or set of tasks) is frequently distributed across people, and distributed across artifacts in the environment such as tools (e.g., Brown & Campione, 1994, 1996; Lave, 1988; Pea, 1993; Salomon, 1993). Decisions about how knowing is going to be distributed are extremely important for theories of instructional design. Two aspects of distributed expertise are discussed next.

Expertise Distributed Across People. When people work collaboratively they can often form a system that is capable of accomplishing goals that no individual could accomplish alone. An example from research by Newman, Griffin, and Cole (1989) provides an excellent example. They developed an after-school cooking club that became very popular with students. Students who joined the club needed to be able to read recipes, and they needed to be organized and stay on task.

Two boys were eventually allowed to joined the cooking club who, initially, appeared to be very poor candidates. One boy could not read (it was later discovered that he was dyslexic). A second boy had severe attention problems and could not stay on task. As individuals, the two boys failed to meet the qualifications for the cooking club. As a team, the two boys did extremely well in the cooking club. The boy who could not read assumed leadership in organizing all the activities. When something needed to be read, he called the other boy for help.

We have seen numerous instances where students have become valuable contributors when allowed to work in teams. For example, some students seem to be excellent group organizers despite not being particularly strong individual learners. Others show evidence of creativity when working in groups that they do not show when working individually. As an illustration, consider Student A, who cannot draw but has great ideas for concepts that can be represented visually, and Student B, who is excellent at drawing what someone tells him to draw, but usually doesn't know what to draw on his own. When students such as A and B are put together we have seen some outstanding products emerge—products that would have been impossible for either one to produce alone.

Distributing Expertise Across People and Artifacts. A second way to distribute knowing is to invent tools that provide support for human cognitive activities. In *Things That Make Us Smart*, Norman (1993) argued for the importance of distributing knowing across people and artifacts such as tools and written symbols. He stated: "The power of the unaided mind is highly overrated. Without external aids, memory, thought and reasoning are all constrained" (p. 42).

Written representations are one form of tools that are especially important for enhancing our mental powers. Norman (1993) made the following argument about oral cultures: "They haven't developed mathematics or science, formal history, or extensive commercial records because they can't without the aid of artificially constructed artifacts. It is things that make us smart" (p. 44).

Things that make us smart include tools that enhance problem solving. In her analyses of everyday environments, Lave (1988) noted that humans attempt to eliminate the need to continually solve repetitive sets of problems by inventing tools that allow them to "work smarter." Examples include calendars, watches, speedometers, charts, graphs, and many types of computer software.

As a simple example, imagine setting up a T-shirt business that sold T-shirts with backscratching grids. It would not be particularly efficient to conduct an inventory every day by counting how many T-shirts of each size, design, and so forth are left over after the day's sales. It would be more advantageous to invent tools that allow one to work smart. A very simple idea is to stack T-shirts in piles in a stockroom according to size and design. On the wall of the stockroom is a line. When the stack of T-shirts falls under the line, the clerk knows it is time to reorder (see Fig. 8.10). Placement of the line involves knowledge about baseline sales of particular types and sizes of T-shirts, plus knowledge about delivery times from the manufacturer. In short, a mathematical model underlies the construction of the inventory system.

Another way to work smart is to design spreadsheet templates that make it easy to calculate costs for each customer. A template can provide

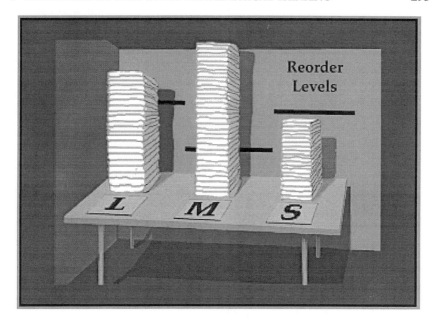

FIG. 8.10. Smart Tool for T-shirt inventory.

a place for cost of each T-shirt, number of T-shirts purchased, any discounts based on volume of purchase, sales tax, and so on. Templates can also be created that allow clerks to instantly determine the postage required to mail packages, rather than to continually have to compute postage. Underlying the creation of appropriate templates are mathematical models of the situation.

Our readings of theorists such as Lave (1988) and Norman (1993) helped us realize that most classrooms are not designed with an eye toward helping students learn to invent tools for working smarter. We now include this goal in our thinking about instructional design.

Summary

Our goal in this section has been to provide an overview of some theoretical analyses principles of understanding and social contexts that are guiding our attempts to design environments that invite students to learn with understanding rather than simply memorize. Dewey's analysis of "brute things" provided a good starting point for our discussion because he made it clear that understanding cannot simply be equated with connecting symbols with concrete referents. People's abilities to understand the meaning of referents can be problematic, and this understanding needs to be explained.

Following Garner, the Gibsons, and others, we argued that *meaning* must be viewed as a place in a general field or relation structure, and that meanings change as semantic fields change. The work in perceptual learning by Garner and the Gibsons shows that what one notices about objects and events depends on the contrast sets within which they are embedded. The example of the backscratchers' grid illustrates the importance of a general "semantic field" that makes the contrasts among individual grids meaningful. We also discussed Buhler's field theory of comprehension, and the fact that comprehension is an active process where people need to test their ideas, receive feedback, and refine what they know.

Additional principles that have affected our thinking about design include explicit attempts to analyze the nature of the social environments in which people operate. This discussion included analyses of distributing knowledge across (a) different individuals and (b) artifacts in the environment. The idea of having students work collaboratively to invent artifacts that help them "work smart" is an idea that has become very important in our thinking about design.

A shortcoming of the preceding discussion is that it simply provides a list of theoretical principles that have guided our thinking about design. These must be combined in particular ways in order to design learning environments that are useful for students. Our goal in the next section is to show how different combinations of these principles lead to different kinds of instructional designs.

AN ORGANIZING FRAMEWORK FOR MAPPING THEORETICAL PRINCIPLES INTO CONCRETE DESIGNS

Discussion in this section is organized around the framework illustrated in Fig. 8.11. Use of this framework allows us to illustrate how our thinking has changed as we incorporated more and more of the theoretical principles discussed in the first section into our thinking. As noted earlier, these changes in thinking have stemmed both from our own research in classrooms (e.g., CTGV, 1996, 1997; cf. Gravemeijer et al., chap. 7, this volume; Nemirovsky & Monk, chap. 6, this volume) and from reading relevant literature—especially by theorists in the situated cognition tradition (e.g., Brown et al., 1989; Cobb, 1994; Greeno, Smith, & Moore, 1993; Lave, 1988; Rogoff, 1990; etc.).

The framework in Fig. 8.10 is based on the intersection of two dimensions of thinking that have guided our work, namely, (a) the nature of the instructional content that forms the basis of instruction, and (b) the social contexts in which learning is situated. For the instructional content

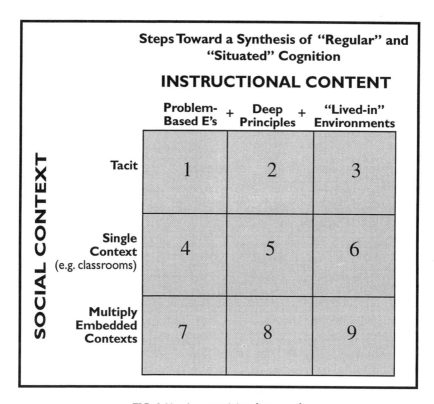

FIG. 8.11. An organizing framework.

dimension, the categories are cumulative. The first column represents the use of problem-based environments to situate learning. The second column involves an addition to these environments by emphasizing the importance of transforming students' specific problem solving experiences into an understanding of more abstract "deep principles" in mathematics.

The third column involves a change from "single-shot problems" to simulations of "lived-in environments," where the latter include multiple encounters with recurring classes of problems. One advantage of placing students in these environments is that it helps them appreciate the value of inventing ways to remove the need for frequent, cumbersome computations (Lave, 1988). The idea of "lived-in environments" should become clearer as our discussion proceeds.

The dimension labeled *social context* includes three different values: tacit, single contexts such as a classroom, and multiply embedded contexts. By *tacit* we do not mean an absence of social context. We include *tacit* as one of the values in Fig. 8.11 because in our early work, social context was left unanalyzed. Gradually we began to understand how different sets of classroom norms affected everything that we developed, so the social context of classrooms became a major concern. As our work proceeded we began to see that there are multiple social contexts within classrooms, and that classroom contexts are affected by teacher communities in which they are embedded, as well as school, district, and larger out-of-school contexts (e.g., Cobb, 1994; Mc Laughlin & Talbert, 1993). We also began to appreciate the role of "outsiders" in helping form a sense of community (e.g., Barron et al., 1995; CTGV, 1997).

Cell 1: Situating Instruction in Meaningful Problem-Solving Environments (With No Explicit Analysis of Social Context)

In retrospect, we now see that our early ideas about design were relevant to Cell 1 in Fig. 8.11. These early ideas were discussed in a 1990 article (CTGV, 1990) that argued for the advantages of situating (anchoring) instruction in meaningful problem-solving environments that helped students understand the meaning or significance of the information they were learning rather than merely memorizing it as a set of facts or procedures. By significance, we included knowledge of why, when, and how the information was useful for solving important problems that people might encounter in life. We stated:

> The major goal of anchored instruction is to overcome the inert knowledge problem. We attempt to do so by creating environments that permit sustained exploration by students and teachers and enable them to understand the kinds of problems and opportunities that experts in various areas encounter and the knowledge that these experts use as tools. We also attempt to help students experience the value of exploring the same setting from multiple perspectives (e.g., as a scientist, historian, etc.). (p. 3)

We discussed the Jasper series as one example of anchored instruction (the other was the Young Sherlock project that focused primarily on literacy). At that time two Jasper adventures had been completed: *Journey to Cedar Creek* and *Rescue at Boone's Meadow*. Both adventures were organized around trip-planning scenarios that involved concepts such as distance, rate, and time. The goal of the adventures was to help students form a "big picture" of a problem space within which particular concepts and tools became useful.

A brief description of *Rescue at Boone's Meadow* (RBM) provides an example. In the adventure, Jasper is on a hiking trip in the wilderness when he discovers an eagle that is seriously wounded. He radios for help. Emily Davidson eventually receives the message and begins to plan the rescue. There are no roads at Jasper's location, and only a small amount of open space (the rest is all treed). Emily eventually decides that she needs to use Larry's ultralight to rescue the eagle. The students' challenge is to help her decide how to do this. What is the fastest route? Does she have enough fuel and can she stay under the payload limit? How much time will the rescue plan require?

Like all the Jasper adventures, RBM includes both irrelevant and relevant data that have been embedded in the story line. Students can use interactive technologies to rapidly return to important places on the video and find the relevant data (e.g., information about fuel consumption, speed of the ultralight, size of landing areas, payload limits). They usually work in groups to generate a solution and then present it to their fellow classmates and sometimes to outside audiences. Data available at the time we wrote the 1990 article indicated that the experience of solving a Jasper adventure had highly positive effects on students' ability to solve transfer problems compared to students who received more traditional instruction in word problems that included concepts such as distance, rate, and time (Van Haneghan et al., 1992).

Cell 2: Adding an Emphasis on "Deep Principles"

As our work on Jasper progressed, we began to realize the importance of going beyond the goal of simply helping students learn to solve complex, authentic problems. We began to focus on "deep principles" or "big ideas" in mathematics that were relevant to their solution strategies. An example for *Journey to Cedar Creek* and *Rescue at Boone's Meadow* is the mathematical concept of rate and its applicability in a wide variety of settings. Additional Jasper adventures focus on other deep principles such as functions, geometric models for "measuring the earth," models of statistical sampling, and inferencing (see Bransford et al., 1996).

We noted earlier that our increased emphasis on deep principles came from several different sources. One was the cognitive literature, which shows that people's representations of problems have powerful effects on transfer (e.g., Anderson, Reder, & Simon, 1996, 1997; Bransford, Vye, Adams, & Perfetto, 1989; Brown & Campione, 1994). When students are helped to represent their experiences at a more general level (e.g., helped to see that a particular solution strategy represents an example of a more general concept such as rate, model building, etc.), their ability to transfer improves.

A second reason for focusing on deep principles emerged from our increased interaction with people in mathematics education (e.g., Cobb, 1994; Schoenfeld, 1985, 1987; Silver, 1986, 1990). As noted elsewhere (Bransford et al., 1996), our initial foray into mathematical problem solving was motivated by a concern with "dynamic assessment." The focus on mathematics was more accidental than planned. Our primary concern was having

students solve everyday problems that required mathematical computation; we paid little attention to "big ideas" in mathematics. As we began to
collaborate with members of the mathematics community, we realized that
our ideas about mathematics had been shaped by our own experiences in
school rather than by a serious study of the mathematics literature. In
retrospect, we now understand statements such as this one made by
Kilpatrick (1992): "Mathematics educators have often been wary of psychological researchers because of what they have been seen as an indifference
to or ignorance of the academic discipline" (p. 5). The cognitive psychologists in our group were indeed ignorant of the mathematical literature
when we first began our work on Jasper. Our attitude was, "After all, each
of us had passed our middle school mathematics courses—what more was
there to know?" (Bransford et al., 1996, p. 204).

A third reason for emphasizing the importance of deep principles
stemmed from our own research, which indicated that students' abilities
to solve new problems after working with a Jasper adventure were not
as flexible as we wished (CTGV, 1992, 1997). Therefore, we developed
analog and extension problems to each Jasper that invited students to
revisit adventures from new perspectives. The goal was to help them
refine their strategies and deepen their understanding of the activities
involved in solving the adventures. For example, after solving *The Big
Splash*, we found that middle school students understood one procedure
for obtaining a random sample and extrapolating to a population, but
that this knowledge was relatively rigid. Students benefited greatly from
opportunities to develop a more general understanding of sampling and
statistical inferencing (Schwartz, Goldman, Vye, Barron, Bransford, with
CTGV, 1998). Data from studies with other Jasper adventures indicate
that opportunities for students to revisit adventures and deepen their
understanding of the mathematical principles also increased their flexibility of transfer (e.g., CTGV, 1997, especially chap. 4; Williams, 1994).

We also became aware of the need to help teachers monitor and shape
how students represented their experiences as they solved Jasper adventures and their respective analog and extension problems. Ideally, students working in a context such as Jasper are able to relate their specific
actions (e.g., calculating fuel consumption for the ultralight) to the overall
goal of the Jasper challenge. Often, however, they became lost in the
specifics of a particular task and needed help relating it to a "bigger
picture." For example, students may state, "we are drawing graphs" rather
than "we are comparing different rates." Data indicate that students'
representations of their experiences have important effects on transfer
(Anderson, Reder, & Simon, 1996). Attention to this aspect of learning
has become an important aspect of our approach to design (e.g., Barron
et al., in press).

Cell 3: Authentic Context and Deep Principles
Transformed Into "Lived-In" Environments

Additional work with Jasper prompted us to move from Cell 2 to Cell 3 in Fig. 8.11. Work in Cell 3 preserves the goal of situating instruction in authentic contexts (Cell 1) coupled with a focus on deep principles in mathematics (Cell 2). However, Cell 3 represents an important change in the nature of the environments in which the students interact. In particular, we have moved from attempts to present students with environments that involve "one-shot" problems to environments where problems tend to reoccur and it becomes useful to invent ways to deal with these reoccurrences (cf. Lehrer et al., chap. 9, this volume; Lesh & Doerr, chap. 10, this volume). As noted earlier, theorists such as Lave (1988), Norman (1993), Rogoff (1990), and others argue that people become smart, in part, by learning to deal with important problems that tend to recur in their environments. One way to do this is through the invention of tools that allow them to "work smarter." Examples of tools that can eliminate cumbersome computations include charts, graphs, computer programs, and gadgets such as watches, speedometers, and proportion wheels (cf. Lehrer et al., chap. 9, this volume; Nemirovsky & Monk, chap. 6, this volume).

We illustrate the idea of smart tools in Jasper by returning to the adventure *Rescue at Boone's Meadow* that was discussed earlier. The challenge in this adventure was to find the fastest way for Emily to rescue the eagle and explain how long that will take. Analog and extension problems that accompany the adventure provide additional experiences by posing additional "what if" questions (What if Emily's plane flew at 45 rather than 30 miles per hour? What if she confronted a 10 mph headwind, etc?). Other extension problems let students apply the same kind of thinking to other adventures such as Charles Lindbergh's trip from New York to Paris, and help them develop more abstract concepts of rate. All of these experiences fall into Cells 1 or 2 of the framework illustrated in Fig. 8.11.

Rescue at Boone's Meadow is transformed when it is situated within Cell 3 of our framework. Instead of confronting an adventure where they are asked to solve a single problem (rescuing the eagle as quickly as possible), students are invited to imagine that Emily becomes an entrepreneur who sets up a pickup and delivery service for people who go camping in her area. She has several different planes to choose from depending on the needs (e.g., some can carry more payload, fly faster, etc.). When customers call in to ask for assistance, Emily asks where they are (or where they want to go) and needs to tell them the trip time and fuel costs as quickly as possible. Different requests embody problems that vary in terms of the location of the destination, windspeed conditions, payload limits that determine which plane must be used, costs due to fuel consumption, and so forth.

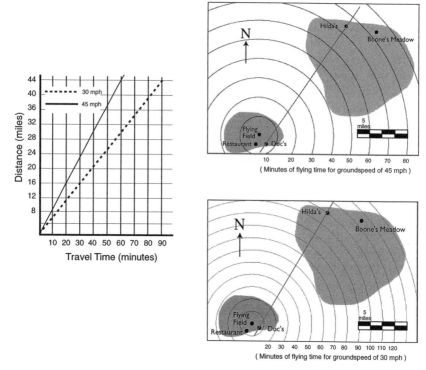

FIG. 8.12. Smart Tools for Emily's Rescue and Delivery Service.

To calculate the answer to each individual problem is cumbersome, and Emily wants to be as efficient as possible. The challenge for students in the classrooms is to invent smart tools that will help Emily solve such problems with efficiency. Some simple smart tools for determining travel time are illustrated in Fig. 8.12.

Each of the adventures in the Jasper series has been repurposed so that it can be approached from the perspective of creating smart tools. Several of the most recently developed Jasper adventures were designed from a smart tool perspective from their very onset. We explore the issue of smart tools in more detail in the next section of this chapter.

Cells 4, 5, 6: Analyses of Single Social Contexts Such as Classrooms

Many readers will have noted that our discussion of Cells 1, 2, and 3 made no mention of the social structure and norms of the classrooms in which our instruction was situated. As noted in the first section, many theorists (e.g., Cobb, Wood, Yackel, & McNeal, 1992; Cobb, Yackel, &

Wood, 1992; Greeno, 1993, 1997) argue that all human activities are socially situated, and we agree. Nevertheless, when we first began our work we left the social context unanalyzed.

As our work has progressed we have discovered that an explicit analysis of the social contexts in which instruction is situated is crucial for a complete understanding of student and teacher learning (cf. Gravemeijer et al., chap. 7, this volume). A number of theorists have helped us move ideas about social context from the realm of the tacit and invisible to the realm of the visible (e.g., Brown & Campione, 1994, 1996; Brown et al., 1990; Cobb, 1994; Cohen, McLaughlin & Talbert, 1993; Lave, 1988; Rogoff, 1990). Several important characteristics of the social context of classrooms that have become part of our thinking about design are discussed next.

General and Subject-Specific Norms. One principle of social analysis is that classrooms can have a variety of different social norms. Some are subject-general; some are subject-specific and apply to particular content areas such as how a group explores history or mathematics (Cobb, Wood, Yackel, & McNeal, 1992; Cobb, Yackel, & Wood, 1992b). Usually these norms reflect teachers' understandings of both pedagogy and content knowledge of a domain (e.g., Bruer, 1993; Shulman, 1987).

We have visited classrooms where the general norms are not conducive to the kinds of instructional environments that we envision. For example, consider the previously described goal of building smart tools that help one solve a variety of problems. The probability that people will have the courage to generate and share their designs is strongly influenced by the norms of the classrooms in which they operate. If the social norms are "always follow the rules and never make mistakes," it is difficult to get students invested in the goal of designing and testing smart tools. In contrast, when everyone's ideas are encouraged and each person is given a chance to make mistakes and learn from them, the probability of successful participation increases noticeably.

Classrooms where students are encouraged to take risks and generate new ideas still do not necessarily encompass the kinds of subject-specific norms that facilitate deep understanding of particular disciplines (e.g., Cobb, Wood, Yackel, & McNeal, 1992; Cobb, Yackel, & Wood, 1992). For example, we have used the *Working Smart* Jasper in classrooms that were excellent at inviting students to generate many kinds of ideas—but not the kinds of ideas that focused on deep content in mathematics. One teacher with whom we worked noted that she first thought of *Working Smart* as a way to teach students to plot points and make graphs. As a result, most of her instruction, and most of the student discussion, focused only on procedures for graph-making. Only later did the teacher realize the importance of emphasizing and discussing mathematical modeling and its role in constructing model-based tools (cf. Nemirovsky & Monk, chap. 6, this volume). Eventually she and her students developed a classroom culture where discussions of the mathematical principles underlying tools such as graphs became the norm.

Social Organization and Participation. The social organization of classrooms can also affect the degree to which everyone participates. Brown and Campione (1994) discussed the advantages of first having students work in "expert" groups where each group develops some degree of expertise in a specific area (e.g, in *Working Smart* each group might develop its own set of smart tools for problem category number 1). After this, students form jigsaw groups that include one member from each of the separate expert groups. Within the jigsaw groups, each person must teach the others about what was discussed and developed in his or her expert group; hence each student must function as a teacher as well as a learner.[1]

Classrooms where students work in groups can be designed to promote individual as well as group accountability. For example, every individual might first be asked to design a smart tool and then meet with his or her expert group and be given chances to revise. Each student can be given chances to revise again after meeting with the jigsaw groups. The important point is that, eventually, each individual must be able to provide mathematical reasons for the tool of his or her choice, plus successfully use that tool to solve problems. Each student might also be asked to evaluate other potential tools.

Alignments of Curriculum, Instruction, Assessment, and Social Organization. Brown and Campione (1996) emphasized that the curriculum, instruction, and assessment materials one uses must fit the desired social organizations of the classroom and vice versa. Materials differ in the degree to which they are jigsawable, and the degree to which they make it easy to assess each student's thinking. For example, asking students to design smart tools provides a visual representation of their thinking that makes their thinking visible and hence relatively easy to assess (see also CTGV, 1997; Schwartz, 1995; cf. Lesh & Doerr, chap. 10, this volume).

Cells 7, 8, 9: Analyses of Multiply Embedded Contexts

Discussion in the previous section tended to treat social contexts such as classrooms as closed systems. Except for the acknowledgment that norms

---

[1]An alternate way to use expert and jigsaw groups is have different expert groups specialize in particular problem types (i.e., problem categories 1–4) and each jigsaw group create smart tools for the entire range of problems to be solved.

for dealing with specific disciplines such as mathematics are embedded within more general classroom norms, little explicit attention was paid to the idea of multiply embedded contexts. It is this idea that separates work in Cells 7, 8, and 9 from Cells 4, 5, and 6. We use the term *multiply embedded contexts* to refer to two important aspects of social structures that need to be explicitly considered when attempting to design effective educational environments. The first is that "outsiders" to a social group can play an extremely important role in facilitating learning. The second is that classroom cultures both affect and are affected by other cultures such as teacher communities within schools, school cultures, and broader community cultures (Barth, 1988; Elmore, Peterson, & McCarthey, 1996; McLaughlin & Talbert, 1993). These two examples of multiply embedded contexts are discussed next.

Roles for Outside Audiences. Our experiences in schools convince us that acts of preparing to interact with outside audiences have an extremely powerful effect on students' and teachers' motivation and a sense of "being in this together." Arranging for "outsiders" to visit classrooms is now an important part of our thinking about design.

One reason for our emphasis on outsiders stems from opportunities to observe their effects on students and teachers. For example, we recently accompanied a group of visitors to an inner-city middle school that had begun the year by solving *Rescue at Boone's Meadow* (RBM). The halls were lined with visual representations that had been constructed to support each group's oral presentation of its solution to RBM. The students actively sought out adults who would listen to their presentations and provide feedback. In each of these interactions, the importance of getting to present to "outsiders" was abundantly clear. We later learned that the teachers were also excited and energized by the fact that outsiders cared enough to want to listen to their students and see what they had learned. We have also had opportunities to visit Brown and Campione's Community of Learners classrooms in California and have seen the powerful effect that "interested outsiders" have on both students and teachers (Brown & Campione, 1994, 1996).

A second reason for our emphasis on outsiders stems from the opportunity to analyze the functioning of our own Learning Technology Center in an effort to see what made it a strong learning community (Barron et al., 1995; CTGV, 1997). An extremely important feature of community building turned out to involve preparation for outside audiences. Preparation for these audiences took a variety of forms, such as presentations to visitors, the collaborative preparation of grant applications, articles written for different kinds of audiences (different people in the center excel in writing for different audiences), and so forth. The fact that most of these challenges included deadlines was especially important. Through our analysis of the LTC it became clear to us that if we were our group's sole audience, much of our sense of community and willingness to exert extra effort would be diminished. We realized that, like us, students and teachers in classrooms need outside audiences as well.

The idea of outside audiences as presenting challenges (complete with deadlines) has been incorporated in our center's SMART Assessment programs, which have been designed to supplement work on problem-based activities such as Jasper. SMART stands for Special Multimedia Arenas for Refining Thinking (e.g., Barron et al., 1995, in press; CTGV, 1994, 1997; Vye et al., 1998). It provides teachers and students with frequent opportunities to "test their mettle" and compare their efforts to others from around the country. Data show a clear value added for Jasper plus SMART compared to Jasper alone (e.g., Barron et al., 1995; CTGV, 1997).

Multiply Embedded Contexts. A second feature characteristic of designs that fit Cells 7, 8, and 9 involves an explicit analysis of the multiply embedded contexts in which one's educational program is situated. Included in this cell is an examination of the classroom and subject-matter norms discussed in Cells 4, 5, and 6. As our work has progressed, it has become clear to us that efforts to sustain and continually improve educational practice also require attention to additional contexts that influence classrooms. Much of what we have learned about this process stems from opportunities to collaborate with McLaughlin and Talbert (1993). Work by Barth (1989) and Elmore et al. (1996) is highly relevant as well.

Teacher Communities. An extremely important aspect of the social environment that affects teachers is the quality of their professional communities. These generally include other teachers and sometimes administrators, researchers and additional members of the broader community. We have learned to appreciate the wisdom of Barth's (1989) statement: "The relationship among adults who live in a school has more to do with the character and quality of the school and with the accomplishments of the students than any other factor" (p. 31).

Studies by McLaughlin and Talbert (1993) demonstrate the importance of this point. They show how different discipline-specific teacher communities within the same high school can differently affect the achievement of the same students (e.g., the mathematics teachers may find the students wonderfully motivated and bright whereas the English teachers may find the same students lazy and underprepared).

Work by Melinda Hall Bray (1996) in our center is documenting the importance of learning communities by studying teachers and researchers involved in Nashville's Schools for Thought project (e.g., Lamon et al., 1996; Secules, Cottom, Bray, & Miller, 1997). Bray is able to show a transformation of teachers' interactions from one of "isolated soloists" to that of a community of learners who readily discuss strengths and weaknesses and strive to improve. This transition from a soloist culture to a learning community is especially important for areas such as middle school mathematics because many of the teachers have never had the benefit of exploring mathematics from the perspective of a quest for deep understanding. No single-shot workshop is sufficient to help them achieve this kind of understanding. As a result, the development of teacher learning communities is a prerequisite for effective education reform, and one of the key elements in our current thinking about design.

Broader Community Support. Teacher learning communities are also supported (or undermined) by other aspects of the social environment such as the degree of support from school administrators and community members. If left unattended, it is very easy for reform efforts to flourish for a short while but never sustain themselves. Issues that can make or break such efforts include the degree to which principals allow flexible time blocks so that students can engage in sustained thinking about important issues, and the degree to which members of the community as a whole support new approaches to assessment that reveal deep understanding.

The idea of anchoring instruction in authentic problem-solving environments such as the Jasper series has turned out to be extremely beneficial for community building (CTGV, 1997). College students, parents, business partners, and others can watch a Jasper adventure and get a solid idea of what the students are exploring. They can then (a) help students solve the problems and prepare their presentations; (b) serve as outside audiences during students' presentation; or (c) create additional materials and experiences that link to themes in the anchor (e.g., after seeing RBM, community members have let students visit their personal ultralight fields; students have also visited wildlife centers that house injured eagles and other species).

An event that has proved to be especially powerful for community building has been to let a group of adults see a Jasper adventure and attempt to solve it, and receive help from students. The students get to see that adults also struggle with these problems, yet don't give up. The adults get to see that young students are able to think and communicate much better than they typically imagined. Procedures for building community have become a very important part of our thinking about design (CTGV, 1997).

Cultural Flexibility.   The idea of multiply embedded contexts also includes another component that we feel is important for teachers as well as students. It involves the ability to analyze key characteristics of one's immediate social environment and see how it differs from other possible environments. For example, in some environments (e.g., during well-planned professional development sessions) it can be comfortable for adults to emphasize what they don't know. In other environments (e.g., appearing before the school board) it can be important to look competent and keep many questions and doubts to oneself. Similarly, in some environments (hopefully most classrooms), students feel free to explore particular concepts deeply (e.g., the concept of nonlinear and linear functions that may underlie the design of different smart tools). In other environments (e.g., a business environment), the emphasis may be on efficiency. In this context it is probably not wise to spend a great deal of business time exploring something as deeply as one would explore it in a mathematics classroom. Alternatively, getting 80% of the problems on a quiz correct may be acceptable performance in a classroom but totally unacceptable in a business context where the customer expects problem solving that is error free.

We believe that cultural flexibility is an important aspect of transfer. The cognitive literature (e.g., Anderson, Reder, & Simon, 1996) tends to focus on learning that leads to abstract representations of important subject-matter concepts (e.g., functions, rate) as a primary source of positive transfer. The situated cognitive literature (e.g., Lave, 1988) tends to focus on learning as assimilation to existing sets of cultural norms, often with little attention to how adaptation to one set of norms affects adaptation to other norms. We believe that the strongest transfer will occur when people acquire "big ideas" of content, plus "big ideas" of how to analyze social settings and see how to best adapt to these settings. It is in this sense that the idea of cultural flexibility is part of the design principles that we currently use.

AN ILLUSTRATION OF A DESIGN
FOR CELLS 6 AND 9

Our goal in this section is to provide more detail about a design involving Jasper that fits into Cell 9 in our framework (see Fig. 8.11). We do so by discussing one of our Jasper Adventures that was specially designed for Cell 9: *Working Smart.* The major mathematical goal of *Working Smart* is to introduce middle school students to important pre-algebra concepts such as functions—including their visual and symbolic representations. Our goal for the adventure is to help students understand and appreciate the power of mathematics (and especially functions) for "modeling the world."

Overview of Working Smart

Working Smart consists of a 17-minute story on videodisc or CD ROM that ends with a challenge. Students are challenged to create mathematical "smart tools" (e.g., graphs, tables, templates for spreadsheets) that will help them quickly and easily solve classes of problems that have been highlighted in the video. An overview of *Working Smart* is provided in Fig. 8.13.

Set in 1968, *Working Smart* is a story about three teenagers, Jasper, Emily, and Larry. Jasper and Larry start a business building and delivering birdhouses. To help them determine a fair price to charge for delivery, Grandpa shows them a Smart Tool that he used when he had a similar business. The Smart Tool is a graph showing delivery times and distances for 3 different modes of transportation: walking, riding a bicycle, and driving a truck.

Emily arrives with exciting news. There is going to be a contest at a local travel agency. All student teams who do well in the contest will receive an all-expense paid trip anywhere in the country. Jasper suggests that the three of them study geography in order to have an edge in the contest. Grandpa suggests that they should create some Smart Tools like his to help them answer questions about travel time.

Ignoring Grandpa's advice, the three friends diligently study geography to prepare for the contest. But when they arrive at the travel agency for the preliminary round, they discover that none of the questions are about geography. They are about travel time (including overtake problems), cost of renting vehicles, and fuel consumption. As a result, Jasper, Emily, and Larry do not do as well as they had hoped in the preliminary round. Disappointed and discouraged, the three leave the travel agency to ponder what to do next.

As they are discussing their options for the next round of the contest, Grandpa returns from delivering birdhouses. He mentions that his Smart Tool is still helpful in determining the time it will take to deliver a birdhouse. Emily realizes that Grandpa's Smart Tool would be helpful in answering questions for the contest at the travel agency, and she convinces Jasper and Larry that they should create Smart Tools.

Challenge: Create Smart Tools to help Larry, Jasper, and Emily pass the final interview.

FIG. 8.13. Story summary of the Jasper Adventure, *Working Smart.*

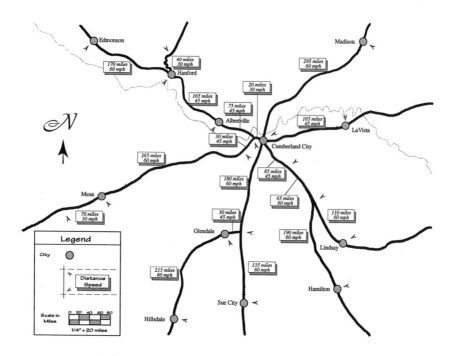

FIG. 8.14. Map for the category, "Are We There Yet?"

In order to solve *Working Smart*, students need to revisit the adventure and gather information about the types of problems they can expect to encounter. Students usually proceed by dividing into groups. Four different problem types are featured in the video—two involve rate, time, and distance, and two involve other types of relationships. Functions generated for several of the categories involve linear relationships; others are nonlinear.

Preparing for a Particular Class of Problems. Consider preparing smart tools to answer questions about the category "Are We There Yet?" Problems in this category relate to a map (see Fig. 8.14) that is given to students and shows relevant distances and speed limits. Given the map and their smart tools, students are asked to solve problems such as the following (which are all based on leaving from Cumberland City):

1. How long should it take me to get to Sue City by car?
2. I've been driving for 2 hours at 60 mph and I'm in the country. Can you tell me the nearest town?
3. If I drive 45 mph rather than 60 mph, how much longer will it take me to get to Hanford (which is 260 miles away)?

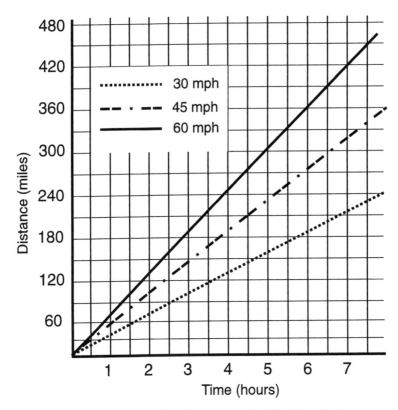

FIG. 8.15. Smart Tool for the category, "Are We There Yet?"

A graph like the one illustrated in Fig. 8.15 provides an excellent smart tool for helping students answer a variety of questions about the Category "Are We There Yet?"

Like all Jasper adventures, *Working Smart* includes "embedded teaching" scenes that students can return to in order to begin to understand the idea of smart tools. One scene features Grandpa's smart tools that he uses to determine the delivery time for birdhouses, depending on the distance he must travel and whether he will walk, ride his bicycle, or drive his old truck (see Fig. 8.16). Students cannot simply copy Grandpa's smart tool and use it to solve the challenge because it does not contain the relevant information. However, it provides a model of the value of smart tools.

The Need for Active Inquiry, Feedback, and Opportunities to Revise

We noted earlier that even for an easy-to-communicate idea such as backscratcher T-shirts, a thorough understanding of the value of different types of grids requires opportunities to make conjectures about design and

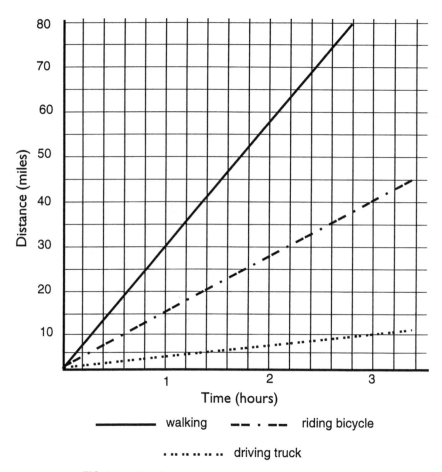

FIG. 8.16. Grandpa's Smart Tool for delivering birdhouses.

to receive feedback. The need for opportunities for inquiry and feedback is even greater for *Working Smart*. The adventure is motivating and provides a good foundation for understanding the idea of creating smart tools. The embedded teaching scenes are helpful to most students and teachers. Nevertheless, most middle school students are used to thinking about mathematics as "what you do to solve a particular problem that someone gives you." This is very different from attempting to select or invent tools and procedures that will help one solve an entire class of problems. Our experience is that students must attempt to use and then revise smart tools several times before they begin to grasp the idea that they are solving entire classes of potential problems rather than only a single problem.

Figure 8.17 shows data from a group of seventh graders who used their smart tools to help them solve the "Are We There Yet?" category of problems from *Working Smart*. Their initial performance was not very good. After testing the mettle of their tools, students received a chance to revise their tools and try again. Their performance improved substantially (see Fig. 8.17).

An interesting aspect of students' thinking in the context of *Working Smart* involves their initial assumptions about what counts as "acceptable performance." On their first chance to test their mettle, many of the students argued that getting 75% correct should be acceptable because it counts as a "pass."

Working Smart helped set the stage for discussions of how errors on roughly 25% of the problems one confronts would be quite unacceptable in a real setting such as a travel agency. If people are counting on you for advice that affects their vacation planning, they expect performance that is essentially error free. This example illustrates why we include cultural flexibility as one of the design principles that are important for Cells 7, 8, and 9.

Additional Cycles of Inquiry, Feedback, and Revision. Following several passes at the "Are We There Yet?" problems, students then develop smart tools for other categories of problems such as "Burning Bucks" and

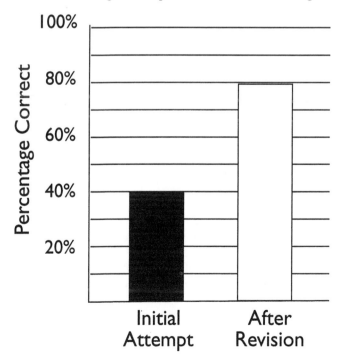

FIG. 8.17. Questions answered correctly with Smart Tool on initial attempt and after revision.

"Catch Em If You Can." Our experiences in classrooms indicate that students' abilities to prepare for new categories of problems, and to explain the mathematical basis of their smart tools, improve over time.

The cycles of inquiry, feedback, and revision built into *Working Smart* are also designed to help students learn to differentiate linear from nonlinear functions. For example, mathematical models for questions in the category "Beat This Deal!" are piecewise defined functions. Working with nonlinear functions provides opportunities for students to compare properties of linear functions with nonlinear ones and helps them understand how the functions are alike or different.

As an illustration, consider a student presenting ideas about her group's discussions. She noted that the graph of a piecewise defined function did not allow her to extrapolate in the same way that she did with a linear function to find values for points outside the range of the graph. The student recognized the constant rate of change for the linear function and used this insight to help her determine values outside the range of the graph. She recognized that piecewise defined functions did not possess the same constant rate of change that was captured by her comment. Her teacher described the situation as follows:

> There's one group that has this [pointing to a graph-based smart tool where the vertical axis had the wrong range for the class of problems that students were asked to solve] ... and it was really good—she was testing her smart tool today and she kept having problems. She said, "Well, I can't do it with this because this is 300 miles and this only goes up to 140 and before I could just take half [referring to the smart tool she used for the category "Are We There Yet?"; for this category if the range of the smart tool was not big enough she could find the distance traveled in half the time and multiply by 2 to get the correct distance] ... But I don't know ..." You have U-Steer beginning to really increase there and she said, "And I don't know what U-Steer is going to do now."
>
> And I said to the student: " are you going to persuade the class to buy your smart tool." And she said, "No!" And I said, "What are you going to do?" And she said, "I'm going to persuade them not to use my smart tool." And I said, "Good job!" And I said, "What are you going to do when other people are persuading?" And she said, "I'm going to listen."

This is an excellent example of mathematical reasoning, plus it illustrates a very positive attitude toward wanting to learn and improve.

Contrasting Cases as Scaffolds

In many classrooms where we have tested *Working Smart*, we find that it can be extremely difficult to have students attempt to invent smart tools from scratch. It's too big a leap. As a scaffold for inventing smart tools, we have used the theory of contrasting cases discussed in section 1 of this paper. In particular, we have presented students with a catalog of contrasting smart tools that they can use to solve particular classes of problems such as the "Are We There Yet?" problems (Fig. 8.18). Their job is to work in groups to choose a smart tool and then explain why they

Smart Tools Catalog

This catalog contains possible **Smart Tools** for the category "Are We There Yet?" and "Catch 'Em if You Can!" Your group must select one Smart Tool to "buy." Once you have selected your Smart Tool, write a paragraph to describe what you thought about as you decided which Smart Tool to buy. Also explain why you selected your tool.

Item A:
Grandpa's Smart Tool

This is an expanded version of the Smart Tool that served Grandpa so well for so many years. Guaranteed to be Distance (miles)Time (hours) accurate and reliable.

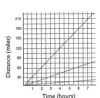

Item E:
Multiple Speed Chart

Time (hours)	Miles for Rate 1	Miles for Rate 2	Miles for Rate 3	Miles for Rate 4	Miles for Rate 5	Miles for Rate 6	Miles for Rate 7
1/2	5	10	15	20	25	30	35
1	10	20	30	40	50	60	70
1 1/2	15	30	45	60	75	90	105
2	20	40	60	80	100	120	140
2 1/2	25	50	75	100	125	150	175
3	30	60	90	120	150	180	210
3 1/2	35	70	105	140	175	210	245
4	40	80	120	160	200	240	280
4 1/2	45	90	135	180	225	270	315
5	50	100	150	200	250	300	350
5 1/2	55	110	165	220	275	330	385
6	60	120	180	240	300	360	420
6 1/2	65	130	195	260	325	390	455
7	70	140	210	280	350	420	490
7 1/2	75	150	225	300	375	450	525
8	80	160	240	320	400	480	560

Don't be caught without the right speed. This Smart Tool tells you distances for seven different speeds. You'll be able to plan just about any trip with this Smart Tool. Tool comes on a 5 1/2" by 8 1/2" page.

Item B: Table of Distances

With this Smart Tool you can quickly determine the distance from Cumberland City to any other city on the map. Saves time and effort! Smart Tool comes on a 5 1/2" by 8 1/2" page.

From Cumberland City to:	Distance (miles)
Albertville	95
Edmonson	430
Glendale	210
Hamilton	340
Hanford	260
Hillsdale	425
LaVista	165
Lindsay	260
Madison	295
Mesa	285
Sue City	315

Item C:
Time on My Side Smart Tool

Distance (miles)	Time (min) Rate 1	Time (min) Rate 2	Time (min) Rate 3	Time (min) Rate 4	Time (min) Rate 5	Time (min) Rate 6	Time (min) Rate 7
10	20	17	15	13	12	11	10
20	40	34	30	27	24	22	20
30	60	51	45	40	36	33	30
40	80	69	60	53	48	44	40
50	100	86	75	67	60	55	50
60	120	103	90	80	72	65	60
70	140	120	105	93	84	76	70
80	160	137	120	107	96	87	80
90	180	154	135	120	108	98	90
100	200	171	150	133	120	109	100
110	220	189	165	147	132	120	110
120	240	206	180	160	144	131	120
130	260	223	195	173	156	142	130
140	280	240	210	197	168	153	140
150	300	257	225	210	180	164	150

When you ask someone, "How far is it to Albertville?" what do they say? "Three hours," of course. Time is what's important when you travel, not distance. So use a Smart Tool that highlights time. It's the real, natural way to talk about travel.

Item D:
Basic Smart Tool

Here's a Smart Tool that will help you plan lots of trips. Easy-to-read scales make it simple to determine times or distances. Smart Tool comes on an 8 1/2" by 11" page.

Item F:
Precision Smart Tool

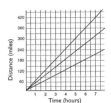

Know exactly how long or how far your trip is. This Smart Tool lets you determine the time of your trip to the nearest minute or the length of your trip to the nearest mile. Smart Tool comes on an 8 1/2" x 11" page.

Item G:
Eternity Smart Tool

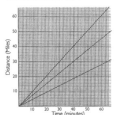

This is the Smart Tool for a lifetime. With three different speeds to choose from, you'll always know how far you've gone and how long you've got left. Because there are three different lines, you can even track more than one speed at a time!

FIG. 8.18. A catalog of contrasting Smart Tools for the category, "Are We There Yet?"

chose it and how it will be used. Some of the smart tools in the catalog won't work at all. Others vary in terms of elegance and ease of use.

As noted in the first section, an emphasis on particular sets of contrasts affects the kinds of dimensions and features that students notice. For example, using different rates of speed in a chart focuses students' attention on speed. When students look at a graphical smart tool, they usually have conversations about how and what speed is represented on each graph. Similarly, the contrast of reading exact data for selected values in a chart verses a graph provides opportunities for students to identify what a reasonable degree of precision might be for their estimates of time and distance.

We are finding that the use of catalogs of contrasting cases helps teachers develop classroom communities that result in more effective learning. First, students are highly motivated to look through the catalog. Second, students' conversations are focused because they organize their discussions around the design features that differentiate the contrasting tools. Third, students receive more chances for feedback because the catalogs help structure their presentations and make their current thinking clear and more visible so it is easier to give feedback.

A teacher who has collaborated with us for several years first taught *Working Smart* without a catalog and found that all her students tended to generate the same "smart tool" each time. When she later used a smart tool catalog, there was much more variability in the students' initial choices and hence much better and more meaningful discussion. After thinking about her teaching the teacher realized that the first time she had taught *Working Smart*, she had led her students to create a particular type of smart tool without realizing that she had done so. The use of the catalog made it much easier to keep from being too directive, and it motivated exciting discussions among students, who then became eager to test the mettle of their particular tools.

From Selection to Adaptation to Invention. Instruction in *Working Smart* is designed to move students from processes of (a) selecting tools, to (b) adapting existing tools, and eventually (c) inventing new tools from scratch. For example, the tool shown in Fig. 8.19 requires that students add their own information—it is basically a shell for more generative activities. Eventually they work on parts of the problem where they generate their own tools from scratch.

As students gain insights that help them learn to generate their own tools, it can be useful to have them return to previous problem sets where they simply selected smart tools and attempt to create tools that are better than any shown in the catalog. Figure 8.20 illustrates a student-generated smart tool (the student was an eighth grader) for solving problems of

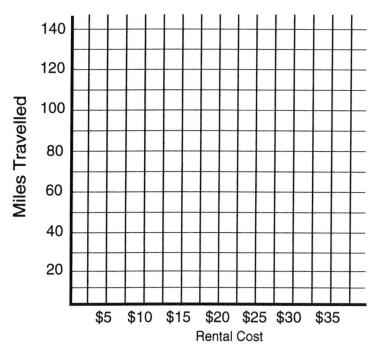

FIG. 8.19. Template for Smart Tool for category, "Beat This Deal!"

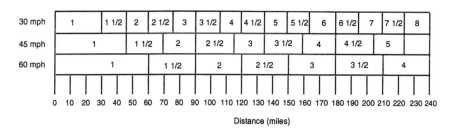

FIG. 8.20. A student's Smart Tool for the category, "Are We There Yet?"

distance, rate, and time in *Working Smart*. No one in our research group had thought about designing this particular tool.

Additional extensions to *Working Smart* are designed to help students experience a number of situations where they can create smart tools by beginning with mathematical models. Many of these extensions revisit earlier Jasper adventures. For example, in *Rescue at Boone's Meadow*, Larry's ultralight is used to rescue a wounded eagle. How might one create a smart tool that lets Larry quickly see if his ultralight has enough range (hours of flying time on a tank of gasoline) depending on where he wants to go and whether there are headwinds and tailwinds? In *The*

Big Splash, how might one create a smart tool that make it easy to determine the rate of filling different size pools depending on different flow rates of water in the school hose?

Eventually, we want to help students understand that a general model for concepts such as rate can apply to a wide variety of concrete situations. The model can be transformed into useful smart tools when it is calibrated for particular contextual conditions (e.g., when it takes into account the appropriate values for range and speed that fit Larry's ultralight, or the flow rate for the school hose and volume for the pool in *The Big Splash*).

We also want to help students learn to move from visual representations of mathematics to symbolic representations. Helping students create special templates for spreadsheets is one way to help them begin to make this transition. It is especially useful to help them to see that symbolic, computer-based representations are especially helpful when the range of values one has to deal with is large. Additional Jasper adventures in the algebra strand (see Fig. 8.4) are designed to move increasingly toward an appreciation of how visual representations of functions map into symbolic representations. For example, *The General Is Missing* is explicitly designed to help students see the symbolic power of algebra as a language—for communicating both with other humans and with machines such as computers. (Features of this adventure are described in Bransford et al., 1996, and CTGV, 1997.)

Engineering the Social Environment

Our experiences with *Working Smart* clearly illustrate the importance of classroom and subject-specific norms, which are emphasized in Cell 6 of the framework in Fig. 8.11. *Working Smart* can look very different depending on whether teachers emphasize "always find the right answer" or encourage a diversity of thinking and reasoning. Teachers' understandings of the goals of *Working Smart* have a strong effect on the classroom culture. For example, we noted earlier that one teacher initially thought that the purpose of the adventure was to teach students how to draw graphs. Her classroom that year looked very different than it did in subsequent years when we did a better job of helping her understand the kinds of mathematical understanding that the adventure might help students achieve.

Working Smart takes on added dimensions when it is incorporated into Cell 9 of the framework in Fig. 8.11. As noted earlier, Cell 9 includes an emphasis on multiply embedded social contexts, which include roles for outside audiences in building classroom communities, plus the importance of thinking about classroom environments as being embedded in teacher communities, school-based communities, and the broader community (e.g., McLaughlin & Talbot, 1993). Examples are provided next.

The SMART Challenge Series. *Working Smart* is ideal for incorporating into our center's SMART Challenge Series, which provides outside challenges that invite teachers and their students to "test their mettle," see how other classes around the country perform, and make revisions as necessary. SMART stands for Special Multimedia Areas for Refining Thinking. Data indicate a clear value added in terms of achievement when we use Jasper and others adventures in a SMART context compared to using Jasper without SMART (Barron et al., 1995, in press; CTGV, 1997; Vye et al., 1998). The ability to design and test the mettle of particular classes of smart tools is an activity that is ideally suited for SMART Challenges.

Outside Audiences. *Working Smart* is also excellent for helping outside audiences interact with students and teachers in the classroom. Outsiders (which in the past have included college students, business partners, parents, and others) can watch the adventure so that they understand what the students are doing. They then have a more concrete basis for interacting with the students to help them test their mettle and improve their abilities to communicate. The idea of creating smart tools in *Working Smart* is particularly appealing because it represents a novel approach to mathematical thinking that most people find exciting. In addition, the fact that discussions can be organized around the mathematical properties of particular tools makes it easier for visitors to understand what the students are talking about.

The idea of "tools for working smart" is also a topic that allows outsiders to share tools that they use in their work. Our experiences indicate that students are intrigued with opportunities to learn about tools that people have invented to "work smart" in a wide variety of environments (fascinating examples include aviation, carpentry, artistic activities such as color matching and quilt making, and tools for business environments). An introduction of these tools raises a series of additional questions. For example, to what extent must tools be redesigned when they are moved from one setting to another? To what extent are cultural norms transformed as new tools are introduced? How much emphasis is placed on relating tools to formal bodies of knowledge such as mathematics or physics in different types of settings? These are fascinating issues that can be very useful for students to explore and articulate.

Questions like these help develop skills of cultural flexibility—a concept that we discussed earlier. For example, the adventure helps students compare classroom cultures with business cultures and other everyday activities. In the process, they can learn a great deal about how to move from one culture to the another. We noted earlier, for example, that classroom cultures often encourage a deep examination of ideas that in a business environment often does not happen because of the need to be cost-effective and time-efficient. We also noted that students who are used to a classroom culture initially assume that 75% correct is perfectly acceptable as a passing grade. In a business setting, however, it would usually be far from acceptable.

SUMMARY AND CONCLUSIONS

Our goal in this chapter was to discuss our current thinking about designs that invite and sustain mathematical thinking. We noted that, as a research group, we are interested in designing environments for all disciplines, including science, literature, and history, as well as mathematics. We believe that there are important principles of understanding and learning that are common across disciplines, but we also believe that there is also a great deal of domain specificity. Our focus in the present chapter has been in the area of mathematics for students in the middle school years.

We divided our discussion into three major sections. In the first section we focused on theories of understanding and socially situated learning that have had a major impact on our thinking. Our discussion of understanding included work by Dewey (1933) on differences between "meaningful objects" and "brute things"; work by Buhler (cf. Blumenthal, 1970) on the importance of shared knowledge for comprehension; and work by Garner (1974) and J. Gibson and Gibson (1955) on the development of differentiated knowledge. We emphasized that people's perception and understanding of individual objects and events depend on their place in a field of alternatives. An important implication is that simply knowing the referent of various symbols is insufficient to understand their overall significance.

Our discussion of socially situated learning included an emphasis on both general and discipline-specific norms that characterize the social contexts of learning (Cobb, 1994), and on the fact that knowing is often distributed across other people and artifacts (e.g., Norman, 1993; Pea, 1993; Salomon, 1993). We also emphasized the importance of embedded contexts (McLaughlin & Talbert, 1993) and the need to explicitly take these into account in approaches to design.

We ended our discussion in the first section by noting that its major shortcoming was that it simply involved a list of principles. The purpose of the second section was to explore how these principles could be combined to create different kinds of instructional environments. We used the 3×3 matrix in Fig. 8.11 to illustrate nine different design environments, and we explained how and why our own work in design has moved from Cell 1 in that matrix to Cell 9. These changes were motivated by our experiences in classrooms (e.g., CTGV, 1996, 1997), plus our increasing familiarity with other research literatures such as the literature on situated cognition and the literature on mathematics education. Each of these has helped us deepen our understanding of design.

In the third section of this chapter we discussed a particular example of an instructional environment that was designed to fit Cell 9 of the matrix shown in Fig. 8.11. Based on the Jasper adventure *Working Smart*, this environment helps students focus on mathematical modeling as a way to create solutions that solve entire classes of problems rather than simply solve a single problem, and it invites students to think visually as well as symbolically as they attempt to invent mathematical tools that help them "work smart" in these environments. We also discussed how the theory of contrasting cases has guided our attempts to help scaffold students' thinking in this domain.

We envision several "next steps" in our attempts to develop environments that invite and sustain mathematical thinking. A major goal is to increase the resources available with the Jasper adventures so that they can move from a supplement to the curriculum to a full curriculum in areas such as algebra and geometry (see CTGV, chap. 7, 1997). As support for achieving this goal, we have created a software shell that can help both students and teachers grasp the "big picture" of their inquiry; download from the World Wide Web a number of text, video, and interactive resources that are relevant to their inquiry; and continually "test their mettle" as they explore important mathematical concepts (Schwartz, Lin, Brophy & Bransford, in press).

A second "next step" is to continue our research in classrooms, plus our collaboration with colleagues in mathematics education. The goal of this step is to find ways to further improve our approach.

ACKNOWLEDGMENTS

The research reported in this chapter was supported, in part, by grants from the National Science Foundation (NSF) for development and research on the Jasper series (MDR-0050191 and ESI-9252990), and from the Office of Educational Research and Improvement (OERI; 305F60090) for research on contrasting cases. The ideas expressed in this chapter are those of the authors, not the granting agencies.

The Cognition and Technology Group at Vanderbilt (CTGV) refers to an interdisciplinary group of individuals at the Learning Technology Center, Peabody College at Vanderbilt University. Members of the CTGV contributing to the work discussed in this chapter are the following (in alphabetical order): Melinda Bray, Kay Burgess, Susan R. Goldman, Ted Hasselbring, Xiaodong Lin, Allison Moore, Tom Noser, James W. Pellegrino, Teresa J. Secules, and Susan M. Williams.

REFERENCES

Adams, L., Kasserman, J., Yearwood, A., Perfetto, G., Bransford, J., & Franks, J. (1988). The effects of facts versus problem-oriented acquisition. *Memory & Cognition, 16,* 167–175.

American Association for the Advancement of Science. (1989). *Science for all Americans: A project 2061 report on literacy goals in science, mathematics, and technology.* Washington, DC: Author.

Anderson, J. R. (1982). Acquisition of cognitive skill. *Psychological Review, 89,* 369–406.

Anderson, J. R. (1987). Skill acquisition: Compilation of weak-method problem solutions. *Psychological Review, 94,* 192–210.

Anderson, R., & Ortony, A. (1975). On putting apples into bottles—A problem of polysemy. *Cognitive Psychology, 7,* 167–180.

Anderson, J. R., Reder, L. M., & Simon, H. A. (1996, May). Situated learning and education. *Educational Researcher, 25*(4), 5–11.

Anderson, J. R., Reder, L. M., & Simon, H. A. (1997). Rejoinder: Situative versus cognitive perspectives: Form versus substance. *Educational Researcher, 26*(1), 18–21.

Bacon, F. (1620). *Novum organum.* First book, Aphorism 2.

Barclay, J. R., Bransford, J. D., Franks, J. J., McCarrell, N. S., & Nitsch, K. E. (1974). Comprehension and semantic flexibility. *Journal of Verbal Learning and Verbal Behavior, 13,* 471–481.

Barron, B., Schwartz, D. L., Vye, N. J., Moore, A., Petrosino, A., Zech, L., Bransford, J. D., & Cognition and Technology Group at Vanderbilt. (in press). Doing with understanding: Lessons from research on problem and project-based learning. *Journal of Learning Sciences.*

Barron, B., Vye, N. J., Zech, L., Schwartz, D., Bransford, J. D., Goldman, S. R., Pellegrino, J., Morris, J., Garrison, S., & Kantor, R. (1995). Creating contexts for community-based problem solving: The Jasper challenge series. In C. N. Hedley, P. Antonacci, & M. Rabinowitz (Eds.), *Thinking and literacy: The mind at work* (pp. 47–71). Mahwah, NJ: Lawrence Erlbaum Associates.

Barth, R. (1988). School: A community of leaders. In A. Lieberman (Ed.), *Building a professional culture in schools.* New York: Teachers College Press.

Barth, R. (1989). The principal and the profession of teaching. In T. J. Sergiovanni & J. H. Moore (Eds.), *Schooling for tomorrow: Directing reform to issues that count.* New York: Teachers College Press.

Blumenthal, A. L. (1970). *Language and psychology.* New York: John Wiley and Sons.

Bransford, J. D. (1979). *Human cognition: Learning, understanding, and remembering.* Belmont, CA: Wadsworth.

Bransford, J. D., Franks, J. J., Vye, N. J., & Sherwood, R. D. (1989). New approaches to instruction: Because wisdom can't be told. In S. Vosniadou & A. Ortony (Eds.), *Similarity and analogical reasoning* (pp. 470–497). New York: Cambridge University Press.

Bransford, J. D., & Johnson, M. K. (1972). Contextual prerequisites for understanding: Some investigations of comprehension and recall. *Journal of Verbal Learning and Verbal Behavior, 11,* 717–726.

Bransford, J. D., & Johnson, M. K. (1973). Considerations of some problems of comprehension. In W. G. Chase (Ed.), *Visual information processing* (pp. 383–438). New York: Academic Press.

Bransford, J. D., & McCarrell, N. S. (1974). A sketch of cognitive approach to comprehension. In W. Weimer & D. Palermo (Eds.), *Cognition and the symbolic processes* (pp. 189–229). Hillsdale, NJ: Lawrence Erlbaum Associates.

Bransford, J. D., & Stein, B. S. (1993). *The IDEAL problem solver* (2nd ed.). New York: Freeman.

Bransford, J. D., Vye, N., Adams, L., & Perfetto, G. (1989). Learning skills and the acquisition of knowledge. In A. Lesgold & R. Glaser (Eds.), *Foundations for a psychology of education* (pp. 199–249). Hillsdale, NJ: Lawrence Erlbaum Associates.

Bransford, J. D., Zech, L., Schwartz, D., Barron, B., Vye, N., & Cognition and Technology Group at Vanderbilt. (1996). Fostering mathematical thinking in middle school students: Lessons from research. In R. J. Sternberg & T. Ben-Zeev (Eds.), *The nature of mathematical thinking* (pp. 203–250). Mahwah, NJ: Lawrence Erlbaum Associates.

Bray, M. H. (1996). *The changing role of teachers as they implementing a constructivist approach to learning.* Unpublished manuscript, Vanderbilt University, Nashville, TN.

Brown, A. L., Bransford, J. D., Ferrara, R. A., & Campione, J. C. (1983). Learning, remembering, and understanding. In J. H. Flavell & E. M. Markman (Eds.), *Handbook of child psychology: Vol. 3. Cognitive development* (4th ed., pp. 78–166). New York: Wiley.

Brown, A. L., & Campione, J. C. (1994). Guided discovery in a community of learners. In K. McGilly (Ed.), *Classroom lessons: Integrating cognitive theory and classroom practice* (pp. 229–272). Cambridge, MA: MIT Press.

Brown, A. L., & Campione, J. C. (1996). Psychological theory and the design of innovative learning environments: On procedures, principles, and systems. In L. Schauble & R. Glaser (Eds.), *Innovations in learning: New environments for education* (pp. 289–325). Mahwah, NJ: Lawrence Erlbaum Associates.

Brown, J. S., Collins, A., & Duguid, P. (1989). Situated cognition and the culture of learning. *Educational Researcher, 18*(1), 32–41.

Bruer, J. T. (1993). *Schools for thought.* Cambridge, MA: MIT Press.

Chi, M. T. H., Glaser, R., & Farr, M. (1991). *The nature of expertise.* Hillsdale, NJ: Lawrence Erlbaum Associates.

Chi, M. T. H., & Koeske, R. D. (1983). Network representation of a child's dinosaur knowledge. *Developmental Psychology, 19*(1), 29–39.

Cobb, P. (1994). Where is the mind? Constructivist and sociocultural perspectives on mathematical development. *Educational Researcher, 23*(7), 13–20.

Cobb, P., Wood, T., Yackel, E., & McNeal, B. (1992). Characteristics of classroom mathematics traditions: An interactional analysis. *American Educational Research Journal, 29*, 573–604.

Cobb, P., Yackel, E., & Wood, T. (1992). A constructivist alternative to the representational view of mind in mathematics education. *Journal for Research in Mathematics Education, 19*, 99–114.

Cognition and Technology Group at Vanderbilt. (1990). Anchored instruction and its relationship to situated cognition. *Educational Researcher, 19*(6), 2–10.

Cognition and Technology Group at Vanderbilt. (1992). The Jasper series as an example of anchored instruction: Theory, program description, and assessment data. *Educational Psychologist, 27*, 291–315.

Cognition and Technology Group at Vanderbilt. (1993). Toward integrated curricula: Possibilities from anchored instruction. In M. Rabinowitz (Ed.), *Cognitive science foundations of instruction* (pp. 33–55). Hillsdale, NJ: Lawrence Erlbaum Associates.

Cognition and Technology Group at Vanderbilt. (1996). Looking at technology in context: A framework for understanding technology and education research. In D. C. Berliner & R. C. Calfee (Eds.), *Handbook of educational psychology* (pp. 807–840). New York: Simon & Schuster MacMillan.

Cognition and Technology Group at Vanderbilt. (1997). *The Jasper project: Lessons in curriculum, instruction, assessment, and professional development.* Mahwah, NJ: Lawrence Erlbaum Associates.

Cognition and Technology Group at Vanderbilt. (in press). Designing environments to reveal, support, and expand our children's potentials. In S. A. Soraci & W. McIlvane (Eds.), *Perspectives on fundamental processes in intellectual functioning.* Norwood, NJ: Ablex.

Cohen, D. K., McLaughlin, M. W., & Talbert, J. E. (Eds.). (1993). *Teaching for understanding: Challenges for policy and practice*. San Francisco: Jossey-Bass.

Dewey, S. (1933). *How we think, "a restatement" of the relation of reflective thinking to the educative process*. Boston: Heath.

Elmore, R. F., Peterson, P. L., & McCarthey, S. J. (1996). *Restructuring in the classroom: Teaching, learning, and school organization*. San Francisco: Jossey-Bass.

Franks, J., Bransford, J., Brailey, K., & Purdon, S. (1991). Understanding memory access. In R. Hoffman & D. Palermo (Eds.), *Cognition and the symbolic processes: Applied and ecological perspectives* (pp. 281–299). Hillsdale, NJ: Lawrence Erlbaum Associates.

Gagné, R., & Gibson, J. J. (1947). Research on the recognition of aircraft. In J. J. Gibson (Ed.), *Motion picture training and research* (pp. 113–168). Washington, DC: U.S. Government Printing Office.

Garner, W. R. (1974). *The processing of information and structure*. Potomac, MD: Lawrence Erlbaum Associates.

Gibson, J., & Gibson, E. (1955). Perceptual learning: Differentiation or enrichment. *Psychological Review, 62*, 32–51.

Gick, M. L., & Holyoak, K. J. (1980). Analogical problem solving. *Cognitive Psychology, 12*, 306–365.

Gick, M. L., & Holyoak, K. J. (1983). Schema induction and analogical transfer. *Cognitive Psychology, 15*, 1–38.

Gragg, C. I. (1940, October 19). Because wisdom can't be told. *Harvard Alumni Bulletin*, 78–84.

Greeno, J. G. (1993). For research to reform education and cognitive science. In L. A. Penner, G. M. Batsche, H. M. Knoff, & D. L. Nelson (Eds.), *The challenge in mathematics and science education: Psychology's response* (pp. 153–194). Washington, DC: American Psychological Association.

Greeno, J. G. (1997). Response: On claims that answer the wrong questions. *Educational Researcher, 26*(1), 5–17.

Greeno, J. G., Smith, D. R., & Moore, J. L. (1993). Transfer of situated learning. In D. K. Detterman & R. J. Sternberg (Eds.), *Transfer on trial: Intelligence, cognition, and instruction* (pp. 99–167). Norwood, NJ: Ablex.

Hanson, N. R. (1970). A picture theory of theory meaning. In R. G. Colodny (Ed.), *The nature and function of scientific theories* (pp. 233–274). Pittsburgh, PA: University of Pittsburgh Press.

Kilpatrick, J. (1992). Problem formulating: Where do good problems come from? In A. H. Schoenfeld (Ed.), *Cognitive science and mathematics education* (pp. 3–8). New York: Macmillan.

Lamon, M., Secules, T. J., Petrosino, T., Hackett, R., Bransford, J. D., & Goldman, S. R. (1996). Schools for thought: Overview of the project and lessons learned from one of the sites. In L. Schauble & R. Glaser (Eds.), *Innovations in learning: New environments for education* (pp. 243–288). Mahwah, NJ: Lawrence Erlbaum Associates.

Lave, J. (1988). *Cognition in practice: Mind, mathematics, and culture in everyday life*. Cambridge, UK: Cambridge University Press.

Lindberg, M. (1980). The role of knowledge structures in the ontogeny of learning. *Journal of Experimental Child Psychology, 30*, 401–410.

Lockhart, R. S., Lamon, M., & Gick, M. L. (1988). Conceptual transfer in simple insight problems. *Memory & Cognition, 16*, 36–44.

McLaughlin, M. W., & Talbert, J. E. (1993). *Contexts that matter for teaching and learning: Strategic opportunities for meeting the nation's education goals*. Stanford, CA: Center for Research on the Context of Teaching.

Moore, J. L., Lin, X., Schwartz, D., Petrosino, A., Hickey, D. T., Campbell, O., & Cognition and Technology Group at Vanderbilt. (1996). The relationship between situated cognition and anchored instruction: A response to Tripp. In H. McLellan (Ed.), *Situated learning perspectives* (pp. 213–221). Englewood Cliffs, NJ: Educational Technology Publications.

National Academy of Sciences. (1996). *National science education standards*. Washington, DC: National Academy Press.

National Council of Teachers of Mathematics. (1996). *Professional standards for teaching mathematics*. Reston, VA: Author.

Newman, D., Griffin, P., & Cole, M. (1989). *Construction zone: Working for cognitive change in school*. New York: Cambridge University Press.

New Standards. (1995). *Performance standards draft 5.1*. Washington, DC: Author.

Norman, D. A. (1993). *Things that make us smart: Defending human attributes in the age of the machine*. New York: Addison-Wesley.

Pea, R. D. (1993). Learning scientific concepts through material and social activities: Conversational analysis meets conceptual change. *Educational Psychologist, 28*(3), 265–277.

Rogoff, B. (1990). *Apprenticeship in thinking*. New York: Oxford University Press.

Salomon, G. (Ed.). (1993). *Distributed cognitions: Psychological and educational considerations*. New York: Cambridge University Press.

Schoenfeld, A. H. (1985). *Mathematical problem solving*. Orlando, FL: Academic Press.

Schoenfeld, A. H. (Ed.). (1987). *Cognitive science and mathematics education*. Hillsdale, NJ: Lawrence Erlbaum Associates.

Schwartz, D. L. (1995). The emergence of abstract representations in dyad problem solving. *Journal of the Learning Science, 4*, 321–354.

Schwartz, D. L., & Bransford, J. D. (in press). *A time for telling*.

Schwartz, D. L., Goldman, S. R., Vye, N. J., Barron, B. J., & Bransford, J. D., with the CTGV. (1998). Aligning everyday and mathematical reasoning: The case of sampling assumptions. In Susanne P. Lajoie (Ed.), *Reflections on statistics: Learning, teaching, and assessment in grades K–12* (pp. 233–273). Mahwah, NJ: Lawrence Erlbaum Associates.

Schwartz, D. L., Lin, X., Brophy, S., & Bransford, J. D. (in press). Toward the development of flexibly adaptive instructional designs. In C. M. Reigeluth (Ed.), *Instructional design theories and models: Volume II*. Mahwah, NJ: Lawrence Erlbaum Associates.

Secules, T., Cottom, C., Bray, M., & Miller, L. (1997). Creating schools for thought. *Educational Leadership, 54*(6), 56–60.

Shulman, L. S. (1987). Knowledge and teaching: Foundations of the new reform. *Harvard Educational Review, 57*, 1–22.

Silver, E. A. (1986). Using conceptual and procedural knowledge: A focus on relationships. In J. Hiebert (Ed.), *Conceptual and procedural knowledge: The case of mathematics* (pp. 181–189). Hillsdale, NJ: Lawrence Erlbaum Associates.

Silver, E. A. (1990). Contribution of research to practice: Applying findings, methods, and perspectives. In T. J. Cooney (Ed.), *Teaching and learning mathematics in the 1990s: 1990 Yearbook of the National Council of Teachers of Mathematics* (pp. 1–11). Reston, VA: National Council of Teachers of Mathematics.

Simon, H. A. (1980). Problem solving and education. In D. T. Tuma & R. Reif (Eds.), *Problem solving and education: Issues in teaching and research* (pp. 81–96). Hillsdale, NJ: Lawrence Erlbaum Associates.

Van Haneghan, J. P., Barron, L., Young, M. F., Williams, S. M., Vye, N. J., & Bransford, J. D. (1992). The Jasper series: An experiment with new ways to enhance mathematical thinking. In D. F. Halpern (Ed.), *Enhancing thinking skills in the sciences and mathematics* (pp. 15–38). Hillsdale, NJ: Lawrence Erlbaum Associates.

Vye, N. J., Schwartz, D. L., Bransford, J. D., Barron, B. J., Zech, L., & Cognition and Technology Group at Vanderbilt. (1998). SMART environments that support monitoring, reflection, and revision. In D. Hacker, J. Dunlosk, & A. Graesser (Eds.), *Metacognition in educational theory and practice* (pp. 305–346). Mahwah, NJ: Lawrence Erlbaum Associates.

Whitehead, A. N. (1929). *The aims of education*. New York: Macmillan.

Williams, S. M. (1994). *Anchored simulations: Merging the strengths of formal and informal reasoning in a computer-based learning environment.* Unpublished doctoral dissertation, Vanderbilt University, Nashville, TN.

Zech, L., Vye, N. J., Bransford, J. D., Swink, J., Mayfield-Stewart, C., Goldman, S. R., & Cognition and Technology Group at Vanderbilt. (1994). Bringing geometry into the classroom with videodisc technology. *Mathematics Teaching in the Middle School, 1,* 228–233.

9

The Interrelated Development of Inscriptions and Conceptual Understanding

Richard Lehrer
Leona Schauble
Susan Carpenter
David Penner
University of Wisconsin–Madison

In this chapter, we describe two episodes from elementary classrooms where children are learning through design. The focus and goal of the design vary across these cases, but the episodes share an emphasis on modeling and on the related issue of mathematizing the theoretically important elements of a problem as one route toward constructing a solution. In the first classroom case, second graders are working to design combinations of Lego cars and downhill "racetracks" (inclined planes) so that the cars will traverse a fixed distance either "really fast" or "really slow." In the second case, third-grade children are designing experiments to explore the factors that affect the growth rate of Wisconsin "Fast Plants." These design cases are presented as a backdrop against which we illustrate the importance of inscription and symbolization for teaching and learning mathematics and science.

Our interest in design has been inspired partly by recent highly enthusiastic accounts of teaching experiments that feature design contexts for mathematics and science learning (Greeno, Knudsen, Lachapelle, Lauman, & Merris, 1996; Harel, 1991; Kafai, 1995; Pea, Sipusic, Allen, & Reiner, 1990). In our view, there is some basis for this optimism. Because design problems are generally ill-structured, they more effectively represent the kinds of problems that actually occupy scientists and mathematicians than do well-structured "textbook problems" with one right answer. Although much school time is spent merely computing solutions to problems, design focuses attention on other important phases of problem solving that are typically overlooked, such as analyzing the problem, exploring the space of possible solutions, and deciding when a good enough solution has been achieved. In professional communities that are organized around design, such as architectural firms, landscaping companies, and highway engineers, the activity of design has a cyclical nature, suggesting that design can provide students with valuable opportunities to generate multiple design possibilities, explore their implications, settle on a provisional plan, carry out the plan, evaluate the outcome, and then perhaps carry out one or more repetitions of these phases as cycles of revision (Lawson, 1990). These cycles of planning and revision are consistent with the idea that problem solution often looks more like successive approximation than like the application of known algorithms (cf. Lesh & Doerr, chap. 10, this volume; Bransford et al., chap. 8, this volume). Good design problems invite multiple solutions, thus increasing the probability that students will construct, debate, and evaluate alternative solution strategies. Finally, design implies functionality, and so includes built-in feedback loops. Observing how well one's design suits its purpose can provide a standard for evaluating learning and problem solving.

Yet, in spite of their promise, we do not believe that design problems—or, for that matter, any kind of classroom tasks—are sufficient alone to produce conceptual change. Rather than casting our bets too narrowly on the nature of design tasks themselves, we prefer to keep our focus on the way that such tasks are orchestrated in classrooms (cf. Gravemeijer et al., chap. 7, this volume; Nemirovsky & Monk, chap. 6, this volume). Although it is useful to study what makes an effective design task, that question is arguably secondary to a more fundamental consideration: What needs to be considered in developing classrooms in which design fosters learning, not just doing? We believe that the most promising agents of educational change are teachers, not tasks. Hence, we are interested in the ways that teachers use and embroider design tasks—with tools, talk, notation, and modes and means of argumentation—to develop classrooms where thinking and reflection, shared critical standards, evaluation, and revision are elements considered integral to the process of design. For example, one feature that distinguishes design from mere tinkering is the development of effective means for fixing and composing the process of design in replicable plans and outcomes. Unless actions can be accurately captured in inscriptions, they are unlikely to be communicated to others, to be replicable, or to be improved by cycles of evaluation and revision (cf. Lesh & Doerr, chap. 10, this volume). Good design depends on such practices, so to support them, designers rely on forms of symbolization that support the representation and composition of important aspects of the phenomenon being investigated, the actions taken in the design process, or both. Inscriptions are especially important for a design community (like a classroom), in which members work together to negotiate plans, processes, and critical standards for design (Erickson & Lehrer, 1998). As inscriptions take a more central role in the classroom, it is increasingly the inscriptions, and not just the designed artifacts themselves, that become subject to the critical analysis of the design community. A central focus of the work that we present here is to document the process by which inscriptions develop, spread, and evolve in the classroom, including the means by which they become increasingly conventionalized, general, and powerful. In so doing, we explore the progressive mathematization of important ideas, track the evolution of inscriptions during both cases, and discuss how inscriptions, in turn, govern the evolution of children's thinking.

INCLINED PLANES AND FREE FALL

In the first case, children worked over the course of a week to explore the features that affect the speed at which objects (a) roll down inclined planes and (b) fall when dropped from a fixed height. For purposes of this instruction, two second-grade classrooms were configured into three groups of a dozen to 15 children each. These groups rotated through a series of design activities about force and motion, one of which was the set of explorations concerning inclined planes and free fall (the others involved designing and constructing wind-up toys, tops, mobiles, and balancing toys). Each group worked on the inclined planes unit for approximately 7 hr within the boundaries of one school week. In the following sections, we begin by describing problems that emerged in the context of these relatively brief design tasks that could best be solved by representing aspects of the problem mathematically. We then describe in more detail two groups' diagrams for representing steepness and discuss the implications for interrelations between the development of symbolization and the development of students' thinking.

Representing the Design Problem Mathematically

Students were posed the design task of working in teams of two to three children to invent and construct two Lego cars—one that would traverse a downhill racetrack "as quickly as possible," and one that would travel "as slowly as possible." During work on this problem, students encountered three conceptual problems: how to operationalize speed, how to conceptualize the nature of a trial, and how to represent steepness.

Operationalizing Speed. At the outset of the investigation, the second graders seemed to consider speed to be a self-evident property of a car, that is, something that would be obvious on inspection. Deciding which car was fastest was regarded as a simple matter of observing each car as it rolled down a "racetrack" (a plank inclined against a chair). A faster car would just "look" faster than a slower car. This heuristic probably works for most of the speed judgments that second graders need to make, but it had clear limitations in this situation, because to the unassisted eye, many of the Lego cars seemed to roll equally fast (although, of course, designers reliably observed their own cars as being "just a bit faster" than the others).

The children's proposed way to resolve these disputes was to run cars down a racetrack in pairs. Had they found this strategy feasible, we might have encouraged them to construct an algorithm for generating all possible pairs. However, the racetracks were too narrow to permit an unobstructed race to the finish line, and even when children did (rarely) succeed at getting two cars to complete a run without crashing into each other, there were still discussions about how to be sure that each was released at exactly the same moment, or how to determine which one crossed the finish line first. Hence, we introduced a timing device, the optical sensors that are part of a standard Lego Logo kit. One set of sensors was taped to the "starting line" of the racetrack and was programmed to start a computer timer when a car broke the beam of light by rolling over the starting line. A second set of sensors was taped to the "finish line." When the light beam at the finish line was broken, the computer timer turned off, and the total time for the trial was posted on the computer screen in hundredths of a second.

The optical sensors are more convenient than timing with stopwatches and forestall disputes about error of human timers, but they highlight some of the same fundamental issues about measurement. For example, when the second graders completed the design of their "fast" cars and brought them to the racetrack, some children were dissatisfied with the outcome of their "run," claiming, for example, that a car was inadvertently positioned so that it failed to take the shortest route down the "racetrack." Hence, it was decided that each group would have the chance to conduct five trials for their "slow" car and five trials for their "fast" car.

In sum, the very idea of measuring speed emerged only after "eyeball" judgments failed to discriminate among trials. Children readily accepted "time of travel" as an appropriate measure for speed. They originally expected measuring devices (e.g., optical sensors) to produce a perfect, reliable, and undistorted measure of the speed of a car. Only with experience and observation in comparing speeds of different cars did children begin to question the relation between any given measure and its "fairness" in determining which of two cars was faster. Having considered the possibility that there might be variance in measure, children were now posed with the problem of deciding which measure was the best representative of the group or, as they described it, the "most typical."

The Meaning of a Trial. The computer posted times in tenths of a second for each trial, and these trial times were recorded on the board. Table 9.1 shows the times for "slow" and "fast" cars for each of the subgroups (Group A, B, and C) in the initial group of 12 students. The variability in these measures raised the question, "What's the best way of saying how fast or slow a car is?" The teacher (in this case, one of the researchers, RL) suggested that the children consider that question with respect to the times for Group B's "slow" car. He rewrote Group B's data on the board in a column arranged by ascending order of time: 10, 15, 22, 28, 44. One second grader suggested that the best way of handling the problem was to use the "middle number."

Tracy: Use the middle number—22.

RL: What do you mean by the middle?

Tracy: Two above and two below. 10, 15 and 28, 44.

Susan: No, use the middle one here, 28 [pointing to the raw data as originally arrayed on the board and duplicated in Table 9.1].

TABLE 9.1
Time (in Tenths of Seconds) for Each of Five Trials of the "Slow"
and "Fast" Car Designed by Group A, Group B, and Group C

Group	"Slow" Car	"Fast" Car
Group A	42	6
	339	6
	397	6
		5
		6
Group B	44	6
	10	5
	28	5
	22	5
	15	5
Group C	43	9
	77	7
	24	8
	165	8
	9	8

Note. Some of the trials of the slow cars (especially for Group A) did not move at all—children had to nudge the vehicle down the ramp.

Matt: The different groups could talk and decide what they want.

Jeff: . . . or groups could just pick their slowest number.

In this brief exchange, students first brought up the ideas that reappeared over the course of the unit when questions of "typicality" were raised. A few students, like Tracy, were willing to subscribe to an idea like median, although we never saw a student endorse this value unless we rearranged the values in ascending or descending order. As Susan's comment clearly shows, some students did not understand why the "middle number" was a good choice for representing all five trials. To her, the "middle number" of the unordered set of data was equally acceptable—probably more acceptable, because the value was higher, and thus was consistent with the goal of achieving the slowest possible car.

The remaining two comments in the discussion also reflect this concern for matching the top-level goal, a bias that we frequently observed in the second graders. Matt appeared to believe that the best way to resolve the dispute was to let each group decide which value they wanted to use to represent their car. This solution shows no regard for consistency in the rule applied. Jeff's solution was very characteristic of those offered by these young children: If you are trying to make a slow car, then the best value to pick is the one that is consistent with achieving that objective. This same concern surfaced in discussion of the data for the "fast" cars, as the discussion here illustrates:

RL: Let's look at Group C's fast car data. [RL writes these data in ascending order on the board: 7, 8, 8, 8, 9.] Which one should we choose?

Linda: 7, because it's the fastest.

RL: Is that the fairest?

Linda: Yeah.

RL: Really? I see one 7 but three 8s. Is that fair?

Linda: Yeah, because it's the one that's the fastest.

Roy: I think if you have lots of one number you should use that.

RL: So we have three different ideas: Pick the one that's the best, the one in the middle, and the one that is the most frequent? Well, what if we did this? [RL rewrites the data on the board in the form illustrated in Fig. 9.1.]

RL: So what should we do?

LS: What rule should we use? Should it be the same for all the cars?

Students: One rule.

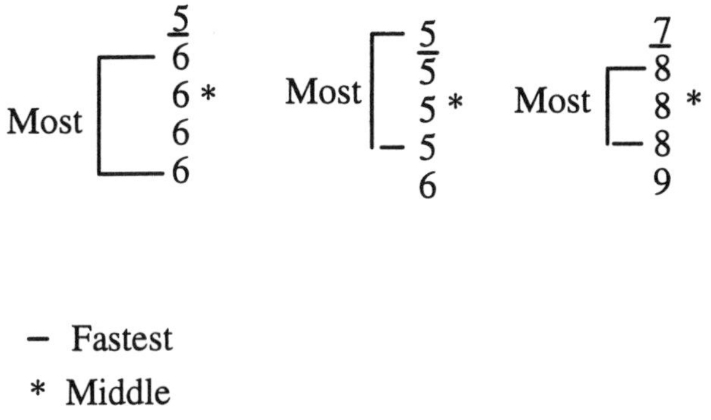

$$\text{Most} \begin{bmatrix} \dfrac{5}{6} \\ 6 \\ 6 \\ 6 \end{bmatrix} * \qquad \text{Most} \begin{bmatrix} \dfrac{5}{5} \\ 5 \\ 5 \\ 6 \end{bmatrix} * \qquad \text{Most} \begin{bmatrix} \dfrac{7}{8} \\ 8 \\ 8 \\ 9 \end{bmatrix} *$$

— Fastest

* Middle

FIG. 9.1. RL's inscriptions capturing the "fastest," "middle," and "most frequent" values for children's car speeds.

LS: So which rule should we use—the most? the middle? the fastest?

In the ensuing discussion, it became evident that in spite of their original agreement that "one rule" was fairest, the students in fact felt it was OK to use more than one rule, that is, to make decisions about each case on a different basis. Later in instruction, we raised this issue of typicality again, both with this group and with the other two instructional groups. Ideas of mode (most frequent measure) and optimal measure (the fastest or the slowest) continued to remain salient for the children.

In sum, the utility of multiple trials was not apparent to children. When multiple trials were run, it was not immediately clear how to decide what measure would be best for representing the set of measures. Children's choices of "most typical value" were influenced by their overriding goal (e.g., making the fastest or slowest car). Comparisons were frequently made on the basis of only one measure among many trials taken. Children did not usually consider variability of measure, even though the data posed some interesting questions about variability—for example, the variability of the trials for "slow" cars was considerably greater than that for "fast" cars. Their relative lack of interest in these issues may have been a result of the fact that the design goal (optimization of speed) collided with the instructional goal of describing variability and typicality. In the second part of this chapter, we describe a case in which the instructional goals and the design goal are in better synchrony. In that case, students found more ways and more flexible ways to represent variability and typicality.

Representing Steepness. As children revised their designs, we gave each team a different-length plank of wood to serve as a trial racetrack.

TABLE 9.2
Facsimile of Whiteboard Table Recording Values (in Inches) for
Variables of an Inclined Plane at Three Different Levels of Steepness

		Steep			
	No Steep	A Little	Middle	Very	Most Steep
Length	38	38	38	38	38
Height	0	11	20	27	38
Push-out	38	35	32	25	0

The need for several trial racetracks was motivated by the crowding around the "true" racetrack equipped with the optical sensors and the consequent waiting for a turn to run the five trials required for each car. However, and in our view more important, we provided multiple racetracks as a way of provoking questions about how properties of the racetracks might affect the speed of cars. Because the children expected cars to run faster on a steep racetrack than a shallow one, they quickly raised the question of how comparable these different racetracks really were. Specifically, how could the teams ensure that all the trial racetracks were equally steep?

In a whole-class discussion devoted to this question, the children in Group 1 spent $1\frac{1}{2}$ hr discussing what makes inclined planes more or less steep. The children's original reactions were similar to those concerning questions about car speed—that is, they acted as if there were nothing to explain, as if steepness were a self-evident property of ramps. For example, when pressed to describe how steep their racetrack was to someone in one of the other groups, students made hand gestures that communicated tilt or angle. However, over the course of the discussion, they eventually began to talk about the components of steepness—specifically, the height of the ramp and its "pushed-outness." They finally concluded that one could describe the steepness of an inclined plane by specifying three values: "how long it is," "how high it climbs," and "how far pushed out it is at the bottom." Children next used a tape measure to measure values of "length," "height," and "pushed-outness" at three different levels of steepness that they defined as "a little steep," "middle steep," and "very steep." The values were entered on a whiteboard table, duplicated in Table 9.2. The teachers, RL and LS, spent considerable time discussing with the children what it meant to change the steepness of the ramp. For example, after measuring length, height, and "pushed-outness" for a ramp that the children judged "a little steep," RL raised the height of the ramp to represent "middle steep," and the following discussion occurred.

LS: So what do we have to measure?

Jill: How high.

LS: Want to come up and measure how high for me? OK, I'll hold it [the tape measure] down and you pull it up.

Jill: About 20.

LS: About 20 inches, Mr. Lehrer. [RL writes that value in the table on the board.] Is it higher than it was before?

Students: Yeah.

RL: What do you think is going to happen to pushed-outness? Is it going to go up?

Peter: Down!

RL: . . . or down?

Students: Down, down, down.

Jenna: It's higher up and, um . . . and when it was lower it had more longer under it and now it's shorter.

RL: OK, Zach, want to add onto that?

Zach: It's shorter because, um, the more high it gets, I mean the higher it gets . . . (moves pencil upward in a slantwise direction) . . .

RL: I see what you're doing with your pencil. Could you hold your pencil where everyone could see what you're doing?

Zach: If I can get it steeper, push-out gets pushed in more.

Later in the discussion, children were challenged to find the case in which the inclined plane was "as steep as possible" and the case in which it showed "the least possible amount of steepness." One child demonstrated the former case by standing a plank at an angle perpendicular to the floor, while another child demonstrated the latter by placing the plank horizontally on the floor. Both of those values for "steepness" are included in Table 9.2.

Notable is the rather extended route the children took toward mathematizing an aspect of the physical world—a plank made of wood—and how much the plank itself got in the way, obscuring the forms of thinking that permitted children to regard each racetrack as a different instance of "steepness." The variable that the children labeled "pushed-outness" was especially difficult for many children to perceive as part of the system, perhaps because it was not explicitly marked by the ends of the board (as was length) or the crate against which it was propped (as was height). "Pushed-outness" had to be mentally constructed before it could be measured and included in a "number rule" that summarized the relations among the variables that comprise steepness (see Fig. 9.2, later). Our decision to spend so much time helping children make the transition from physical gesture to mathematization to a general rule was motivated by our judgment that "steepness" is a concept that has wide application in mathematics and science. Of course, it is central to rolling objects, inclined planes, and free fall, but it plays a role as well in other contexts, including understanding graphs, which are critical to the second example that we discuss later in the chapter.

Because three different groups of students cycled through this investigation, the teaching varied somewhat from group to group. One of these variations highlighted an important issue regarding the development and use of representational drawings for solving problems. Specifically, the first group (Group 1) was invited to invent a sketch that could effectively capture the features of inclined planes that they had identified as definitive of steepness: height, length, and "pushed-outness." In contrast, Group 2 was *provided* a representational device and invited to use it to reason about the same problem. This difference in the teaching might seem trivial. However, we next spend some time elaborating the contrast because we believe it sheds light on common instructional practice. A widely used instructional strategy among teachers and researchers trying to foster model-based reasoning is to provide a model that embodies conceptually important distinctions and relations, and then to ask students to solve a series of problems with the model (e.g., Smith, Snir, & Grosslight, 1992; White, 1993). Those who take this approach center much of their research around the problem of developing models that can serve as a bridge between students' understanding and the conceptual distinctions represented in mathematical or scientific theory. However, as we describe next, our experience with these second graders suggests that, at least in some circumstances, giving children models may be less helpful than fostering their propensity to construct, evaluate, and revise models of their own to solve problems that they consider personally meaningful. In particular, we next describe some emerging contrasts between the thinking of Group 1, who were trying to develop an adequate way to represent, and Group 2, who were primarily struggling to find a way to apply a representational convention suggested by a teacher.

We invited Group 1 to make a sketch that could represent the steepness of their "racetrack," which was a plank of wood propped against a crate.

RL: I wondered if someone could think of, if they were thinking about this thing as a shape, what shape does that you remind you of, when you look at the whole thing?

Brett: Triangle.

RL: A triangle?

Megan: Triangle.

Kyle:	Rectangle.
RL:	And a rectangle?
Kyle:	It's a rectangle.
Linnea:	It's a rectangle, but I think it's a triangle.
RL:	OK, you are thinking about the board as a rectangle? Alright, but I, but what I'm trying to get you to think about is, what's the whole thing look like? The boxes *and* the board?
Kyle:	Um, a triangle.
Scott:	Yeah, it does look like a triangle.
Kaitlin:	I think it looks like a triangle.
Students	(lots of kids talking at once): Hey, that's what I said, a triangle.
RL:	Could you draw that triangle? Let's see the triangle for, like, a little bit steep. Can somebody come up and try that for us? Who hasn't gone to the board yet? You haven't, Maggie? OK, come on up. OK, the triangle for a little bit steep. Go ahead [pause while Maggie draws the sketch illustrated on the top left in Fig. 9.2]. OK, so this is Maggie's way of showing a little bit steep. OK, can somebody show me a different way to show it? Kaitlin? You want to show a little bit steep? [Kaitlin draws.] OK, how is yours different?
Kaitlin:	It's more pushed out.
RL:	So Maggie's is a little more pushed in; Kaitlin's is a little more pushed out? Linnea? Can you come up and show us a way of showing not very steep? [Linnea draws.] Zach? You got a different way? [Zach draws.]
RL:	OK, How is Zach's way different than anything else that's been done here? Maggie?
Maggie:	Um, it's pushed out a lot.

In each case, RL asked children to describe the sketch drawn and then invited someone to revise the convention for representing "a little steep." Next he challenged children to develop and critique conventions for showing a ramp that is "a lot steep." These drawings are in the right-hand column of Fig. 9.2.

The sketches are intriguing both for what they do and do not represent. Basically, the progression from top to bottom of the column in Fig. 9.2 preserves the sequence of the children's drawings (so that the triangle at the bottom of each column was the last one drawn in the sequence). Note that the drawings toward the top of the column, including Maggie's on the left, fail even to explicitly represent "pushed-outness" with a line as steepness ↑   height ↑   push-out ↓

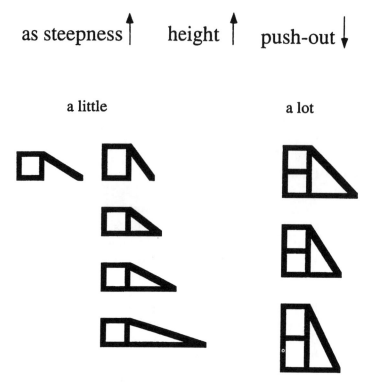

a little   a lot

FIG. 9.2. Facsimile of Group 1 diagrams for showing "a little steep" and "a lot steep."

marking the base of the triangle. These sketches seem in accord with the general rule, "If you can't see it, don't draw it." Moreover, the outstanding feature of these earlier drawn triangles is that they are small, reflecting the children's description of the ramp as "a little steep." In contrast, as the discussion and critiquing continued, the figures toward the bottom not only explicitly depicted "pushed-outness"; they also exaggerated its value. The final triangle in the column, drawn by Zach, clearly exaggerates the "amount of push-out." We also find it intriguing that although the children agreed that the situation could be represented as a triangle, their diagrams were not schematic triangles. Instead, they found it important to continue to represent the crate as a box, rather than abstracting it into a line that forms one leg of the triangle. So important was the crate (which the children perhaps regarded as the "source" of "height"), that in the triangles representing "a lot steep" on the right-hand side of the figure, all of the children included two stacked crates in their sketch. Possibly the children were not thinking of "height" as a continuous variable, but instead were considering these as examples of a "one-crate" ramp and a "two-crate" ramp.

In Group 2, the features and growth of diagrams looked quite different. As we explain later, we believe that the sketches of Group 2 are less representational, because we inadvertently began the discussion by providing the children with a solution to a problem that they had not yet accepted as problematic. As before, we invited the children to draw a sketch representing steepness (at the same point in the instruction as Group 1 tackled this problem). But note the difference in the invitation:

LS: I want someone to come up here and I want them to take this red pen that I'm going to give you, and I want them to show me a triangle of what our ramp looks like when it's not very steep. Suppose I was going to look from the side and think of that as a triangle. What kind of triangle would I draw to show a ramp that isn't very steep?

As Fig. 9.3 shows, there is some evidence that these instructions did not really elicit representations of the situation at all, but instead elicited drawings of triangles. The children in Group 2 did not attempt at any point to represent important features in the situation, like the crates. Moreover, there was little progressive abstraction over the course of the discussion, or indeed little change of any kind in their diagrams. Instead, having heard the suggestion to draw a "triangle," these children tried to oblige by drawing their best version of the prototypical isosceles or equilateral triangle sitting on its base. Instead of "show me what's important about this situation," the task became "draw me a triangle." In fact, some of these triangles were elicited by requests to represent ramps that are "a little steep," and others by requests to show "a lot steep," but it is difficult to tell which are which. Except for the one on the bottom right of the figure, none of the triangles even is a right triangle.

In our view, this episode illustrates the danger of being too quick to provide students with notations, conventions, or models. Our experience suggests that although drawings, diagrams, and notations can be important tools for thought, they are also cognitively demanding for novices of any age, but especially for young children. Envision what is required to represent aspects of a situation in a notation, diagram, graph, map, or model: One must be able to conceptualize a complex physical situation, which often entails mentally constructing aspects (like "amount of push-out") that are not explicitly marked in the situation itself. Simultaneously, one must negotiate the conventions of the representational system, sometimes inventing them as one goes (e.g., deciding whether "push-out"

FIG. 9.3.   Group 2 diagrams for showing "a little steep" and "a lot steep."

should be represented by a line or whether the crate that props the ramp needs to be drawn). Finally, one must coordinate the two by mapping objects and relations from the former onto those of the latter. Choosing the best timing for encouraging children to represent a situation is one among many important decisions that teachers must make. If representation is imposed too early, the resulting notation, model, or inscription may end up failing to represent at all, or failing to represent the critical parts of the situation for the majority of students. Children may become concerned with internal features of the representation, or if it is notational, may become lost in its syntax and lose sight of the meaning that it potentially carries, resulting in an overconcern with procedure at the expense of meaning. On the other hand, neglecting or postponing inscription for too long may result in a group of students who fail to lift principles out of the "stuff" of their ongoing activity. Models and representations denote theoretically important similarities between cases; hence, teachers must give careful consideration to the best ways of orchestrating students' developing coordination between the cases and the abstractions (cf. Gravemeijer et al., chap. 7, this volume).

DESIGNING EXPERIMENTS ABOUT GROWTH

In this second section, we explore the role played by inscriptions in a different kind of design: Third-grade students designed and conducted a series of experiments about growth. During the course of these experiments, inscriptions emerged and became central ingredients in the development of children's models for describing and explaining the growth of plants. In contrast to the brief teaching experiment described in the previous section, here children's inquiry evolved over several months. The prolonged duration allows us to describe the periodicity and mutual constitution of inscriptions and conceptions in the context of the classroom. The teacher, Carmen Curtis, is unusual in that she promotes geometry and spatial reasoning in her teaching of third-grade mathematics (Lehrer et al, 1998); moreover, she is considerably more skilled than we are in the craft of teaching.

Lynch (1990) suggested that scientists work in a world of inscription, manipulating and transforming inscriptions to describe the natural world. He noted that visual displays are particularly important forms of inscription, a generalization borne out by the children participating in this study. Over the course of several months, children developed a "cascade" (Latour, 1990) of visual inscriptions. Children's inscriptions were guided by their questions about growth, and, in turn, their questions about growth were revised and refined in light of their increasingly inscribed view of the world. As the nature of the representational functions of the inscriptions changed, so, too, did the dimensionality of the inscriptions. First inscriptions were unidimensional, followed by a series of two-dimensional and finally three-dimensional inscriptions. These transitions in dimensionality afforded opportunities for children to describe growth in new ways, and inscriptional variation helped children revise and refine the questions and arguments they made.

From the several months of inquiry, we have selected episodes that exemplify children's efforts to inscribe growth. We describe transitions in children's reasoning in the context of two successive life cycles of Wisconsin "Fast Plants," a species of fast-developing brassica (cabbages) that undergo a complete life cycle within 35–40 days. In the first cycle, children inquired about and observed the growth of plants. In the second, children conducted an experiment to test the effects of level of fertilizer on plant growth. Our efforts to describe children's inscriptional activity necessarily foreshorten the roles played by teacher assistance, the development of classroom norms about the value of a good argument, and other elements of the classroom culture that sustained inquiry, although they were central to the events reported here (Lehrer, Jacobson, Kemeny, & Strom, 1999).

First Life Cycle

Posing Questions. Children first posed questions about the growth of Fast Plants and recorded them in their journals. These initial questions focused on aspects of growth related to endpoints, such as ultimate height (e.g., "How tall can Fast Plants be?"), number of leaves (e.g., "I wonder how many leaves they can get?"), and number of seeds produced ("I wonder how many seeds a single plant can get?"). Other, less frequently posed questions focused on conditions of growth, such as the presence of light (e.g., "I wonder if they could grow with no light?"). Only one or two questions were directed toward characterizing growth itself ("How fast do plants grow?").

Predicting Growth. To orient children toward consideration of the entire life cycle, the teacher asked them to predict the pattern of growth over time. She provided a two-dimensional grid with axes labeled "days of growing" and "height." This was not the students' first experience with two-dimensional graphs. During previous classroom activity (the context was plotting the length and width of similar rectangles), they had investigated the qualities of two-dimensional graphs. Their investigations encompassed the relationship between the measure of dimensions of objects in the world and the representation of these measures on the graph (e.g., should a 3-inch by 9-inch paper rectangle be represented on inch grid paper, or can the number denoting each interval be in a different measure, like cm?), the meaning of equal intervals for each axis, the idea that a point instead of a drawing can represent an object like a rectangle, and the construction of the origin. Construction of the origin proved especially problematic. Some children suggested using the highest value on the ordinate as the origin; this proposal was abandoned when they realized that the location of a point so determined would be ambiguous. For instance, one child noted that "if the long side (of a rectangle) is 9 and we start at the top and count down 9 (from 16) and get 7, how will people know that the long side is 9, and not 7?" Another child pointed out that even if they could find a way to communicate this feature of the "count from the top way," values like 7 would vary with the scale: "Suppose we marked it up to 20 instead of 16. What then?"

These conversations and experiences underlay the graphs that children drew to illustrate their predictions about the growth of Fast Plants. Most of the predictions were linear. Two examples are displayed in Fig. 9.4. In one example, growth is represented as increasing at a constant rate throughout the life cycle, and in the other, the initial growth rate is constant but then ceases. Most children interpreted the line of growth as

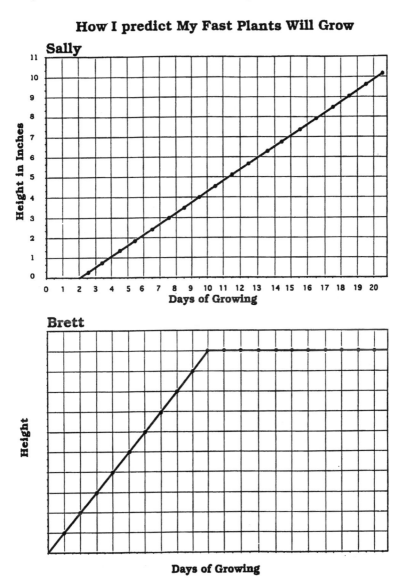

FIG. 9.4. Student predictions of growth for Fast Plants.

representing a constant difference; that is, they expected plants to grow the same amount every day.

Collecting and Structuring Data. Each of the children grew a plant and in light of the questions he or she posed, made decisions about what data to collect. All students measured the height of their plants as they grew, resulting in discussions about how to measure height and what might be a good unit of measure. Eventually, it was agreed that height would be measured in millimeters from the soil base to the tip of the highest leaf. Throughout the plant's life cycle, each child measured his or her plant's height, made drawings, and noted other features of interest. For example, Fig. 9.5 shows the top view constructed by one child and the side view constructed by another. The primary form of inscription was a table denoting height, day, and text about observations, as displayed in Fig. 9.6. These observations led to new questions that reflected children's emerging knowledge of the growth of this species. For example, children noticed that the plants' first leaves were different from the "true" leaves that followed: "Why do Fast Plants have two kinds of leaves?" The classroom teacher uprooted and pressed a plant in a plant press at each of several points in the life cycle, and then photocopied the pressed plants for display (see Fig. 9.7). This new form of inscription characterized a prototypical pattern of growth and also preserved a visual record of change.

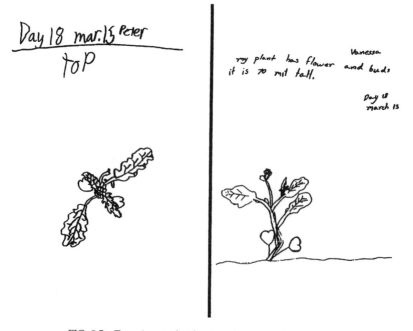

FIG. 9.5. Top view and side view drawings of Fast Plants.

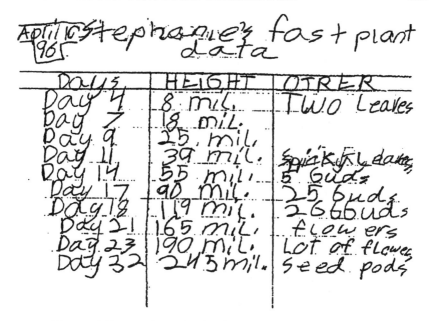

FIG. 9.6. Table recording plant height and observations on successive occasions of measure.

FIG. 9.7. Xerox record of pressed plants.

Inscribing Diversity. At the end of the life cycle, children began to consider the variation among plants. Initial consideration focused on single dimensions of difference, such as variation in height at day 32 of the life cycle:

Sara: They grew differently and I can prove that. My plant was 140 millimeters when it stopped growing and Katie's was

260, and Kelly's plant was 275. Those are 3 different measurements [on the same day], so that's proof that our Fast Plants did not all grow the same.

However, partly because children worked in pairs, the conversation soon shifted toward comparing growth between pairs of plants, inscribed as two-dimensional graphs of height and time, as displayed in Fig. 9.8. This notation afforded opportunities to describe rates of growth and to compare rates, as children discovered that differences between the heights of pairs of plants were not constant because the rates of growth were not constant. In addition, some children became interested in relationships among different kinds of growth, for example, noting that the width of plants did not covary continually with height:

Brynn: When my plant was 60 millimeters tall it was 90 millimeters wide, then it was 80 millimeters tall, then it was still 90 millimeters. The height went 60, 80, 120 and the width did not change, it stayed at 90.

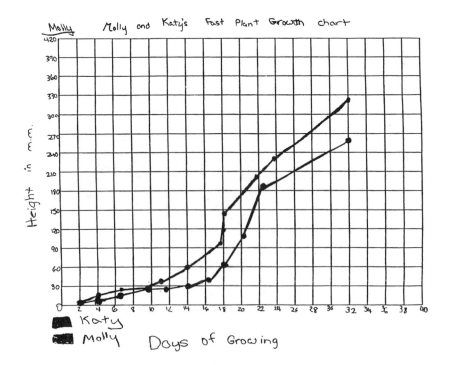

FIG. 9.8. Graph comparing growth rates for two students' Fast Plants.

Inscribing Typicality. At the end of the first round of growth, the teacher displayed all of the children's plots of height versus time and invited them to try to "make some general statements" about growth to inform the expectations of a second-grade class just beginning to work with Fast Plants. The need for a more general or "typical" description was fueled by the teacher's proposal to "pick just one" of the displayed graphs as representative of those made by the class. Some children objected to this instruction because no single graph "matched exactly" an "S" pattern (see Fig. 9.8), yet most "came close." In response, the teacher invited children to try to generate a typical growth curve without matching precisely any of the cases they had constructed: "Could we draw one line that does do a good job of giving a lot of information? It won't fit exactly, but it will be a pretty good match." Although the emphasis in this suggestion was on the generality of the inscription, the teacher also introduced a tacit criterion of model fitting—it was clear that the line was to be taken as a model of growth, not as a replication of any particular instance of growth. This inscriptional sense of the general, displayed in Fig. 9.9, was highlighted by the teacher, who asked children to verbally describe the patterns of growth depicted on the graphs, for example, "It goes up slow, then it goes up really fast, then it goes up slow again."

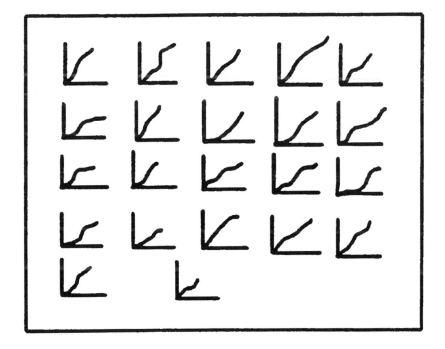

FIG. 9.9. Children's representations of "most typical" growth curve.

Although statements like this characterized only the appearance of the changing slopes of the growth curve, children also interpreted the changes in slope as evidence of rates of growth: "Like, when you just plant your Fast Plant, it will start growing up slowly, but then it takes space to have the flowers. It needs to grow pretty big, so it takes a big jump and then it starts to slow down a little."

As children sketched their models of typical growth, they reflected on their predictions and compared their initial graphs with those obtained empirically. Rather than simply noting the contrast in appearance, they used the initial graph to compare how they "used to think" about plant growth with "how they think now." Many students noted that their first estimates assumed "that the plants will grow the same amount every day," whereas the "S-curve" clearly indicated periods of nonuniform growth.

In sum, children's first questions about plant growth focused primarily on unidimensional quantities, such as the ultimate height of a plant. Students employed a variety of inscriptions to characterize growth, and the variation helped to recast their views. The pressed-plant notation served as a visible record of growth, preserving a visual history that would otherwise be lost as the plants grew. This inscribed history served to anchor other systems of inscription, like tables and graphs, because the visual display served as a ready reference point for interpreting pairs of numbers in tables or growth curves in graphs. Inscriptions organized both typicality and diversity and suggested their mutual dependence. The use of a table transformed simple changes in length to a two-dimensional structure involving length and time of measure. By inscribing these variables in a graphical display, children could see something not immediately obvious in the table—that is, that growth was characterized by an "S" pattern. The detection of this pattern in specific cases and its reification as a "typical" growth curve triggered the beginnings of a search for an explanation that continued into the next round of experimentation. Moreover, the multiple forms of inscription made it evident that diversity was the rule, not the exception; children could compare their plants rapidly and see that no two were exactly the same. This experience with variation invoked the very idea of a model (the ideal "S" growth curve), an attempt to characterize commonalities in ways that fit, albeit imperfectly, the world observed. Interestingly, the model of growth described rate, a derived quantity.

Second Life Cycle: Designing an Experiment

Posing Questions. The first cycle of inquiry served as a springboard for new questions. Some of these questions concerned new aspects of growth, such as how the root system grows, and others were concerned with new factors influencing growth, like temperature, light, and "food." Among the factors suggested, the class decided to focus on what effect "food" might have on plants. They designed an experiment contrasting "regular amounts" (6 pellets) and "a lot" (18 pellets) of fertilizer. Children's speculations about the effects of fertilizer included: "Maybe high-fertilizer plants will have more buds or pods," "Maybe high fertilizer means more seeds in the pods," and "Maybe high fertilizer means the plants get wider or get wider more quickly." As these examples show, children's speculations often included aspects of rate. Molly: "Maybe in the life cycle, maybe the high fertilizer will make them grow faster." Michael responded, "Maybe the high-fertilizer plants will grow faster right from the beginning." Some children were skeptical about fertilizer: "There will be no difference between pots with 6 pellets and pots with 18 pellets. They'll be about the same." The experiment was viewed as a means of testing these and related conjectures; the class agreed that they could not otherwise reasonably decide among the alternatives.

Collecting and Structuring Data. The children decided to revise their data tables to include new aspects of growth, such as each plant's "width" (distance between tips of leaves on opposite sides of the stem), number of leaves, number of buds, and number of pods. Each of these additions to the original table provoked discussion about their measure. For example, children debated whether or not to count all leaves or just "true" leaves (those other than the cotyledon) and considered what would constitute a valid measure of width (the furthest extension of the canopy of the plant).

Inscribing Rate. In the previous cycle of growth, children developed two-dimensional plots of plant height and day of measurement, qualitatively described the changing slope of the growth curve, and related qualitative changes in the graphs' "diagonality" or "steepness" to growth. During the second growth cycle, children revisited this issue and developed a more precise notation for rate, inspired in part by their newfound questions about the effects of fertilizer on rates of plant growth. To focus attention on intervals of growth instead of endpoints, the teacher encouraged verbal descriptions of growth, like: "From day 23 to day 32 was 35 millimeters, so it grew 35 millimeters in 9 days." Children then reexpressed this statement numerically as millimeters/day. For example, to reexpress the 35 millimeters in 9 days, they said: "So then we tried four 9's—that was our closest, and that got us 36. And it was just one off, so we knew one less 9 would make 27. So we knew we had to do 8/9, 8 of them (millimeters) divided over the 9 days, so it was $3\frac{8}{9}$ millimeters per day." Children annotated their growth curves accordingly, as displayed in Fig. 9.10.

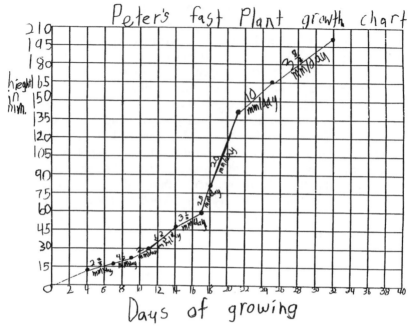

FIG. 9.10.   Growth curve annotated with rates of growth in millimeters per day.

Reinscribing Growth. Observing more aspects of growth created additional opportunities for reasoning about relationships; for example, many children investigated the relationship between plant width and height. One child noted that "perhaps right before it takes the big jump up, maybe right before the growth spurt, the height equals the width." Another child agreed, and many in the class observed that the growth was more "rectangular" after the growth spurt, meaning that the height far exceeded width at that point in the life cycle. The classroom teacher referred to the pressed plant inscription to validate this conjecture, and children drew squares and rectangles to inscribe the relationships they were considering. Next the teacher challenged children to go beyond two dimensions to "think about the space it takes up."

Most children thought that a cylinder would be a good model for the volume of a Fast Plant. Some arrived at this decision on the basis of resemblance ("the stem is like a cylinder"), whereas others reasoned that the cylinder would provide a more accurate estimate of volume than other solids, like rectangular prisms, whose properties they understood well enough to calculate volume. Nevertheless, the majority of the class ultimately decided to represent change in volume with models of rectangular prisms, as displayed in Fig. 9.11. This decision was based partly on

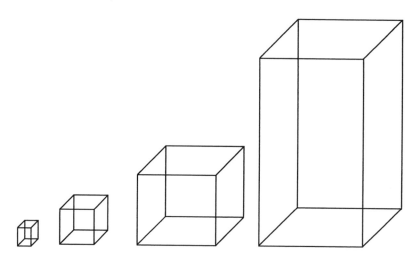

FIG. 9.11. Rectangular prism models of plant volume at different days of measure.

the realization that these models circumvented the problem of determining the relationship between their measure of plant width and the circumference of the cylinder (although this problem eventually was resolved by those who decided to use cylinders).

Children's three-dimensional models of the "growth space" provided yet another inscription, one that invited new conjectures about the form of growth and new explanations for the transitions in growth that are so evident in models like those in Fig. 9.11. For example, one pair of students used the nesting property of the models (one model fits inside another) to develop and test the conjecture that growth fit the geometric property of similarity. These students noted that over the first time interval, the width and height each doubled, leading to an eightfold increase in volume: "Day 7 was like a cube. When we grew this cube [doubled the length for both height and width], 8 of these cubes fit into it at Day 11." The children noted that the fit wasn't "perfect," but it was a good approximation. They also commented that this was like "growing cubes," a reference to previous classroom work on similar figures. However, as they continued to pursue their conjecture, they realized that eventually the notion of geometric growth ("growing" similar forms) failed: "And from day 11 to day 16, again volume increased 8 times, but day 16 to day 21, it didn't change as much." (This student demonstrated by nesting the day 16 model inside the day 21 model, showing that the rate of increase was less than eight). Other students in the class noted that at this last point, the plant had entered its growth spurt. This observation set the stage for a round of discussion about the functions for the growth patterns they were observing, with most of the children's explanations centered on resources available to the plant:

Peter: To grow, the plant needs food, so the leaves grow (they make food), so at first, they really need to grow out wide to get the plant the food it needs. It just has to wait until it gets cultivated later.

Teacher: So it doesn't take as much energy later in its life cycle?

Kyle: No, that can't be right. It's making seeds.

Another child speculated that the change in height associated with the growth spurt might serve the function of "pushing flowers up where the bees can get to them." (The children were aware of the role of bees in pollination because they used "bee sticks" to pollinate the plants during flowering.) Children also plotted root growth over time (a small number of plants were grown in a root chamber) and found that the most rapid phase of root growth ("the steepest part of the line") occurred as the plant was germinating. One child explained, "That's because that is when the plant is coming out of the soil and it needs water (presumably, provided by roots) to do that."

Reinscribing Typicality. During the first cycle, typical growth was inscribed as an S-shaped curve that was mentally composed as a prototype over the individual growth curves plotted by students. Typicality emerged in this inscription, but the criteria for typicality were not made explicit. During the second cycle of growth, children decided to create another plot of height versus time to compare growth in the second round to that in the first. They decided to use only those plants that had received six pellets of fertilizer for purposes of comparison to the first cycle, and they plotted every plant's height during each interval as a point (see Fig. 9.12).

Once the points were plotted, the class cast about for ways to "sum up" how plants grew during the second cycle. The teacher asked children to come up with some strategies to accomplish this objective; her goal was to make criteria for typicality more visible. A number of candidates were generated by the children, including connecting all the top points, all the bottom points, the bottom points for the first six measurements and the top points for the remaining six measurements, the middle point (median) of each time of measurement, and the midpoint of the range for each time of measurement. Children's justifications included selecting a strategy that would make the "best" (most easily seen) S-curve or selecting one where the line generated would come closest to all the points. Just as in the design context involving cars, not all children adopted the instructional goal of "best fit"—some took as the goal depicting what

Height of Round Two Fast Plants
(6 pellets fertilizer)

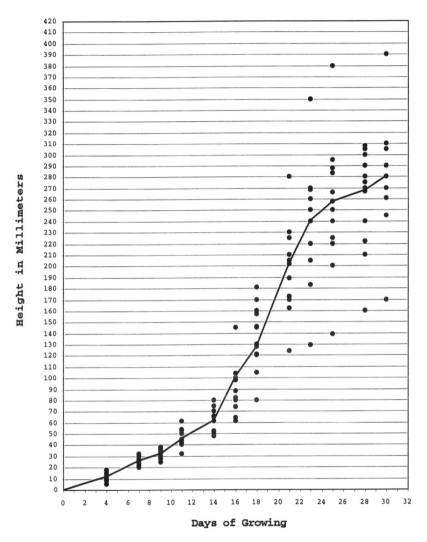

FIG. 9.12. Growth points for low-fertilizer plants at each day of measure.

they had found before, albeit in a new way. After further discussion about whether or not drawing a nice-looking S-curve was a "fair" goal, children voted to select the midpoint of each range. Several children objected on the grounds that sometimes this would not include *any* of the points plotted, but their objections were overruled on the grounds that the goal was only to "come close."

Reinscribing Diversity. Children explored the effects of fertilizer on plant growth, raising the issue of whether differences among the two fertilizer conditions reflected mere plant-to-plant variation or systematic difference. This question was explored in a number of ways. After children measured growth on the fourth day in the second cycle, the teacher asked what they might be able to tell another class about fertilizer. She also asked what they were going to do about the "puddle of numbers," which were not ordered, in their lists. One child said, "We'll need to know the lowest and the highest." The class went on to plot the frequency of values for each batch of data. Observing clear overlap in the distributions, children readily concluded that there were no differences in height at this point in the life cycle. They later revisited this issue when making three-dimensional models of the plants, concluding again that there was considerable overlap in the height of the models throughout the life cycle. It was particularly easy to see at a glance that the rectangular prisms representing the plants in both treatment groups were about the same height. It is interesting that they made these judgments on the basis of their models in spite of the ready availability of the plants. Perhaps this occurred because the models represented a form of structured observation. However, while investigating the models for different levels of fertilizer, some children became convinced that although the heights did not vary by condition, the width of the plants appeared to do so. This observation led to a reconsideration of the meaning of overlap of distributions. The classroom teacher helped children construct a histogram for width with color-coded marking (orange, green) indicating the values in each condition. On the histogram, shown in Fig. 9.13, the two distributions clearly overlapped, but nonetheless showed much more

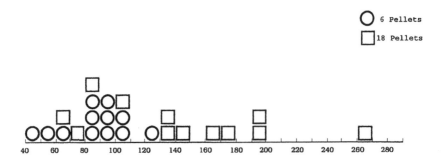

Width of Round Two Fast Plants on Day 30

FIG. 9.13. Width of low-fertilizer and high-fertilizer Fast Plants on the final day of measure.

separation than did the two distributions for height. After viewing the histogram, Kyle began to talk about relative degree of overlap:

Kyle: They look like they're like in two different groups 'cause most of the 6 pellets are right here and most of the 18 are more in the higher area, so I think 18 pellets maybe are wider than the 6 pellets.

Peter sought to quantify the uncertainty:

Peter: Because only 4 of the 12, only $\frac{1}{3}$ of the 18-pellet plants are less (wide) than the widest 6-pellet plants,
Teacher: So you would feel pretty safe in saying to the second-grade class ... ?
Peter: But we're not quite sure, because we only did it once, but I think it's pretty safe to say ... well, we can't be exact like $\frac{2}{3}$ and we only did one round, but we could say that $\frac{1}{2}$ or more of the high-fertilizer plants will be wider than the 6 pellets.

Learning of Individuals

Of course, observing the work of an intact class does not address legitimate questions about the level of understanding of individual children. Therefore, follow-up interviews were conducted with pairs of children to further explore students' understanding of these graphical depictions of rate. Moreover, at the close of the school year, interviews were conducted with each student in the class to develop a clearer portrait of individuals' thinking about growth as represented in various inscriptional forms.

Dyads on Rate. During the interviews of student dyads concerning rate, one of us (SC) worked with students Nicholas and Nadine to identify the period of fastest growth recorded on the graph for Nicholas' plant, which he had whimsically named "Tyler."

SC: Where on your graph would you say he's growing fastest?
Nicholas: [Traces an interval on his graph with his finger] ... right here. It goes from 230 to 305 in only ... [traces up from the X axis, where he has marked intervals] ... in only three days. This other time that it went three days, it only grew from 40 to 70.
SC: So you're comparing two three-day periods ...

Nicholas: Yeah, it went from 40 to 70.

SC: So you're comparing two three-day periods. How much did it grow in this one [the first period]? It started at 230 and eventually it was 305. How much did it grow? How many millimeters?

Nicholas: Um, 75.

SC: So it went 75 in three days. [Explains to Nadine:] That's what Nicholas is saying is the really fast time of growth. The other period, it was also three days, but how much did it grow? It went from 40 to 70.

Nadine: 30.

SC: So let's look at those numbers.

Nicholas: Wait, I may have something coming in. It's 305 to 340, that's only 35 millimeters [identifying yet a third interval on the graph]. If it was close to, well, this is in a two-day period I think. 35 in two days. That would be actually faster than this [points to the figures in the notebook where he has recorded 30 mm in three days], because this [the 35 mm segment] only grew in two days; this grew in three days.

SC: So you're saying that 35 millimeters . . .

Nicholas: In two days . . .

SC: In two days is faster than . . .

Nicholas: . . . than 30 in 3 days.

SC: How do you know?

Nicholas: Well, this one's lower than this one [e.g., the number 30 is "lower than" 35], and this had a longer time to grow than this one [referring again to the figures in the notebook]. . . . So that means this had to grow faster; otherwise it wouldn't have been higher.

SC: . . . OK, Nick, was it growing faster in this period than in this period [pointing to graph and indicating the 75 mm in three-days segment vs. the 35 mm in two-days segment]? 75 in three days or 35 in two days?

Nicholas: I'll have to think about that. 'Cause we'll have to split 35 in half, that would give us down to . . . I don't know. Well, it looks like 17 and a half.

SC: So 17 and a half millimeters, but like in how . . .

Nicholas: That's in one day.

Susan: OK.

Nicholas: So, um, what you do is just add 17 onto 35, 'cause that one day and two days equals three days. If 17 is higher than 75

> [he means if 17 + 35 is greater than 75], that means this one [the 75 mm in three days] would have grown faster.

SC: This one would have grown faster?

Nicholas: Yes.

SC: How about if you take a look at how much this ... you took a look at how much it would have to grow each day to grow this much in two days, right? Now, how much would it have to grow in one day to get to be 75 in three days?

Nicholas: ... I'm trying to think ... [rocks back and forth]. Oh, I know! 25 millimeters per day.

SC: Okay ...

Nicholas: Well, actually, guess what? I just pretty much figured out that this one is faster. Because this one is 25 millimeters per day, and this is 17 and a half millimeters per day. This is higher.

SC: So your original idea that this is the fastest ...

Nicholas: ... is true.

Although Nicholas' way of comparing the rates of two growth periods was somewhat unusual (e.g., he apparently found it easier to think about identifying the amount each plant grew in three days rather than identifying rate of growth per day), the capability to compare linear sections of the graph in this way was reasonably well established among many of the children.

Individuals on Changes in Geometric Models. We presented each child with three rectangular prisms, arranged to depict three points of the growth cycle of the Fast Plants (each point separated by 5 days), and a metric ruler. The measurement occasions spanned the relatively linear increase in growth characteristic of the early phase of the life cycle of the Fast Plants (Times 1 and 2 in the models presented to the children), as well as the more exponential phase of growth characteristic of the later phase of the life cycle (Time 3). We asked each child to examine the three models and to tell the interviewer what the models "tell you about the growth of Fast Plants." We coded children's responses to characterize the ways in which they used the models to describe growth. We were most interested in descriptions that explicitly focused on changing quantities (e.g., differences in height) and on changes in those changing quantities (e.g., on different differences between the first and second, and the second and third points in time).

All but two of the children in the class explicitly noted that the changes in attributes of height, width (recall the previous discussion of children's definition of this attribute), and volume, all of which were explicitly inscribed in the classroom work, were not identical: Volume changed the most and width the least over the course of the portion of the plant's life cycle depicted. Moreover, all of these children noted that the rates of increase in each attribute were not identical over the three points in time. For example, after measuring the heights of the prisms at each point in time, one child noted that "from 85 (time 2) to 210 is a big spurt," to mark the relatively large difference she had noted between the second and third points compared to the more modest difference she observed between the first two points of height measure. Other children noted that if one thought of multiples, the multiple describing the change in height between the first two times of measure increased, but the multiple describing that of width decreased.

Forty percent of these children who noted variable change coordinated the changes in the measures of the attributes by characterizing the change over time as a geometric form, noting that change was initially "squarish" (the measurements of length and width were approximately equal during the first two occasions of measure) or "cubic," but then became more "rectangular" (reflecting the acceleration in rate of growth for height, but not for width). Reflecting on the transition from linear to exponential growth, one child said: "Fast Plants have like a rule they follow [a reference to previous class work in geometry with linear relationships], like a pattern, and sometimes they, like, have a pattern for a long time and then it starts breaking." Generally, then, we found that transitions in growth were inscribed not only collectively and publicly, but also individually.

In summary, then, over the course of children's investigations with the Fast Plants, a cascade of inscriptions was accompanied by a cascade of conceptual change. As children inscribed growth, their ideas about growth became both more varied and more differentiated, and also became more tightly coupled to potential explanations, such as resource allocation in plants. In spite of occasional detours, the overall trajectory of inscription was toward increasing dimension. One-dimensional inscriptions of length (e.g., height) were transformed into two-dimensional inscriptions involving length and time, so that growth itself became an object for inspection. Three-dimensional models provided a means for coordinating multiple dimensions of growth (e.g., height, width, volume). Moreover, the arrangement of the three-dimensional models along an axis of elapsed time afforded some children the opportunity to test the feasibility of a mathematical model of similarity as a guideline to predicting patterns of growth. The ultimate failure of the model does not detract from the value of the attempt. Like working scientists, children increasingly worked in a world of inscription, so that, over time, the natural and inscribed worlds became mutually articulated, albeit not indistinguishable (Lynch, 1990; Werner & Kaplan, 1963).

DISCUSSION

In both of these classroom cases, children were engaged in the process of design, and in both, diagrams and inscriptions played a central role in the reasoning. Yet, although the two cases are similar in some ways, their differences are informative as well. We have found both the comparisons and the contrasts to be instructive as we think about what makes an effective design task and as we consider the role that inscription can play in the context of design and ultimately in the conceptual development of students.

Both cases underline the importance of history, in two senses. The first has to do with the history of the inscription itself. Not only was the inclined planes unit very brief, but perhaps more important, the diagrams that evolved there had no standing in the history of the classroom. They did not build on children's previous classroom experience, and as far as we know, they were not picked up, elaborated, or used further in the children's ongoing work. In contrast, the third graders' work with the Fast Plants built on a rich history of experience with these inscriptions: graphs; representations of length, area, and volume; and other varied ways of inscribing both large- and small-scale space. Recall also how the inscriptions in this classroom changed, evolved, and built on each other during the course of this study. No inscriptional invention was wasted because inscriptions were not evoked as one-shot solutions to solve a problem of the moment. Instead, they were continually edited, composed, and elaborated to do additional work (cf. Lesh & Doerr, chap. 10, this volume). The children's representations for growth began as one-dimensional recordings of height, expanded to become two-dimensional graphs relating time and height, and finally evolved to three-dimensional models of plant volume. Inscriptions in this classroom not only have a past; they also clearly have a future.

The second sense in which inscriptions underline the importance of history is that they can be used to preserve history, a role that was exploited in both cases. In the inclined planes unit, inscription captured and quantified both trials (speed of cars) and the conditions under which trials were run (length, height, and "pushed-outness" of the racetracks), making it possible and meaningful to draw comparisons. In the Fast Plants work, the photocopy of pressed plants captured the appearance of plants that were changing in time, and the other displays—graphs and rectangular prisms—made it easy to notice features of change (like patterns of growth and amount of space that plants occupy) that would not otherwise be evident. As Latour (1990) explained, inscriptions, notations, and diagrams can serve to "fix" change, effectively freezing and preserving it so that it can serve as the object of reflection. Lynch (1990) added that inscriptions not only preserve change, they edit it as well: Inscriptions reduce and enhance information. In this sense, the classroom history that was preserved was not a simple succession of events, but rather an account that revised and edited events into a coherent conceptual framework. Moreover, somewhat unlike other descriptions of the evolution of children's inscriptions (e.g., Meira, 1995), this history reflects evidence both of children's invention with the inscriptions and of guidance by the teacher, who played an important role in negotiating discussions about inscriptional possibilities and ideas worthy of inscription.

A second issue concerns the alignment between the design task and the inscriptional form. In the inclined planes unit, children were primarily concentrating on the design task as posed to them—that is, optimizing speed, an activity that presumes one best solution. Under these circumstances, it was difficult to make much headway in getting them to consider, and hence to notate, typicality. A good design task encourages variability, and inscription is most useful when the variability is of a kind that can be captured by inscription. Inscription that focused around variability (e.g., steepness of racetracks) was more fruitful than inscription that focused around optimization (e.g., the outcome of trials). In contrast, during the Fast Plants unit, there was a much smoother match between the design goal (e.g., explore the variability in growth of plants) and the forms of inscription that were used. In retrospect, it is little wonder that the result was greater flexibility and power in the notation.

Third, it is important to remember that inscription and notation have an overhead cost. Children must either invent or learn the syntactical and semantic conventions of the inscription, and must do so thoroughly enough so that the inscription eventually becomes transparent (see Nemirovsky & Monk, chap. 6, this volume for a discussion of transparency). This achievement entails not only becoming able to navigate within the inscriptions smoothly, but also coordinating changes in the inscription with changes in the referent. Notational fluency does not come for free, and the cost (in learning and processing effort) raises the question, what is worth inscribing? In our view, students should work to inscribe fundamental or "big ideas," those with generality and power. In these classroom cases, children were working to develop satisfactory ways of inscribing important physical and biological concepts. One cannot, for example, develop evolutionary models about diversity without a handle on ways of inscribing typicality and variation. Similarly, in both classroom cases, children worked to represent and mathematize a general idea of steepness, applicable to inclined planes, rates of growth portrayed on graphs, and many other situations as well. Interestingly, in both cases, the children had to overcome similar stumbling blocks to understanding steepness, for example, confusing the rate of change with the highest value of a variable, and mentally constructing ideas like "push out" and time interval, that are not immediately apparent in the situation.

Finally, both of these classroom cases highlight the importance of introducing a notation, diagram, or inscription only when a need for it has "ripened" in the work of the children and is widely acknowledged in the classroom community. Inscriptions serve functions—for example, to support activities such as communication, planning, recall, or problem solving. Yet their functions are easily obscured if they are introduced in a heavy-handed way (see Gravemeijer et al., chap. 7, and van Oers, chap. 5, this volume, for further discussion). In the inclined planes unit, we observed the rigidity in students' reasoning that occurred when inscriptions were given to children as the solution to a problem that they did not yet recognize. The triangles that they drew at our invitation had no function; they did not really represent, and they did not evolve over their brief period of use. In contrast, when children identified triangles on their own as the solution to the problem of representing steepness, their diagrams showed considerable change over a brief period. Similarly, in the Fast Plants case, children developed inscriptions of increasing complexity and power to solve problems that emerged as they investigated questions of their own posing. Coming to understand the function of inscriptions is arguably more important than amassing a large library of representational devices that can be used only rigidly and within the narrow boundaries of their original acquisition. Rather than transmitting inscriptions—even powerful inscriptions—we may do better by taking a longer term perspective, concentrating instead on trying to help our students understand over the long term what inscriptions are good for: They allow you to plan and compose what would otherwise be incommunicable, to make evident what would otherwise not be seen, and to keep a trace of what otherwise would disappear. All of these functions are indispensable to good argument in mathematics and science, and, more generally, to coming to know the world.

ACKNOWLEDGMENTS

We gratefully acknowledge the assistance of Carmen Curtis, Susan Wainwright, Elizabeth LaHam, and their students in the Country View Elementary School. This research was supported by the National Science Foundation and the James S. McDonnell Foundation.

REFERENCES

Erickson, J., & Lehrer, R. (1998). The evolution of critical standards as students design hypermedia documents. *Journal of the Learning Sciences, 7*, 351–386.

Greeno, J. G., Knudsen, J., Lachapelle, C., Lauman, B., & Merris, K. (1996, April). HABITECH: A modeling environment for middle-school students learning to reason about functions. In F. C. Smith (Chair), *Tools for learning: Computer-based representational tools for mathematics instruction.* Symposium presented at the annual meeting of the American Educational Research Association, New York.

Harel, I. (1991). *Children designers.* Norwood, NJ: Ablex.

Kafai, Y. B. (1995). *Minds in play: Computer game design as a context for children's learning.* Mahwah, NJ: Lawrence Erlbaum Associates.

Latour, B. (1990). Drawing things together. In M. Lynch & S. Woolgar (Eds.), *Representation in scientific practice* (pp. 19–68). Cambridge, MA: MIT Press.

Lawson, B. (1990). *How designers think. The design process demystified.* Boston: Butterworth Architecture.

Lehrer, R., Jacobson, C., Thoyre, G., Kemeny, V., Strom, D., Horvath, J., Gance, S., & Koehler, M. (1998). Developing understanding of geometry and space in the primary grades. In R. Lehrer & D. Chazan (Eds.), *Designing learning environments for developing understanding of geometry and space.* (pp. 169–200). Mahwah, NJ: Lawrence Erlbaum Associates.

Lehrer, R., Jacobson, C., Kemeny, V., & Strom, D. (1999). Building on children's intutions to develop mathematical understanding of space. In E. Fennema & T. Romberg (Eds.), *Mathematics classrooms that promote understanding.* (pp. 63–87). Mahwah, NJ: Lawrence Erlbaum Associates.

Lynch, M. (1990). The externalized retina: Selection and mathematization in the visual documentation of objects in the life sciences. In M. Lynch & S. Woolgar (Eds.), *Representation in scientific practice* (pp. 153–186). Cambridge, MA: MIT Press.

Meira, L. (1995). The microevolution of mathematical representations in children's activity. *Cognition and Instruction, 13*, 269–313.

Pea, R. D., Sipusic, M., Allen, S., & Reiner, M. (1990, April). Dynagrams for reasoning about light. In L. B. Resnick (Chair), *Dynamic diagrams for model-based science learning.* Symposium presented at the annual meeting of the American Educational Research Association, Boston.

Smith, C., Snir, J., & Grosslight, L. (1992). Using conceptual models to facilitate conceptual change: The case of weight-density differentiation. *Cognition and Instruction, 9*, 221–283.

Werner, H., & Kaplan, B. (1963). *Symbol formation.* New York: Wiley.

White, B. Y. (1993). ThinkerTools: Causal models, conceptual change, and science education. *Cognition and Instruction, 10*, 1–100.

10

Symbolizing, Communicating, and Mathematizing: Key Components of Models and Modeling

Richard Lesh
Purdue University

Helen M. Doerr
Syracuse University

In this chapter, we describe some of the ways that models and modeling provide a unifying theme that is useful for integrating many of the most relevant research traditions in order to gain insight into the growth of student learning. We then share an example of students' developing models while engaged in a model-eliciting task. We have found that the multiple cycles of increasing stability and sophistication that students go through in developing solutions to model-eliciting problems prove to be very valuable forms of information about the growth of student thinking. We conclude by describing how modeling highlights some new issues and suggests some significant changes in direction for traditional lines of research.

HOW DOES THE THEME OF MODELS AND MODELING INTEGRATE WITH OTHER RELEVANT RESEARCH PERSPECTIVES?

One way to begin a discussion of models is by considering the following kinds of questions: What is meant by *model*? How are models and representations related?

What Is a Model?

The terms *models* and *representations* have a variety of everyday meanings as well as a variety of technical meanings that have been given to them by diverse theoretical perspectives. There is no single "correct" meaning of these words. In the case of models and modeling, most of these meanings have enough in common so that even if one person's meanings are not identical to another's, productive discussions can continue to occur. Additional meanings, distinctions, and nuances tend to unfold as discussions take place. This latter characteristic is important because it is useful to avoid inventing new jargon in places where well-known terminology is already available, and it is useful to begin with terms that are simple, but whose meanings invite further refinement, rather than to begin with words that seem to have abstruse or technically "correct" meanings while carrying little intuitive meaning.

What is a model? The following first-iteration answer is familiar to people in fields such as mathematics, physics, chemistry, or other physical sciences. A model is a system consisting of (a) *elements*, (b) *relationships* among elements, (c) *operations* that describe how the elements interact, and (d) *patterns* or *rules*, such as symmetry, commutativity, or transitivity, that apply to the preceding relationships and operations. However, not just any old system functions as a model. To be a model, a system must be used to describe some other system, or to think about it, or to make sense of it, or to explain it, or to make predictions about it. Also, to be a *mathematically* significant model, it must focus on underlying structural characteristics of the system being described.

One issue that tends to confuse people about models is whether they are intended to refer to systems that reside inside or outside the mind. The confusion arises because there is a sense in which it is natural to speak of mathematical models and conceptual systems as though they were pure systems somehow disembodied from any tools, representations, or external artifacts. Yet, in practice, beyond the most trivial situations, it is clear that these conceptual systems seldom function without the support of powerful tools or representational systems, each of which emphasizes and deemphasizes (or ignores, or distorts) somewhat different aspects of the underlying conceptual system. The conceptual systems that humans develop often are partly embedded in conceptual tools that may involve electronic gadgets, but that also may involve specialized symbols, language, diagrams, organizational systems, or experience-based metaphors (cf. Dörfler, chap. 4, this volume). Thus, in speaking of students conceptualizing or reasoning with tools, the use of the tool is integral to the act of reasoning; the tool is not outside the reasoning process and the reasoning process is not entirely in the head (Lesh, 1987; see Nemirovsky & Monk, chap. 6, this volume, for a discussion of symbol use and symbolizing).

Humans are continually projecting their conceptual systems into their environments in the form of communication systems, economic exchange systems, and other types of systems that strongly influence our daily lives.

For example, when a business manager uses a graphics-linked spreadsheet to make predictions about maximizing cost–benefit trends, this model enables the manager to create completely new types of business systems that did not exist before the tools were available. In turn, the manager's conceptual and procedural capabilities are both changed and amplified when dealing with these newly introduced external systems. The cost–benefit system becomes an artifact that gets projected into the experienced world of others. Consequently, among the mathematical "objects" that impact everyday lives, many of the most important are human systems—complex, dynamic, interacting systems—which range in size from large-scale communication and economic systems, to small-scale systems for scheduling, organizing, and accounting in everyday activities. These systems are artifacts that have been projected into the world and become part of the experienced world of others (Lesh, 1981; see Gravemeijer et al., chap. 7, this volume, for a contrasting discussion of models).

How Are Models Related to Representations?

The meaning of a model, or conceptual system, tends to be distributed across a variety of interacting representation systems that may involve written symbols, spoken languages, pictures or diagrams, concrete manipulatives, or experience-based metaphors. But although the term *models* tends to emphasize the dynamic and interacting characteristics of the systems being modeled, the term *representations* tends to draw attention to the objects within these systems. Models tend to refer to functioning whole systems, whereas representations tend to be treated as inert collections of objects to which manipulations and relationships must be added in order to function.

Modeling involves the interactions among three types of systems: (a) internal conceptual systems, (b) representational systems that function both as externalizations of internal conceptual systems and as internalizations of external systems, and (c) external systems that are experienced in nature, or that are artifacts that were constructed by humans. When taking this perspective, it is essential to emphasize that the boundaries between these systems are fluid, shifting and at times ambiguous (see Fig. 10.1). Conceptual systems, in a Piagetian sense, seem to exist mainly inside the head. Another kind of system seems to be embedded in the spoken language, written symbols, pictures, diagrams, and concrete models that people use to both express their internal systems and to describe external systems. These are often referred to as representation systems. A third kind of functioning system is that which humans create in the world, such as economic systems, communications systems, and mechanistic systems. As described earlier, these artifacts are projected into the

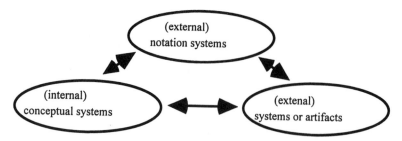

FIG. 10.1. Modeling interactions among three types of systems.

world and become part of the experienced world of others. Although there are distinctions between these three systems, these systems are partly overlapping, interdependent, and interacting. It is these interactions that are brought to the foreground and are central to our analyses of student learning from a models and modeling perspective. Thus although cognitive systems seem to be largely internal, when students use powerful conceptual tools, it is clear, as we show later, that a large part of their abilities is embedded in their tools. Although the representation systems that students use seem to reside outside their minds and in a form that can be shared with others, it is also the case that a part of the meaning of these representation systems cannot simply be shared with others. In fact, the person who generates a representation tends to read out somewhat different information than the person put in (Lesh, 1983).

Representations function partly as externalizations of internal conceptual systems, and they also function partly as descriptions and simplifications of external systems in an experienced world. The constructs that humans develop to make sense of their experiences also are used to mold and shape the very world in which those experiences occur. Therefore, the constructs and conceptual systems that are in human minds today may be used to create systems that function as objects in the world tomorrow, and systems that are created for their own sake today may be used to make sense of other systems tomorrow.

How Is a Models and Modeling Perspective Related to Learning and Instruction?

The kinds of models that we are talking about in this chapter are those that students develop in attempts to produce mathematical descriptions or explanations of structurally interesting systems (e.g., Lehrer et al., chap. 9, this volume). If these descriptions and explanations are shareable and reuseable, then the ways of thinking that they involve represent important forms of learning. We believe that helping students develop powerful conceptual models should be among the most important goals of mathematics instruction (Confrey, 1994; Lehrer, Horvath, & Schauble, 1994; Lesh & Lamon, 1994).

In science, it has tended to be obvious that some of the most important goals of instruction are to help students develop powerful models for making sense of their experiences involving light, gravity, electricity, and magnetism; it has also been obvious that young students invent models of their own and that changing students' ways of thinking must involve challenging and testing these models. But in mathematics, where the emphasis has been on representations, it is often assumed that students do not (and cannot) develop metaphors, language, and symbol systems for making sense of systems that involve mathematical entities such as directed quantities (negatives), multivalued quantities (vectors), ratios of quantities, changing or accumulating quantities, or locations in space (coordinates). This assumption comes about in part because the mathematical representations that are associated with the preceding kinds of systems often are so deep and profound that it seems very unlikely that youngsters would ever invent them by themselves. However, as we further describe later, when confronted with the need to create meaningful models of experientially real situations, learners can invent significant mathematics.

How Is a Models and Modeling Perspective
Related to Cognitive Constructivism?

Models are interacting systems based in complex conceptual systems, and as such these models cannot simply be handed to students in a meaningful form. This is the basis for the claim that models (constructs) must be constructed. But it is also the case that: (a) construction can lead to a great many things (such as complex systems of low level facts and skills) that are not models for making sense of experiences, and (b) construction isn't the only process that contributes to the development of models. For example, models evolve by being sorted out, refined, or reorganized at least as often as they evolve by being assembled (or constructed). Furthermore, sorting out and refining unstable conceptual systems is not at all the same thing as assembling stable conceptual systems.

We wish to avoid the error of turning model development into an end in itself; the misplaced emphasis of some enthusiasts for "discovery learning" often emphasizes the process of discovery without paying much attention to what it is that is being discovered. If instruction and learning focus on models and modeling, then it is absolutely critical to focus on models that correspond to the "big ideas" or main constructs and conceptual systems that underlie the curriculum in mathematics and science (cf. Gravemeijer et al., chap. 7, this volume). Models that describe patterns or systems of quantitative and spatial relationships in the experienced world should be emphasized throughout the mathematics and science curriculum (cf. Lehrer et al., chap. 9, and Nemirovsky & Monk, chap. 6, this volume).

How Is a Models and Modeling Perspective Related to Social Constructivism?

Models are often developed by groups and not just individuals. The development of models often involves social as well as cognitive functions. Of course, the sharing of models does not necessarily mean that each of the individuals who participated in the creation of the shared model or artifact has the same understanding of that system. Or, to put it differently, individuals' personal models or artifacts may be somewhat different from the shared model. We make no claim that any one individual has direct access to the model of another individual. In fact, in the following sense, individuals do not even have direct access to their own models or conceptual systems. The internal, conceptual system that I had in my mind that enabled me to produce an external representation or artifact quite often changes as I experience the representation that I have created. In fact, during attempts to solve problems, one of the main reasons for drawing pictures or for developing other descriptions of the problem is that students' early conceptualizations often fail to recognize the proverbial forest because of the trees, or vice versa—or, when they focus on one type of detail, other details may be conceptually neglected. Thus, when I draw a picture, the meaning that I had in mind that I put into the picture often changes as I see my picture, which in turn changes the picture that I see. When I look at my own picture, my ideas may have already changed and my view of my picture may not be so different than yours in the sense that the picture no longer represents some direct mapping of what is in my mind. In principle, there is often very little difference between viewing a picture that another person has created and viewing a picture that you yourself have created. Therefore, seeing my own picture is in fact more problematic than a constructivist perspective would have led us to believe, but seeing the picture of another may be less problematic.

How Is a Models and Modeling Perspective Related to Mathematizing?

Mathematizing (e.g., quantifying, visualizing, or coordinatizing) is a form of modeling; it usually involves using specialized languages, symbols, graphs, pictures, concrete materials, and other notation systems to develop mathematical descriptions and explanations that make obvious heavy demands on learners' representational capabilities. Therefore, focusing on mathematizing meaningful situations brings to the foreground activities in which representational abilities are salient. Yet in the past, when researchers investigated the roles that representations play in mathematical reasoning, most focused on how students make sense of word problems or symbolic computations. Few investigated how students mathematize real-life situations.

MATHEMATIZING VERSUS DECODING

As Fig. 10.2 suggests, when mathematics is used in real-life situations, the processes that are needed often emphasize almost exactly the opposite kind of processes of those needed to make sense of most to the symbolic computations or word problems (exercises) that occur in traditional text-books, tests, and teaching (see Lehrer et al., chap. 9, this volume for a discussion of design tasks). For example, for traditional textbook word problems, the problematic aspects tend to involve trying to make meaning out of symbolically stated questions; however, when students use mathematics in real-life situations, the processes that are needed tend to emphasize the need to make symbolic descriptions of situations that are already meaningful.

An Example of Average Ability Students
Developing a Powerful Model

To focus on representational systems and mathematizing, we carefully examine a modeling activity whose goal is to stimulate and elicit the development of some construct. In the analysis that follows, we show

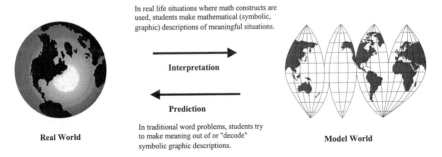

FIG. 10.2. Processes that are needed for mathematics in real-life situations versus the exercises that occur in traditional teaching.

how the solutions to such problems involve a series of modeling cycles in which progressively more sophisticated ways of thinking are introduced, tested, and refined. The purpose of representations in this development is not only for students to communicate with one another; it is also for students to communicate with themselves and to externalize their own ways of thinking so they can be examined and improved. Thus, the meanings and functions of students' representations are not static; they are continually evolving. The same is true for the underlying mathematical constructs that the representations embody, as well as for the external systems that they describe.

An important characteristic of the Summer Jobs Problem (Katims & Lesh, 1994) that follows is that it is intended to be addressed by three-person groups of students. The Summer Jobs Problem assumes that relevant tools, such as calculators and graph paper, are readily available to the student. The task makes heavy demands on communication capabilities and representational fluency for purposes such as: (a) analyzing problems, and planning solutions involving multiple steps and multiple resources and constraints, (b) justifying and explaining suggested actions, and predicting their consequences, (c) monitoring and assessing progress, and (d) integrating and communicating results in forms that are useful to others. As a model-eliciting activity, the goal of the task is to produce an operational definition that stimulates and expresses the learners' notion of how to measure some construct, such as "productivity" at summer jobs. Descriptions, explanations, and justifications are not simply accompaniments to useful responses; they are the heart of useful responses. Model development is what solutions to such problems is all about.

The members of the three-person team whose work is described in this section were all considered to be "average ability" mathematics students in an "average ability" inner-city, seventh-grade classroom. Because of the teacher's emphasis on portfolio-based assessment, the students had considerable prior experience working on projects similar in scope to the Summer Jobs Problem. This problem was based on a context that was described in a "math rich newspaper article" that was discussed by the class as a whole on the day before the Summer Jobs Problem was presented (Fig. 10.3). The students worked at small tables where a "tool kit" was available that included three TI-92 calculators; a Macintosh computer with software for word processing, spreadsheets, drawing, and making geometry constructions; and other standard classroom tools. Although this particular group made somewhat greater use of the technology, the actual result that they produced is not significantly different from that of other groups. What is prototypical of this group is the process of progressing through multiple modeling cycles. The analysis of the student activities over two class periods yielded evidence for 14 distinct cycles.

Last summer Maya started a concession business at Wild Days Amusement Park. Her vendors carry popcorn and drinks around the park, selling wherever they can find customers. Maya needs your help deciding which workers to rehire next summer. Last year Maya had nine vendors. This summer, she can have only six – three full-time and three half-time. She wants to rehire the vendors who will make the most money for her. But she doesn't know how to compare them because they worked different numbers of hours. Also, when they worked makes a big difference. After all, it is easier to sell more on a crowded Friday night than on a rainy afternoon.

Maya reviewed her records from last year. For each vendor, she totaled the number of hours worked and the money collected – when business in the park was busy (high attendance), steady, and slow (low attendance). (See the table.) Please evaluate how well the different vendors did last year for the business and decide which three she should rehire full-time and which three she should rehire half-time.

Write a letter to Maya giving your results. In your letter describe how you evaluated the vendors. Give details so Maya can check your work, and give a clear explanation so she can decide whether your method is a good one for her to use.

HOURS WORKED LAST SUMMER

	JUNE			JULY			AUGUST		
	Busy	Steady	Slow	Busy	Steady	Slow	Busy	Steady	Slow
MARIA	12.5	15	9	10	14	17.5	12.5	33.5	35
KIM	5.5	22	15.5	53.5	40	15.5	50	14	23.5
TERRY	12	17	14.5	20	25	21.5	19.5	20.5	24.5
JOSE	19.5	30.5	34	20	31	14	22	19.5	36
CHAD	19.5	26	0	36	15.5	27	30	24	4.5
CHERI	13	4.5	12	33.5	37.5	6.5	16	24	16.5
ROBIN	26.5	43.5	27	67	26	3	41.5	58	5.5
TONY	7.5	16	25	16	45.5	51	7.5	42	84
WILLY	0	3	4.5	38	17.5	39	37	22	12

MONEY COLLECTED LAST SUMMER (IN DOLLARS)

	JUNE			JULY			AUGUST		
	Busy	Steady	Slow	Busy	Steady	Slow	Busy	Steady	Slow
MARIA	690	780	452	699	758	835	788	1732	1462
KIM	474	874	406	4612	2032	477	4500	834	712
TERRY	1047	667	284	1389	804	450	1062	806	491
JOSE	1263	1188	765	1584	1668	449	1822	1276	1358
CHAD	1264	1172	0	2477	681	548	1923	1130	89
CHERI	1115	278	574	2972	2399	231	1322	1594	577
ROBIN	2253	1702	610	4470	993	75	2754	2327	87
TONY	550	903	928	1296	2360	2610	615	2184	2518
WILLY	0	125	64	3073	767	768	3005	1253	253

FIG. 10.3. The Summer Jobs Problem. Figures are given for times when park attendance was high (busy), medium (steady), and low (slow).

We describe the significant characteristics of the evolution of the students' interpretations and representations through those cycles.

Some Characteristics of Students' Early Interpretations. Early interpretations often consist of a hodgepodge of several disorganized and sometimes inconsistent ways of thinking about givens, goals, and possible solution steps, as can be seen as the first modeling cycle begins:

Alan: Oh god. We've gotta add up all this stuff ... You got a calculator?

Barb: They're in here [the toolkit] ... Here [she finds two TI-92 calculators in the toolkit].

[Students calculated independently for about 5 minutes.]

Carla: [looking at Barb] What'd you get? ... I got 159.

Barb: Yep ... um ... That's what I got.

Alan: I got, let's see, ... 116.

Barb: You punched them in wrong.... Here, you read them [the numbers] and I'll punch 'em in.

Alan: [pointing to the numbers in the table] 12.5, 5.5, 12, 19.9, 19.5 ...

Carla: Huh! ... Not those, you dummy.

Alan: Why?

Barb: Here, ... read these [pointing to the first row of the table].

This first cycle is characterized by the inconsistent use of several unstated and uncoordinated ways of thinking. In this team's first interpretation of the problem, they tended to worry most about "What should I do?" rather than "What does this information mean?" Their first interpretations focused on computation, and the information that was given was treated as though no data interpretation or mathematization was necessary. They tended to focus on only a small subset of the information, and they tended to focus on isolated pieces of information rather than focusing on underlying patterns and regularities. For example, Alan, Barb, and Carla focused on only the first information that they noticed. This emphasis was not based on a thoughtful selection about which information was most important. It was simply the first information that came to their attention. They tended to focus only on numbers, and ignored quantity types. For example, the quantity "12.5 hours" usually was read as "twelve point five," emphasizing "how much" but ignoring "of what."

At the beginning of Modeling Cycle 2, the students created a table that accumulated more meaningful data, the total number of hours for each worker:

Barb: Here, read these [again pointing to the first row of the table].

Alan: OK ... 12.5, 15, 9, 10, 14, 17.5 12.5, 33.5, and 35 ... [pause] ... What is it? [pause]

Barb: It's 159.

Carla: [As Alan was reading numbers, Carla was checking off the numbers in her table. So, when Barb gives the result, Carla recorded it in a new column on the right side of her table of data.]

Alan: OK, so who should we hire? [Alan was looking at Carla's table of sums.]

Barb: Robin looks good . . . [pause] So does Tony.

Alan: Maybe Kim . . . [pause]

In the very next cycle, the students computed a table that showed the total number of dollars that each worker earned. Because this problem involves both "too much" and "not enough" information, the students' first representations and ways of thinking often focused on only a subset of the information, and students often tended to be preoccupied with finding ways to simplify or aggregate (sums, averages) all of the available information. These students focused on hours worked and earnings while ignoring work schedules.

At the same time that students were preoccupied with finding ways to simplify or reduce information, they also expressed concerns about not knowing additional information that they believed was relevant. For example, the Summer Jobs Problem does not include information about the needs, flexibility, or friendliness of potential employees, or their willingness to work. Yet, even though this information is not available, it tends to be clear that the client in the problem would not find it useful if students refused to respond to her request for help simply because some relevant information was not available. Therefore, even at early stages of thinking about the problem, students generally recognize that, to solve the problem, a simplified description (or model) needs to be developed that focuses on significant relationships, patterns, and trends, and that simplifies the information and puts it into a useful form, while avoiding distractions related to surface-level details or gaps in the data. Consequently, these purposes tend to be reflected in the representations that they produce.

Some Characteristics of Students' Intermediate Interpretations.   Later, more sophisticated ways of thinking tended to go beyond organizing and processing isolated pieces of data to focusing on relationships, or patterns, or trends in the data. The students saw that different workers earned different amounts of money each month and they shifted their attention to trends across time. This shift marked the beginning of Modeling Cycle 5:

Barb: OK, let's, like, line 'em up for each month.

Alan: You started doing that.

Barb: OK, you [Alan] read 'em off and I'll write 'em down.

Alan: OK, here's August. . . . We got Kim, Tony, Robin . . . Cheri
          . . . Willy, Chad, and Jose. Then, Maria and Terry.

The students focused on trends in rank across time. For about five
minutes, Alan, Barb, and Carla worked together to get a list of "top money
makers" each month. Then they noticed that the rankings were somewhat
different each month, so the table shown in Fig. 10.4 was used as an
attempt to reduce this information.

Approximately five minutes passed while each of the three students
nominated workers that they believed should be hired, based on rankings
and trends in the preceding table. In most cases, when students spoke in
favor of a given worker, they made up some sort of "cover story" to
account for the "ups" and "downs" in the performance of the worker.
These stories involved the following kinds of possibilities: Some workers
learned and improved, whereas others got bored; some weren't able to
work as much as others; some were good during busy periods, but not
during slow periods. In these discussions, the students started to pay
attention to the fact that the months might not be equally important (e.g.,
July is the busiest month, but August might be the best indicator of current
abilities) and that busy, steady, and slow periods might not be equally
important (e.g., the part-time workers wouldn't be hired during slow
periods). Finally, as Carla was looking at the three-column chart that
showed trends, she got the idea to make a similar graph using the
computer. This idea led to Modeling Cycle 6:

Carla: I can make a graph like that [pointing to the table that was
          used in cycle 5] with the computer. Want'a see.

Alan: Sure, um, what's it look like.

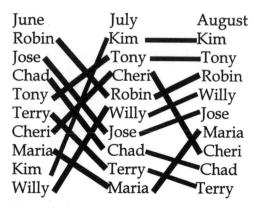

FIG. 10.4. List of "top money makers" each month.

Barb: . . . Let me see.

Carla: Wait a minute. . . . [long pause] . . . Wait a minute. . . . [long pause] . . . Here's one. No. . . . [long pause] . . . Ah, here. No. . . . [long pause] . . . OK, look at this.

Alan: Wow! Neat! How'd you do that?

[Carla explains again how she made the graphs using the computer.]

Alan: Now who do we pick. . . . Who's this?

Carla: Um, let's see, it's Kim. . . . And, this is . . . um . . . Tony.

Alan: Who's this?

Barb: Let me see.

Carla: Oh, it's Robin.

Barb: So, we've got Kim . . . Tony, and Robin. Who's next? [pause]

Carla: What about this guy? . . . Who is he? . . . Um, it's Cheri. . . . Look, she was really good here. But, then she screwed up.

Barb: How we gonna decide which of these guys to hire? They were all good some and bad some. . . . [long pause] . . . How many were we supposed to hire anyway? . . . [pause] . . . Look at the problem [speaking to Alan]. What does it say? . . . [long pause].

Alan: We're supposed to hire three full time and three part time. . . . [pause] . . .

Alan: I think we should hire Willy. He was good here [pointing to July and August] . . . and he didn't get to work much here [pointing to June].

Neither their chart nor their graph was sufficient for them to produce a list that successfully ranked the workers from "best" to "worst." This mismatch between their current results and the desired products led them to consider relationships involving both time and money. It is important to note here that this shift in their model development was driven by the mismatch that the students themselves perceived between their current results and the desired outcomes. Modeling Cycles 8 through 10 reflect their shift to constructing relevant rates for each worker.

Barb: Look you guys. Some of these people got to work a lot more than others. . . . That's not fair. Look, Willy didn't get to work at all back here [in June].

Carla: So, what're we gonna do?

[Mumbling. More than 1 minute passes.]

Alan: Here. I'm trying something. . . . I'm subtracting how much
            each guy worked. That'll kind of even things out. . . . I
            worked for a guy who did that once. We were cleaning up
            trash and he wanted us to work fast.

Barb: Hey, that's a good idea! We could figure out dollars-per-
            hour. . . . I did that for my jobs last summer.

In addition to their own sense-making about the desired outcomes, the
students drew on their own experiences in out-of-school situations. These
experiences seem to serve as prototypes for actions in the summer jobs
situation.

Some Characteristics of Students' Final Interpretations. The final
results that students produced went beyond simple, static solutions to
include conditional statements about a variety of options or mechanisms
for taking into account additional information. Their results were built
on an understanding and use of rate and aggregated quantities that
emerged in the final modeling cycles. The students produced a letter to
the client with an accompanying graph (Fig. 10.5) that showed dollar-per-
hour monthly trends for busy and steady periods for each worker.

In essence, then, we claim that the students have created a model that
they themselves can think with and that can be shared with their client.
The solution that is given enables the client to assign different "weights"

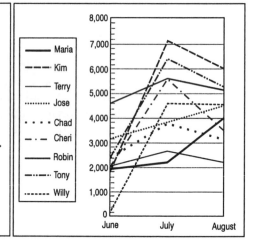

FIG. 10.5. Students' letter to the client, with accompanying graph showing
trends in money earned for June, July, and August.

to reflect the client's own views about the relative importance of information about different months and different periods of work. Rather than using only a single rule that is applied uniformly across all of the possible employees, the procedure that students used involved a series of dependent procedures. One approach was used to select employees that are in a "must hire" category; then a different procedure was suggested to select employees among the possibilities that remained. Thus, the students considered the realistic constraints of the model and the conditions under which their model applies.

The richness that we saw in the development of the students' model, through multiple cycles, contrasted sharply with the somewhat more barren final product created by the students. This has important implications for both practice and research. On the one hand, we see the need for teachers to be able to examine students' developing models in order to assess student knowledge and understanding and to foster continued model development in ways that evolve as the student models evolve. For example, the final product created by the students reveals little about the rejected or modified ideas that influenced the final interpretation or about the roles played by the various students. We see the need for research that will create and examine new and effective ways to capture the richness of the students' model development. An important characteristic of the model development is that students' later models are characterized by greater stability than their earlier models. There is evidence of increasing stability as the students are able to explain how they accounted for the data as well as missing information. In the later cycles, they were able to modify their model without losing their earlier work. It would appear that they are poised to modify and/or extend their own thinking, perhaps incorporating good ideas that they may hear from other students, but without abandoning their own work. Further research is needed to understand how teachers can themselves develop conjectures about how those ways of thinking might evolve and about the means of supporting those processes.

Our research with model-eliciting problem situations has led us to four insights that drive our continued work. First, because model-eliciting tasks emphasize the process of mathematizing meaningful situations, they emphasize representational abilities that tend to be overlooked in stereotypical textbook word problems. For example, learners need to explain and predict structurally complex systems, to monitor and assess their progress, to construct tools, symbols, and resources, and to integrate and communicate meaningful results. Consequently, if the posed tasks involve a much broader range of mathematical and representational competencies, it should be no surprise that a broader range of capable students emerge. Second, in cases where it is possible for students to recognize the need for a targeted construct, they often invent it (Lesh, Hoover, & Kelly, 1993). Such problems enable researchers to go beyond descriptions of static states of development to focus on mechanisms that contribute to development from one state to another. Third, when students develop a model, they often do so using a rich array of interacting representations, many of which tend to involve idiosyncratic diagrams and notational systems that are introduced by students themselves. Furthermore, students who are able to invent powerful constructs often include many who have been labeled "below average in ability" based on their performance in situations involving traditional tests, textbooks, and teaching, where only a narrow and shallow range of mathematical abilities tend to be emphasized (Lesh et al., 1993). Fourth, experiences like the Summer Jobs Problem provide stories or experiences that often function in symbolic and metaphoric ways. Students use these experiences as prototypes for thinking about other similar problem-solving situations (Schank, 1990; Doerr, 1994).

Implications of a Modeling Perspective

A modeling perspective, and the kind of observations that were made in the preceding sections, imply significant shifts for our views of learning, problem solving, and teaching, as well as new opportunities for gaining insight into the mechanisms that drive learning. This section discusses some of these challenges and opportunities, and focuses on implications that these changes have for future research on representational systems.

Model Development Is Learning. To develop models is to learn. For example, when students produce responses to model-eliciting activities, of the type described in the preceding section, what they produce is not just a solution—it is a powerful conceptual tool. The products that they produce are not simply answers to questions. They involve descriptions, explanations, and justifications that explicitly reveal important aspects of students' ways of thinking. Furthermore, if these ways of thinking are embedded in "smart tools" (see Bransford et al., chap. 8, this volume) that can be shared and reused in other situations, then they are conceptual systems that represent significant forms of learning; if care is taken to focus on models that are mathematically significant, then the models that are constructed often provide the conceptual foundations for the most important cognitive objectives of mathematics instruction. Consequently, when students develop solutions to such problems, they tend to both learn and document what they are learning. The documentation provides a trail of development that helps teachers become familiar with students' ways of thinking, and that helps students go beyond thinking *with* these conceptual systems to also thinking *about* them (Skovsmose, 1990). In this way, students are better able to modify, refine, and extend their ways of thinking. An assumption underlying the modeling perspective described in this chapter is that the most important goals of mathematics instruction are to help students develop powerful models for making sense of the kind of complex systems that are ubiquitous in our modern technology-based society.

How Is a Models and Modeling Perspective Related to Developmental Psychology? Piaget inspired a great deal of the best research on the nature of students' developing mathematical knowledge. For example, just as Piaget described the sequences of stages that children go through to develop general cognitive structures for making sense of everyday experiences, mathematics educators described the sequences of stages that students go through in topic areas ranging from whole number arithmetic (Carpenter, Fennema, & Romberg, 1993; Fuson, 1988; Steffe, 1994), rational number and proportional reasoning (Lesh, Post, & Behr, 1989), to early algebra (Kaput, 1990). However, recent research has shown that learning is a great deal more unstable, piecemeal, and situated than the preceding unfolding linear sequences of development suggested. For example, descriptions of children's whole number arithmetic concepts appeared complete and sensible until researchers in different topic areas began to compare their results and conclusions. At the same time that early number concepts are developing, children are also developing ideas about continuous measures, fractions, ratios, rates, accumulating quantities, coordinates, and a host of other constructs; it is only at relatively late stages of development that these topic areas are sorted out into separate but linked conceptual domains.

During model-eliciting activities, it is often possible to describe how the relevant ways of thinking develop from intuitions to formalizations, or from concrete to abstract relationships or actions, or from situated to decontextualized understandings. So, researchers can describe: (a) what it means for given models to develop, (b) dimensions along which development occurs, and (c) mechanisms that drive development (from the perspective of the child) or that stimulate or facilitate development (from the perspective of the teacher). But in general, for any given conceptual model, there tends to be no such thing as a "stage n child," at least not if such statements are intended to imply that the child should be expected to give a "stage n" level response on all tasks that a mathematician or a psychologist might consider to characterize the same structure. Even when seemingly superficial changes are made in the context or content of such tasks, students' levels of development often vary significantly depending on factors such as experience and the other developing conceptual systems at play.

New Ways of Thinking About Generalizing and Sharing. A modeling perspective on student learning brings a new perspective on generalizing and sharing. The kinds of model-eliciting tasks described in this chapter require as part of their solution meaningful descriptions, explanations, and procedures for predictions that can be used by others. The solution to such a task is not just a simple answer to someone else's well-formulated question; it a tool that can be used to make sense of a collection of situations, and it is a tool that can be shared and reused by others.

In our own research, when we have asked students to develop such reusable and sharable tools, then we have found that their constructs have generalizability, transportability, and/or modifiability (Lesh, 1998; Doerr, 1995, 1997; see also Bransford et al., chap. 8, this volume). By contrast, in most textbook problems, students are rarely asked to produce any models at all. Most often these problems simply provide the relevant, usually invariant, model to the student and then the student is directed to produce single-number answers. Even many applied problems, which are intended to involve "real-life" situations, usually require no more than specific answers to particular, often complex, questions. It is a rare situation where textbook problems call for mathematical descriptions, explanations, or justifications, and it is even rarer to find solutions that are intended to be useful for a whole class of situations.

To build a general model does not guarantee that the builder will be able to generalize. We wish to distinguish carefully between claiming that the students have built a general model or a transferable tool and claiming that the students who created it can transfer the knowledge or use the tool in a variety of contexts. On the other hand, it is well known that when a person has a hammer in the hand, lots of things tend to look like nails. So, with models, the key learning problem is not necessarily acquiring the ability to generalize, but rather the key problem is for students to become more discerning about identifying situations where the model is appropriate. Effective model construction tasks can serve as powerful prototypes by providing rich, memorable contexts for learning and discussing important mathematical ideas. During the school year, these model-eliciting episodes can become an important part of the culture and history of the classroom. It is common to hear mathematical discourse in which students and teachers refer back to these prototypes—"Remember when we used rates in the Summer Jobs Problem?" A model thus becomes a powerful tool for students when they encounter structurally similar situations while simultaneously becoming part of the shared language of the classroom.

New Ways of Thinking About the Mechanisms That Drive Construct Development. For model-eliciting activities like the Summer Jobs Problem described in the preceding section of this chapter, students develop progressively more robust and powerful ways of thinking by going through a series of modeling cycles. In a modeling cycle, when a description is produced, it may involve a combination of spoken words, written symbols, pictures or diagrams, or references to other models or real-life experiences. But, in any case, the representation tends to organize and simplify the situation so that additional information can be noticed, or so that attention can be directed toward underlying patterns and regularities, which may, in turn, drive changes in conceptions. This new information often creates the need for a more refined or more elaborate description, and this new description again tends to make it possible for another round of additional information to be noticed. Internal conceptual systems and external representational systems both tend to be unstable, interacting, and continually evolving. The general cycle of development repeats until the match between the model and the modeled is experienced as being sufficiently close and sufficiently useful to produce the desired results without any further adaptations. We saw that in the students' intermediate interpretations of the Summer Jobs Problem, they found that neither their chart nor their graph was sufficient for them to produce a list that ranked the workers. This led to a refinement of their model that included both time and money. In this way, the meanings of both models and representational systems tend to be unstable. This lack of stability, together with adaptations that are made that are aimed at increasing stability, are some of the most important driving forces behind model development. Cognitive conflict, or the need to develop increased conceptual stability, is a primary factor that creates the need for conceptual adaptation; representation systems facilitate the progressive differentiation and integration of relevant conceptual systems.

New Ways of Thinking About Problem Solving. The application of a modeling perspective to problem solving is a relatively new phenomenon within mathematics education research. Much of the problem-solving research of the past three decades has largely been based on variants of Polya-like processes that proceed from givens to goals, with more recent research attending to the metacognitive processes in which expert problem solvers engage (Schoenfeld, 1985, 1994; Charles & Silver, 1989). As a result, problem solving has been defined as getting from givens to goals when the path is not immediately obvious or it is blocked. Students are often asked to learn some general heuristics that essentially answer the question: What can you do when you are stuck? These generalized heuristics and problem solving processes are then applied to "real-life" problem situations that may involve "messy" data and additional "real-life" information in order to solve a particularized problem. Applied problem solving is thus conceived of as a special case of generalized, content-independent, problem-solving processes.

When attention focuses on model-eliciting activities, the essence of problem solving becomes finding ways to mathematically interpret meaningful problem situations. Nonroutine problems involve more than a single modeling cycle of getting from givens to goals; traditional problem solving is a special case where only one modeling cycle is needed. In model-eliciting tasks, there are of necessity multiple modeling cycles, with multiple ways of thinking about givens, goals, and solution paths (Bell, 1993; Doerr, 1996; Lesh & Zawojewski, 1987). It is crucial to recognize that these ways of thinking evolve over the course of the activity in ways that are increasingly stable. Modeling activities are much more than the mapping of problem information (givens) onto an invariant model in order to reach a solution (goals). In modeling, it is the interpretation and the model itself that are constructed, modified, refined, or extended.

When attention focuses on model construction, it becomes much more important for students to find ways to adapt, modify, and refine ideas that they do have, rather than to try to find ways to be more effective when they are stuck, that is, when they have no relevant ideas, as often happens in one-cycle problems and mathematical puzzles. To develop useful responses to modeling tasks, the kinds of heuristics and strategies that are most useful tend to be quite different from those that have been emphasized in traditional problems where the solution involves only a single interpretation cycle. For example, model-eliciting activities place greater demands on students' abilities to introduce, modify, and adapt useful representations. In model-eliciting tasks, the mathematical abilities that are highlighted often emphasize communication, planning, monitoring, and other types of higher order thinking that emphasize representational abilities (diSessa, Hammer, Sherin, & Kolpakowski, 1991). Students must go beyond thinking with a given mathematical representation or model to also think about the relative strengths and weaknesses of alternative representations.

New Ways of Thinking About Teaching. A modeling perspective on learning and problem solving is a shift that views the student learner not as a traditional problem solver but rather as a model builder, and this necessitates a corresponding shift in views about effective teaching. The model building that we have examined is characterized by the development of models (or tools) that are both generalizable and shareable; modeling is seen not as a linear progression from givens to goals but rather as multiple cycles of modification, refinement, and extension, with increasing stability through the modeling cycles. The shift that views learners as model builders brings new issues for teaching and teachers into the foreground.

The metaphor of a teacher as a facilitator, guide, or coach has been widely used in recent years. However, transforming traditional teacher roles into the role of facilitator has proven to be an often vague and unclear charge. In the model-eliciting tasks we have discussed, the critical role for the teacher is to create the need for students to create significant models in the first place. The symbolizing, communicating, and mathematizing that need to occur among learners must be centered in tasks that are meaningful to the students and that evoke the need for the students to create a significant construct. Hence the role of the teacher is to effectively set the stage for this activity to occur. Lest this seem like an overly simplistic view of teaching, we are quick to add that this activity implies that teachers develop great skill in attending to what it is that students already know. This shifts the focus from what students need to be taught (as prerequisite skills and knowledge) to understanding more deeply the student knowledge that can be built on, extended, and refined by the student (cf. Nemirovsky & Monk, chap. 6, this volume).

As we have seen in our work, students can bring a great deal of diversity to modeling tasks (Confrey & Doerr, 1994; Doerr & Confrey, 1994). Moreover, because such tasks require different abilities than traditional, symbolic tasks, new students emerge as capable (Lesh et al., 1993). The challenge then, for the teacher, is not in terms of assisting students in finding a predetermined single solution, but rather is in terms of maintaining and nurturing the diversity in student approaches. Facilitating the development of student models requires that teachers carefully and closely attend to students' ways of thinking about problem situations, but it is not necessary to classify such thinking in predetermined, linear next steps. Rather, the task confronting the teacher is to ensure that the mechanisms that drive model development can occur. This means that the teacher is in the role of hearing students' own voices but not giving students the next step that would appear to be useful from the teacher's perspective. The teacher needs to create the situations that provide students with conflicts that they need to resolve or with alternatives that they might test.

Finally, from a models and modeling perspective, we see the role of the teacher as creating the need for students to share their tools and representations. These representations become ways for a learner to communicate with himself or herself, within the group, and within the larger class setting. It is within this larger classroom setting that the teacher plays an especially critical role. Sharing alternative models, fostering discussion, creating and nurturing diverse approaches, creating meaningful and powerful prototypes through classroom discourse, and building on the connections that students make to their out-of-school mathematics experience are all activities that will support students as they extend, apply, and explore the models they themselves have built. Teachers will need to develop the collaborative classroom settings in which such activities are most likely to occur. At the same time, more research needs to be done on the design of effective instructional sequences for learners.

CONCLUSIONS

The purpose of this chapter has been to describe a theoretical perspective that emphasizes models and modeling. It also pointed out how a modeling perspective leads to significant ways to rethink issues about learning, problem solving, and teaching. This perspective suggests several significant new directions for future research efforts.

Preparation for success in a technology-based society demands that students must learn to think about a multiplicity of systems, often of significant complexity. Students will need to mathematize systems that involve far more than simple counts and simple measures. They will need to develop representational fluency for dealing with mathematical entities such as signed quantities, ratios and rates, accumulating quantities, continuously changing quantities, measures associated with frequencies of events (probabilities), patterns and trends, logical statements, and control statements. As human conceptualizing and processing capabilities are increasingly embedded within powerful technology-based tools (such as computers and calculators), some of the most useful representational systems are those that are dynamic and functionally linked. From a modeling perspective, representational fluency will be an essential component of what it means to understand the kind of constructs that underlie elementary mathematical reasoning.

REFERENCES

Bell, M. (1993). Modelling and applications of mathematics in the primary curriculum. In T. Breiteig, I. Huntley, & G. Kaiser-Messmer (Eds.), *Teaching and learning mathematics in context* (pp. 71–80). London: Ellis Horwood.

Carpenter, T. P., Fennema, E., & Romberg, T. A. (1993). *Rational numbers: An integration of research.* Hillsdale, NJ: Lawrence Erlbaum Associates.

Charles, R. I., & Silver, E. A. (Eds.). (1989). *The teaching and assessing of mathematical problem solving.* Hillsdale, NJ: Lawrence Erlbaum Associates.

Confrey, J. (1994). Splitting, similarity, and rate of change: A new approach to multiplication and exponential functions. In G. Harel & J. Confrey (Eds.), *The development of multiplicative reasoning* (pp. 293–332). Albany, NY: State University of New York.

Confrey, J., & Doerr, H. M. (1994). Student modelers. *Interactive Learning Environments, 4,* 199–217.

diSessa, A. A., Hammer, D., Sherin, B., & Kolpakowski, T. (1991). Inventing graphing: Meta-representational expertise in children. *Journal of Mathematical Behavior, 10,* 117–160.

Doerr, H. M. (1994). *A model building approach to constructing student understandings of force, motion and vectors.* Unpublished doctoral dissertation, Cornell University.

Doerr, H. M. (1995). Negotiating conjectures within a modeling approach to understanding vector quantities. In L. Meira & D. Carraher (Eds.), *Proceedings of the Nineteenth*

International Conference for the Psychology of Mathematics Education (Vol. 3, pp. 168–175). Recife, Brazil: Universidade Federal de Pernambuco.

Doerr, H. M. (1996). Integrating the study of trigonometry, vectors and force through modeling. *School Science and Mathematics, 96,* 407–418.

Doerr, H. M. (1997). Experiment, simulation and analysis: An integrated instructional approach to the concept of force. *International Journal of Science Education, 19,* 265–282.

Doerr, H. M., & Confrey, J. (1994). A modeling approach to understanding the trigonometry of forces: A classroom study. In J. D. da Ponte & J. F. Matos (Eds.), *Proceedings of the Eighteenth International Conference for the Psychology of Mathematics Education* (Vol. 2, pp. 264–271). Lisbon, Portugal: University of Lisbon.

Fuson, K. C. (1988). *Children's counting and concepts of number.* New York: Springer-Verlag.

Kaput, J. (1990). Applying the computer's representational plasticity to create bridging notations from the concrete to the abstract. In B. Bowen (Ed.), *Designing for learning* (pp. 114–148). Cupertino, CA: Apple Computer.

Katims, N., & Lesh, R. (1994). *PACKETS: Performance Assessments for Grades 6–8.* Lexington, MA: D. C. Heath.

Lehrer, R., Horvath, J., & Schauble, L. (1994). Developing model-based reasoning. *Interactive Learning Environments, 4,* 218–232.

Lesh, R. (1981). Applied mathematical problem solving. *Educational Studies in Mathematics, 12,* 235–264.

Lesh, R. (1983). Conceptual analyses of problem solving performance. In E. Silver (Ed.), *Teaching and learning mathematical problem solving* (pp. 309–329). Hillsdale, NJ: Lawrence Erlbaum Associates.

Lesh, R. (1987). The evolution of problem representations in the presence of powerful conceptual amplifiers. In C. Janvier (Ed.), *Problems of representation in teaching and learning mathematics* (pp. 197–206). Hillsdale, NJ: Lawrence Erlbaum Associates.

Lesh, R. (1998). The development of representational abilities in middle school mathematics: The development of student's representations during model eliciting activities. In I. Sigel (Ed.), *Development of mental representation* (pp. 323–349). Mahwah, NJ: Lawrence Erlbaum Associates.

Lesh, R., Hoover, M., & Kelly, A. (1993). Equity, technology, and teacher development. In I. Wirszup & R. Streit (Eds.), *Developments in school mathematics education around the world: Volume 3* (pp. 117–134). Reston, VA: National Council of Teachers of Mathematics.

Lesh, R., & Lamon, S. (Eds.). (1994). *Assessment of authentic performance in school mathematics.* Washington, DC: American Association for the Advancement of Sciences.

Lesh, R., Post, T., & Behr, M. (1989). Proportional reasoning. In M. Behr & J. Hiebert (Eds.), *Number concepts and operations in the middle grades* (Vol. 2, pp. 93–118). Reston, VA: National Council of Teachers of Mathematics.

Lesh, R., & Zawojewski, J. (1987). Problem solving. In T. Post (Ed.), *Teaching mathematics in grades k–8: Research-based methods* (pp. 49–88). Boston: Allyn & Bacon.

Schank, R. C. (1990). *Tell me a story: A new look at real and artificial memory.* New York: Charles Scribner's Sons, Macmillan.

Schoenfeld, A. H. (1985). *Mathematical problem solving.* Orlando, FL: Academic Press.

Schoenfeld, A. H. (Ed.). (1994). *Mathematical thinking and problem solving.* Hillsdale, NJ: Lawrence Erlbaum Associates.

Skovsmose, O. (1990). Reflective knowledge: Its relation to the mathematical modelling process. *International Journal of Mathematical Education in Science and Technology, 21,* 765–779.

Steffe, L. (1994). Children's multiplying schemes. In G. Harel & J. Confrey (Eds.), *The development of multiplicative reasoning in the learning of mathematics* (pp. 3–40). Albany: State University of New York Press.

11

Postscript: Integrating Themes on Discourse and Design

Janet Bowers
San Diego State University

The rich and varied perspectives included in this book provide a broad view of contemporary philosophies concerning mathematics education. The goal of this postscript is to draw together the preceding chapters by outlining three common themes that cut across the two divisions of the book. These include:

1. The interrelations between the role of community and communication in establishing common interpretations.
2. The characterization of learning as a process of progressive refinement and reorganization.
3. Assumptions regarding the coemergence of meaning and symbolizations.

THREE COMMON THEMES IN THE CHAPTERS

Theme 1: Interrelations Between Mathematizing, Symbolizing and Communicating Within a Community

In *Democracy and Education*, Dewey (1916/1944) described the interrelations between the notions of commonalties, community, and communication. He wrote, "Men live in a community in virtue of the things which they have in common; and communication is the way in which they come to possess things in common" (Dewey, 1916/1944, p. 4). Although stated differently in different chapters, the perspectives in this book all appear to be consistent with Dewey's premise in that what students come to have in common evolves through successive iterations of symbolizing, mathematizing, and communicating. The implication of this assertion leads many of the contributors to call for analyses that incorporate both cultural and psychological processes when attempting to account for individual activity within a given classroom microculture. For example, Bransford et al. (chap. 8) conclude:

> During the past several years, our research group has become increasingly aware of the need to move beyond an exclusive focus on the individual and pay careful attention to the assumption that all human endeavors are socially situated. . . . One way to characterize the impact of this work is to conclude that "culture is not an option." Classroom, school, and community cultures are always present, irrespective of whether they are explicitly analyzed.

Sfard (chap. 3) contends that a coordination of social and cultural factors may lead to a reconceptualization of earlier views of symbolizing. She argues that although symbolizing was once viewed as a one-way process in which one "baptized an object" or attached a linguistic placeholder to an already extant object, she, and many of the authors in this book have come to characterize the relationship between symbolizing and learning as reflexive. In this reconceptualization, symbolizations and meanings are continually revised as students reorganize their current ways of knowing while communicating with others in their classroom community. This is aptly captured in Sfard's metaphor describing the relationship between discourse and meaning as "two legs that make the movement forward possible thanks to the fact they are never in the same place, and at any given stage, one of them is ahead of the other." This is also echoed in van Oers' view (chap. 5) that "meanings and signs inextricably go together and develop concurrently."

One implication that arises from this reconceptualization is that the ontological question regarding the existence of mathematical objects can be recast. That is, although students cannot talk about the existence of a function in the same way they can talk about the existence of a chair, their shared communication creates a space in which mathematical objects do, at least from the conversants' point of view, exist. Sfard calls this shared negotiation space the virtual reality (VR) of mathematical discourse. Moreover, she suggests that although the virtual reality of mathematical discourse does not support discussions that parallel discourse in the physical world (i.e., you can hand me a pencil, but you cannot hand me a function), students can talk about mathematical objects (such as functions) in meaningful ways. In sum, Sfard's notion of VR discourse can be used to demonstrate the role of the community in establishing common understandings through communication. She states (chap. 3):

> It is the discursive activity, including its continuous production of symbols, that creates the need for mathematical objects; and these are mathematical objects (or rather the object-mediated use of symbols) that, in their turn, influence the discourse and push it into new directions.

In contrast to Sfard's focus on the community's role in the construction of symbols and meaning, Dörfler (chap. 4) emphasizes the role of individual construction in communal discourse. He states, "I consider communication to be the social medium for the individual construction of prototypes and protocols and also for the development of what I call an as-if attitude." Here, Dörfler indicates that individuals create prototypes (idiosyncratic images that serve as templates for classes of objects) and protocols (idiosyncratic schemas of action) based on their efforts to participate in the practices of the wider mathematical discourse. As Dörfler notes, one of the main functions of these tools is to support students' discussions and reflections on mathematical objects "as if" they exist. It is, of course, assumed that individual student's prototypes and protocols are not necessarily closely aligned. That is, Dörfler does not assume that everyone forms identical prototypes for, say, a function. Instead, these prototypes serve as discursive tools to establish taken-as-shared ways of talking about and reflecting on mathematical objects.

In short, for Sfard and Dörfler, participation in mathematical discourse involves negotiating common meanings. Dörfler suggests that such discussions enable students to discuss mathematical objects "as if" they exist. For Sfard, the issue is epistemological rather than ontological. She notes that, to the discussants, the objects do exist because they are experientially real.

From the perspective of instructional design, the triadic relationship between community, communication, and common referents is essential to the discussions of Gravemeijer et al. (chap. 7), Bransford et al. (chap. 8), Lehrer et al. (chap. 9), and Lesh and Doerr (chap. 10). For example, Gravemeijer et al. describe a vision of the communal mathematical practices that serves as the basis for developing instructional sequences. The authors note (chap. 7):

> The task for the instructional designer, in our view, is to create sequences of instructional activities that take account of both the evolving mathematical practices of the classroom community and the development of individual students as they participate in those practices.

This view suggests that the classroom community (including the teacher and students) supports its own development by discussing and revising models through collective negotiations. In this way, the authors suggest that learning can be viewed as a process by which individuals construct meaning as they participate in and contribute to communal practices.

Lehrer et al. (chap. 9) describe how one such negotiation process occurred in a classroom in which students were asked to describe the growth of "Fast Plants." Over the course of several weeks, the students discussed and revised their symbolic inscriptions several times. The authors conclude:

> We found that transitions in growth were inscribed not only collectively and publicly, but also individually. In summary, then, over the course of the children's investigations with Fast Plants, a cascade of inscriptions was accompanied by a cascade of conceptual change.

These arguments suggest the critical role of the community in supporting the evolution of individual learning. By communicating with each other, students can develop a cascade of inscriptions which emerges through successive iterations of discussion and refinement. This parallels the descriptions presented by Bransford et al. and Lesh and Doerr, both of whom claim that when students discuss and revise models communally, they gain deeper insight into the processes they are modeling. In particular, Lesh and Doerr (chap. 10) state:

> Models are often developed by groups and not just individuals. The development of models often involves social as well as cognitive functions. Of course, the sharing of models does not necessarily mean that each of the individuals who participated in the creation of the shared models or artifact has the same understanding of that system.

In sum, the chapters illustrate Dewey's view of the critical relationship between community, communication, and the establishment of common meanings. From a theoretical point of view, this supports an epistemology in which learning is viewed as each individual's contribution to and participation in the negotiation of common practices. This theory informs pedagogical and design perspectives by suggesting that it is essential to anticipate the ongoing processes of collective reflection and generalization. In regard to this goal, several authors (e.g., van Oers, Gravemeijer et al.) take as their starting point Freudenthal's assertion that doing mathematics can be viewed as a human activity. If the role of community is integrated into this view, then learning mathematics can be seen as a communal human activity. The implication from this reconceptualization is that although designers cannot know how any one particular student will interpret any given instructional activity, they can make curricular decisions based on predictions of how the collective discourse will support the negotiation of taken-as-shared meanings. For example, Nemirovsky and Monk (chap. 6) suggest that the designer's goal is not to determine any individual path, but to delimit a "territory" for trail making and to develop tools for supporting this exploration.

Theme 2: Multiple Perspectives on Learning as a Process

A second theme implicit in the book focuses on defining learning as an ongoing process of progressive refinement. This focus was first proposed by the symposium organizers who chose to emphasize the actions of symbolizing, modeling, and communicating, rather than focusing on the meanings that might be inherent in symbols, models, or words. For my part, I use the word *process* here to indicate the authors' views regarding the importance of shifting from documenting the accumulation of knowledge to documenting the ways in which students can be seen as developing knowing-in-action. In general, this knowing-in-action can be viewed as a process of progressive reflection and reorganization. This analytic shift is elaborated, for example, in Lehrer et al.'s (chap. 9) description of how one class revised their models of plant height as they revised their own ideas about what they were measuring. Similarly, Gravemeijer et al. (chap. 7) describe a shift in the ways that students discussed relationships between numbers up to 20. The value of case studies such as these is that they provide insight into the process by which groups of students develop taken-as-shared understandings of "big mathematical ideas." These insights can inform designers' efforts to anticipate possible ways in which other communities will negotiate norms, expectations, and taken-as-shared mathematical meanings.

Although the contributors to this book appear to share the analytic view of learning as a process of progressive refinement, they offer a variety of theoretical positions regarding the nature of this process. These positions range from sociocultural to more psychological in nature. For example, based on a Vygotskian perspective that supports sociocultural views, van Oers (chap. 5) argues that "the structural endpoint of any mature activity needs to be present in the interaction between child and adult as a precondition for this new structure to appear as an individual psychological function in the child." Here, van Oers describes the process of learning in terms of a transition from the inter- to the intramental planes that occurs as students interact with more knowledgeable others in the zone of proximal development. For van Oers, learning may be seen as an iterative process of engaging in, reflecting on, and eventually personalizing cultural practices (including the use of cultural tools). One implication of this view is that it emphasizes the importance of semiotic exploratory activity as a basis for supporting students' engagement in formal practices such as culturally recognized ways of notating.

Assuming a more cognitively based approach, authors such as Bransford et al. and Lesh and Doerr focus on the ways in which students can develop general models that can be applied in a variety of different situations. For example, Bransford et al. (chap. 8) describe several studies to support the claim that "people's representations of problems and experiences have strong effects on the degree to which they will transfer their knowledge to new settings." Similarly, Lesh and Doerr (chap. 10) argue that the models students produce when engaging in model-eliciting problems are not just solutions to the problem at hand, but instead stand as more generalized conceptual tools that can be "shared and reused in other situations." To this end, authors in both chapters discuss ways to design instructional tasks that activate relevant knowledge and affect students' abilities to discriminate between cases.

Nemirovsky and Monk offer a third approach to characterizing the process of learning. Their phenomenological perspective attempts to document the ways in which students actually experience their symbol use. To this end, they describe one interview with Lin, a fifth grader, who draws a graph to represent the motion of a toy bear. The importance of a phenomenological position rests on the ways in which the authors describe the student's experiences. They claim that Lin did not experience her symbol use as a representation of the toy bear's movement. Instead, she experienced her symbol use as fused with the toy bear's movement. That is, "the symbol user points out events and qualities of her lived-in space taking up a distinct perspective, a perspective ambiguously ascribed to herself and the tools at hand." Later in the interview, Nemirovsky and Monk offer a second construct to describe Lin's experiences with the graph. Here, Lin was seen as "trail-blazing," which involved interacting with her environment such that various aspects of the problem setting became tools that were ready-at-hand. By way of contrast, the authors describe the experience of "path-following" and note that although this perspective more aptly describes most school-based activities, the experiences of trail-blazing often open new opportunities for learning. In sum, the phenomenological approach attempts to account for students' activity in terms of the lived-in world, which, by definition, includes the social and cultural aspects as part and parcel of the unit of analysis. This perspective thus rejects assumptions of Cartesian dualism and by-steps the entire debate over whether the individual or culture should gain prominence in analyses.

Although approaching the process of learning from slightly different epistemological positions, all of the chapters appear to view learning as a process of activity reorganization in which students continually revise their ways of knowing as they interact with others in their community and surrounding culture. Given this generalized definition, the question of how to support this process can be viewed as a search for activities and tools that will promote the development of collective meaning through progressive refinement. For example, Lehrer et al., Sfard, Gravemeijer et al., and van Oers all describe the progression of symbolizations in semiotic terms as moving from icons to symbols, or from signifiers to signs. As Sfard (chap. 3) notes, "It is through interaction that public signifiers are turned into private signs." The question of how and when these public signifiers should enter the discussion serves as the basis for the third theme, which addresses the issue of whether symbols should precede or follow the introduction of mathematical concepts.

Theme 3: The Invent Versus Explore Dichotomy

A third theme that figured prominently in many of the chapters can be characterized as the "invent" versus "explore" dichotomy. This question may be seen as the perceptual chicken and egg paradox for mathematics education in that it concerns asking whether mathematical symbols should be introduced before, during, or after students have engaged in activities in which the mathematical ideas that the symbols portend to signify may arise. This question formed one of the major foci in the design chapters written by Gravemeijer et al., Lehrer et al., and Nemirovsky and Monk, and also the theoretical chapters written by Sfard and Dörfler.

Sfard's theoretical description of the tension that arises if one accepts the view that discourse and mathematical objects are mutually constitutive and coemerge in discussion may set the stage for this debate. She asks (chap. 3), "How does the ongoing process of coemergence begin? According to what has been said, structural symbols cannot become meaningful before they are used; however, how can one use a symbol before it becomes meaningful?" In her conclusion, Sfard addresses this issue by noting that "starting with mathematical signifiers may sometimes be the right thing to do. Not only abstract mathematical objects, but also real-world structures, do not come into existence by themselves, but rather have to be 'symbolized into being.'"

In arguing this position, Sfard claims that the introduction of new symbols opens an opportunity for students to discursively construct (or negotiate meanings for) new mathematical objects. To illustrate this process, she offers the metaphor of a pump that operates in two phases. In the first phase, the introduction of a new symbol equates to the lifting of the piston, thereby creating an opportunity for discussing meanings, what Sfard calls *the semantic space*. At this point, students can frame conversations around an object about which they know very little. For example, although students may not know what the symbol "π" means, they can frame discussions around it because they know that it refers to a quantity, rather than, say, a polygon. Sfard describes this use of the new term as *template-driven* or operational in nature in that students are able to frame discussions by following a template for discourse that fits quantities instead of polygons. In the second phase of the pump, these discursive negotiations lead to an ontological transition wherein the operational use becomes more structural in nature. By structural, Sfard indicates that a type of reification has occurred in which the process-based discussions have led to the creation of an object on which other operations can now be performed. At this point, mathematical objects can be discussed in ways that, in many respects, remind one of AR discourse; in spite of the relative weakness of perceptual clues, the participants feel that their conversation is being mediated by objects, a process that Sfard refers to as *object mediation* (Sfard, personal communication). Thus, the second stage involves filling the semantic space created in the pump. This pump metaphor enables the discussion of symbols to transcend the traditional dualism wherein meaning is assumed to be carried by symbols in that it locates meaning-making in social discourse rather than in any individual's mind. On the other hand, although collective conversations can frame a taken-as-shared view of the newly introduced symbol, each individual forms his or her own ways of thinking, knowing, and acting with it.

Sfard's theoretical argument sets the stage for discussing the tension that arises when one attempts to design an instructional sequence. The issue of whether instructional activities should begin with the *exploration* of symbolizations or whether activities should be designed around the *invention* of symbolizations was addressed by several of the design chapters. One example of an argument calling for the exploration of symbolizations rather than their invention was made by Bransford et al. These authors base their view on their extensive research with the Jasper series, a collection of video-based instructional scenarios that engage students in situated problem solving. Based on their recent research, these authors report that although they initially attempted to embed enough information to support students' invention of "smart tools" to solve problems (e.g., inventing a linear graph to figure out distance–time problems), they found it more productive to present students with catalogs describing various smart tools (e.g., graphs) that were available for use and then ask students to discuss which were most useful for their purposes at hand. They support this decision by noting,

> An emphasis on particular sets of contrasts affects the kinds of dimensions and features that students notice. For example, using different rates of speed in a chart focuses students' attention on speed. When students look at a

graphical smart tool, they usually have conversations about how and what speed is represented on each graph.

This argument is consistent with the general claim that it is unrealistic to expect that students will create representations that echo the underlying conventions and concepts that have evolved in the course of mathematical history.

In sum, Bransford et al. argue that the introduction of symbols may be a fruitful and productive approach for initiating the process of negotiation through which meaning and symbolizations emerge. On the other hand, Nemirovsky and Monk emphasize the importance of engaging students in activities that involve opportunities to invent symbolizations. For example, when reflecting on their efforts to design the "Patterns of Change" curricular unit (Tierney, Nemirovsky, & Noble, 1995), Nemirovsky and Monk argue that introducing students to the fundamental ideas of calculus through engagement in physical activities and then making representations of them was an essential aspect of the planning and implementation of the unit.

> A crucial activity to "set the stage" for the students' encounter with mathematical ideas is, we believe, the students' invention of mathematical representations (Bednarz, Dufour-Janvier, Poirier, & Bacon, 1993; diSessa, Hammer, Sherin, & Kolpakowski, 1991). We have found these activities important not because we would expect that students would necessarily develop the mathematical ideas in question spontaneously and autonomously, but because these inventing activities can generate a context for a meaningful encounter with them.

Although these two positions appear to be in conflict, one must analyze the assumed relations between the development of symbolizations and the development of meaning. In both cases, the authors argue that a critical aspect of their work is to involve students in activities in which the need for symbolizations arise from the mathematical experiences in which the students are engaged. As such, both perspectives appear to suggest that meanings cannot be experienced outside of situations that call for mathematizing, and, conversely, situations that involve mathematizing can become learning opportunities with the use or development of symbolizations. In the Bransford et al. case, the students were asked to determine which smart tool might help them express a mathematical relationship between two variables they were attempting to coordinate. For these researchers, the objective appears to have been to support students' efforts to interpret conventional graphs. In Nemirovsky and Monk's case, the authors emphasize the importance of generating meaningful encounters with mathematical ideas. The objective here was to set the stage for later encounters with more conventional symbolizations by first involving students in situations that could be mathematized.

Chapter 9 by Lehrer et al. also emphasizes the value of having students invent their own symbolizations in an effort to set the stage for later development of more formal and conventional symbolizations. Like Nemirovsky and Monk, Lehrer et al. do not appear to aim toward supporting the emergence of conventional symbolizations. Instead, their goal appears to be to engage students in situations that offer possibilities for supporting the emergence of rich mathematical discussions. The main characteristic of these discussions is that they focus on describing and revising informal models of various phenomena. Their overall claim is that these informal symbolizations and their revisions are vital for supporting the emergence of mathematical meanings. To support this claim, they offer reflections based on observations taken from one teaching experiment. During this project, two groups of students were each asked to describe the steepness of different ramps used to race small toy cars. In the first group, the teacher asked the students to invent ways to describe the various inclined planes. These inscriptions evolved from literal drawings of the crates used to hold the planks to more generalized drawings of triangles. In the second group, the teacher inadvertently told the students to represent steepness by drawing triangles. The authors note that the sketches from the second group were less representational because the children in this latter group had been provided a solution to a problem that was not yet problematic to them. Based on these differences in richness, Lehrer et al. conclude:

> A widely used instructional strategy among teachers and researchers trying to foster model-based reasoning is to provide a model that embodies conceptually important distinctions and relations, and then ask the students to solve a series of problems with the model (e.g., Smith, Snir, & Grosslight, 1992; White, 1993). . . . However, . . . our experiences with these second graders suggest that, at least in some circumstances, giving children models may be less helpful than fostering their propensity to construct, evaluate, and revise models of their own to solve problems that they consider personally meaningful.

This approach is consistent with the modeling perspective advanced by Lesh and Doerr (chap. 10), who go even further to claim that "model development is learning." For these authors, the activity of modeling implies a broad process in which students create and revise a series of systems that represent the objects, relationships and patterns that exist between the quantities involved in a given mathematical situation.

This view of modeling shares several similarities with that of Gravemeijer et al. In both cases, the underlying epistemological view is based on a non-dualist perspective in which mathematical meanings are not seen as inherent in models. Instead, meanings are seen to arise as students act with them (cf. Cobb, Yackel, & Wood, 1992). One of the main tenets of the view of Gravemeijer et al. is that the process of modeling is seen as reflexively related to students' evolving ways of knowing. Thus, when the authors talk about the transition from model *of* to model *for*, they do not necessarily envision a change in the physical inscription system. Instead, what changes is the students' views of what they are modeling. One critical aspect of this transition is that the role of the model shifts from being a model *of* a given situation to serving as a model *for* more generalized mathematical activity. To illustrate this transition, Gravemeijer et al. (chap. 7) describe one teaching experiment involving the arithmetic rack, an abacus-like device containing 20 beads. When using this device, students initially moved beads to show ways in which various configurations of passengers could be seated on a double decker bus. The authors state that the students' activity with this model shifted from initially serving as a model *of* their situated activity (i.e., modeling people on a bus) to serving as a model *for* their more generalized mathematical reasoning (i.e., creating different configurations of addends that would constitute the same sum). In this case, the physical form of the rack did not change. Instead, it was the students' activity (by which I mean their observable actions based on their evolving interpretations) that shifted from model *of* to model *for*. Moreover, the students reorganized their activity and, in so doing, their views of the rack. The basis for this shift was the students' construction of a framework of number relations, which itself emerged in the modeling activity. Thus, these authors, along with the other design contributors, can be said to fall somewhere along the continuum between favoring pure invention of symbolizations and complete exploration of meanings. From the Gravemeijer et al. perspective, the critical aspect of design involves beginning with students' current ways of knowing, but keeping an eye on target endpoints: the construction of personally meaningful ways of symbolizing that are consistent with conventional symbolizations.

In sum, one of the criteria all authors use to evaluate aspects of the invent/discover continuum is that students will develop insights into the conventions of representations that others who are already familiar with the concept may take for granted or overlook altogether. In other words, the authors appear to agree that the traditional practice of handing students ready-made tools or symbolizations and assuming that they can decode the math that experts see embodied in them is not as effective as encouraging students to engage in activity, reflection, and discussion regarding the tool's use in-action.

A second similarity between the contributors' views is the assumption that learning does not occur in a vacuum. Instead, as themes 1 and 2 are intended to illustrate, all contributors to this book maintain that learning can be viewed as an inherently social process of reorganizing one's ways of knowing through participation in communal activities. Thus, they describe other aspects of the learning experience that must be considered when discussing issues of instructional design that reach beyond the present invent/discover dichotomy. Two of these aspects include the role of the teacher and the role of the norms established in the microculture of the classroom. For example, Lesh and Doerr (chap. 10) note:

> It is within [the] larger classroom setting that the teacher plays an especially critical role. Sharing alternative models, fostering discussion, creating and nurturing diverse approaches, creating meaningful and powerful proto- types through classroom discourse, and building on the connections that students make to their out-of-school mathematics experiences are all activi- ties that will support students as they extend, apply, and explore the models they themselves have built. Teachers will need to develop the collaborative classroom settings in which such activities are most likely to occur.

These critical elements are not merely add-ons but, in fact, form the very basis on which theory and design revolve.

A LOOK FORWARD: THEORIES INFORMING DEVELOPMENT AND RESEARCH

This postscript has highlighted three themes arising from current devel- opment and research projects in mathematics education. It is hoped that these ideas will inform future efforts to create tools and activities to support students' collective negotiation of meaning and that these devel- opment efforts will, in turn, initiate calls for research documenting the meaning that students construct as they act with the tools in the social setting of the classroom. As we approach the 21st century, advances in technology and shifts away from conventional classroom settings will naturally generate new tools and novel social environments. The genera- tive ideas contained in this volume form a sound basis to blaze trails along which, to borrow Sfard's imagery quoted earlier, the two legs of discourse and meaning may head.

REFERENCES

Bednarz, N., Dufour-Janvier, B., Poirier, L., & Bacon, L. (1993). Socioconstructivist viewpoint on the use of symbolism in mathematics education. *Alberta Journal of Educational Research, 39*, 41–58.

Cobb, P., Yackel, E., & Wood, T. (1992). A constructivist alternative to the representational view of mind in mathematics education. *Journal for Research in Mathematics Education, 23*, 2–33.

Dewey, J. (1944). *Democracy and education.* New York: Free Press. (Original work published 1916)

diSessa, A. A., Hammer, D., Sherin, B., & Kolpakowski, T. (1991). Inventing graphing: Meta-representational expertise in children. *Journal of Mathematical Behavior, 10*, 117–160.

Tierney, C., Nemirovsky, R., & Noble, T. (1995). *Patterns of change: Tables and graphs.* Palo Alto, CA: Dale Seymour.

Author Index

Y

Yackel, E., 46, *95*, 136, 141, 146, 171, *172*,
  176, 225, 238, 250, 251, 252,
  260, 262, *271*, *273*, 290, 300,
  301, *321*, 395, *397*
Yearwood, A., 281, *320*
Young, M. F., 297, *323*

Z

Zawojewski, J., 380, *383*
Zech, L., 114, 141, 214, 225, 233, 280, 290,
  291, 296, 297, 298, 303, 304,
  316, 317, *320*, *321*, *323*, *324*,
  326, 376, 378, 386, 387, 390

Subject Index

A

Abbreviation, 144, 145, 149, 150, 154-156
Abstract object, 32, 57, 78-86, 93, 105, 106, 123-130, 168, 339
Abstractness, 32, 57, 67, 76, 105, 160, 196, 229, 306, 377
Actions, 32, 137, 182, 197, 207, 220, 281
  Children's play and, 162-165, 168-171
  Culturally mediated, 139-144
  Cycles of, 288
  Structure of, 143-146
  Symbols and, 151-156, 265
Action psychology, 133, 138, 142, 144, 153
Activity, 178, 204-207, 210, 266
  Agent of, 141, 142
  Approach, 133-138
  Culturally organized, 20-22, 25, 26, 35, 134, 139-141, 149, 389
  Discursive, 6, 7, 19, 47, 49, 101, 387
  Mathematical, 2, 17-35, 136, 152-154, 159, 161, 169-171, 209, 226, 235-237, 242, 243, 250, 251, 264, 270
  Predicating, 7, *see also* Predication
  Semiotic, 7, 22, 23, 26, 146-153, 155, 158-163, 167-171, 389
  Sociocultural, 2, 20, 26, 139, 141, 159, 169, 225
  Symbolizing, 8, 11, 12, 18, 94, 136, 151, 181, 230-232, 263
Actor's viewpoint, 20, 21, 26, 28, 33, 34

Appropriation, 7, 20, 21, 26, 27, 133-137, 154, 156, 169, 170, 230, 235
Arithmetic rack, 244-269, 395
Artifacts, 25, 26, 48, 212-214, 291-294, 318, 363, 364
As-if attitude, 6, 102, 122-130, 149, 387
Assessment, 305
Associationism, 21-24, 180-182, 186, 190, 191
Authentic experience, 9, 228-231, 305
Autopoietic system, 59-61, 91

B

Boundaries, 215-218, 220

C

Cartesian dualism, 45, 134, 390, 392
Certainty, 165-168, 236
Chains of signification, *see* Signification
Classroom microculture, 10, 238, 240, 246, 251, 316, 340, 386, 396
Cognitive conflict, 379, 391
Cognitive psychology, 25, 276, 298, 306
Cognitive science, 1, 10
Communicating, 2-4, 7, 11, 12, 385-387
  Capabilities, 368
  Meaning making and, 101-112, 135, 146, 150, 171, 191, 282
  Object mediation and, 40
  Participation and, 141
  Role of symbols in, 17, 48, 171
  Sociocultural theory and, 134
Constructing objects, 69, 85, 137